# THE LIFE OF CHARLES DICKENS
## HIS LIFE, WRITINGS,
## AND PERSONALITY

## BY

## FREDERIC G. KITTON

## PUBLISHED BY

## LEXDEN PUBLISHING LTD

Edited and typeset by Lexden Publishing
Typographical and editorial copyright © 2004
Lexden Publishing
Cover design by Lexden Publishing

ISBN: 1-904995-02-0
A part of the Revisiting History series

First published in 1902
This edition published August 2004 by:

Lexden Publishing Ltd
23 Irvine Road
Colchester
Essex
CO3 3TS
UK

**phone:** (01206) 533164
**website:** www.lexden-publishing.co.uk
**email:** info@lexden-publishing.co.uk

Printed by Lightning Source UK Ltd
and
Lightning Source Inc. (US)

# PREFACE TO THE FIRST EDITION

In preparing this Life of "Immortal Boz," it has been my endeavour faithfully to register, chronologically, the incidents and achievements appertaining thereto, and, in so doing, I have adopted a course previously unattempted by biographers of England's most popular Novelist. In striving to maintain an absolute sequence of events, difficulties have occasionally opposed themselves, compelling me to abandon, for the moment, such an arbitrary plan; I have completed, for example, the bibliographical accounts of certain books in preference to giving a disjointed relation by interpolating irrelevant matter. I trust, nevertheless, that so slight a departure from strict consecutiveness does not seriously impair the continuity of the narrative.

To approach such a formidable task as that involved in writing the biography of one who, like Dickens, crowded so many activities into his life requires not a little courage, application, and patience; indeed, to produce the biography of any man that shall be at once a true portrait, of the inward as well as the outward of him, demands qualifications which are rarely discoverable. The possession of those qualifications I do not pretend to have acquired; but I may claim for the present work that it is a faithful chronicle of facts and data, obtained from trustworthy sources, and compiled by an ardent student and disciple of that mighty Magician who so effectually wielded his pen in the great cause of Humanity.

There have appeared from time to time critical and instructive commentaries upon "Boz," considering him not only in his capacity as Author, but also as Stenographer, Journalist, Editor, Actor, Public Reader, Orator, Art Critic, Political Economist, and Social Reformer. In order to conceive what manner of man he was, it is evidently essential that this *"unique of talents"* (to borrow Carlyle's phrase) should be comprehensively studied, and I have therefore ventured, in the two concluding chapters of this volume, to dilate upon his characteristics and idiosyncrasies—to make manifest his views and opinions on Literature, Art, Science, and Politics, and reveal his habits, methods of work, taste in dress, &c. Intelligence of this nature, supplemented by a series of portraits and word-pictures, should enable the reader to understand the real Dickens, and to obtain an accurate perception of his personality.

It is obvious that no biographer of Dickens can dispense with the information afforded by Forster's Life, and to avow my indebtedness to those fascinating pages for material to which the author had the exclusive right of access seems a superfluous acknowledgment. It has been contended that Forster's book is complete and sufficing; so much of importance, however, has transpired since its publication (thirty years ago) as to justify the production of a "new" Life, and I trust that the result of my effort to embody here a large proportion of this wealth of fresh matter may be regarded as an acceptable contribution to the literature of the subject. The printed Letters of Charles Dickens (the majority of which were unknown to Forster) alone constitute an immense field for research—yielding those autobiographical touches which prove so useful to the historian—and by quoting therefrom I have occasioned Dickens himself to fill in details relating to a considerable portion of his marvellous career. To other writers besides Forster I am under obligations, especially to the late Mr. Robert Langton, whose "Childhood and Youth of Charles Dickens" contains many interesting particulars concerning the early years of the Novelist. From intimate friends of the Author of "Pickwick" I have also gleaned personal reminiscences, the inclusion of which conspicuously enhances the value of this record.

FREDERIC G. KITTON.

ST. ALBANS.

*To*

# THE PRESIDENT

(LORD JAMES OF HEREFORD)

## AND

## MEMBERS OF THE "BOZ" CLUB

*THIS BIOGRAPHY*

IS RESPECTFULLY INSCRIBED BY THEIR FELLOW-MEMBER

# THE AUTHOR.

# PREFACE TO THIS EDITION

This 2004 edition is as faithful to the original 1902 publication as possible. It is therefore likely that some facts recorded in 1902 may have since changed.

For further information on Charles Dickens please visit our website, www.lexden-publishing.co.uk.

# CONTENTS

# LIST OF ILLUSTRATIONS

Charles Dickens

*From a photograph by Ben Gurney, 1868*

# CHAPTER 1

# EARLY YEARS

When, in the year 1809, John Dickens was transferred from the Navy Pay Office at Somerset House, London, to resume his clerical duties at Portsmouth Dockyard, he little imagined that the unpretentious abode on the island of Portsea which then became his home would, in after years, be reverently regarded as a literary shrine; it seemed, indeed, beyond the range of probabilities that a son would be born to him who was destined to achieve a worldwide fame, and whose name would become a familiar household word. Had John Dickens been endowed with the prophetic instinct of Joseph Bagstock, he might have uttered with justifiable pride the words used by the gallant Major with reference to the future prospects of Paul Dombey—"That boy, Sir, will live in history. That boy, Sir, is not a common production."

The name of John Dickens first appears in the books of the Navy Pay Office in 1805, as seventh assistant-clerk, with an annual salary of eighty pounds, he being then nineteen years of age. Four years later (June 13, 1809) he married the sister of one of his fellow clerks, Elizabeth Barrow, and the ceremony was performed in the Church of St. Mary-le-Strand, over against Somerset House. After a brief honeymoon the young couple went to South Hampshire, John Dickens having received orders to attend the paying-off of ships at Portsmouth, and made their home at No. 387 Mile End Terrace, Commercial Road, Landport, Portsea. Here, in the following year, was born their first child, Frances Elizabeth (Fanny), and here, on the 7th of February 1812, the subject of this biography first saw the light. "I was born on a Friday," observes David Copperfield, and this is literally true of his creator. Baptized, when less than a month old, at the parish church of Portsea,[1] he received the names of Charles John Huffam, the first being the Christian name of his maternal grandfather, the second that of his father, while the third was the surname of his godfather, Christopher Huffam (incorrectly spelt "Huffham" in the church register), who is described

[1] Locally and popularly known as St. Mary's, Kingston. The present vicar of All Saints, Portsea (the Rev. W. C. Hawksley, M.A.), who resides in the house adjoining Dickens's birthplace, informs me that the borough of Portsmouth comprises almost the whole of the isle of Portsea, and includes the old parishes of Portsmouth and Portsea. The old Portsmouth parish is quite a small place, and to this day is still but a single parish; whereas Portsea is of great area and divided into several parishes. Landport is one of those divisions of the ancient parish of Portsea, and the church in which Charles Dickens was baptized preceded the present modern edifice, the actual font being now in St. Stephen's Church Portsea.

I am indebted to Mr. William Pearce (a son of John Dickens's land-lord) for the interesting fact that the father of the Novelist rented the house (No. 387, now No. 393) in Mile End Terrace, from June 24, 1808 (not 1808 as hitherto stated), and that he entered into possession shortly after his marriage, his tenancy continuing just three years. The room in which the future Novelist was born is furnished in the most ordinary style of old-fashionedness! One of the streets near the birthplace has been appropriately named "Dickens Street," and a presentation portrait of him has been placed in the Town Hall, Portsmouth.

Birthplace of Charles Dickens, 1812

(Now known as No. 393 Old Commercial Road,
Portsmouth)

*Photographed by F. J. Mortimer*

No. 18 St. Mary's Place, Chatham

("The House on 'The Brook' ")

Residence of John Dickens and His Family,
1821-1823

*Photographed by Catharine Weed Ward*

in the London Post-Office Directory of that time as "Rigger to his Majesty's Navy," with a residence at Limehouse Hole, near the lower reaches of the Thames, that portion of London's great waterway, which afterwards played a significant part in "Our Mutual Friend." The author of "Pickwick," however, never favoured his second and third baptismal names, subscribing them on very rare occasions; curiously enough, they are not even included in the autograph signature upon his marriage certificate, and the stone slab which marks his last resting-place is simply inscribed, "Charles Dickens." [1]

Like Walter Scott, Charles Dickens was blessed with a marvellously retentive memory, and late in life could remember minor incidents of his childhood, such as his first attempts at walking, when his fond mother and her servant stooped down or knelt on the floor while he toddled unsteadily from one to the other. The Dickens family left Mile End Terrace on the 24th of June 1812, and went to live in Hawke Street, Portsea; here was born another son, Alfred (who died during infancy), and here they remained until Charles was two years old. Forster, the biographer of Dickens, intimates that John Dickens, with wife and children, then left Portsea for London, in accordance with official instructions from Somerset

---

[1] According to that learned philologist, the late Canon Bardsley, the surname "Dickens" is descended from a far-away ancestor who was Richard, and was nicknamed indifferently Hick and Dick. Both Forster and Mr. Langton are silent regarding the ancestry of Charles Dickens. In a work called "The Rambler in Worcestershire," 1854, appears the following statement:—"The Dickens family of Bobbington [Staffordshire] were lords of this manor from 1432 to 1657, and it is said that from this family Mr. Dickens, the author, is descended."

House, and that they went into lodgings in Norfolk
Street (now Cleveland Street), on the east side of
Middlesex Hospital. They did not long remain in the
Metropolis, however, for the elder Dickens was again
"detached" and placed on duty in Chatham Dockyard.
The date of their departure from London is given by
Forster as, 1816, during which year their fourth child,
Letitia Mary, came into the world; they probably again
took lodgings, for nothing can be discovered as to the
situation of their home in Chatham earlier than the
following year. After an exhaustive search in the
parish rate-books, the late Mr. Robert Langton has
recorded that from 1817 (probably midsummer) until
Lady-day 1821 the Dickens abode was at No. 2 (since
altered to No. 11) Ordnance Terrace; here two more
children were born, Harriet Ellen (who followed
Alfred to an early grave) and Frederick William. John
Dickens's income (ranging from £200 to £350 per
annum) enabled him at this period to grapple
successfully with the responsibilities incurred by him
as the father of a young and increasing family, and to
provide adequately for the comfort of wife and
children. At Ordnance Terrace, little Charles Dickens
passed some of the happiest years of his childhood,
and it was at Chatham in those juvenile days that he
received the most durable of his early impressions.
Even at that tender age his power of observation
asserted itself, and in after years he remembered the
idiosyncrasies of certain neighbours in Ordnance
Terrace, and noted them in "Sketches by Boz"; for
example, the Old Lady in "Our Parish"; was a Mrs.
Newnham, who lived at No. 5 in the Terrace, and the
original of the Half-Pay Captain (in the same sketch)
was another near neighbour; again, Steerforth

(in "David Copperfield") he probably portrayed from George Stroughill, "a frank, open, and somewhat daring boy," who lived at No. 1, and was his greatest friend at that time, while his golden-haired sister, Lucy Stroughill (said to have been Charles's little sweetheart) figures as "Golden Lucy" in one of his Christmas Stories.[1]

The name of Charles's nurse was Mary Weller (familiar cognomen!), who married Thomas Gibson, a shipwright in Chatham Dockyard. Her death occurred but a few years ago, and to the last she had a vivid recollection of the accomplishments of her young charge.[2] Through Mr. Langton she placed on record the fact that little Charles was "a terrible boy to read," fond of reciting and singing comic songs, and performing parts of plays with his friend George Stroughill. One of his favourite pieces for recitatation was "The Voice of the Sluggard," from Dr. Watts, and this he would give with great effect "and with *such* action and *such* attitudes"; he was therefore a decided acquisition at children's parties and picnics. He lived in her memory as "a lively boy of a good, genial, open disposition, and not quarrelsome as most children are at times." He could read well, thanks to the thorough teaching he received at home from his aunt and mother, the latter being (in the words of Mrs. Gibson) "a dear, good mother, and a fine woman." His paternal grandmother was the much-respected housekeeper at Crewe Hall (in the time of the first Lord Crewe), and Lady Houghton told her husband that among the chief pleasures

---

[1] "The Wreck of the Golden Mary" (Christmas Number of *Household Words*, 1856).

[2] Mrs. Gibson died at Chatham, in April 1888, having nearly attained her eighty-fourth year.

of her childhood there was to go to the housekeeper's room and listen to Mrs. Dickens's endless and diverting stories.[1] From her it is more than likely the Novelist inherited his talent as a writer of fiction. Dickens afterwards described himself at this period as "a very queer small boy," and we have Forster's assurance that he was a very sickly boy, subject to attacks of violent spasm which disabled him for any active exertion. "He was never a good little cricket player. He was never a first-rate hand at marbles, or peg-top, or prisoner's base. But he had great pleasure in watching the other boys, officers' sons for the most part, at these games, reading while they played; and he had always the belief that this early sickness had brought to himself one inestimable advantage, in the circumstance of his weak health having strongly inclined him to reading."

Early in 1821, John Dickens relocated with his family from Ordnance Terrace to a less expensive residence, No. 18 St. Mary's Place (otherwise called "The Brook"), Chatham. The fact is, the elder Dickens (who had by nature a generous disposition, inclining him to be too lavish in his expenditure) found it necessary to economise. Their new home was a small tenement, with a plain-looking whitewashed plaster-front and a small garden before and behind—and stood next to a Baptist meeting-house called Providence Chapel, now a Drill Hall of the Salvation Army; while the house itself remains unaltered, the neighbourhood has since sadly deteriorated. Here

---

[1] An account of this episode imparted especial interest to the dinner party given in 1870 by Lord and Lady Houghton, at which Charles Dickens was presented to the King of Belgian and Prince of Wales (later King Edward VII).

they lived from 1821 to 1823, in close proximity to the old parish church of St. Mary, where three of the Dickens children were baptized, viz., the before mentioned Harriet Ellen and Frederick William, and a third son, Alfred Lamert, born at St. Mary's Place, 1822. From the upper window in the side of their house the church and churchyard were plainly visible—a circumstance which Dickens recalled some thirty years later when writing that charming little story, "A Child's Dream of a Star"—a touching reminiscence of his own and his sister Fanny's childhood.

While at Chatham, little Charles was fond of roaming about the great Dockyard, watching the rope-makers, anchor-smiths, and others at their labours, gazing with curious awe at the convict hulks (or prison-ships), and delighting in the varying scenes and incidents to be observed in that locality, at one time witnessing the bright displays of military tactics, at another enjoying a sail with his father to Sheerness in the Navy-pay yacht. He was thus unconsciously storing up impressions that were to prove of inestimable service by-and-by. The time was now ripe for bestowing attention upon his education, and, in order that he should receive instruction of a more systematic character than usually appertains to home studies, he (with his sister Fanny) was sent to a small preparatory school kept by William Giles, minister of the Baptist meeting-house aforesaid, who lived in Clover Lane (now Clover Street), Chatham.[1] The following doggerel rhyme still survives in the neighbourhood, in allusion to the four

[1] Forster gives the address of the school as Rome Lane (now Railway Street), but Mr. Langton states that there is no available evidence to corroborate this.

principal scholastic establishments in Strood, Rochester, Chatham, and Brompton:—

> "Baker's Bull Dogs
> Giles's Cats,
> New-road Scrubbers,
> Troy Town Rats."

Mr. Giles, declared to have been an accomplished scholar and a conscientious teacher, quickly detected the exceptional degree of intelligence possessed by his new pupil, and not only gave him every encouragement to study, but made a companion of him; it is, therefore, fair to conjecture that Dickens's knowledge and felicitous use of the English language in after life was greatly due to this worthy pedagogue's kind influence and careful training. The boy is described as being very handsome, with long curly hair of a light colour, and as possessing an amiable disposition; he was capital company, too, and "quite at home at all sorts of parties, junketings, and birthday celebrations," taking especial delight in Guy Fawkes festivities of the orthodox kind. When, some fifteen years later, Charles Dickens had achieved fame as the author of "Pickwick," it was natural that his old schoolmaster should experience a sense of pride in his former disciple, and, as a token of his admiration, he sent the young author a silver snuff-box, the lid of which bore a suitable inscription "to the Inimitable Boz." For a considerable time afterwards Dickens humorously alluded to himself, in letters to intimate friends, as "the Inimitable."

Of the many little experiences which entered into his life at Chatham, that which undoubtedly produced the most marked effect in preparing him for the career for which he was destined is discoverable in the fact that adjoining his bedroom in his father's house was another little room ("about which nobody else ever troubled") containing a small library, consisting of the works of Fielding, Smollett, Defoe, Goldsmith, and such classics as the "Arabian Nights" and "Tales of the Genii." These were perused by the boy with avidity, over and over again, and concerning them he said (speaking as David Copperfield), "They kept alive my fancy, and my hope of something beyond that place and time . . . and did me no harm; for, whatever harm was in some of them, was not there for me; *I* knew nothing of it."

After residing in Chatham about six years, John Dickens was recalled to Somerset House. Accordingly, in the winter of 1822-23, the family left for London, with the exception of little Charles, who apparently remained a few weeks longer in the care of Mr. Giles. At the expiration of that time the boy was conveyed to the Metropolis by coach, the "Commodore," driven by old Cholmeley (or Chumley), said to have been the original of Tony Weller—while the coach was the identical vehicle by which Mr. Pickwick and his companions travelled from London to Rochester, as duly set forth in the opening chapter of "The Pickwick Papers." It is undoubtedly a reminiscence of his own solitary journey that finds its way into one of Dickens's minor writings: "As I left Dullborough, in the days when there were no railroads in the land, I left it in a stagecoach. Through all the years that have since passed have I ever lost the smell of the damp straw in which I was packed—like game—and forwarded, carriage paid, to the Cross Keys, Wood Street, Cheapside, London? There was no other inside passenger, and I consumed my sandwiches in solitude and dreariness, and it rained hard all the way, and I thought life sloppier than I expected to find it."[1] Forster often heard Dickens remark, with reference to this incident, that he seemed to be leaving "everything that had given his ailing little life its picturesqueness or sunshine;" for (says the biographer) Chatham was "the birthplace of his fancy, and he hardly knew what store he had set by its busy varieties of change and scene, until he saw the falling cloud that was to hide its pictures from him for ever."

Soon after the return of the elder Dickens to London, a crisis came in his affairs in the shape of money embarrassments, resulting in a composition with creditors. This was the "falling cloud," which now began to obscure the brightness of Charles's young life. John Dickens had left service at Somerset House, and severe retrenchment in domestic affairs became imperative. The family abode at this juncture was "a mean small tenement" in Bayham Street, Camden Town—one of the poorest parts of London now; in those days, however, the newly-built cottages (about forty in number, erected in 1812) stood in the midst of a comparatively rural environment, for Camden Town was then but a suburban village, with

---

[1] "Dullborough Town," in "The Uncommercial Traveller," 1860. *Apropos* of Charles Dickens's first coach journey, it is interesting to quote the following advertisement (dated 1756), in which the "Cross Keys" is mentioned: "The Old Canterbury, Dover, and Deal Stage Coaches go throughout all the year, and set out every day at five in the morning, with six horses and a man well armed to guard them, from the Spread Eagle and Cross Keys Inns in Gracechurch Street, London. Each passenger pays 16s., and is allowed 40lb. of weight baggage," In "Dullborough Town" the name of the coach is given as "Timpson's 'Blue-eyed Maid'" —a veritable coach owned by one Simpson, which started from Brompton, near Chatham, and Mr. Langton points out that it would therefore be more convenient for the Dickens family, when resident on "the Brook" at Chatham, than the "Commodore" mentioned by Forster.

a meadow at the back of the principal row of houses, in which haymaking was carried on in its season, and there was a beautiful walk across the fields to Copenhagen House; amongst the first inhabitants of Bayham Street were retired tradesmen and professional men, the latter including the two well-known engravers, Engelhart and Francis Holl, Charles Rolls (an artist of note), Henry Selous (the painter), and Angelo, Selous (the dramatic author).[1] We must conclude, therefore, that the miseries of the locality to which Dickens subsequently alluded arose from sufferings and privations, and not from the house or the neighbourhood in which he lived with his parents, for he doubtless felt crushed and chilled by the contrast from the life at breezy Chatham. Their house, No. 16, with its "wretched little back garden abutting on a squalid Court" still exists, but its number is changed to 141; it was then rated at £22 a year.[2] Dickens frequently mentioned to Forster that "a washerwoman lived next door, and a Bow Street officer lived over the way," and described how he seemed at once to fall into a solitary condition apart from all other boys of his own age, and to sink into a neglected state at home. "As I thought," he said on one occasion very bitterly, "in the little back garret in Bayham. Street, of all I had lost in losing Chatham,

[1] "Saint Pancras: Past and Present," by Frederick Miller, 1874.

[2] I am indebted for many interesting particulars concerning the early homes of Dickens to Mr. R. B. Prosser, editor of "St. Pancras Notes and Queries," and an old inhabitant of the parish, to the history of which he has devoted much attention. Mr. Prosser informs me that in the parish Rate-book for October 8, 1823, John Dickens appears at No. 16 Bayham Street, and also at No. 18; in the next Rate-book (January 21, 1824), No. 16 is marked "empty." In 1866 the Metropolitan Board of Works renumbered Bayham Street (then consisting of about a hundred and fifty tenements), incorporating therewith Bayham Street South and Fleming Place.

what would I have given, if I had had anything to give, to have been sent back to any other school, to have been taught something anywhere!" Forster gives a sufficiently complete account of the Bayham Street days—a pathetic story it is—and justly reminds us that "the self-education forced upon him was teaching him, all unconsciously as yet, what, for the future that awaited him, it most behoved him to know."

Towards his father Charles Dickens entertained a feeling of love and respect, declaring him to be "as kind-hearted and generous a man as ever lived in the world;" as a husband and parent he showed great affection; he was respected by his friends, sympathetic and helpful to those in distress, zealous and conscientious in all business dealings, honourable in fulfilling duties for the discharge of which he became responsible. His easy temperament, coupled with a want of means, seems to have caused the elder Dickens (who was a compound of Wilkins Micawber and William Dorrit) to forget at this sorrowful time what was due from parent to offspring, especially in regard to the important question of education. By a stroke of good fortune the daughter, Fanny, who had a decided talent for music, was admitted a pupil at the then recently established Royal Academy of Music, through the recommendation of a pianoforte maker in Soho; whereupon the son felt more desolate and neglected than ever. Although John Dickens continued, for the present, to draw his salary at Somerset House, a large proportion of it doubtless went to the importunate creditors, and thus compelled the strictest economy at home. Charles, still a very small boy for his age (eleven years), degenerated into cleaning boots and running errands, and made himself useful in looking after his younger brothers and sisters. Happily, a few pleasant events tended to minimise the depressing effect of such an existence. A cousin by marriage, James Lamert, then lodging with the family, made and painted a little theatre for him, and the boy paid occasional visits to his godfather, Christopher Huffam, who lived in "a substantial handsome sort of way, and was kind to the child." He encouraged his precocious godson to sing comic songs, much to the amusement and delight of the Rigger and his boatbuilding friends, and the mention by Dickens in after years of this *penchan*t of his boyhood induced him to express a fear that "he must have been a horrible little nuisance to many unoffending grownup people who were called upon to admire him." Another of the few enjoyments afforded him was the loan of some books to amuse him, the lender being the landlady of his uncle, Thomas Barrow, and the widow of a bookseller named Manson, father to the partner in the celebrated firm of Christie & Manson (now Christie, Manson, & Woods). It is interesting to note that Charles Dickens's very first efforts in authorship date from this period, for he essayed a description of his uncle's old barber—a very odd specimen of humanity; he similarly tried his hand at portraying a deaf old woman who waited on the Dickens family, "and who made delicate hashes with walnut ketchup." He thought these immature sketches extremely clever, but nevertheless was too bashful to allow anyone to see them.

In the meantime, affairs in Bayham Street went from bad to worse. John Dickens's resources became so circumscribed that all ordinary expedients for soothing his creditors having been exhausted, it needed some special effort to save the situation.

Mrs. Dickens herself courageously resolved to attempt the solution of the difficulty by means of a school for young ladies, and suitable accommodation having been found at No. 4 Gower Street North, the family relocated thither in 1823.[1] The house, known in recent times as No. 147 Gower Street, was demolished a few years ago, and an extension of Messrs. Maple's premises now occupies the site. A large brass plate announced "Mrs. Dickens's Establishment," but, alas, to no purpose, notwithstanding the fact that little Charles left "at a great many doors a great many circulars." "Nobody ever came to school," observed Dickens to his biographer, when recalling the forlorn situation, "nor do I recollect that anybody ever proposed to come, or that the least preparation was made to receive anybody." The project, therefore, speedily failed, and the prospect seemed more hopeless than ever. Creditors could no longer be kept at bay, and at length arrived the inevitable climax—John Dickens was arrested and conveyed to a debtors' prison, his last words to his heart-broken son before he was carried off being those which were afterwards despondingly uttered by Micawber under similar circumstances, to the effect that the sun had set upon him for ever! Then, with the breadwinner in the clutches of the law, followed miserable struggles at home for daily subsistence, eked out by small sums accruing from the sale, at the pawnbroker's or elsewhere, of everything that could be thus disposed of,

[1] Verified by Mr. R. B. Prosser from the Rate-book of the Paving Board for the Southampton Estate, St. Pancras, which body was abolished in or about 1852. The record shows that No. 4 (Gower Street North) and adjoining houses were unfinished in 1822, and that the name of the tenant of No. 4 (from Michaelmas 1823 to Lady-day 1824) is entered as "Mrs. Dickens," the annual rent being £50. The family apparently left Bayham Street at Christmas 1823.

little Charles acting as the principal agent in these distressful transactions—even the cherished books he brought from Chatham ("Humphrey Clinker" and the rest) parted company, and we can easily conceive it to have been a bitter experience for the boy when, for a trivial sum, he relinquished his treasures to a drunken bookstall keeper in the Hampstead Road. At length, nothing remained but a few bits, of furniture, mother and children encamping in the two parlours of the emptied house; the boy's own little bed (with a brass coalscuttle, a roasting-jack, and a birdcage "to make a Lot of it") went for a song—"so I heard mentioned, and I wondered what song; and thought what a dismal song it must have been to sing." [1]

It now became the obvious duty of Charles (as the eldest boy, and precocious for his age) to endeavour to provide daily subsistence for those near and dear to him. Their relation, James Lamert, hearing of this misfortune, interested himself in procuring a situation for him in a blacking warehouse, of which he was chief manager. This business was a commercial speculation of George Lamert (cousin and brother-in-law of James), who bought the right and title of the then celebrated firm of Warren, whose premises—"a crazy, tumble-down old house, overrun with rats"— were at Old Hungerford Stairs, abutting on the Thames near the present railway bridge at Charing Cross. The proposal was that Charles should make himself generally useful in the blacking warehouse, for the modest pittance of six or seven shillings a week —an offer which, in an "evil hour" for him (he often bitterly thought), his parents readily accepted. Accordingly he went to the warehouse

---

[1] "The Haunted House" (Christmas Number *of All the Year Round,* 1859).

"to begin my business life," as he autobiographically expressed it—and became "a poor little drudge;" for his work was to cover the pots of paste-blacking, "first with a piece of oil-paper, and then with a piece of blue paper; to tie them round with a string; and then to clip the paper close and neat all round until it looked as smart as a pot of ointment from an apothecary's shop"; the final process being to attach a printed label to each bottle. A monotonous occupation, truly, and particularly uncongenial for one conscious of the fact that he was (as he afterwards described himself) "a child of singular abilities; quick, eager, delicate, and soon hurt, bodily and mentally." "No words can express the secret agony of my soul," he observed, when relating how he thus sank into the companionship of boys so much beneath him, intellectually and socially; and the bare recollection of what is usually referred to as "the blacking-bottle period" for ever caused him pain and a sense of humiliation.[1] We learn that Alphonse Daudet, who may be described as the French Dickens, began life in a similarly discouraging manner, being obliged to gain his daily bread before he was sixteen years of age; *apropos* of which he says, "I feel in my heart the love that Dickens felt for the unfortunate and the poor, and for childhoods spent in the wretchedness of large cities." Miss Mamie Dickens tells us that her father never alluded to these early experiences

[1] John Payne Collier, in his privately printed "Diary of an Old Man," states that Dickens (when a youth) told him that he had written puff verses for Warren, and quotes the following as a specimen:

"I pitied the dove, for my bosom was tender,
I pitied the sigh that she gave to the wind;
But I ne'er shall forget the superlative splendour
Of Warren's Jet Blacking, the pride of mankind."

in his children's hearing, and it was not until after his death that they knew the little history of that sad episode in his life.

But, distasteful as the work must have been to the sensitive lad, and in many ways unsuited to such a nature as his, it must be admitted that it was far preferable to the demoralising environment at home; for at Warren's he not only acquired some knowledge of business habits, but earned a weekly stipend that proved a welcome addition to the family's finances. "It was a grand thing," observes Forster, "to walk home with six shillings in his pocket, and to look in at the shop windows and think what it would buy." That these few shillings had to be carefully husbanded and expended to the best advantage is indicated in the following fragment of autobiography: "My mother and my brothers and sisters (excepting Fanny, in the Royal Academy of Music) were still encamped, with a young servant girl from Chatham workhouse, in the two parlours in the emptied house in Gower Street North. It was a long way to go and return within the dinner hour, and, usually, I either carried my dinner with me, or went and bought it at some neighbouring shop. In the latter case, it was commonly a saveloy and a penny loaf; sometimes a fourpenny plate of beef from a cook's shop; sometimes a plate of bread and cheese and a glass of beer. . . . Once I remember tucking my own bread (which I had brought from home in the morning) under my arm, wrapped up in a piece of paper like a book, and going into the best dining-room in Johnson's alamode beef-house in Clare Court, Drury Lane, and magnificently ordering a small plate of alamode beef to eat with it."

As we have seen, failure to propitiate creditors

brought dire consequences in its train. The home in
Gower Street North was broken up, and Mrs. Dickens,
with her younger children, went to live in the
Marshalsea with the father. For Charles a lodging was
procured in Little College Street, Camden Town, at the
house of a reduced old lady named Roylance,[1] who
unconsciously posed for the portrait of Mrs. Pipchin,
in "Dombey and Son." He and his sister Fanny passed
their Sundays in prison, the boy making mental notes
of his surroundings, which are to be found faithfully
recorded in the pages of "David Copperfield."
Although suffering in secret, he continued to perform
his duties at the blacking warehouse with expedition
and skill, endeavouring to forget for the nonce those
sorrows and trials which overshadowed him. In order
to be nearer his kith and kin, a back attic was found for
him in Lant Street, Borough, and this he thought "a
Paradise." It will be remembered that Bob Sawyer, of
"Pickwick" fame, lived in Lant Street, humorously
described in that work as a by-street whose "dullness
is soothing" and the population of which is migratory,
"usually disappearing on the verge of quarter-day, and
generally by night." Charles's landlord in Lant Street,
and the wife and lame son, who were kindly disposed
towards the lonely lad, are honourably immortalised as
the Garland family in "The Old Curiosity Shop."

    After his retirement from duty at Somerset

---

[1] Little College Street became College Street West on July 31, 1828,
and this name was changed in 1887 to College Place, that is to say the
portion of that thoroughfare north of King Street. In the Rate-book
(under date January 21, 1824), No. 37 (rated at £18) was occupied by
Elizabeth Raylase, and it is fair to assume (from the fact that entries were
carelessly made at the time referred to) that the correct name was
Roylance, which is still well known in the neighbourhood. College Place
was rebuilt in 1890.

House, John Dickens was in receipt of an official pension due to him for long service. By a fortunate circumstance, a rather considerable legacy from a relative accrued to him, and had been paid into court during his incarceration, thus enabling him to leave the Marshalsea, and, with his family, take up his abode with Mrs. Roylance in Little College Street, where they remained for a brief space, that is, until their relocation to a small house in Johnson Street, Somers Town.[1] Just at this time the blacking business was transferred to Chandos Street, Covent Garden, where little Charles and his colleague, Bob Fagin (whose surname was subsequently bestowed upon the Jew in "Oliver Twist"), carried on the work of tying up the pots in a window facing the street, compelling, by their dexterity, an admiring crowd of passers-by to stop and look in. When relating this incident to Forster, the Novelist added: "I saw my father coming in at the door one day when we were very busy, and I wondered how he could bear it." The, boy still remained solitary and self-dependent, indulging his taste, when opportunity offered, in wandering about the streets in the neighbourhood and quietly regarding the various types of humanity

[1] Johnson Street runs east from the north end of Seymour Street, and it is believed, from the evidence afforded by the Rate-book, that the house occupied by John Dickens (and rated at £20) was No. 29, at the east end of the north side. In 1825 the numbering of the houses was altered, when 29 became 13—its present number. In July 1824 the name of the tenant was entered in the Rate-book as Caroline Dickens, and it so remained until January 1829, when the house is marked "empty." On July 30, 1827, Caroline Dickens "applied for time to pay, or relief." Johnson Street has undergone but little change since that date, and there is no doubt that it tallied better with the description—"a poverty-stricken street"—than did Bayham Street. It was the last street in Somers Town, and adjoined the fields between it and Camden Town.—*See* Miller's "Saint Pancras: Past and Present," 1874.

with which they were peopled. But brighter, happier days were imminent. John Dickens and James Lamert quarrelled about the boy, with the result that he was withdrawn from the blacking warehouse and again sent to school.

Forster reminds us that, notwithstanding such miserable trials, little Charles never lost "his precious gift of animal spirits, or his native capacity for humorous enjoyment," his chequered experiences giving the decisive bent to his genius. He was about twelve years old when he became a day scholar at the Wellington House Academy, at the north-east corner of Granby Street, Hampstead Road; the house is still standing, but doomed to be presently demolished; the schoolroom and large playground disappeared in 1835, on the formation of the London and Birmingham railway, as it was then called.[1] The proprietor of this "Classical and Commercial Academy" was a Welshman named William Jones, who proves to have been, by all accounts, both ignorant and tyrannical, and whose chief employment was to scourge the boys. There can be no doubt that Jones and his establishment were revived by Dickens in "David Copperfield," as Creakle and Salem House, and that he had both in his mind when, in one of his minor writings, he says: "It was a school of some celebrity in its neighbourhood, nobody could say why—the master was supposed among us to know nothing, and one of the ushers was supposed to know everything."[2] Taylor, the English master, figures as Mr. Mell in "David Copperfield," and a gruff serving-man, who nursed the boys in scarlet fever, was the prototype

---

[1] In Mornington Place, close by, lived for many years the famous draughtsman and etcher, George Cruikshank.
[2] "Our School" (*Household Words*, October 11, 1851).

Wellington House Academy, Hampstead Road
Where Charles Dickens went to school, 1824-1826

*Photographed by Catharine Weed Ward*

No. 15 St. Furnival's Inn, Holborn

Residence of Charles Dickens, 1835-1837

*From a drawing by the Author*

of Phil Squod, in "Bleak House," who, it will be borne in mind, similarly tended poor Jo Dickens was remembered, by the old schoolfellows who survived him, as "a healthy looking boy, small but well built, with a more than usual flow of spirits. He usually held his head more erect than lads ordinarily do, and there was a general smartness about him." He and his fellow pupils invented a lingo by adding a few letters of the same sound to every word, and, by using this gibberish, pretended to be foreigners; they also kept bees, white mice, and other living things clandestinely in their desks. Charles took to writing short tales, which he lent to his schoolfellows on payment of marbles and pieces of slate pencil; and he and the other boys mounted small theatres with gorgeous scenery, the plays (such as "The Miller and his Men") being presented "with much solemnity" before a juvenile audience and in the presence of the ushers. It is fair to surmise that Dickens's aftertaste for theatricals had its origin in these performances, at which he was always a leading spirit. Dr. Danson, who was a pupil at Jones's with Dickens, recollects that on one occasion the high-spirited lad acted as ringleader in waylaying passers-by, especially old ladies; they, pretending to be poor boys, asked for charity, and their impudence so staggered the elderly dames, that Dickens could not refrain from exploding with laughter, whereupon the little impostors would take to their heels. From the same source we learn that Master Dickens was very irreverent during divine service at Seymour Street Chapel (then called Somers Chapel), and once narrowly escaped ejection. It is affirmed that he did not particularly distinguish himself at school, for he carried off no prizes. He remained at Wellington House Academy

about two years, and it is recorded by Mr. Langton that
the lad was then transferred to a school kept by
Jonathan Dawson at 19 Compton Street, Brunswick
Square, where he stayed but a short time.[1] Mr. John W.
Bowden, a fellow pupil of Dickens at Jones's
Academy, states, however, that Taylor, the headmaster,
who had taken a fancy to Dickens, left Jones's to open
a school on his own account at "The Retreat," South
Lambeth, whither young Dickens accompanied him.
But another schoolfellow, Mr. Owen P. Thomas,
asserts that, in one of his interviews with Dickens in
after years, he asked the Novelist whether he went to
another school after leaving Jones's, and he replied in
the negative; "indeed," adds Mr. Thomas, "it could not
be considered at that time any improvement to do so
and the error respecting Dawson's seems to have
arisen from the fact that it was a *brother* of Charles
Dickens who entered that seminary. Confronted with
such authoritative evidence, we must conclude that
Dickens's educational training terminated at
Wellington House Academy. As truly observed by Mr
John Leighton, F.S.A., who was a pupil at the same
establishment after Dickens left it: "Genius wants no
school. A classical education might have 'done for'
Dickens. 'Boz,' like Burns, might have found all
necessary in a Board school."

It was now considered by his parents that the
time had arrived when Charles ought to make another
and more promising start in life. Accordingly we find
him installed as clerk in a solicitor's office (Mr.

---

[1] The building (now a temperance hotel) still exists at the northeast
corner of Compton Street, at the junction of Hunter Street with Judd
Street. Jonathan Dawson was the father of George Dawson, who was
born here—not George Dawson the trainer of horses, but the preacher
and essayist.

[LONDON 1827-28]

Molloy's), New Square, Lincoln's Inn, and before
many months had expired he entered the office of
Messrs. Ellis & Blackmore, attorneys, of Gray's Inn,
where he secured regular employment from May 1827
to November 1828. According to Mr. George Lear,
one of his fellow clerks, the Dickens family were at
that time living in the now vanished Polygon, Somers
Town,[1] and a son, Augustus (their last child) had just
been born.[2] Mr. Lear distinctly remembers the boy's
talent as a mimic, and says: "He could imitate, in a
manner that I have never heard equalled, the
low population of the streets of London in all their
varieties . . . and the popular singers of that
day, whether comic or patriotic; as to his acting,
he could give us Shakespeare by the ten minutes, and
imitate all the leading actors of that time. . . . He told
me he had often taken parts in amateur theatricals
before he came to us. Having been in London two
years, I thought I knew something of town, but after a
little talk with Dickens I found that I knew

[1] The Polygon (so called from the arrangement of the houses in a
circle) stood within Clarendon Square, and, on completion, became the
aristocratic portion of Somers Town; many successful artists resided
there, including Dr. Wilde, one of the best engravers of his day. The
name of Dickens as a tenant in the Polygon does not appear in the Rate-
book of 1827-28, but, curiously enough, we find No. 17 entered as being
"let to lodgers," such an entry (Mr. Prosser informs me) being a very
unusual one and previously unknown to him. Remembering the comparatively high rents of the Polygon houses, it is fair to assume that the
Dickens family were lodgers only, at No. 17.

[2] John Dickens's family consisted of eight children, five boys and
three girls: Frances Elizabeth (born 1810), Charles John Huffam (1812),
Alfred (1813), Letitia Mary (1816), Harriet Ellen (1819), Frederick
William (1820), Alfred Lamert (1822), and Augustus (1827). Alfred and
Harriet Ellen died in childhood. Letitia (Mrs. Henry Austin) was the only
survivor of the family in 1872; she died in 1893.

nothing. He knew it all from Bow to Brentford. . ."[1]
During the brief interval of eighteen months at Ellis
and Blackmores, Dickens's exceptional powers of
observation were ever on the alert, and that he made
good use of the opportunities thus afforded him of
studying the peculiarities of lawyers, their clerks and
clients, is apparent to all who are familiar with his
writings. Forster alludes to an account-book—a book
in which the petty disbursements of the office were
regularly entered. Here we find that his own weekly
salary began at ten shillings, increasing to fifteen
shillings during the last three months; the clerks kept
this book in turns, and it is in Dickens's handwriting
from the beginning of January to March 1828, the fly-
leaf bearing his autograph signature; it is worthy of
remark that the book contains such names as Weller,
Mrs. Bardell, Corney, Rudge, and Newman Knott. One
of Dickens's fellow clerks, named Potter, was very
fond of theatricals, and the two youths frequently went
together to a minor theatre, where, it is said, they
occasionally engaged in parts. Potter afterwards
figured in "Sketches by Boz," namely, in the papers
entitled "Making a Night of it" and "Misplaced
Attachment of Mr. John Dounce;" in the latter he is
referred to as a barrister's clerk, "capital company, full
of anecdote!" and with a *penchant* for the play; his
personality also suggested the character of Alfred
Jingle, in "Pickwick." Dickens's position at
Blackmore's was inferior to Potter's, for he was merely
"one of the office-lads in their first surtouts," who (as
described in the thirty-first chapter of "Pickwick")
felt "a befitting contempt for boys at day-schools, club
as they go home at night for saveloys, and

[1] "Charles Dickens by Pen and Pencil," by F. G. Kitton, 1889-90.

porter, and think there's nothing like life."
Circumstances enforced the conclusion that young
Dickens's prospect of attaining prominence in the
legal profession was very remote; realising this, and
aspiring to greater things than were likely to accrue
from his clerical labours in an attorney's office, he
began assiduously to study shorthand (Gurney's
system) in the reading-room of the British Museum.
His own endeavours to master that difficult subject are
amusingly reflected in "David Copperfield," where we
read that David having purchased a book on the
subject, "plunged into a sea of perplexity" that brought
him in a few weeks to the confines of distraction. "The
changes that were rung upon dots, which in one position meant one thing, and in another position
something else; the wonderful vagaries that were
played by circles; the unaccountable consequences
that resulted from marks like fly's legs; the tremendous effect upon a curve in a wrong place, not only
troubled my waking hours, but reappeared before me
in my sleep"; and when he had fixed in his mind one
set of characters he found that he had forgotten others,
and so had to begin again. "In short, it was almost
heartbreaking." Like his hero he resolutely determined
to overcome all obstacles"—"Whatever I have tried to
do in life," he causes David to observe, "I have tried
with all my heart to do well. What I have devoted
myself to, I have devoted myself to completely." This
was likewise Charles Dickens's golden maxim, to
which he consistently adhered; so it is not surprising
that he should succeed not only in taming "that savage
stenographic mystery," but in rapidly acquiring such
extraordinary skill as to justify the verdict of experts
that "there never was such a shorthand writer!"

## CHAPTER 2

# REPORTER AND JOURNALIST— "SKETCHES BY BOZ" AND "PICKWICK"

Leaving Ellis & Blackmore's office in November 1828, Dickens abandoned the pursuit of the Law forever. That profession he seems to have regarded in a distinctly unfavourable light, judging by the following quotation from a letter written to a friend in 1870: "I have that opinion of the law of England generally, which one is likely to derive from the impression that it puts all the honest men under the diabolical hoofs of all the scoundrels."[1] John Dickens (whose resources had now improved) went with his family to reside at No. 18 Bentinck Street, Manchester Square, Charles accompanying them. The official pension received by the father from Somerset House being insufficient to meet general expenses, he was compelled to follow an occupation that would be likely to yield the necessary addition to his income; whereupon he resolved, thus late in life (and to his credit be it said), to attempt the same task as that which his son was then rapidly accomplishing, namely, the study of shorthand, and his efforts were so far successful as to enable him to attain a place in the reporters' gallery of the House

---

[1] *See* Letter to Mrs. Frederick Pollock, May 2, 1870 ("The Letters of Charles Dickens," edited by his Sister-in-law and his Eldest Daughter).

of Commons. Whereupon the son felt a natural inclination to follow his father's example and become a newspaper parliamentary reporter; so, with this object in view, he practised stenography in the Law Courts for nearly two years. After this period of probation an opening was found for him on the staff of a London morning journal called the *True Sun*, and it is interesting to know that it was in the office of this paper that Dickens, when acting as spokesman in a general strike of reporters, first met his future friend and biographer, John Forster, who thus heard his name for the first time. The personal appearance of the future Novelist (then nineteen years of age) made a very favourable impression on Forster, who saw in him a young man "whose keen animation of look would have arrested attention anywhere."

At that period the work of a newspaper reporter was not unattended by difficulties and even danger. Railways were as yet unknown, and the electric telegraph had not come into operation. In the course of a memorable speech delivered by Dickens in 1865, at the second annual dinner of the Newspaper Press Fund, he delighted his audience with a thrilling account of his experiences and adventures as a reporter—how he travelled by post-chaise to remote parts of the country to record important speeches, and how, on the return journey, he transcribed his notes on the palm of his hand by the light of a dark lantern, while galloping at fifteen miles an hour at the dead of night, through a wild district. "Returning home from exciting political meetings in the country to the waiting press in London," he said, "I do verily believe I have been upset in almost every description of vehicle known in this country. I have been, in my time, belated on miry byroads, towards the small hours, forty or fifty miles from London, in a wheelless carriage, with exhausted horses and drunken post-boys, and have got back in time for publication." We are assured that prior to 1840 the labours of a press reporter proved so excessive that only those who were very rarely qualified to sustain the wear-and-tear could bear the brunt of it without succumbing. It was the wholesome training of severe newspaper work, however, to which Dickens constantly attributed his early success in literature.

It was of course in the *old* Houses of Parliament, not the present Palace of Westminster, that Dickens followed the avocation of reporter, first for the *True Sun*, then for the *Mirror of Parliament* (conducted by his uncle Barrow), and finally for the *Morning Chronicle*. The accommodation provided for the representatives of the Press was most unsatisfactory, the "gallery" in the House of Lords being no better than "a preposterous pen" (as Dickens himself described it) in which the reporters were "huddled together like so many sheep." If those journalists could revisit the scene of their labours, they would be astounded at the changes that have lately been effected, for instead of the dark lobby or "preposterous pen," they would find three large writing-rooms, a smoking- and reading-room, a tearoom, a dining-room, lavatories, a dressing-room, a stationer's shop, post-office, and a refreshment-bar of fair dimensions. One who was thus engaged with Dickens (Mr. James Grant) averred that among the eighty or ninety reporters he "occupied the very highest rank, not merely for accuracy in reporting, but for marvellous quickness in transcribing." The only personal intimacy he then formed among his colleagues was with Thomas Beard, a *Morning Herald* reporter, who eventually received the appointment of Court Newsman, and who not unfrequently accompanied him on reporting expeditions as "associate-in-chief." In 1833, that is, about two years before Dickens joined the staff of the *Morning Chronicle*, his exceptional skill in stenography led to an introduction to Mr. Stanley (afterwards Lord Derby), who had just made an important political speech; a *verbatim* report being required, the young parliamentary scribe was sent to take it down *in extenso* from the lips of the orator, who repeated the speech for that purpose. During the parliamentary recess his services were utilised in the general work of the paper, such as reviewing new publications and writing notices of theatrical performances; but the principal editor, John Black, recognising his exceptional talents, spared him this kind of drudgery as much as possible. "Any fool," he said, in his usual broad Scottish accent, "can pass judgment, more or less just or unjust, on a book or a play—but 'Boz' can do better things; he can create works for other people to criticise. Besides, he has never been a great reader of books or plays, and knows but little of them, but has spent his time in studying life. Keep 'Boz' in reserve for great occasions. He will *aye* be ready for them."[1] His last appearance at the House of Commons in the capacity of reporter was at the close of the session of 1836, when, in the words of David Copperfield, he "noted down the music of the

---

[1] Dr. Charles Mackay, in "Charles Dickens by Pen and Pencil." The old *Morning Chronicle* building (No. 332 Strand) has recently been demolished in the course of the Holborn-Strand improvement scheme.

parliamentary bagpipes for the last time." It is interesting to add that many of his colleagues in the
"gallery" of Parliament afterwards achieved eminence
either in the literary or the legal profession; such as,
for example, John Payne Collier, F.S.A. and
Shakespeare commentator, William Hazlitt (son of the
famous essayist), and others of lesser note, who
succeeded in making the "gallery" a steppingstone to
worldly advancement.

Before his reporting career had closed, Charles
Dickens distinguished himself in another direction. He
took "with fear and trembling" to authorship, and
wrote "a little something, in secret, and sent it to a
magazine, and it was published in the magazine." The
"little something" was a humorous paper entitled "A
Dinner at Poplar Walk" (afterwards called "Mr. Minns
and his Cousin"), and concerning this, his first
published piece of writing, he has recorded how, in the
dusk of the evening, he stealthily dropped the
manuscript into "a dark letterbox, in a dark office, up
a dark court in Fleet Street." It was the office of the
*Monthly Magazine* in Johnson's Court, and when, in
December 1833, his little effusion appeared "in all the
glory of print," he walked down to Westminster Hall,
and turned into it for half-an-hour, because his eyes
"were so dimmed with joy and pride, that they could
not bear the street, and were not fit to be seen there."
In a letter to an intimate friend, informing him of his
success, he said: "I am so dreadfully nervous that my
hand shakes to such an extent as to prevent my writing
a word legibly." Upon the success or failure of that
maiden effort a great deal depended, inasmuch as the
result would enable him to determine whether or not
he should continue to wield his pen as a writer of

fiction. His good fortune, therefore, acted as an incentive, encouraging him to contribute other Sketches (nine in all), chiefly of a humorous character, to the same journal, the last appearing in February 1835. They bore no signature until August 1834, when he adopted the pseudonym of "Boz"—a very familiar household word to him, being the nickname of his youngest brother Augustus, whom he had dubbed Moses, in honour of tile Vicar of Wakefield—this, being facetiously pronounced through the nose, became Boses, and, when shortened, became Boz. Early in 1835, one of the editors of the *Morning Chronicle*, Mr. George Hogarth, made arrangements for an evening edition of that paper, and, desiring to stimulate its sale, expressed a wish that Dickens should prepare an original article for the first number. Whereupon the young author suggested a series of articles in the style of his Sketches in the *Monthly Magazine*, stipulating that he should receive some remuneration for them in addition to his salary as a reporter. This proposition was cordially acceded to by John Black (sometimes called the "father" of the London Press), to whom Dickens afterwards referred as his "first hearty out-and-out appreciator." It was agreed that his weekly stipend should be raised from five guineas to seven, and on January 31, 1835, was launched the initial number of the *Evening Chronicle*, containing, under the heading of "Sketches of London—No. 1," an article on "Hackney coach Stands," signed "Boz," similar papers appearing at brief intervals until the following August. Those published in the *Monthly Magazine* were contributed gratuitously, and were discontinued because the editor, James Grant, could not afford to act upon

the author's hint that if he received no compensation
for them, negotiations must cease. Even the modest
sum of half-a-guinea per page, as proposed by
Dickens, proved too heavy a tax on the pecuniary
resources of the magazine, which was not then in a
flourishing condition. "Only imagine," wrote Mr.
Grant when, several years later, he recalled these facts,
"Mr. Dickens offering to furnish me with a continuation, for any length of time I might have named, of his
'Sketches by Boz' for eight guineas a sheet, whereas in
little more than six months from that date he could—
so great in the interval had his popularity
become—have got a hundred guineas per sheet of
sixteen pages from any of the leading periodicals of
the day!"

In 1836, four Sketches were published in the
*Morning Chronicle* and reprinted in the *Evening
Chronicle*. During the interval that had elapsed since
the appearance of the final Sketch, contributed to the
*Evening Chronicle* in the previous year, the author
supplied other papers (signed "Tibbs") to *Bell's Life in
London*, these having the general title of "Scenes and
Characters." In 1836 he also wrote two articles in the
same humorous vein for "The Library of Fiction,"
published by Chapman & Hall, with which firm he
was destined to become intimately connected; these
papers were respectively called "The Tuggses at
Ramsgate" and "A Little Talk about Spring and the
Sweeps." It has transpired that the earlier Sketches did
not immediately attract special attention, although
considered clever and graphic by those moving in
literary circles.

Dickens, having wisely retained the copyright of
his "Sketches by Boz," disposed of it to John
Macrone, *the* publisher, for a hundred pounds.

Early in 1836 a selection from the published articles, supplemented by eight new papers, was issued by Macrone in two volumes, with etchings by the renowned George Cruikshank. The venture proved so satisfactory that other editions followed in rapid succession, and in 1837 there appeared a second series of the "Sketches" with Macrone's imprint, similarly illustrated with plates by Cruikshank. The first Complete Edition (containing both Series) was issued by Chapman & Hall in monthly parts in 1837-39, the designs being re-etched by the artist on a larger scale. This edition included the two papers originally written for "The Library of Fiction." In his preface to the first Cheap Edition (1850), the author stated that he had "not felt it right either to remodel or expunge, beyond a few words and phrases here and there," although he fully realised that these "Sketches" had a good many imperfections, "often being extremely crude and ill-considered, and bearing obvious marks of haste and inexperience."

In 1834, while still on the staff of the *Morning Chronicle*, Dickens left his father's house in Bentinck Street with the intention of starting a home of his own. He elected to live in bachelor apartments, and rented chambers in Furnival's Inn, Holborn, recently demolished and the site now occupied by extensive business premises. At first he became the tenant of a "three pair back" at No. 13, where many of the "Sketches" were written, and later he relocated to more cheerful rooms at No. 15, residing there from 1835 until 1837. On a certain memorable day in the early part of 1836 there called at the chambers of this rising author Mr. William Hall (partner in the then young firm of publishers, Chapman & Hall), in whom, oddly enough, Dickens recognised the very man who, two years previously, had sold him the copy of the *Monthly Magazine* containing his first printed piece of writing.

Mr. Hall's object in visiting "Boz" was for the purpose of discussing a proposal to publish "a monthly something" which should be the vehicle for certain plates by Robert Seymour, an artist of repute in his day, who had then recently completed some humorous designs of a sporting character for "The Squib Annual," under the auspices of Chapman & Hall. On Seymour expressing a wish to produce a series of cockney sporting plates of a superior sort, Charles Whitehead, who edited "The Library of Fiction" for Chapman & Hall, remembered the two clever and amusing Sketches which Charles Dickens had contributed to that work, and recommended him to the firm as the very man for writing the letterpress to accompany Seymour's plates. The idea propounded to Dickens was that a Nimrod Club, the members of which were to go out shooting, fishing, and so forth, and whose want of dexterity would result in all kinds of misadventures, seemed the best means of introducing the illustrations. This, however, did not meet with Dickens's approval. In the first place, he knew nothing of sport; secondly, the idea was somewhat hackneyed, and he considered that it would he infinitely better for the plates to arise out of the text. He naturally preferred not to be restricted in any way, and, on his views being deferred to, he says: "I thought of Mr. Pickwick, and wrote the first number." Thus originated that world-famous classic. "The Pickwick Papers."

"Pickwick" appeared in twenty numbers, each enclosed in a green paper wrapper bearing a design in which were incorporated incidents of a sporting kind, thus foreshadowing the intended character of the work; but the sporting element was afterwards considerably modified. An advertisement in *The Times*, March 26, 1836, thus announced the project:—

"THE PICKWICK PAPERS.—On the 31st of March will be published, to be continued monthly, price One Shilling, the first number of the POSTHUMOUS PAPERS OF THE PICKWICK CLUB, containing a faithful record of the Perambulations, Perils, Travels, Adventures, and Sporting Transactions of the Corresponding Members. Edited by Boz. Each Monthly Part embellished with four Illustrations by Seymour. Chapman & Hall, 186 Strand, and of all Booksellers."

The first portion of "Pickwick" was written at Furnival's Inn, and the opening number is dated April 1836. The launching of the initial instalment of the work that brought the author both fame and a moderate fortune was signalised in a memorable manner, for on the second of April he took unto himself a wife—not the Dora, however, of whom he became enamoured in 1829. The lady of his choice was Miss Catherine Thomson Hogarth, eldest daughter of George Hogarth,[1] his fellow worker on the *Morning Chronicle*, the marriage ceremony (a very unpretentious affair) taking place in the church of St. Luke, Chelsea, of which parish the Rev. Charles Kingsley (father of the author of "Westward Ho!") then officiated as rector. The bridegroom's old friend, Thomas Beard, acted as "best man," and concerning this auspicious event the late Mr. Henry

---

[1] George Hogarth married Georgina, daughter of George Thomson, "the friend of Burns."

Burnett (the Novelist's brother-in-law, and husband of Fanny Dickens) has placed on record the following reminiscence: "As for the wedding, even Boswell could have nothing to say, unless he had invented it. Mr. Dickens had not yet taken hold, as soon after he did, of the busy and talented men [that is to say, he did not yet number them amongst his personal friends]. . . The breakfast was the quietest possible. The Dickens family, the Hogarth family, and Mr. Beard . . . comprised the whole of the company. A few common, pleasant things were said, healths drunk, with a few words said by either party—yet all things passed off very pleasantly, and all seemed happy, not the least so Dickens and his young girlish wife. She was a bright, pleasant bride, dressed in the simplest and neatest manner, and looked better perhaps than if she had been enabled to aim at something more."[1] Her father was a most unassuming man, and a gentleman in feeling and education. The honeymoon was spent in the secluded little village of Chalk, about five miles from Rochester and two from Gravesend, and the farmhouse in which they lodged still stands—a corner house on the southern side of the road, advantageously situated for commanding views of the river and the far stretching landscape beyond. The house is interestingly associated with "Pickwick," for in it were penned some of the earlier chapters.

Before the completion of the second number of "The Pickwick Papers" a tragic event happened—the suicide of Seymour, the artist engaged as illustrator, whose brain had given way under pressure of overwork and worry. Part II contained an address to the public announcing the sad incident, and apologising for a reduction in the number of plates—

[1] Charles Dickens by Pen and Pencil," 1889-90.

three instead of four: "When we state that they comprise Mr. Seymour's last efforts, and that on one of them in particular (the embellishment of the Stroller's Tale) he was engaged up to a late hour of the night preceding his death, we feel confident that the excuse will be deemed a sufficient one." Much difficulty was experienced in finding another designer capable of carrying on the Seymour traditions; eventually Robert W. Buss, "a gentleman already well known to the public as a humorous and talented artist" (says the Address in the third number), was employed, but, being unaccustomed to the technicalities of etching on copper or steel, the two plates produced by him proved unsatisfactory, and were cancelled after only a few copies of the part containing them had been circulated—hence the eagerness of collectors to secure these rare impressions. It is interesting to note that among the applicants for the post rendered vacant by the dismissal of Buss was William Makepeace Thackeray, who, in those early days, desired to adopt art as a profession; he accordingly submitted specimens of his draughtsmanship, which Dickens, "strange to say, did not find suitable," as Thackeray himself explained many years afterwards. John Leech similarly proved to be an unsuccessful aspirant to the honour of illustrating "Pickwick," the privilege being presently accorded to a young artist named Hablot K. Browne, who had recently been awarded a Society of Arts medal for a spirited etching of John Gilpin. This facile designer and draughtsman afforded great satisfaction as the illustrator of "Pickwick," and, under the now familiar pseudonym of "Phiz" (adopted, probably, to harmonise with that of "Boz"), he forthwith became artist-in-chief in respect to nearly the whole of the Novelist's works. For some time Dickens continued to write under his *nom de guerre*, the wrappers of the monthly numbers of "The Pickwick Papers" proclaiming that they were "edited by Boz"; but in Part XVII (September 1837) appeared an advertisement announcing that the publisher had "completed arrangements with Mr. Dickens for the production of an entirely new work" in the same form as "The Pickwick Papers." This was apparently the first authoritative intimation affording a clue by which the public were enabled to attribute the authorship of "Pickwick" to Charles Dickens; but, some seven months previously, the secret was divulged in the second number of *Bentley's Miscellany* (March 1837), which contained the following clever "impromptu":—

> "Who the *dickens*, 'Boz' could be
> Puzzled many a learned elf,
> Till time unveiled the mystery,
> And 'Boz' appeared as *Dickens'* self."

About the same date a reviewer in *Chambers's Edinburgh Journal*, in criticising "The Pickwick Papers," observed: "Boz is the fictitious signature of a young man named Dickens, who was for some years engaged as a writer on one of the London newspapers, which he enlivened with his humorous and graphic sketches. We are not aware that he is a native of London, but he has, at least by his residence there, made himself intimately familiar with the peculiarities of the people, chiefly of the middle and lower ranks, which he has the knack of hitting off in a singularly droll and happy manner."

Respecting Dickens's financial arrangements with his publishers, it was agreed that he should receive nine guineas a sheet of sixteen pages, and that, if the work proved successful, he would be further remunerated. In a letter to his future wife (from Furnival's Inn, Wednesday Evening, 1835), he said: "I have had a visit from the publishers this morning, and the story cannot be any longer delayed; it must be done tomorrow, as there are more important considerations than the mere payment for the story involved too. I must exercise a little self-denial and set to work. They [Chapman & Hall] have made me an offer of fourteen pounds a month to write and edit a new publication they contemplate, entirely by myself, to be published monthly, and each number to contain four woodcuts. I am to make my estimate and calculation, and to give them a decided answer on Friday morning. The work will be no joke, but the emolument is too tempting to resist."[1] According to the still existing voucher (dated March 29, 1836), Dickens received the sum of twenty-nine pounds for the first two numbers of "The Pickwick Papers," which makes the payment fourteen pounds ten shillings for each number, consisting of a sheet and a half; and it is interesting to note that he received this payment in advance, for he was about to be married and required money for his honey-moon. Presently he announced to his fiancée: "I have at this moment got Pickwick and his friends on the Rochester coach, and they are going on swimmingly, in company with a very different character from any I have yet described" [Alfred Jingle], "who I flatter myself will make a decided hit. I want to get them from the ball to the inn before I go to bed; and I think that will take until one or two o'clock at the earliest. The publishers will be here in the

---

[1] "The Letters of Charles Dickens."

morning, so you will readily suppose I have no alternative but to stick to my desk."[1] The incidents here referred to appertain to the second chapter of the book.

The expectations entertained of the possible success of "Pickwick" were modest in the extreme. "Boz," as yet, was practically unknown except as the author of some extremely original and amusing articles in newspapers and magazines, so that his publishers were doubtless justified in acting cautiously. In regard to Part I, the first order transmitted to the binder was for four hundred copies only, and the publishers sent out, "on sale or return," fifteen hundred copies of each of the first five numbers to all parts of the provinces, the result being an average sale of only fifty copies of each number. So far the venture seemed likely to prove a failure; indeed, the publishers, beginning to repent of their bargain, seriously debated whether the work should be continued or not. The author's friends, too, spoke slightingly of the production, which they described as "a low, cheap form of publication," by which he would ruin all his rising hopes! Cheap it certainly was, being about one-third the price of ordinary novels of that day. Happily, at this juncture, neither author nor publishers felt discouraged by unfavourable comments or by the apathy of the public. They decided to proceed, and when Part IV duly appeared, it proved to be the turning point, for in that number the author introduced Samuel Weller, who called forth such admiration by the freshness and originality of the conception, that the sale of the ensuing numbers increased enormously, eventually attaining a

[1] "The Letters of Charles Dickens."

circulation of forty thousand copies! Messrs.
Chapman & Hall were naturally delighted, and, when
the twelfth number was reached, expressed their gratification by presenting the author with a cheque for
£500. In fact, during publication, Dickens received
from the firm the sum of £3000 in addition to the stipulated payments, the publishers themselves making a
clear profit of £14,000 by the sale in numbers only—
and this from a work which they very nearly
abandoned as hopeless. The failure of "Pickwick"
would, in all probability, have determined Charles
Dickens to relinquish the idea of adopting literature as
a profession, so we may consider it due to the creation
of the immortal Sam that the world is enriched by the
writings of "Boz."

It is, perhaps, not generally remembered that
Dickens, when twenty years of age, thought to
encourage his taste for the stage, and so earnestly
entertained the idea of becoming a professional actor
that he wrote to Bartley, the stage-manager at
Covent Garden, telling him exactly what he believed
he could do. "There must have been something
in the letter that struck the authorities," he afterwards
said to Forster, "for Bartley wrote to me, almost
immediately, to say that they were busy getting up
'The Hunchback' (so they were!), but that they would
communicate with me again." An appointment was
made for him to give at the theatre a specimen of his
histrionic ability in the presence of Charles Kemble,
but when the day arrived he was rendered *hors de
combat* through a terribly bad cold and an
inflammation of the face. He therefore resolved to
resume his application during the following season;
meanwhile, however, his attention was directed to
reporting and journalism, he "began to write, didn't

want money, had never thought of the stage but as a means of getting it," and gradually abandoned the idea. "See," he remarked, "how near I may have been to another sort of life."

Successful as "Pickwick" quickly proved to be, its issue by instalments met with hindrances as sad as they were unexpected. In the first place, as already intimated, the suicide of Seymour caused a difficulty with respect to an illustrator; another serious trouble presented itself when, on the eve of the publication of the fifteenth number, Dickens was prostrated with grief owing to the terribly sudden death, at the age of seventeen, of a favourite sister-in-law, Mary Hogarth, to whom he was tenderly attached. At this time, his prospects having improved, he and his pretty young wife relocated from the chambers in Furnival's Inn, where a son (Charles) had been born to them, to take up their residence at No. 48 Doughty Street, Mecklenburgh Square[1]; here his wife's youngest sister (Mary) also made her home, and it was on returning one night from the theatre, well and happy, that the "young and lovely girl" (whose charming personality is revived in Rose Maylie, of "Oliver Twist") was suddenly seized with a fatal illness, expiring in Dickens's arms a few hours afterwards. Her untimely end completely paralysed

---

[1] This locality is not unknown to literary fame. Shirley Brooks was born in Doughty Street, and Sidney Smith lived there, as did Edmund Yates at No. 43, opposite Tegg, the publisher of the delightful "Peter Parley" series of juvenile books. "It was a broad, airy, wholesome street," observes Mr. Yates; "none of your common thoroughfares, to be rattled through by vulgar cabs and earth-shaking Pickford vans; but a self-included property, with a gate at each end, and a lodge with a porter in a gold laced hat and the Doughty arms on the buttons of his mulberry coloured coat, to prevent anyone, except with a mission to one of the houses, from intruding on the exclusive territory." It is not so "exclusive" now.

his mental faculties, and in a letter to Harrison Ainsworth he said: "I have been so much unnerved and hurt by the loss of the dear girl whom I loved, after my wife, more deeply and fervently than anyone on earth, that I have been compelled for once to give up all idea of my monthly work, and to try a fortnight's rest and quiet." He thereupon suspended, for a brief space, the writing of "Pickwick," and the interruption in the hitherto regular appearance of the monthly numbers caused many strange conjectures to be circulated. Rumour sagely declared it to be impossible that a work "so varied, so extensive, and yet so true in its observations, could be the production of any single individual; that it was the joint production of an association, the different members of which transmitted their various ideas and observations; that one of their number, whose province it was to reduce them to a connected form, was, and had for many years been, a prisoner in the King's Bench!" It was likewise surmised that the author was a youth of eighteen who had been bred to the Bar, and whose health had so seriously suffered through his literary exertions that there was not the slightest chance of his ever publishing another number of "Pickwick." On hearing of these "idle speculations and absurdities," Dickens decided to issue an address in the fifteenth number, explaining the actual reason of the delay, and from that time matters went smoothly until the publication of the final instalment. Dickens tells us that nearly every number was written "almost as the periodical occasion arose," that is to say, with the printer close at his heels—a plan which afterwards yielded to a better system. "The Pickwick Papers" were received with a fervour so astounding that it may without exaggeration be averred that, in this regard, the author enjoyed an experience unique in literary annals. The book fell into everybody's hands; the judge on the bench revelled in its pages with as much delight as did the boy in the street; while tradesmen, availing themselves of the enormous popularity it achieved, bestowed its name upon various articles in the shop windows, in which were displayed Pickwick chintzes, Pickwick canes, hats, coats, gaiters, and Weller corduroys; Boz cabs rattled through the streets, Pickwick clubs were inaugurated, and portraits of the young writer were pasted up in omnibuses. Even today we have the Pickwick pen, the Pickwick cigar, the Pickwick biscuit, and the Pickwick bicycle club,—the first of its kind—and the "Bil Stumps" match box. Sala, in alluding to the days of what people called "Bozomania," says that dogs and cats used to be named "Sam" and "Jingle," and "Mrs. Bardell" and "Job Trotter."

"The Pickwick Papers" are, and always have been, regarded by the majority of readers as a mere collection of humorous episodes. The book is more than this, however, and concerning it Thackeray (who was among the first to recognise the fact) said: "I am sure that a man who, a hundred years hence, should sit down to write the history of our time, would do wrong to put that great contemporary history of 'Pickwick' aside as a frivolous work. It contains true character under false names; and, like 'Roderick Random,' an inferior work, and 'Tom Jones' (one that is immeasurably superior), gives us a better idea of the state and ways of the people, than one could gather from any more pompous or authentic history" Although years must elapse before the centenary of "Pickwick" can be celebrated, yet many of the social customs there chronicled have become obsolete.

Several characters in "Pickwick" (as in later works) were drawn from life, and in particular instances their prototypes have been identified. The name "Pickwick" was accidentally seen by Dickens on the door of a Bath coach owned by Moses Pickwick, while the hero's physique, costume, and benign expression were suggested by the personal appearance and dress of John Foster (a friend of Edward Chapman, the publisher), who is described as "a fat old beau, who would wear, in spite of ladies' protests, drab tights and black gaiters," and who lived at Richmond. Satisfactory evidence justifies the assumption that the original of Sam Weller was a character in a play by Beazeley, called "The Boarding House"—the role being assumed by Samuel Vale, a popular low comedian of that time, who, in that particular impersonation, highly amused his audiences by quaint sayings and out-of-the-way comparisons, such as Sam Weller was wont to indulge in. Concerning other personages in "Pickwick," it is acknowledged that Serjeant Buzfuz was a fairly accurate likeness of Serjeant Bompas, an eminent counsel then living, and that the peculiarities of Mr. Justice Stareleigh were suggested by those of Mr. justice Gaselee. The real name of the original of the Fat Boy was James Budden, whose father kept the "Red Lion" at the corner of Military Road and High Street, Chatham; the cognomen of Budden will also be found in one of the "Sketches by Boz."

*Apropos* of "The Pickwick Papers," it may be mentioned that an impertinent claim was made by

Mrs. Seymour, widow of the artist who designed the earlier illustrations for the work. Labouring under the strange delusion that, but for a severe illness, her husband would have written as well as embellished "Pickwick," Mrs. Seymour printed a pamphlet (in or about 1854), in which she vainly endeavoured to demonstrate that the entire credit of originating the book belonged to the deceased artist. Only two copies of this extraordinary pamphlet (which apparently was never published) are known to exist, and one of these realised £64 in a London auction room a few years ago. Notwithstanding the fact that Dickens, in his preface to the first cheap edition of "Pickwick" (1847), presented a detailed account of the conception and subsequent realisation of that work, he continued to be harassed by attempts on the part of Seymour's widow to extort money from him "by insisting that he [Seymour] had some inexplicable and ill-used part in the invention of 'Pickwick'!!!" In 1866 Seymour's son revived the monstrosity in a letter to the *Athenaeum*; whereupon Dickens, opining that the time had arrived for a formal and authoritative denial of the whole story, inserted a letter in the same Journal, which suffices, once for all, to dispose of such incoherent assertions.

# CHAPTER 3

## "OLIVER TWIST" AND "NICHOLAS NICKLEBY"

Before the last instalment of "Pickwick" reached the multitude of readers who had waited impatiently, month by month, for each new number, the fame of Charles Dickens was assured. He who, some twelve years previously, filled a subordinate position in a blacking warehouse, an unhappy drudge, had become at the age of twenty-four, the most popular author of the day. With "Pickwick," so freshly and brightly written, so spontaneous in its wit and humour, and withal so original in treatment, "Boz" had judged the public taste to a nicety, and the people were emphatic in expressing their appreciation of his efforts to entertain them. Such phenomenal success, thus triumphantly won, is seldom conceded to youthful aspirants in the thorny paths of literature.[1] Stronger heads than his have been turned by such unmistakable evidence of public favour; but, happily for him, Charles Dickens did not allow himself to be overcome by emotion, although, no doubt, he experienced a pardonable pride in the absolute victory he had gained.

We are indebted to Forster for an excellent pen-portrait of "Boz" as he appeared at this time. "A look of youthfulness first attracted you, and then

---

[1] Thackeray's first success, "Vanity Fair," was achieved at the age of thirty-six; George Eliot's at forty, with "Adam Bede"; Sir Walter Scott's at forty-three, with "Waverley."

a candour and openness of expression which made you sure of the qualities within. The features were very good. He had a capital forehead, a firm nose with full wide nostrils, eyes wonderfully beaming with intellect, and running over with humour and cheerfulness, and a rather prominent mouth strongly marked with sensibility. The head was altogether well formed and symmetrical, and the air and carriage of it were extremely spirited. The hair so scant and grizzled in later days was then of a rich brown and most luxuriant abundance, and the bearded face of his last two decades had hardly a vestige of hair or whisker; but there was that on the face as I first recollect it which no time could change, and which remained implanted on it unalterably to the last. This was the quickness, keenness, and practical power, the eager, restless, energetic outlook on each several feature, that seemed to tell so little of a student or writer of books, and so much of a man of action and business in the world. Light and motion flashed from every part of it." "*It was as if made of steel*," said Mrs. Carlyle some four or five years later, and Leigh Hunt remarked that it had "the life and soul in it of fifty human beings."

While engaged upon "Pickwick," Dickens's pen was in request in various directions; indeed, it is marvellous how he could devote attention to several tasks simultaneously without losing his grip of any particular subject.

A small brochure, entitled "Sunday under Three Heads; As it is: As Sabbath Bills would make it: As it might be made," belongs to this date (1836), and was written under the pseudonym of "Timothy Sparks," with illustrations by Hablot K. Browne ("Phiz"). It constituted a strong plea for the poor, with direct reference to a Bill "for the better observance of the Sabbath," which the House of Commons had then recently thrown out by a small majority. Sir Andrew Agnew, M.P., brought about an agitation advocating the enforcement of more rigid laws respecting Sunday observance, and Dickens, believing that such legislation would press more heavily on the poor than on the rich, pleaded for the encouragement of excursions and other harmless amusements on the Sabbath, as likely to counteract the tendency towards certain forms of dissipation which plebeian Londoners might favour in the absence of innocent recreation. Thanks to the National Sunday League and kindred bodies, that which Dickens so warmly advocated in 1836 has been in a measure realised, such as the opening of Museums and picture galleries on the Lord's Day.[1]

The fascination which the stage exercised over "Boz" induced him, in 1836, to take considerable interest in the then newly built St. James's Theatre, and he even essayed to write ("as a practical joke," he afterwards explained) a small farce in aid of the enterprise. This "comic burletta" was called "The Strange Gentleman," it being an adaptation of "The Great Winglebury Duel" in "Sketches by Boz"—a whimsical little production in which the humour arose from mistakes made at an inn on the North Road. The initial performance took place on the first night of the season of 1836, the play continuing for sixty nights, although it must be confessed that its popularity was mainly due to the clever assumption of the title role by J. P. Harley, the stage

---

[1] A copy of "Sunday under Three Heads" (now exceedingly, scarce) has realised as much as £15 by auction.

manager, and for whom the farce was expressly written.[1] Dickens was a constant visitor at the theatre during the run of the piece, and it is said that he once took part in it. A short time previously (that is, in 1835) Dickens became acquainted with John Hullah; a musical composer of the same age as himself, who had set to music some portions of an opera called "The Gondolier." Dickens thought it preferable to convert the opera into an English one, and agreeing to the proposal that he any Hullah should combine forces, offered to dramatise a little unpublished story for the object in view. Hullah consented, the title of "The Gondolier" was abandoned, and a novel subject having presented itself to Dickens, it was put forward as "The Village Coquettes," which assumed the form of a "comic opera" consisting of songs, duets, and concerted pieces. The first performance of "The Village Coquettes" took place at the St. James's Theatre on December 6, 1836, with Braham in the cast, and, after several representations in London, was transferred to Edinburgh. The play was well received, and duly praised by prominent musical journals. Dickens himself thought but little of his own share of the production, and described the *libretto* as being, to a certain extent, "a mere vehicle for the music," so that (quoting his own words) "it is scarcely fair or reasonable to judge it by those strict rules of criticism that would be, justly applicable to a five-act tragedy, or a finished comedy." When, in 1843, it was proposed

[1] This is probably the rarest of Dickens's writings. In 1892, a copy of the play (in the original wrapper) realised in the auction room the sum of £45, and seven years later another copy, containing the original drawing by "Phiz" for the frontispiece, was purchased under the hammer at nearly twice that amount.

No. 48 Doughty Street, Mecklenburgh Square

Residence of Charles Dickens, 1837-1839

*Photographed by Catharine Weed Ward*

No. 1 Devonshire Terrace, Regents Park
Residence of Charles Dickens, 1839-1851
*Photographed by Catharine Weed Ward*

to revive "The Village Coquettes," he vigorously
objected, begging that it might be allowed to "sink into
its native obscurity," and averring that both the
operetta and the farce of "The Strange Gentleman"
were done "without the least consideration or regard
for reputation." About a year before his death, he was
asked by Frederick Locker (Lampson) whether he
possessed a copy of "The Village Coquettes," and the
reply was, "No; and if I knew it was in my house, and
if I could not get rid of it in any other way, I would
burn the wing of the house, where it was!" The fact is,
he devoutly wished to draw a veil over these "dramatic
bantlings," which he had written for Hullah "in a fit of
damnable good nature"; "I just put down for everybody," he explained to R. H. Horne, "what everybody
at the St. James's Theatre wanted to say and do, and
that they could say and do best, and I have been most
sincerely repentant ever since." Forster, who makes
but bare reference to "The Strange Gentleman" and
"The Village Coquettes," entirely omits to mention a
third play by Dickens at this period—namely, a comic
burletta entitled "Is She His Wife? or, Something
Singular!" which first saw the light at the St. James's
Theatre on March 6, 1837, with J. P. Harley in the
principal role. No author's name appeared on the playbill until a week later, when it transpired that "Boz"
was responsible for the little farce, not a single copy of
which, in its original form, is believed to exist in this
country. The manuscript of a fourth play, called "The
Lamplighter," is in the Forster Library at South
Kensington: it was written in 1838, at Macready's
desire, for performance at the Covent Garden Theatre,
but never acted. Three years afterwards, Dickens

converted this farce into a humorous narrative entitled "The Lamplighter's Story,"[1] which represents his contribution to a collection of stories, essays, poems, &c., issued under the general title of "The Pic Nic Papers," and gratuitously produced and published for the benefit of the widow and children of Macrone, the publisher, who died in great poverty.

The overwhelming popularity of "Pickwick" speedily brought about a host of "imitators." The work was ruthlessly seized upon by certain unscrupulous publishers ("gutter hacks," as Sala significantly termed them), who plagiarised *ad nauseam* the book which so stirred the public mind. Many of these cunningly devised imitations purported to be continuations or sequels of Dickens's admired production, and nearly all were issued in monthly parts, with wrappers and illustrations in the style of the famous original. Thus there appeared such obvious imitations as G. W. M. Reynolds's "Pickwick Abroad; or, a Tour in France"; "Posthumous Papers of the Cadgers' Club"; "The Posthumous Notes of the Pickwickian Club"; "The Penny Pickwick"; "Pickwick in America"; "Pickwick in India"; and so forth. Dickens naturally felt disgusted at this unblushing effrontery, but for the present took no action in checking the abuse.

The pronounced success of Dickens's first book indicated with considerable certainty that future writings by him would prove a sound financial venture. His "Sketches by Boz" had already brought him about £400 from Macrone, who purchased the copyrights, and, profiting by the

[1] A parallel case of conversion occurred in respect of Thackeray's unacted play of "The Wolves and the Lamb," changed by the author into a story, "Lovel the Widower."

popularity of "Pickwick," netted some £4000 by them. Macrone then entertained the idea of publishing an edition in monthly parts, in the style of "Pickwick," being both legally and morally justified in so doing; but Dickens, imagining that it might be supposed that he intended to presume upon the success of "Pickwick" in thus foisting an old work upon the public in a new dress for the mere purpose of putting money into his own pocket, emphatically protested against the scheme, whereupon negotiations were opened for the repurchase of the copyright. Accordingly, he hastily arranged with Chapman & Hall to acquire it, jointly with himself and Forster, at the much enhanced sum of £2250, and, having thus secured all rights, he consented to the re-issue of the "Sketches" in monthly parts, the initial number appearing in November 1837. This, the first Complete Edition, included all the papers in the first and second series, and one additional article, viz., "The Tuggses at Ramsgate" from "The Library of Fiction," fifty-six papers in all, with the original designs by George Cruikshank, re-etched on a larger scale than previously, to accord with the increased dimensions of the new issue.

On August 22, 1836, Dickens entered into an agreement with Richard Bentley, the well-known publisher, to edit a new monthly magazine, *Bentley's Miscellany*, and to contribute thereto a serial story. The fact that, while still occupied with "Pickwick," he thus indicated his preparedness to undertake additional responsibilities of a most exacting nature, testifies to his abundant energy, as well as to the vigour of his intellect. The first number of the *Miscellany* was issued in January 1837, synchronising with the tenth instalment of "Pickwick," and in the second number appeared the opening chapter of "Oliver Twist," one of the most dramatic stories ever penned, the effect of which was heightened by George Cruikshank's powerful illustrations. Forster tells us that as the story shaped itself in the Author's mind it took an extraordinary hold upon him, and he could hardly leave it, working more frequently after dinner and until later hours than was his custom with any other of his novels. It is curious how, in the midst of friends, he could concentrate his ideas and fancies, even when a chatty conversation was proceeding; his brother-in-law, Henry Burnett, calling at Doughty Street on an occasion of this kind, when "Oliver Twist" was in progress, watched with great interest "the mind and the muscles working (or, if you please, *playing*) in company, as new thoughts were being dropped upon the paper—and to note the working brow, the set of mouth, with the tongue tightly pressed against the closed lips, as was his habit."

The domestic bereavement caused by the death of Mary Hogarth, which temporarily disturbed the continuity of the issue of "Pickwick," similarly affected the regular appearance of "Oliver Twist" (written contemporaneously), and a note was inserted in the June number stating that the author was so prostrated with grief that he was compelled to seek an interval of rest before resuming the story. In Forster, his life-long friend, he found a wise counsellor, who, from this time forward, lightened his literary labours by suggesting improvements in manuscripts and revising proofs. It was Forster, too, whom the Novelist invited to accompany him, either on horseback or on foot, to Hampstead, Barnet, and other rural places, these enjoyable jaunts acting as

Dickens reading "The Chimes" to his friends at No. 58 Lincoln's Inn Fields

On December 2, 1844

*From a pencil drawing by D. Maclise, R.A., 1844*

Charles Dickens ("Boz")

*From the drawing by S. Laurence, 1838*

a stimulant to fresh exertion, and preventing failure of health likely to accrue from excessive mental tension. "I knows a good 'ous there, where we can have a red-hot chop for dinner, and a glass of wine," —such was the kind of message which Dickens would send him, the "good 'ous" being "Jack Straw's Castle" on Hampstead Heath, famous also for its associations with Thackeray, Du Maurier, and Lord Leighton. Or, uncertain where to go, he would ask despairingly, "Where shall it be — *oh where* — Hampstead, Greenwich, Windsor? WHERE?????? While the day is bright, not when it has dwindled away to nothing! For who can be of any use whatsomdever such a day as this, excepting out of doors?" It sometimes happened that, owing perhaps to his being behindhand with "copy," nothing would tempt him from his desk. "No, no," he replied to one of Forster's invitations, when nearing the end of "Oliver Twist," "don't, don't let us ride till tomorrow, not having yet disposed of the Jew, who is such an out-and-outer that I don't know what to make of him." Here is a delightful instance of the reality which all the creatures of his fancy assumed for him—he regarded the people in his books as actual personages, and not merely of his own creating, following their careers with that eager interest which must necessarily be the outcome of so regarding them, laughing when they laughed, and weeping when they wept. In the first week of September 1838, he desired Forster to lunch with him, "and sit here, and read, or work, or do something, while I write the LAST chapter of "Oliver," which will be arter a lamb chop." "How well I remember that evening!" Observes Forster, "and our talk of what should be the fate of Charley

Bates, on behalf of whom (as indeed for the Dodger too) Talfourd[1] had pleaded as earnestly in mitigation of judgment as ever at the bar for any client he had most respected."

About four months before its *completion* in *Bentley's Miscellany*, "Oliver Twist" was published in three volumes, with Cruikshank's plates, and when the final chapter appeared in serial form, Dickens yielded the editorship of the *Miscellany* to his friend Harrison Ainsworth. For writing "Oliver Twist" the Novelist at first agreed to accept £500, afterwards increased to £750—an inadequate remuneration, as Dickens considered; indeed, he described it as "a paltry, wretched, miserable sum," and, surmising that the publishers were profiting very considerably by the sale of the story in volume form, he determined to repurchase the copyright, to which proposal Bentley magnanimously consented, thus releasing the Author from his covenant. So valuable an asset had Dickens's name become, even thus early in his career, that Bentley offered to pay him £40 monthly for merely lending it to the *Miscellany* for two years, with no writing or editing—an offer which he accepted.

No account of the production of "Oliver Twist" would be complete without reference to the remarkable claim made many years subsequently by its illustrator, George Cruikshank, who averred (as did Mrs. Seymour with respect to the "Pickwick Papers") that he conceived the idea of the story and suggested its principal characters and incidents. In a letter to the

[1] His and Forster's friend, Serjeant Talfourd, to whom "Pickwick" was dedicated. In Talfourd's "Tragedies" (1844) may be found a laudatory sonnet "To Charles Dickens, on his 'Oliver Twist,'" which story he declared to be the most delightful be had ever read.

*Times*, and in a pamphlet entitled "Artist and Author—a Statement of Facts" (1872), the artist affirmed, moreover, that in the presence of Dickens and Ainsworth he described and performed the character of one of the Jew receivers, this being (he insisted) the origin of Fagin. The whole allegation is dismissed by Forster as "a marvellous fable"; it nevertheless seems probable that Cruikshank, aided by his extensive knowledge of the byways of London life, offered valuable hints to the youthful "Boz," the importance of which the artist's vivid imagination caused him to exaggerate. It is interesting to know that in this powerful tale the author wrote out of office a Clerkenwell magistrate named Laing, who (like Mr. Fang) became conspicuous by reason of his coarseness and ill-temper.[1]

That the indefatigable "Boz" felt greatly worried by stress of work during his connection with *Bentley's Miscellany* is not surprising when we remember that he was simultaneously engaged upon several literary

---

[1] The following letter, dated from Doughty Street (1837-39), and recently printed for the first time, seems to indicate that Dickens was then associated with William Jerdan and the *Literary Gazette*. Writing to Jerdan (the Editor), he said: "I had feared you were not going to introduce me to the victim at all, so long have I expected him without avail. I think the best plan will be to have him set up at the end of the month, and a proof sent to you, which you will be able to keep a week or two, and correct at your leisure. Do you think so, too? It is really very unfair of you to charge any mistakes in your last paper upon me. I exerted myself about it at the very last moment, when there was no time to take it away from the printer's, at your own special request. I can have no object but to please the contributors to the best of my power, more especially yourself, and this is very discouraging indeed. I have not yet had time to read your friend's paper, but I will do so, and return you an answer before the close of the month. I have another paper about Ceylon you sent me, which I will return. . . ." It may be inferred that Dickens acted as literary adviser for Jerdan, who, however, makes no reference to the matter in his autobiographical reminiscences.

productions. For, besides "Oliver Twist" and the latter half of "Pickwick," he edited for Bentley the "Memoirs of Joseph Grimaldi" (the famous clown), and wrote several minor works, including articles for Bentley's magazine, afterwards published under the general title of "The Mudfog Papers." Among those minor works was a collection of humorous papers written as a kind of protest against a very ungallant attack upon the fair sex, in the form of a booklet entitled "Sketches of Young Ladies" (Chapman & Hall, 1839). The author was E. Caswall, who hid his identity under the pseudonym of "Quiz," each little essay purposing to describe, in a satirical manner, the peculiar idiosyncrasies of "Young Ladies." Taking up the cudgels on their behalf, Dickens (of course anonymously) similarly made fun of the "Young Gentlemen," summing them up in the same arbitrary fashion. About two years later he became responsible for a second collection of papers, entitled "Sketches of Young Couples," much resembling the previous papers in manner and treatment—his own comment upon it being, "a poor thing of little worth, published without my name."

In the seventeenth number of "Pickwick" an advertisement announced that the publishers had "completed arrangements with Mr. Dickens for the production of an entirely new work, to be published monthly, at the same price and in the same form as the "Pickwick Papers." This was "Nicholas Nickleby," the Novelist's third great effort in fiction. In the summer of 1837, before commencing this new story, he and his wife (accompanied by Hablot K. Browne, the illustrator of "Pickwick") enjoyed a ten days' holiday in Flanders, travelling by post-coach to Ghent, Brussels, Antwerp," and a hundred other places that I cannot recollect now and couldn't spell if I did," as he jocosely observed in a letter to Forster. A later seaside holiday was passed at Broadstairs, his favourite English seaside town, until its quietude and seclusion were disturbed by organ grinders and similar annoyances, attracted thither by the ever increasing crowds of visitors during the summer season.[1] Then, at the end of 1837, came a delightful dinner in town, with "Boz" himself in the chair and Serjeant Talfourd in the vice chair, to celebrate the success of the completed "Pickwick." In March 1838 a daughter[2] was born to him, and, to signalise the occasion, he and Forster "rode out fifteen miles on the Great North Road, and. after dining at the 'Red Lion' in Barnet on our way home, distinguished the already memorable day by bringing in both hacks dead lame."

The time had now arrived for Dickens, after this brief interval of repose, to direct his thoughts to the writing of "Nicholas Nickleby." According to his agreement with Chapman & Hall, it was stipulated that he should deliver the manuscript of the opening chapters on March 15th; for, as in the case of "Pickwick" and nearly all subsequent stories, the new tale was issued in monthly parts, the first appearing in April 1838 and the last in October 1839. Having been away from town when the first instalment of "Pickwick" came out, Dickens made it a superstition to be absent on all similar occasions. Therefore, on the eve of the publication of No. 1 of "Nickleby," Forster received from him a peremptory summons to meet him on the following

---

[1] Described by Dickens in a paper entitled "Our Watering Place" (*Household Words*, August 2, 1851). A portion of "Pickwick" was written at No. 12 High Street, Broadstairs.

[2] Mary (Mamie) Dickens.

(Saturday) night, and one o'clock on Sunday morning found the two friends starting for a ride on horseback, carrying "the news that lightened every part of the road," for the sale of the number had amounted that day to nearly fifty thousand copies.

With "Oliver Twist" not yet finished, and "Nickleby" well in hand, we may imagine that the author's brain was working at high pressure. All doubt as to the future welfare of "Nickleby" being dispersed by the enormous demand for the first instalment, the writing progressed under most promising conditions. The following was the full title of the story when first launched: "The Life and Adventures of Nicholas Nickleby, containing a Faithful Account of the Fortunes, Misfortunes, Uprisings, Downfallings, and Complete Career of the Nickleby Family." As in "Oliver Twist" the Novelist exposed the short-comings of the Poor Law system, so he determined to make "Nicholas Nickleby" the medium for calling public attention to the horrors of cheap boarding schools in Yorkshire. Of these institutions he had heard dreadful accounts during his boyhood, and these so stirred his emotions that he seized the opportunity now afforded him of investigating the subject. In January 1838, with this special object in view, he and his artist friend, Hablot K. Browne, journeyed by coach, in severe winter weather, to the locality where schools of the worst repute were situated. Forewarned that the Yorkshire pedagogues might resent, for obvious reasons, his sudden appearance in their midst, Dickens consulted a solicitor friend (Mr. Smithson) who had a Yorkshire connection, and between them a "pious fraud" was concocted in the form of letters of introduction having reference to "a supposititious little boy who had been left with a widowed mother" anxious to place him at a school in the neighbourhood, one of these missives being addressed to a certain individual who subsequently appeared in the story as honest John Browdie. Information thus gathered concerning typical boarding-schools near the borderline of Yorkshire and Durham enabled the Novelist to arrive at definite conclusions regarding the manner in which such seminaries were conducted, and to depict, with consummate force and skill, the memorable scenes at Dotheboys Hall which, though but "faint and feeble pictures of an existing reality" (as the author himself characterised them), so strongly excited public indignation that the particular institutions so justly denounced by him were doomed to rapid extinction. Perhaps no literary subject (with the exception of the oft-recurring Shakespeare-Bacon theory) has proved so controversial as the question of the identity of Dotheboys Hall and its worthy proprietor, the notorious Wackford Squeers. In the original preface to "Nicholas Nickleby," Dickens stated that it afforded him "great amusement and satisfaction, during the progress of this work, to learn, from country friends and from a variety of ludicrous statements concerning himself in provincial papers, that more than one Yorkshire schoolmaster lays claim to being the original of Mr. Squeers." The author ventured to suggest that the various assumptions to which the supposed portraiture gave rise may be due to the fact "that Mr. Squeers is the representative of a class, and not of an individual," and he added that "where imposture, ignorance, and brutal cupidity are the stock-in-trade of a small body of men, and one is described by these characteristics, all his fellows will recognise something belonging to themselves, and each will have a misgiving that the portrait is his own." Available evidence, however, proves fairly conclusively that, in delineating Dotheboys Hall and Squeers, Dickens had in his mind a particular Yorkshire school and its master, namely, Bowes Academy, kept by William Shaw, whose advertisement, among others of a similar character, may be found in contemporary issues of *The Times*, as follows:—

"EDUCATION.—By Mr. Shaw at Bowes Academy, Greta Bridge, Yorkshire, YOUTH are carefully INSTRUCTED in English, Latin, and Greek languages, Writing, Common and Decimal Arithmetic, Bookkeeping, Mensuration, Surveying, Geometry, Geography, and Navigation, with the most useful branches of the Mathematics, and provided with Board, Clothes, and every necessary, at 20 guineas per annum each. No extra charges. No vacations. Further particulars may be known on application to Mr. J. Metcalfe, agent, 38 Great Marylebone Street. Mr. Shaw attends at the George and Blue Boar, Holborn, from 12 to 2 daily."

Here is Dotheboys Hall to the life, even in the matter of "no vacations," while in Shaw's business card there is a notification, in the handwriting probably of Shaw himself, that he "leaves the Saracen's Head, Snow Hill [the London headquarters of Squeers], half-past seven o'clock, Thursday morning, 25th July."[1] As regards advertisements relating to these boarding schools, it is probable that Dickens generalised; but corroborative evidence of the identity of Squeers is afforded by the Novelist's notebook,

[1] Reproduced in "Charles Dickens by Pen and Pencil."

where, under date February 2, 1838, he entered the following memorandum:—

"Shaw, the schoolmaster we saw today, is the man in whose school several boys went blind some time since from gross neglect. The case was tried, and the verdict went against him. It must have been between 1823 and 1826. Look this up in the newspapers."

The case here referred to was the charge of cruelty brought in 1823 against Shaw by parents of children who had been his pupils, the verdict of the special jury being against the defendant, who was cast in heavy damages. Another link in the chain of evidence is discoverable in "Phiz's" illustrations, where his portrayal of Squeers is declared to be a tolerably accurate representation of Shaw. But the strange part of the business is that William, Shaw, who suffered seriously in consequence of the exposure in "Nicholas Nickleby," has been described, by certain people who knew him intimately, as a man of a kind and humane disposition, the charges levelled at his school being simply so many "artistic untruths"— statements deriving some confirmation from the circumstance that, after Shaw's death in 1850, his neighbours placed a stained-glass window in the village church to his memory! How, then, are we to consider those actions-at-law in which the defendant, Shaw, was mulcted in damages? A writer in the *Athenaeum* informs us that the charge of starving the boys broke down, the verdicts going against the schoolmaster on the charges of carelessness and neglect; and, although Bowes Academy left much to be desired, it is locally acknowledged to have been far above the class of schools which Dickens did so much to abolish. These leading facts, strengthened by others to which I have eluded elsewhere,[1] compel

---

[1] See *Literature*, June 22, 1901.

us to arrive at the conclusion that both Dickens and "Phiz," in their enthusiasm for the admirable cause they had so much at heart, unintentionally induced the public to believe that William Shaw was the worst of his tribe, with the inevitable result that he was made a scapegoat for the sins of others who more richly deserved chastisement.

The prototypes of at least three of the principal personages in "Nicholas Nickleby" were undoubtedly near relatives of the author. The portrait of Mrs. Nickleby was based upon the personality of his mother, who is described by a familiar acquaintance as "a little woman, who had been very nice looking in her youth. She had very bright, hazel eyes, and was as thoroughly good natured, easy going, companionable a body as one would wish to meet with. The likeness between her and Mrs. Nickleby is simply the exaggeration of some slight peculiarities. She possessed an extraordinary sense of the ludicrous, and her power of imitation was something quite astonishing." Mrs. John Dickens evidently did not detect the resemblance between herself and Mrs. Nickleby, for, in a letter to R. J. Lane, A.R.A., in 1844, *apropos* of some people who looked upon certain of his characters as grotesque impossibilities, Dickens said: "Mrs. Nickleby herself, sitting bodily before me in a solid chair, once asked me whether I really believed there ever was such a woman!" His sister Fanny inspired the creation of Kate Nickleby, and her husband, Henry Burnett, assured the present writer that the original of Nicholas, the hero of the story, had been identified with himself;[1] the figure

---

[1] The death of Mr. Henry Burnett took place, at the age of eighty-one, on February 7, 1893, which, by a curious coincidence, happened to be the eighty-first anniversary of the birth of his famous brother-in-law.

and dress of Nicholas, as delineated by "Phiz" in his illustrations, so much resembled Mr. Burnett's that many came to the conclusion that he posed for the hero of the novel. "I remember," observes Mr. Burnett, "going one night into a room at the English Opera House before dressing for the opera, and then for the first time hearing a shout, 'Welcome, Nicholas Nickleby.' After that it was common to address me so in many places. . . ." Those amiable and humane twins, the Cheeryble Brothers, were also drawn from life, their prototypes being the brothers Grant (Daniel and William), of Ramsbottom and Manchester, who had risen by their own exertions from comparative penury to a foremost position in the commercial world. A memorial, called "Grants' Stone," marks the spot where the penniless youths rested (like Dick Whittington of old) while taking their first look at the town in which they were afterwards to make a name and a fortune. Dickens possessed for many years a portrait of Daniel Grant, who died in 1855. On the decease of William Grant in 1842 (that is, nearly three years after the completion of the story), the Novelist (writing from Niagara Falls) thus informed his American friend, Professor Felton, of the fact: "One of the noble hearts who sat for the Cheeryble Brothers is dead. If I had been in England I would certainly have gone into mourning for the loss of such a glorious life. His brother is not expected to survive him. I am told that it appears from a memorandum found among the papers of the deceased that in his lifetime he gave away in charity £600,000, or three million dollars!" In his preface to the first cheap edition of the story, the Novelist declares that he never interchanged any communication with the Cheeryble Brothers, so that his admirable presentments must have been produced with the aid of those who were intimately acquainted with the Grants.

With regard to the writing of "Nickleby" we learn that Dickens commenced the story, from hastily scribbled notes and memoranda, on the very day of his return home from the north of England, where (as we have seen) he had been diligently collecting material concerning the cheap boarding schools. On February 7, 1838 (the twenty-sixth anniversary of his birthday), he said to Forster: "I *have* begun! I wrote four slips last night, so you see the beginning is made. And what is more, I can go on: so I hope the book is in training at last." As in the case of "Pickwick," he was never a single number in advance, but came up to time with astonishing and unfailing regularity. On September 9, 1839, he informed Forster that the end was imminent:— "I am hard at it," he said; "but these windings-up wind slowly, and I shall think I have done great things if I have entirely finished by the 20th." On the 18th he wrote: "I shall not entirely finish before Friday. . . . I have had pretty stiff work, as you may suppose, and I have taken great pains. The discovery is made, Ralph is dead, the loves have come all right, Tim Linkinwater has proposed, and I have now only to break up Dotheboys and the book together." The story was completed on the 20th at Broadstairs, and the event is thus recorded in his private diary: "Finished 'Nickleby' this day at two o'clock, and went over to Ramsgate with Fred [his brother] and Kate [his wife] to send the last little chapter to Bradbury and Evans. Thank God that I have lived to get through

Charles Dickens

*From the painting by D. Maclise, R. A., 1839*

Charles Dickens, his wife and sister

*From the pencil drawing by D. Maclise, R. A., 1843*

it happily." In honour of the occasion there was a dinner celebration at the "Albion" in Aldersgate Street, the guests including Forster, Serjeant Talfourd, Maclise (who painted the beautiful portrait of Dickens which forms the frontispiece to the story),[1] Sir David Wilkie, R. A., and Macready. Thus we see that he numbered among his intimate friends some of the most distinguished men of the day; for he now began to have his place as a writer conceded to him, and ceased to be regarded as a mere phenomenon or marvel of fortune.[2]

The payment originally agreed upon for "Nickleby" (based on the financial results of the sale of "Pickwick") was made in twenty monthly instalments of £150, that amount being the Author's fee for each number, the copyright reverting in five years to the Author, who, at the conclusion of the story, received from the publishers a handsome honorarium of, £1500 over and above the sum named in the bond. Long before the final chapters of the story

[1] This portrait was given to Dickens by his publishers, and now hangs in the National Gallery. Thackeray thought that, as a likeness, it was "perfectly amazing—a looking glass could not render a better facsimile. Here we have the real identical man, Dickens: the artist must have understood the inward Boz as well as the outward before he made this admirable representation of him."

[2] It is not, perhaps, generally known that George Borrow ("The Romany Rye") was numbered among the admirers of Dickens. Writing to a friend from Madrid in 1839, he said: "On my arrival in London [September 1838], everybody was in raptures over a certain 'Oliver Twist' that had just come out, and the 'Memoirs of the Nickleby Family,' which was appearing in fortnightly numbers. I was not long in getting both, and confess I was, like everybody else, delighted with them, especially with 'Oliver Twist.'" He considered Fagin "a frightful character—the most diabolical creation ever engendered by the human brain," and exhorted his friend to read, as soon as he could, all the writings of "Boz"—"and I am sure you will thank me all your life for having disclosed to you a mine of such delectable reading."—"Life, Writings, and Correspondence of George Borrow," by William I. Knapp, Ph.D., L L. D., 1899.

fell into the hands of his readers, a theatrical adapter named Edward Stirling made what Forster terms "an indecent assault" upon the book; that is to say, he seized upon it, "hacked, cut, and garbled its dialogue, invented a plot of his own," and produced it at the Adelphi Theatre.[1] This naturally provoked the indignation of the outraged Author, whose curiosity to witness the performance of so remarkable an adaptation induced him to visit the theatre, at which Forster felt amazed, especially when Dickens praised the making-up and management of certain characters and scenes. Edmund Yates points out, as a matter of fact, that so far from feeling displeased or annoyed by Stirling's version of "Nickleby," the Novelist expressed to Frederick Henry Yates (who impersonated Mantalini) his admiration and approval of the representation, and even proposed himself to dramatise "Oliver Twist" for the Adelphi boards! With regard to the adapters, Dickens speedily revenged himself in the forty-eighth chapter of "Nickleby," where he causes Nicholas to indulge in a violent tirade against their malpractices.

What with the misdeeds of these enterprising dramatists and the bastard productions of literary pirates, Dickens suffered much annoyance. Anticipating

---

[1] "Nicholas Nickleby. A Farce, in Two Acts. Taken from the popular work of that name by 'Boz.' By Edward Stirling, Esq." The play was dedicated to Charles Dickens, and, strange to relate, the imprint was that of Chapman & Hall, Dickens's own publishers! The first performance took place on November 19, 1838, when only about one-third of the story had appeared, and doubtless the clever acting of Yates, O. Smith, and Wilkinson in the "Nickleby" farce had much to do with the undoubted success of the piece. By a curious coincidence, the initial performance of a dramatic rendering of "Oliver Twist" was given on the same night at the Royal Surrey Theatre, the representation of which Dickens also witnessed; but it distressed him so much that in the middle of the first scene he laid himself down upon the floor in a corner of the box and never rose from it until the drop-scene fell.

that, as in the case of "Pickwick" and "Oliver Twist," the vendors of cheap literature would regard "Nicholas Nickleby" as legitimate spoil, the Novelist attempted to frustrate their intentions by issuing, on the eve of the appearance of the first number, the following emphatic "Proclamation," which he caused to be inserted in various reviews and magazines:—

"WHEREAS we are the only true and lawful 'Boz,' and WHEREAS it hath been reported to us, who are commencing a New Work to be called 'The Life and Adventures of Nicholas Nickleby,' that some dishonest dullards, resident in the cellars and bye-streets of this town, impose upon the unwary and credulous, by producing cheap and wretched imitations of our delectable Works. And WHEREAS we derive but small comfort under this injury, from the knowledge that the dishonest dullards aforesaid, cannot, by reason of their mental smallness, follow near our heels, but are constrained to keep along by dirty and little frequented ways, at a most respectful and humble distance behind.

"And WHEREAS, in like manner, as some other vermin are not worth killing for the sake of their carcases, so these kennel pirates are not worth the powder and shot of the law, inasmuch as whatever damages they may commit, they are in no condition to pay any.

"THIS IS TO GIVE NOTICE

"*Firstly,*

"To PIRATES.

"That we have at length devised a mode of execution for them, so summary and terrible, that if any gang or gangs thereof presume to hoist but one thread of the colours of the good ship Nickleby, we will hang them on gibbets so lofty and enduring, and their remains will be a monument of our just vengeance to all succeeding ages; and it shall not lie in any power of any Lord High Admiral on earth to cause them to be taken down again. . . ." [&C.]

Apparently this curious threat produced no immediate effect, as the objectionable plagiarisms became as numerous as ever, that exasperating form of literary piracy continuing some years longer. A raid of this kind was made in 1841 upon "Master Humphrey's Clock," and Dickens at once brought an action against the "dishonest dullards" who produced the "wretched imitation," and completely crushed them, but not before they had issued a valedictory address, stating their grievances and posing as "injured innocents"! Owing to this prompt proceeding on the part of the Novelist, and the very strong view taken of the case by Vice-Chancellor Knight Bruce, who gave judgment without even hearing Serjeant Talfourd (engaged for the prosecution), these catchpenny publications were suppressed, and their proprietors "beaten flat, bruised, bloody, battered, smashed, squelched, and utterly undone."

In March 1839, Dickens went to Devonshire, to seek a cottage home for his parents, his father having long given up his reporting duties. A suitable house was discovered at Alphington, one mile from Exeter and on the high-road to Plymouth. "You would laugh," he remarked in a letter to Thomas Mitton, an old schoolfellow who afterwards became his friend and solicitor, "if you could see me powdering away with the upholsterer, and endeavouring to bring about all sorts of impracticable reductions and wonderful arrangements."[1] He had recently celebrated his twenty-seventh birthday by an impromptu dinner, with Leigh Hunt, Ainsworth, and Forster as guests, and, informing J. P. Harley of the auspicious event, he added, "Lord bless my soul! Twenty-seven years old. Who'd have thought it? I *never* did! But I grow sentimental." At the end of October another daughter was born to him, and christened Kate Macready—the second name being taken from the famous actor, who was asked to be her sponsor.

"Nicholas Nickleby" was written for the most part at 48 Doughty Street;[2] a few chapters, however, were penned at a cottage in Twickenham Park during the summer of 1838, and some of the later numbers in the prettily situated Elm Cottage, Petersham, which he rented for the summer of 1839. In a letter of this date he referred to his "living in these remote and distant parts, with the charm of mountains formed by Richmond Hill presenting an almost insurmountable barrier" between himself and the busy world; and in this secluded retreat he frequently enjoyed the society of his friends—Maclise, Landseer, Ainsworth, Talfourd, Thackeray, Jerrold, and the rest, many of whom joined in the fun of athletic competitions organised by Dickens in the extensive grounds—bar-leaping, bowling, quoits, and such lighter recreations as battledore and bagatelle being freely indulged in, the genial host himself

[1] "The Letters of Charles Dickens."

[2] This, the only London home of Charles Dickens which remains unchanged, ought certainly to be marked with a memorial tablet, and it seems probable that the Historical Records and Buildings Committee will carefully consider its claim to this distinction as soon as they decide upon the mode of procedure to be adopted in such cases.

distancing every competitor in those feats requiring sustained energy. Among other frivolities at Twickenham, Forster recalls a balloon club for children, of which he was elected president on condition of supplying all the balloons. Writing to Macready in November 1839, Dickens said, "You must come and see my new house when we have it to rights." "Nickleby" was completed by this time, and the Novelist was about to leave Doughty Street for a more commodious residence at No. 1 Devonshire Terrace, Regent's Park—still existing in an altered condition— which he occupied until 1851; "a house of great promise (and great premium), undeniable situation, and excessive splendour," to quote his own concise description of the home in which many of the happiest years of his life were spent.

## CHAPTER 4

## "MASTER HUMPHREY'S CLOCK"

With "Nicholas Nickleby" and "Oliver Twist" engaging Dickens's attention, it might reasonably be imagined that, for the moment, he had sufficient to occupy his thoughts; yet another story, however, simmered in that active brain, but of which a word was not written until the autumn of 1839, when he had completed "Nickleby." Some two years previously this story had been frequently advertised by Macrone (who agreed to publish it) as "Gabriel Vardon"; owing to stress of work its preparation was unavoidably deferred *sine die*. It was afterwards proposed that the tale might follow "Oliver Twist" in *Bentley's Miscellany*, but, in consequence of certain disputes between Dickens and Richard Bentley respecting financial arrangements, the project was abandoned. According to a letter in Dickens's autograph, the amount of the honorarium offered by Macrone for the work was £200 for the first edition of one thousand copies. In the meantime, Dickens had entered into business relations with Chapman & Hall respecting "Pickwick," which ensured for him much higher remuneration than he had hitherto received, and caused him to regard with dissatisfaction such a comparatively modest fee as that named by Macrone. Being released by that publisher and by Bentley from all obligations, he was left free to make fresh negotiations with Chapman & Hall in the matter of the projected story, upon which (as will presently be seen) he decided to bestow the title of "Barnaby Rudge."

The Novelist now began to consider the advisability of temporarily discontinuing the plan of issuing his works in monthly parts, for he feared the public might tire of it, and believed that by publishing at briefer intervals the "wretched imitators" and plagiarists would be circumvented. The thought also occurred to him that the establishment of a cheap weekly publication, not necessarily to be written entirely by himself, would somewhat relieve him of the labour involved by the preparation of a long serial story, while proving remunerative at the same time. Having decided upon a new form of issue, he proposed to start the next venture in a manner similar to Addison's *Spectator*—that is (as explained by him to Forster), "with some pleasant fiction relative to the origin of the publication; to introduce a little club or knot of characters, and to carry their personal histories and proceedings through the work; to introduce fresh characters constantly; to reintroduce Mr. Pickwick and Sam Weller, the latter of whom might furnish an occasional communication with great effect; to write amusing essays on the various foibles of the day as they arise; to take advantage of all passing events, and to vary the form of the papers by throwing them into sketches, essays, tales, adventures, letters from imaginary correspondents, and so forth, so as to diversify the contents as much as possible. . . ." In order to impart further novelty to the undertaking, Dickens expressed his readiness to go, at any specified time, to Ireland or America, and

to write thence a series of descriptive papers, introducing local tales and traditions in the manner of
Washington Irving's "Alhambra." The proposal, in its
broader aspects, met with the approval of the
publishers, and at the end of March 1840 an agreement
was drawn up, in which, however, no particular work
is specified. That he had already begun the writing of
"Barnaby Rudge" is indicated by letters to Forster at
the end of the previous year. "Thank God, all goes
famously. I have worked at 'Barnaby' all day"; again,
"'Barnaby' moves, not at racehorse speed, but yet as
fast (I think) as under the unsettled circumstances
could possibly be expected"—he was then house
hunting, and on the point of leaving Doughty Street. It
was fated, however, that "Barnaby Rudge" should be
further delayed, giving precedence to yet another
story.

Although Dickens could not at first satisfy
himself with a title for his forthcoming production,
he had formed a notion as to the manner in which the
work might begin. He thought the first scene might
depict an "old file" in a "queer house, opening the
book by an account of himself, and, among other
peculiarities, of his affection for an old quaint queer
cased clock"; it was intended that the clock should
be a receptacle for odd manuscripts, and that a club
of old cronies should be formed, the members to
meet together in the room of the "old file," to be
known as Master Humphrey, who would read aloud
to them the manuscripts. "And thus I shall call the
book," he wrote presently to Forster, "either
'Old Humphrey's Clock'" or 'Master Humphrey's
Clock'." A few days later he intimated that he
inclined rather more to the latter title, "if so be

there is no danger of the pensive confounding master with a boy." So "Master Humphrey's Clock" gained the day, and in a week he had finished the first number. The work was announced in an original fashion—"Now wound up and going, preparatory to its striking on Saturday, the 28th March, Master Humphrey's Clock, maker's name—'Boz.' The Figures and Hands by George Cattermole, Esq., and 'Phiz.'" The numbers were to be published at weekly intervals, price threepence each,[1] and the announcement thus continued:—

"MASTER HUMPHREY hopes (and is almost tempted to believe) that all degrees of readers, young or old, rich or poor, sad or merry, easy of amusement or difficult to entertain, may find something agreeable in the face of his old Clock. That, when they have made its acquaintance, its voice may sound cheerfully in their ears, and be suggestive of none but pleasant thoughts. That they may come to have favourite and familiar associations connected with its name, and to look for it as for a welcome friend.

"From week to week, then, MASTER HUMPHREY will set his Clock, trusting that while it counts the hours, it will sometimes cheat them of their heaviness, and that while it marks the tread of Time, it will scatter a few slight flowers on the Old Mower's path.

"Until the specified period arrives, and he can enter freely upon that confidence with his readers which he is impatient to maintain, he may only bid

---

[1] "Master Humphrey's Clock" was also issued in monthly parts, the price varying from 1s to 1s. 3d., according to the amount of matter.

them a short farewell, and look forward to their next meeting."

There is good authority for stating that Dickens derived the name, "Master Humphrey," from that of a worthy horologist, William Humphreys, at Barnard Castle, Durham, who, when about sixteen years of age (1828-29), made the identical timepiece which afterwards became famous as Master Humphrey's Clock. On completion, the clock was placed inside the door of Humphreys' shop, and thus attracted Dickens's notice when, during his investigations in 1838 respecting the Yorkshire boarding schools, he put up at the "King's Head," Barnard Castle. William Humphreys died in 1887, at the age of seventy-five; he was born during the same year as Dickens, and in his latter days delighted in recounting his recollections of the Novelist.

The first number of "Master Humphrey's Clock" appeared on April 4, 1840, and nearly seventy thousand copies were sold. The critics, however, did not favour the idea of the weekly issue—an innovation that Dickens imagined would be generally appreciated—nor did they regard with approbation the general scheme of the book, which seemed a kind of serial miscellany of tales and sketches, and not the continuous story they anticipated. The circulation, consequently, began to decrease, but recovered when Mr. Pickwick and the Wellers were revived. The Novelist, however, soon perceived that the work, if continued on the original plan, would be inartistic; he speedily abandoned the idea of enlisting the services of other writers, and disposing of the cumbrous machinery that threatened to prove disastrous, at once decided to embark upon a consecutive tale, uninterrupted by the "Clock" chapters. The title for this tale, which commenced in the fourth number gave the Author some trouble, as usually happened in the case of new stories, a number of tentative titles being customarily submitted to Forster for his opinion as to the most suitable. "What do you think of the following double title for the beginning of that little tale?" he queried in this instance: "'Personal Adventures of Master Humphrey: The Old Curiosity Shop.' I have thought of 'Master Humphrey's Tale,' 'Master Humphrey's Narrative,' 'A Passage in Master Humphrey's Life,' but I don't think any does so well as this. I have also thought of 'The Old Curiosity Dealer and the Child,' instead of 'The Old Curiosity Shop.'" The latter, however, was eventually selected, and it has been objected to because there is scarcely anything in the book about old curiosities, the bric-a-brac shop itself disappearing from the scene in the early chapters.

Early in 1840, Dickens and his wife, accompanied by Maclise and Forster, passed three happy days with Walter Savage Landor at Bath. Forster, in his "Life of Landor," records the interesting fact that it was at a celebration of the poet's birthday in his Bath lodgings, 35 St. James's Square, that "the fancy which took the form of Little Nell in the 'Curiosity Shop' first dawned on the genius of its creator." He further assures us that no character in prose fiction was a greater favourite with Landor, who emphatically declared that he had never in his life regretted anything so much as his having failed to carry out an intention he had formed, viz., to have purchased that house, and then and there to have burnt it to the ground, in order that no meaner association should ever desecrate the birthplace of

Dickens's young girl heroine. The Novelist himself was greatly wrapped up in this tender piece of characterisation, for the reason that in Little Nell he had enshrined the memory of his sister-in-law, Mary Hogarth, whose premature death so sadly affected him, and assured his friends that the child was an object of his love,—that he mourned her loss as if one of his own offspring had left a vacant chair. So great a hold had this touching creation obtained upon the public mind that the author received anonymous requests from all quarters imploring him "not to kill" her; but, in view of the best interests of the story, it became essential that Nelly should die, as the sentiment of the conception would be destroyed if she had ended her days in a prosaic manner. The Novelist, by the way, had not thought of killing her until this was pointed out by Forster, who was really responsible for the tragic ending. Perhaps no incident in the romances of Dickens has so stirred the emotions as the passing away of Little Nell. Such a practical man as Daniel O'Connell, the great Irish agitator, was so overcome by its pathos that, with tears in his eyes, he said, "He should not have killed her. She was too good!" and even the stern critic, Lord Jeffrey,[1] sobbed terribly after reading the account of Nell's last hours, her tragic ending likewise filling Macready with grief. Yet there are intelligent persons who regard the incident as a morbid straining after effect, absolutely devoid of pathos!

For change of scene, and to help the story, Dickens went twice to Broadstairs during its progress, in June and September. He so delighted in the companionship of his friends that they were constantly in receipt of cordial invitations to his seaside home, these

[1] *See* page 505.

invitations sometimes including humorous attempts at versification, such as the following addressed to Maclise:—

> "My foot is in the house,
> My bath is on the sea,
> And, before I take souse,
> Here's a single line to thee."[1]

—a parody of Byron's Farewell to Moore, beginning "My boat is on the shore," &c. Maclise, by the way, made one drawing for the tale; he had proposed to furnish more, but circumstances necessitated the employment of other artists, George Cattermole[2] and "Phiz," the illustrations in this instance being drawn and engraved on wood. Writing to Cattermole with respect to his design for Little Nell's death chamber, he said: "I am breaking my heart over this story, and cannot bear to finish it." Forster states that he never knew him to wind up a story with such sorrowful reluctance, lingering over the finale until he realised the imperative need of concentrating himself upon it, and at length completing his labours at four o'clock in the morning of January 17, 1841. "It makes me very melancholy," he confessed, "to think that all these people are lost to me for ever, and I feel as if I never could become attached to any new set of characters."

"The Old Curiosity Shop" proved an extraordinary triumph from the very beginning, maintaining its popularity and greatly increasing the writer's fame. On the day of launching the first number of "Master Humphrey's Clock," Dickens left town according to the rule prescribed for such occasions,

---

[1] "The Letters of Charles Dickens."
[2] George Cattermole (whom Dickens sometimes addressed as "Kittenmoles") married a Miss Elderton, a cousin of the Novelist.

and, with Forster and Maclise as companions, enjoyed a brief holiday tour in the Midland counties. Forster joined him at Birmingham with the welcome news of the sale of sixty thousand copies (representing the first edition), and of orders for ten thousand more! Towards the end of the unexpectedly-prolonged excursion, the members of this merry party were dismayed to find their resources had become so reduced that they were compelled to pawn their watches at Birmingham in order to provide funds for the return journey!

The story of Little Nell was written at Devonshire Terrace and Broadstairs. As soon as the Novelist had settled down in his London home he resumed almost daily his rides with Forster, foregathered with Maclise at Hampstead and elsewhere, and had sociable intercourse with those distinguished in Literature and Art whom his fame and delightful personality inclined to rally round him— Macready, Talfourd, Procter ("Barry Cornwall"), Clarkson Stanfield, R.A., Albany Fonblanque, Sir Emerson Tennent, Count D'Orsay, Sir David Wilkie, R.A., Sir Edwin Landseer, R.A., Samuel Rogers (the banker-poet), Sydney Smith (the witty Canon of St. Paul's), and Lytton Bulwer, for whom he entertained the highest admiration. What greater compliment could be tendered to "Boz" than the close friendship— nay, companionship—accorded him by men of such intellectual attainments? Needless to observe, their sincere interest in the Novelist's various undertakings added zest to his labours, while his own unwearying animal spirits and good fellowship afforded unlimited pleasure to every one with whom he came in contact.

The "new novel by Boz," heralded by Macrone

as already stated, and to be called "Gabriel Vardon, the
Locksmith of London," was originally planned for
publication in three volumes, and subsequently as a
serial in *Bentley's Miscellany*. It was destined,
however, to succeed "The Old Curiosity Shop,"
appearing under the general title of "Master
Humphrey's Clock," and its designation changed to
that of "Barnaby Rudge."[1] Prefaced by a short chapter
headed "Master Humphrey's Reflections," which
introduces the tale; this powerful and dramatic account
of the famous Gordon Riots proceeded without interruption until its conclusion. Dickens had the advantage
of beginning "Barnaby" with plenty of material in
advance, for since 1838 it had been much in his mind.

After visiting Brighton for a week's quiet labour,
a dinner was given on the 10th of April 1841 to
celebrate the completion of the second of the three
volumes of "Master Humphrey," when Talfourd (who
presided) proposed the toast of "The Clock," the
remaining toasts being interspersed with humorous
songs by the comedian, J. P. Harley, who thus added
considerably to the mirth of the evening. A second son
had been then recently born to Dickens,—christened
Walter Landor, after the father's old friend,—and in
June he left for Scotland, taking "Barnaby" with him.
In August we find him at Broadstairs, where he again
attacked the story. From time to time he informed
Forster of his progress, slow at first, but when the
subject was well in hand he said: "I am warming up
very much about 'Barnaby.' Oh! If I only had him
from this time to the end in monthly numbers,"

---

[1] Gabriel Varden (not Vardon) is one of the leading characters in the
tale, and his cognomen may be found in the London Directory of 1780,
the period in which the narrative is laid.

for he felt more than ever, during the closing scenes, the constraints of weekly publication. On the 11th September the announcement came that he had just "burnt down Lord Mansfield's, and played the very devil. Another number will finish the fires and help us on towards the end. I feel quite smoky when I am at work. I want elbow-room terribly." Unhappily, a serious illness now harassed him, but he bore up gallantly, and was still In his sickroom when (on 22nd October) he wrote: "I hope I shan't leave off any more now until I have finished 'Barnaby.'" On the 2nd of November the printers received the final chapters, thus enabling the Author at the end of the year to take a much-needed rest.

In his preface to "Barnaby Rudge," Dickens explains that he was induced to write this stirring romance because no account of the Gordon Riots of 1780 had been to his knowledge presented in any work of fiction; the subject, too, comprised very extraordinary and remarkable incidents. He gathered his materials for the historical portion of the novel from contemporary newspapers and pamphlets at the British Museum, and his description of the principal events will bear the test of comparison with the accounts given in those records. From the preface we also learn that half-witted Barnaby's pet raven, "Grip," is a compound of two originals, of whom Dickens was at different times the possessor; the first of these (also named "Grip") poisoned himself with white lead, his dying words being "Halloa, old girl!"—a favourite expression—while the second (a larger bird) expired from unknown causes, keeping his eye to the last upon the meat as it roasted, and suddenly turning over on his back with a sepulchral cry of "Cuckoo!" The Novelist's partiality for these curious creatures (whose loss proved a domestic calamity) induced a punning friend to remark that he was "raven mad," which gave rise to the absurd rumour that he had become insane, thus necessitating confinement in a lunatic asylum! Dr. A. W. Ward suggests that Dickens may have derived the first notion of "Grip" from the raven "Ralpho"—likewise the property of a demented person who frightened Roderick Random and Strap out of their wits, and into the belief that he actually *was* the personage which "Grip" so persistently declared himself to be;[1] this seems probable, when we remember how Dickens, when a boy, revelled in the works of Smollett. It is not difficult to identify, in the old "King's Head" at Chigwell, the original of the "Maypole" Inn of "Barnaby Rudge," which, although bearing no resemblance to Cattermole's charming but fanciful drawing, is replete with those ancient features that attract both artist and archaeologist. Writing to Forster, the Novelist said: "Chigwell, my dear fellow, is the greatest place in the world. Name your day for going. Such a delicious old inn opposite the churchyard—such a lovely ride—such beautiful forest scenery—such an out-of-the-way rural place—such a sexton! I say

---

[1] "Roderick Random," chap. 13. For a letter from Dickens to his friend, Angus, Fletcher (the "Mr. Kindheart" of one of his minor writings, describing the illness and decease of "Grip," the sum of £50 was recently offered, and refused, merely for the right to publish a *facsimile* of it in an American journal. A similar letter to Forster was transmitted at Dickens's request to Maclise, who immediately produced a sketch purporting to represent the apotheosis of that remarkable bird. "Grip" the first was stuffed, and placed in a glass case, by way of ornament to his master's study, and at the sale of the Novelist's effects in 1870 it realised a hundred and twenty guineas.

again, name your day." Great was his delight when, on arriving at the inn, the landlord recognised him as the author of "Barnaby Rudge."

The final chapter of the story was succeeded by a paper from Master Humphrey, with which the last volume concluded. Soon after publication, the unsold stock of "Master Humphrey's Clock" was divested of the introductory, intercalary, and miscellaneous papers, and "The Old Curiosity Shop" and "Barnaby Rudge" were issued independently.

The book contained a Dedication to Samuel Rogers, to whom the author acknowledged indebtedness for "a beautiful thought" in the last chapter but one, which is taken from "Ginevra," and has reference to "an old man wandering *as in quest of something.*"

## CHAPTER 5

# "AMERICAN NOTES" AND "MARTIN CHUZZLEWIT"

In May 1841, Dickens became the recipient of a letter conveying a requisition from the people of Reading that he should represent that town in Parliament, which flattering proposal he politely and firmly declined, saying in his reply to the correspondent who acted on behalf of the constituency: "My principles and inclinations would lead me to aspire to the distinction you invite me to seek, if there were any reasonable chance of success, and I hope I should do no discredit to such an honour if I won and wore it. But I am bound to add, and I have no hesitation in saying plainly, that I cannot afford the expense of a contested election. If I could, I would act on your suggestion instantly. I am not the less indebted to you and the friends to whom the thought occurred, for your good opinion and approval. I beg you to understand that I am restrained solely (and much against my will) by the consideration I have mentioned, and thank both you and them most warmly." Although confessing to an intelligent interest in the various phases of politics, he never yearned for parliamentary honours; indeed, we shall find that, at a later period, he expressed a somewhat emphatic and decisive opinion on the subject.

During the summer months the Novelist spent a
few weeks in Scotland, at the suggestion of his friend
Lord Jeffrey,[1] who came to London earlier in the year,
and his reception was of a most enthusiastic character.
This visit to the beautiful country of Burns and Scott
proved a memorable one, it being initiated by a public
dinner in Edinburgh, with Professor Wilson
(Christopher North) in the chair, and among the three
hundred guests were Peter Robertson, Adam Black
(the publisher), Dr. Alison, Allan, Colquhoun, and
Lord Meadowbank. His reputation had preceded him
with the result that his hotel was besieged by admirers,
and so forced him "to take refuge in a sequestered
apartment at the end of a long passage." This (as
Forster observes) was "Boz's" first practical experience of the honours his fame had won for him, and it
found him as eager to receive as all were eager to give.
"It [the dinner] was the most brilliant affair you could
conceive," he wrote to Forster; "the completest
success possible from first to last. The room was
crammed, and more than seventy applicants for tickets
were of necessity refused yesterday. . . . I wished to
God you had been there, as it is impossible for the
'distinguished guest' to describe the scene. It beat all
natur'." A few days later, the lord provost, council, and
magistrates voted him by acclamation the freedom of
the city, and the parchment scroll recording the
grounds on which it was voted hung in his study to the
last—a cherished souvenir. A rumour had reached him
that Glasgow also desired to give a public dinner in his
honour, but he hoped to get away before they sent for
him; for his social engagements, breakfasting or
lunching here, dining or supping there, with theatres
and evening parties to follow, were enough to under-
mine the strongest constitution. "The moral of all this

[1] *See* page 505.

is" (he admitted to Forster) "that there is no place like home. . . . I sigh for Devonshire Terrace and Broadstairs, for battledore and shuttlecock; I want to dine in a blouse with you and Mac [Macready]. . . . On Sunday evening the 17th of July I shall revisit my household gods, please heaven. I wish the day were here. . . ." Before leaving Edinburgh he was called upon to make a public appearance at the theatre, and, on entering the building, he and his friends were much amused and amazed by the orchestra improvising "Charley is my Darling," amid tumultuous shouts of delight. An offer to be returned as an M.P. ("free gratis for nothing and qualified to boot") for a Scottish county then going a begging, but declined by him, must also be mentioned as one of the many noteworthy incidents appertaining to his stay in the North. Before returning to London, he and his wife enjoyed a trip to the Highlands under the guidance of an eccentric companion, Angus Fletcher, himself a quasi-Highlander, who wore a white coat and a great Highland cap; the expedition was distinguished by a series of adventures of which a complete narrative was conveyed to Forster, whence we learn that, of all the scenes then witnessed, nothing affected the Novelist so intensely as the Pass of Glencoe—"that awful Glencoe," he called it. "It is shut in on each side by enormous rocks from which great torrents come rushing down in all directions. In amongst these rocks on one side of the pass (the left as we came) there are scores of glens, high up, which form such haunts as you might imagine yourself wandering in, in the very height and madness of a fever. They will live in my dreams for years—I was going to say as long as I live, and I seriously think so. The very recollection of them makes me shudder. . . . Well, I will not bore you with my impressions of these tremendous wilds, but they really are fearful in their grandeur and amazing solitude." As the close of the Highland tour drew nigh, his impatience to behold once more his beloved Devonshire Terrace increased: "I am dying for Sunday," he said, "and wouldn't stop now for twenty dinners of twenty thousand each." The opening of August found him in his London home and soon afterwards he departed for Broadstairs, spending the autumn there and occupying himself with the concluding chapters of "Barnaby Rudge." Early in October he was obliged to submit to a painful operation, which confined him to a sofa and a carriage for nearly a month. Towards the end of the year he went to Windsor for change of air; but, prior to starting for the Royal borough, he had entered into negotiations with Chapman & Hall for a new work in twenty numbers, similar to those of "Pickwick" and "Nickleby," the first of which, however, was not to be published until a year had elapsed. The terms were to be £200 monthly, in addition to a substantial share of the profits.

One of the most important episodes in the life of Charles Dickens now impended. For some time (that is, since 1839) he had entertained a desire to visit America, and this desire was considerably strengthened when, in 1841, he received a hearty and sympathetic letter from Washington Irving in praise of Little Nell. Such commendation from so distinguished a writer gladdened his heart, and, in acknowledging Irving's warmly expressed appreciation of his writings, he intimated how delightful it would be if he (Irving) would visit England, so that they could compare notes "about all those delightful places and people" that "Boz" used to dream of when "a very small and not-over-particularly-taken-care-of boy." Soon after his return from Scotland the idea of journeying to the United States began to take definite shape, and on the 19th of September 1841 he wrote to Forster: "Now to astonish you. After balancing, considering, and weighing the matter in every point of view, I have made up my mind (with god's leave) to go to America and to start as soon after Christmas as it will be safe to go." Nine days later this decision was likewise imparted, with more exactitude, to a Transatlantic correspondent (Mr. L. Gaylord Clark), in the following terms: "On the fourth of next January, if it please God" [a favourite expression], "I am coming with my wife on a three or four months' visit to America. The British and North American Packet will bring me, I hope, to Boston, and enable me, in the third week of the New Year, to set my foot upon the soil I have trodden in my daydreams many times, and whose sons (and daughters) I yearn to know and to be among." He informed Chapman & Hall, who heartily endorsed the resolution, that (like Mr. Pickwick) he meant to keep a notebook, and, on his return, to "publish it for half-a-guinea or thereabouts." Mrs. Dickens, at first very reluctant, at length agreed to accompany her husband, the four children to be left in the care of Mr. and Mrs. Macready. "The American preliminaries are necessarily startling," he wrote to Forster, "and, to a gentleman of my temperament, destroy rest, sleep, appetite, and work, unless definitely arranged." The steamship *Britannia*, in which berths had been taken, brought to the Novelist in December all sorts of cordial greetings

[BRITANNIA 1842]

in anticipation of the welcome awaiting him.

At length came the eventful day, January 4, 1842, when the ship left the Liverpool docks with Mr. and Mrs. Charles Dickens on board; and it should be remembered that sixty years ago a voyage across the Atlantic, especially in the winter season, was usually fraught with considerable inconvenience, not to say danger, the paddle steamers of that period presenting a marked contrast, in respect of both comfort and speed, to the "ocean greyhounds" and "floating palaces" of the present time, when luxurious travelling is considered a *sine qua non*. The Novelist, referring to the lack of accommodation on board the *Britannia*, thus wrote to Thomas Mitton: "Anything so utterly and monstrously absurd as the size of our cabin, 'no gentleman of England who lives at home at ease' can for a moment imagine. Neither of the portmanteaus would go into it. There!.... The ladies' cabin is so close to ours that I could knock the door open without getting off something they call my bed, but which I believe to be a muffin beaten flat." Prominent among the Novelist's numerous well-wishers anxious for his safe return was the kindly humorist, Thomas Hood, who composed the following witty verses to celebrate the occasion:—

> "Pshaw! Away with leaf and berry,
>     And the sober-sided cup!
> Bring a Goblet, and bright Sherry!
>     And a bumper fill me up.—
> Tho' I had a pledge to shiver,
>     And the largest ever was,—
> Ere his vessel leaves our river,
>     I will drink a health to Boz!

["BRITANNIA" 1842]

"Here's success to all his antics,
Since it pleases him to roam,
And to paddle o'er Atlantics,
After such a *sale* at home!
May he shun all rocks whatever,
And the shallow sand that lurks,—
And the *Passage* be as clever
As the best among his works!"[1]

The encouraging prediction, so sagely uttered by the stewardess, that the voyage out would be really a very fine one, proved quite the reverse; for, almost from the start, the weather continued obstinately and almost unprecedentedly bad, and the good ship *Britannia* laboured in a heavy sea against a headwind. "What the agitation of a steam vessel is, on a bad winter's night on the wild Atlantic, it is impossible for the most vivid imagination to conceive," observes the Novelist, in his realistic description of this trying voyage, hit off (Forster tells us) as if he had been all his life a sailor. "To say that she is flung down on her side in the waves, with her masts dipping into them, and that, springing up again, she rolls over on the other side, until a heavy sea strikes her with the noise of a hundred great guns, and hurls her back—that she stops, and staggers, and shivers, as though stunned, and then, with a violent throbbing at her heart, darts onwards like a monster goaded into madness, to be beaten down, and battered, and crushed, and leaped on by the angry sea—that thunder, lightning, hail, and rain, and wind, are all in fierce contention for the mastery—that every plank has its groan, every nail its shriek, and every drop of water in the great ocean its howling voice—is nothing. To say that all is grand, and all appalling and horrible in the last

[1] The *New Monthly Magazine*, February 1842.

degree, is nothing. Words cannot express it. Thoughts cannot convey it. Only a dream can call it up again, in all its fury, rage, and passion." One night, during the gale, the sea crushed the lifeboat like a walnut shell, and tore away the planking of the paddle boxes, leaving the wheels exposed and bare; the next morning the funnel was white with crusted salt, and the rigging all knotted, tangled, wet, and drooping. "A gloomier picture it would be hard to look upon."[1] The climatic conditions were undoubtedly of exceptional severity, and the experienced head engineer acknowledged that he had never seen such stress of weather. At one time Dickens himself apprehended, and with justification, that all was lost—that the *Britannia*, with its living freight, was doomed to destruction—and he quietly waited for the worst. "I never expected to see the day again," he wrote, "and resigned myself to God as well as I could." At the close of the memorable voyage the ship suddenly struck upon a bank of mud, creating the greatest confusion on board, and after much backing of paddles and heaving of lead, anchor was dropped in a strange looking nook, surrounded by banks, rocks, and shoals; the next morning found the ship gliding down a smooth, broad stream, the sun shining brightly, and the officers and crew rigged out in their smartest clothes. Presently they came to the wharf at Halifax, "and leaped upon the firm, glad earth again;" after delivering and exchanging mails, the ship stood off for Boston, where it was telegraphed on the eighteenth day out from Liverpool. The interest with which Dickens strained his eyes "as the first patches of American soil peeped like molehills from the green sea, and

---

[1] "American Notes," chap. 2.

followed them, as they swelled, by slow and almost imperceptible degrees, into a continuous line of coast," was intense. On the day before landing, a meeting of the passengers was held in the vessel's saloon, with the Earl of Mulgrave as chairman and Charles Dickens as secretary and treasurer, and it was unanimously resolved to recognise, in an appropriate manner, Captain Hewett's nautical skill, which enabled the ship safely to accomplish a more than ordinarily tempestuous passage. A subscription was forthwith raised for the purchase of a piece of plate, to be suitably inscribed, testifying to the lasting gratitude of the passengers.

It has probably never been the good fortune of any individual, whether in a public or a private capacity, to meet with such an ovation as that which was accorded to Charles Dickens on his arrival in America. Writing to Forster from Boston, before many days had elapsed, he said: "How can I give you the faintest notion of my reception here; of the crowds that pour in and out [of the hotel] the whole day; of the people that line the streets when I go out; of the cheering when I went to the theatre; of the copies of verses, letters of congratulation, welcomes of all kinds, balls, dinners, assemblies without end? . . . What can I tell you about any of these things which will give you the slightest notion of the enthusiastic greeting they gave me, or the cry that runs through the whole country!" Again, to Thomas Mitton he wrote that no king or emperor was "so cheered and followed by crowds, and entertained in public at splendid balls and dinners, and waited on by public bodies and deputations of all kinds. I have had one from the Far West—a journey of two thousand miles! If I go out in a carriage, the crowd surround it and escort

me home; if I go to the theatre, the whole house
(crowded to the roof) rises as one man, and the timbers
ring again. You cannot imagine what it is. I have five
great public dinners on hand at this moment, and invitations from every town and village and city in the
States." As Dr. Channing observed, in a letter he then
addressed to the hero of the day, "There never was,
and never will be, such a triumph."

And so, during the six months he remained an
esteemed guest in that great country, his progress
through the States—from city to city, from populous
town to remote village—was marked by an
unmistakable expression of sincere admiration and
personal affection on the part of the inhabitants, which
caused the grateful recipient of such homage immense
satisfaction. Referring to the effect upon himself, he
remarked: "I feel, in the best aspects of this welcome,
something of the presence and influence of that spirit
which directs my life, and through a heavy sorrow has
pointed upwards with unchanging finger for more than
four years past. And if I know my heart, not twenty
times this praise would move me to an act of folly."
Forster attributes Dickens's enormous popularity in
America at the time of this visit to "the hearty, cordial,
and humane side of his genius," and to "the cheerful
temper that had given new beauty to the commonest
forms of life"; these characteristics, then so rare,
proved fascinating to the Americans, who regarded the
young English author "as a kind of embodied protest
against what they believed to be worst in the
institutions of England." Daniel Webster (says Forster)
assured his compatriots that Charles Dickens had done
more already to ameliorate the condition of the
English poor than all the statesmen Great Britain had

sent into Parliament, while Dr. Channing emphatically declared that "Boz's" sympathies were such as to recommend him in an especial manner to his (the Doctor's) fellow countrymen. "He shows that life in its rudest form may wear a tragic grandeur; that amidst follies and excesses, provoking laughter or scorn, the moral feelings do not wholly die; and that the haunts of the blackest crime are sometimes lighted up by the presence and influence of the noblest souls. His pictures have a tendency to awaken sympathy with our race, and to change the unfeeling indifference which has prevailed towards the depressed multitude, into a sorrowful and indignant sensibility to their wrongs and woes." Testimonies of this nature, emanating from the leaders of thought in America, could not fail to influence public opinion favourably as regards the subject of them, while the exceedingly friendly attitude of those whose names rank highest in the annals of American literature afforded a convincing proof that the author of "Pickwick" and the creator of Little Nell deserved all the honours that were showered upon him.

Although Dickens went to America with no particular mission, yet it was during this visit in 1842 he began his agitation of the great International Copyright question, which still remains in abeyance.[1] Besides presenting two petitions to American

---

[1] James Spedding, who reviewed "American Notes" in the *Edinburgh Review* for January 1843, stated in effect that, if he had been rightly informed, Dickens had gone to America as a kind of missionary in the cause of International Copyright. Dickens, in a letter to *The Times* promptly repudiated the suggestion, and accused the writer of reporting, without inquiry, a piece of information which he could only characterise "by using one of the shortest and strongest words in the language"—a denial which extorted an apology and a retractation.

Congress, he referred to the matter publicly, both at Boston and Hartford, and was astonished to find that his remarks were received with great resentment in certain quarters; but he had the assurance of the more intellectual class of the community (men like Washington Irving, Bryant, Halleck, and Dana, who were devoted to the cause) that, if only at once followed up in England, a change in the law might be effected. Directly after the delivery of his second speech on this vexed question he was inundated daily with anonymous letters and verbal dissuasions, while newspapers attacked him without mercy, asserting that he was "no gentleman, but a mere mercenary scoundrel!" The Novelist, who claimed to be one of the principal sufferers at the hands of piratical publishers, considered that the effect of the copyright agitation which he thus originated had been at least "to awaken a great sensation on both sides of the subject." "I have lighted up such a blaze," he wrote from New York, "that a meeting of the foremost people on the other side . . . was held in this town 'tother night. And it would be a thousand pities if we did not strike as hard as we can, now that the iron is hot." Carlyle, who had heard of the Novelist's public advocacy of International Copyright, strengthened his hands by an encouraging letter warmly supporting his views, for which Dickens felt extremely grateful. "The greatest men in England," he informed his brother-in-law, Henry Austin, have sent me out, through Forster, a very manly, and becoming, and spirited memorial and address, backing me in all I have done. I have despatched it to Boston for publication, and am coolly prepared for the storm it will raise. But my best rod is in pickle." His earnest pleading on

behalf of the good cause unhappily proved ineffectual;
at a public meeting held in Boston (the very centre of
literary activity in America), a memorial against any
change of the law was adopted, in the course of which
it was stated (as Forster explains) that if English
authors were invested with any control over the repub-
lication of their own books, it would be no longer
possible for American editors to alter and adapt them
to the American taste. Dickens, feeling naturally indignant and disappointed at the impotent result of his
efforts, saw the hopelessness of pursuing the topic
further in America, but determined, on his return to
England, to endeavour to gain the object in view by
other methods. In a letter (half serious and half
humorous) addressed to Forster from Niagara Falls, he
temporarily dismissed the subject, summing up the
position by declaring that, in America, there were two
obstacles to the passing of an International Copyright
law with England, viz., "the national love of 'doing' a
man in any bargain or matter of business," and "the
national vanity." "Both these characteristics," he
observed, "prevail to an extent which no stranger can
possibly estimate."

Another concern respecting which Charles
Dickens would be expected to express emphatic
dissent is that of slavery and the slave trade. He
proudly boasted that during his American tour he
accepted no public mark of respect in arty place where
slavery existed, "and that's something." What he saw
of "the accursed and detested system" (as he termed it)
excited his intense anger, and, although warned
against discussing the evils of the system, he found it
impossible to be silent, for, he said, "They won't let
you be silent. They *will* ask you what you

think of it; and will *expatiate* on slavery as if it were one of the greatest blessings of mankind." One day a hard-looking, unprepossessing individual ventured to remind him that it was not the interest of a man to ill-use his slaves; to which the Novelist quietly replied "that it was not a man's interest to get drunk, or to steal, or to game, or to indulge in any other vice, but he *did* indulge in it for all that. That cruelty, and the abuse of irresponsible power, ever two of the bad passions of human nature, with the gratification of which, considerations of interest or of ruin had nothing whatever to do; and that, while every candid man must admit that even a slave might be happy enough with a good master, all human beings know that bad masters, and masters who disgraced the form they bore, were matters of experience and history, whose existence was as undisputed as that of slaves themselves." To a certain Judge in St. Louis he somewhat forcibly pronounced the opinion that such men as those who spoke of slavery as a blessing were "out of the pale of reason." In "American Notes" he says, referring to the regions near Baltimore where slavery is practised: "I went upon my way with a grateful heart that I was not doomed to live where slavery was, and had never had my senses blunted to its wrongs and horrors in a slave-rocked cradle."[1]

The fact that Dickens, like Richard Swiveller,

---

[1] See also chapter 17 of "American Notes," re Slavery. The Rev. Dr. M. C. B. Mason, a delegate to the recent Methodist Ecumenical Conference in London, states that the negro can scarcely be said to have any civil status at all, even now, in some of the Southern States of America, and not a single hotel south of what is called "the Mason and Dixon Line" would receive a man of colour; for a negro to seek accommodation at a public hostelry would be regarded as an act of madness on his part (*Daily News*, September 12, 1901).

found occasional comfort in performing upon a musical instrument, is perhaps unfamiliar to most people. During his Transatlantic travels he gave Forster a hint of this, which appears to be the only indication of his posing as a musician: "I have bought another accordion," he said. "The steward lent me one on the passage out, and I regaled the ladies' cabin with my performances. You can't think with what feeling I play 'Home, Sweet Home' every night, or how pleasantly sad it makes us." Many weeks were yet to elapse before he would see England again, and there were ardent longings to be once more with the children left behind, as well as to enjoy the society of innumerable friends on this side of the broad Atlantic. When about to start from Baltimore for the Far West ("which includes mountain travelling, and lake travelling, and prairie travelling") he wrote to Thomas Mitton: "In every town where we stay, though it be only for a day, we hold a regular levee or drawing room, where I shake hands on an average with five or six hundred people, who pass on from me to Kate, and are shaken again by her. . . . Think of two hours of this every day, and the people coming in by hundreds, all fresh and piping hot, and full of questions, when we are literally exhausted and can hardly stand! I really do believe that if I had not a lady with me I should have been obliged to leave the country and go back to England. But for her they never would leave me alone by day or night, and, as it is, a slave comes to me now and then in the middle of the night with a letter, and waits at the bedroom door for an answer. . . . Parties—parties—parties of course, every day and night. But it's not all parties. I go into the prisons, the police-offices, the watch-houses, the hospitals, the workhouses. I was out half the night in New York with two of their most famous constables: started at midnight, and went into every brothel, thieves' house, murdering hovel, sailors' dancing place, and abode of villainy, both black and white, in the town. I went *incog.* behind the scenes to the little theatre where Mitchell is making a fortune. He has been rearing a little dog for me, and has called him 'Boz.'[1] I am going to bring him home. In a word, I go everywhere, and a hard life it is."[2] When at Boston, the Novelist promised to do something more than go *behind* the scenes, having undertaken to act at a Canadian theatre with officers of the Coldstream Guards for the benefit of a charity. This private performance took place at the Queen's Theatre, Montreal, on May 24, 1842, and the plays selected for representation were "A Roland for an Oliver," "Past Two o'clock in the Morning," and the farce entitled "Deaf as a Post." Three days before the event Dickens wrote to Professor Felton: "What would I give to see you in the front row of the centre-box, your spectacles gleaming not unlike those of my dear friend Pickwick, your face as radiant, with as broad a grin as a staid professor may indulge in, and your very coat, waistcoat, and shoulders expressive of what we should take together when the performance was over! I would give something (not so much, but

---

[1] This was a white Havana spaniel, which accompanied him on his return to England, and subsequently travelled with the Dickens family in all its migrations (including visits to Italy and Switzerland) until it died of old age. The dog was rechristened "Mr. Snittle Timbery," after an incidental character in "Nicholas Nickleby," which name he considered "more sonorous and expressive," but it was soon abbreviated to "Timber." Writing to Forster after his return to England, he said: "Little doggy improves rapidly, and now jumps over my stick at the word of command."

[2] "The Letters, of Charles Dickens."

still a good round sum) if you could only stumble into
that very dark and dusky theatre in the daytime (at any
minute between twelve and three), and see me with my
coat off, the stage-manager and universal director,
urging impracticable ladies and impossible gentlemen
on to the very confines of insanity, shouting and
driving about, in my own person, to an extent that
would justify any philanthropic stranger in clapping
me into a strait-waistcoat without further inquiry. . . .
This kind of voluntary hard labour used to be my great
delight. The *furore* has come strong upon me again,
and I begin to be once more of opinion that nature
intended me for the lessee of a national theatre, and
that pen, ink, and paper have spoiled a manager." The
Novelist assumed a prominent character in each play,
in addition to his responsibilities as stage-manager; to
Mrs. Dickens was assigned a part in the farce—her
first appearance on the stage. Writing to Forster
immediately afterwards, Dickens said: "The play came
off last night. The audience, between five and six
hundred strong, were invited as to a party . . . and as
the military portion were all in full uniform, it was
really a splendid scene. We 'went' also splendidly;
though with nothing very remarkable in the acting
way. . . . I am not, however, let me tell you, placarded
as stage-manager for nothing. Everybody was told
they would have to submit to the most iron despotism,
and didn't I come Macready over them? Oh, no. By no
means. Certainly not. The pains I have taken with
them, and the perspiration I have expended, during the
last ten days, exceed in amount anything you can
imagine. . . . I really do believe that I was very funny,
at least I know that I laughed heartily at myself. . . .
It went with a roar, all through. . . But only

think of Kate playing! And playing devilish well, I assure you!" The two first pieces were afterwards repeated to a paying audience for the manager's benefit, professional actresses being substituted for the female characters.

Keenly anticipating the delight of returning to the old country, Dickens could not refrain from giving vent to his feelings in his letters: "Oh, how I look forward across that rolling water to home and its small tenantry! How I busy myself in thinking how my books look, and where the tables are, and in what positions the chairs stand relatively to the other furniture; and whether we shall get there in the night, or in the morning, or in the afternoon; and whether we shall be able to surprise them, or whether they will be too sharply looking out for us; and what our pets will say, and how they'll look, and who will be the first to come and shake hands, and so forth!" As the day of departure for England drew nearer, his excitement became intensified. "We get FEVERED with anxiety for home," he wrote about a fortnight before the vessel sailed. "We shall soon meet, please God, and be happier and merrier than ever we were in all our lives. . . . Oh home—home—home—home—home—home—HOME!!!!!!!"

At length the eagerly-looked-for day arrived, and the vessel which steamed out of New York harbour on June 7, 1842, numbered among its passengers the distinguished young author whom the Americans had lionised for the space of six months. Dickens established on board, during the return voyage, a club called the United Vagabonds ("a very hilarious and jovial institution"), which caused considerable amusement. "This holy brother-hood" he explained, "committed all kinds of absurdities, and dined always, with a variety of solemn forms, at one end of the table, below the mast, away from all the rest." The captain being ill when they were three or four days out, Dickens produced his medicine chest and recovered him, and went round "the wards" every day in great state, "accompanied by two Vagabonds, habited as Ben Allen and Bob Sawyer, bearing enormous rolls of plaster and huge pairs of scissors."[1] Such pleasant fooling helped to pass away the time right merrily, and when the members of this cheerful party landed at Liverpool they breakfasted together for the last time, shook hands, and separated most cordially.

The reality did not fall short of the expectations Dickens had formed respecting his return home, which proved to be an occasion of unbounded gratification. He paid surprise visits first of all to his cherished friends Forster and Maclise, to be followed presently by a dinner at Greenwich, this affording him the opportunity of receiving the greetings and congratulations of others besides who loved him— Talfourd, Monckton Milnes, Procter ("Barry Cornwall"), Clarkson Stanfield, R.A., Marryat, Barham (of "Ingoldsby" fame), Tom Hood, and George Cruikshank being among them. The Novelist quickly settled down to his literary labours, and after spending a few days at Devonshire Terrace, he, with wife and family, went to Broadstairs for the autumn months as usual. From this seaside resort he wrote to Professor Felton : "I have looked over my journal and have decided to produce my American trip in two volumes. I have written about half the first since I came home, and hope to he out in October. This is 'exclusive news,' to be communicated to any

[1] "The Letters of Charles Dickens."

friends to whom you may like to entrust it."[1] Two
months later, when the work was nearly completed, he
addressed a letter to Longfellow stating his resolution
to publish the American visit, and adding: "I have
spoken very honestly and fairly; and I know that those
in America for whom I care will like me better for the
book. A great many people will like me infinitely the
worse, and make a devil of me straight away." The
"Notes" punctually appeared on October 18, 1842, and
were immediately in great request. Here, as well as in
his letters to Forster, the Novelist's impressions of
America, of its people, its government, and its public
institutions are fully set forth, and that these
impressions were not entirely favourable we have
ample evidence in the record. He confessed to
Macready that he was disappointed to find that the
republic he went to see was not the republic of his
imagination, being immeasurably below the level he
had placed it upon, and far inferior to the government
of England, "bad and faulty as the old land is"; he
declared "freedom of opinion" to be non-existent, and
intimated that he had been strongly advised to refrain
from writing about America because the Americans
could not bear to be told of their faults. Concerning the
people themselves he entertained a high opinion, and
with many in the towns he formed "perfect
attachments." The natural scenery of this vast country
deeply stirred him—the immensity of its rivers, the
beauty of its mountains, the dreary solitude of its
prairies, and, above all, the magnificent grandeur of
Niagara Falls; indeed, the descriptive passages are in
many respects the most attractive features of his
"American Notes." The book from the first proved

[1] "The Letters of Charles Dickens."

"a most complete and thorough-going success," as the author himself declared, and four large editions were sold by the end of the year. The "Notes" won golden opinions from all sorts of men among them Lord Jeffrey,[1] who in congratulating Dickens on the disposal of three thousand copies in one week, and thus netting a thousand pounds, said: "You have been very tender to our sensitive friends beyond sea, and my whole heart goes along with every word you have written. I think that you have perfectly accomplished all that you profess or undertake to do, and that the world has never yet seen a more faithful, graphic, amusing, kind-hearted narrative." On the other hand Macaulay expressed great dissatisfaction, protesting that he could not praise the book, as it seemed to him a failure. It is perhaps natural that Dickens's candid criticisms of American customs and institutions (when unfavourable) failed to meet with a friendly reception in the States; as a matter of fact the author was abused and vilified unmercifully in nearly every American print. The intellectual people of America, however, regarded the book with approval. Emerson thought that the lesson it inculcated "was not quite lost, that it held bad manners up so that churls would see the deformed," while Longfellow (who a short time previously visited London and became a revered guest of the Novelist) spoke to Sumner of the work as "jovial and good-natured, and at times very severe," adding: "You will read with delight and, for the most part, approbation." In a suppressed chapter, intended to be introductory, the Author revealed "his honest purpose in the use of satire even where his humorous temptations were strongest. . . . He held always the same high opinion of what

[1] *See* page 505.

was best in that country, and always the same contempt for what was worst in it."

Before Charles Dickens embarked upon his next great work of fiction, it was determined to celebrate, in a very special manner, his safe return to England. This took the form of a trip to Cornwall, the select party consisting of Stanfield, Forster, Maclise, and, of course, "Boz" himself. Concerning the delectable pilgrimage, which continued nearly three weeks, the Novelist had the most entertaining incidents to relate, as in the following letter to his American friend Professor Felton: "We went down into Devonshire by the railroad, and there we hired an open carriage from an innkeeper, patriotic in all Pickwick matters, and went on with post-horses. Sometimes we travelled all night, sometimes all day, sometimes both. I kept the joint-stock purse, ordered all the dinners, paid all the turnpikes, conducted facetious conversations with the post boys, and regulated the pace at which we travelled. Stanfield (an old sailor) consulted an enormous map on all disputed points of wayfaring; and referred, moreover, to a pocket-compass and other scientific instruments. The luggage was in Forster's department; and Maclise, having nothing particular to do, sang songs." Thus it seems that the four young men, "out of harness" for a time, were like jubilant schoolboys let loose for a summer holiday. "Heavens! If you could have seen the necks of bottles—distracting in their immense varieties of shape—peering out of the carriage pockets! If you could have witnessed the deep devotion of the post boys, the wild attachment of the hostlers, the maniac glee of the waiters! If you could have followed us into the earthy old churches we visited, and into the strange caverns on the gloomy seashore, and down into the depths of mines, and up to the tops of giddy heights where the unspeakably green water was roaring, I don't know how many hundred feet below! If you could have seen but one gleam of the bright fires by which we sat in the big rooms of ancient inns at night until long after the small hours had come and gone, or smelt but one steam of the hot punch . . . which came in every evening in a huge broad china bowl! I never laughed in my life as I did on this journey. It would have done you good to hear me. I was choking and gasping and bursting the buckle off the back of my stock, all the way. And Stanfield got into such apoplectic entanglements that we were often obliged to beat him on the back with portmanteaus before we could recover him. Seriously, I do believe there never was such a trip. And they made such sketches, those two men" [Maclise and Stanfield], "in the most romantic of our halting places, that you would have sworn we had the Spirit of Beauty with us as well as the Spirit of Fun. But stop till you come to England—I say no more."[1]

After the Cornwall Expedition Dickens immediately set about the story which he had agreed with Chapman & Hall to write, for publication in shilling numbers. The public were informed of the proposed venture in an Address printed on the wrapper of No. 80 of "Master Humphrey's Clock," where, after intimating that it was his intention to

---

[1] "The Letters of Charles Dickens." From one of his sketches Maclise painted the picture of "A Girl at the Waterfall," which included a likeness of Miss Georgina Hogarth, a sister-in-law of Dickens. The artist, by the way, had previously given Dickens a drawing of his (the Novelists) eldest children to accompany him and his wife to America, and, four years later, painted (as a voluntary offering) a portrait of Mrs. Dickens now in the possession of Lady Burdett-Coutts.

take advantage of the respite which the close of that work would afford him, by visiting America, he said: "On the first of November eighteen hundred and forty-two I propose, if it please God, to commence my book in monthly parts, under the old green cover, in the old size and form, and at the old price."[1] On the twelfth of that month Forster received from him the title of the new tale: "Don't lose it," he warningly observed, "for I have no copy." This was "Martin Chuzzlewit," and primarily he entertained the idea of opening the story in the lantern of a lighthouse or mine in Cornwall, but eventually decided to substitute a Wiltshire village. On the Christian name of the hero he determined at once, but the surname formed the subject of considerable discussion, the respective merits of Sweezleden, Sweezleback, Sweezlewag, Chuzzletoe, Chuzzleboy, Chubblewig, and Chuzzlewig being duly considered before that of Chuzzlewit was adopted. The full title, as it appeared on the original wrappers, reads thus: "The Life and Adventures of Martin Chuzzlewit, his Relatives, Friends, and Enemies Comprising all his Wills and his Ways; with an Historical Record of What he Did, and What he Didn't: Showing, moreover, Who inherited the Family Plate, Who came in for the Silver Spoons, and Who for the Wooden Ladles. The Whole forming a Complete Key to the House of Chuzzlewit. Edited by 'Boz.' With Illustrations by 'Phiz.'" In subsequent editions the book was simply called "Martin Chuzzlewit." Its actual origin was the notion of taking Pecksniff (the English Tartuffe) for a

[1] An advertisement in the first edition of "American Notes" announced the forthcoming work as "a new Tale of English Life and Manners, by 'Boz.'"

type of character, and the Novelist's object was "to show how selfishness propagates itself, and to what a grim giant it may grow from small beginnings."[1] In a word, "Chuzzlewit" may be considered as a crusade against "Cant" in its most vicious form. The first instalment appeared in January 1843. He soon got into the swing of the story; writing to Forster on the eighth of that month he said: "I have been hammering away, and at home all day. Ditto yesterday; except for two hours in the afternoon, when I ploughed through snow half a foot deep, round about the wilds of Willesden"; and in March he wrote to Professor Felton: "I am in great health and spirits and powdering away at 'Chuzzlewit,' with all manner of facetiousness rising up before me as I go on." The work proceeded satisfactorily until its completion in 1844, the final (double) number appearing in July of that year, when the story was published complete in volume form, with its full complement of forty etched illustrations by "Phiz." The artist's portrait of Pecksniff, by the way, bore a marked resemblance to Sir Robert Peel, this doubtless suggesting to *Punch*, at the time, the idea of representing (pictorially and otherwise) the eminent statesman as Mr. Pecksniff, a distinction which he shared with Samuel Carter Hall, editor of the *Art Journal*, whose sententious catch-phrase of appealing to "hand, head, and heart" *Punch* delighted in paraphrasing as "gloves, hat, and waistcoat." There is Forster's authority for the statement that the highly amusing, albeit objectionable, creature, Sarah Gamp, was the portrait of a person hired by a distinguished friend of the Novelist; she (as portrayed in Mrs. Gamp) was a true specimen of the

[1] See preface to the first Cheap Edition, 1849.

ordinary sick-nurse (now happily obsolete), and a common habit of that worthy personage was to rub her nose along the top of the tall fender, and to indulge in other Gampish peculiarities. In 1847 Dickens entertained the idea of reviving Mrs. Gamp by writing in her peculiar vernacular a little *jeu d'esprit* in the form of a history of a theatrical tour organised by himself and friends (Cruikshank, Leech, Mark Lemon, &c.), for the purpose of raising a fund for the benefit of Leigh Hunt; but this literary joke perished prematurely when only a few pages of manuscript had been prepared.

As already stated, "American Notes" excited considerable adverse comment on the other side of the Atlantic, in consequence of the Author's candid opinions concerning the manners and customs of the country. In "Martin Chuzzlewit" he made more free and dashing use of his American observations, so we are not surprised to learn that the feeling of anger displayed by a certain section of citizens in the United States became greatly intensified. It is not generally known that Dickens, before many chapters had been written, altered the very structure of the story as originally planned; owing to the severe censure and unkind personalities showered upon himself and the "Notes" by Transatlantic critics, he resolved, as an afterthought, to carry his hero to America in order to obtain an opportunity of further revealing to his English readers "the ludicrous side of the American character." This form of revenge was doubtless legitimate enough; although not ill-natured in spirit, such retaliation had the effect of still further increasing the hostile animus, and the Novelist related in one of his letters (comically, but with a good deal of earnestness too) how three or four years afterwards, meeting some Americans on a ship in the Mediterranean, he was in terror, from their manner, of their throwing him overboard! No sooner had "Chuzzlewit" reached Transatlantic shores than the indignation of those who were morbidly sensitive respecting the American scenes in the book expressed itself in various ways, not the most ludicrous, perhaps, being the method adopted by the actors at the Boston Theatre, New York, who, in a burlesque of "Macbeth" then being performed, exhibited their spleen in the incantation scene by pitching into the witches' cauldron a copy of "Boz's" latest work, together with a miscellaneous collection of what were considered worthless objects, such as Mexican rifles and Pennsylvanian bonds, public opinion regarding "Chuzzlewit" being thus rendered obvious to the delighted audience! Carlyle failed to understand this animosity, and, after perusing Forster's Life of the Novelist, said: "Me nothing in it so surprises as these two American explosions around poor Dickens, *all* Yankee-doodle-dom blazing up like one universal soda water bottle round so very measurable a phenomenon; this, and the way the phenomenon takes it, was curiously and genially interesting to me, and significant of Yankee-doodle-dom."[1] The broader-minded American critics were candid enough to admit the accuracy of the Novelist's presentments, and considered that the satire was richly deserved. "As for the American portraits, painted in 'Martin Chuzzlewit,'" observed the late

[1] "Conversations with Carlyle," by Sir Charles Gavan Duffy, K.C.M.G., 1892. A presentation copy of the first issue of "American Notes," containing the following autograph inscription: "Thomas Carlyle, from Charles Dickens, nineteenth October, 1842," realised £45 at Sotheby's in March, 1902.

Miss Kate Field, an American authoress. "I should as
soon think of objecting to them as I should think of
objecting to any other discovery in natural history."
Happily, any hostility engendered in the "Land of the
Stars and Stripes" by Dickens's strictures was speedily
obliterated   for   the   sensitiveness   of   American
patriotism (as a friend of Mark Twain informed the
present writer) did not brood over them long enough
"to seriously interfere with the tender regard and
enthusiastic admiration that the genius of his literature
had kindled in the universal heart." The late Mr.
Charles Dickens the younger was probably correct in
his contention that the real cause of the provocation
which "American Notes" excited in certain quarters
was the fact that his father was an abolitionist, who
spoke courageously against the slavery system; and in
1887, when travelling in almost every part of the
United States, he found that all the anger and ill-
feeling had passed away, the whole matter being now
regarded in the light of ancient history. It may in truth
be averred that the Americans regarded Charles
Dickens as a friend rather than as an enemy long
before his second visit to the States in the winter of
1867-68, when he was accorded a most enthusiastic
reception at their hands, and the Novelist, in an
admirable speech delivered at a dinner given in his
honour at New York, remarked upon the beneficial
changes, moral and physical, which he then observed:
"This testimony," he said, "so long as I live, and so
long as my descendants have any right in my books, I
shall cause to be republished as an appendix to every
copy of those two books of mine in which I have
referred to America. And this I will do and cause to be
done, not in mere love and thankfulness, but because I

regard it as an act of plain justice and honour."
Accordingly the postscript has since been appended to
every edition of the books in question, and
supplemented by the following asseveration: "I said
these words with the greatest earnestness that I could
lay upon them, and I repeat them in print here with
equal earnestness. So long as this book shall last, I
hope that they will form a part of it, and will be fairly
read as inseparable from my experiences and
impressions of America."[1]

With respect to the writing of "Martin
Chuzzlewit," we are assured by Forster that the
uncertainty as regards the construction of the story
gave the Author much concern, "beginning so
hurriedly as at last he did, altering his course at the
opening, and seeing little of the main track of his
design." Its sale as a serial proved at first to be a
comparative failure, the average number per month
never exceeding 23,000 copies, as against more than
double that of previous novels. The Author, who
thought it, in a hundred ways, immeasurably better
than anything he had yet done, naturally experienced
great disappointment, but recovered his spirits when,
on its conclusion in July 1844, the work appeared in
volume form, the demand for it becoming almost as
great as that which greeted "Pickwick," the half-year's
profits amounting to £750. Not only did the
diminished sale of the story in its serial form cause
vexation, but there were other pecuniary troubles as
between author and publishers which caused a
temporary breach in their business relations. A clause
had been inserted in the "Chuzzlewit" agreement

---

[1] The Appendix to "American Notes" and "Martin Chuzzlewit" was
reprinted in *All the Year Round* on June 6, 1868, under the title "A Debt
of Honour."

to the effect that, in the event of the book not proving remunerative, £50 of the £200 stipulated to be paid monthly to the Author might be withheld; and on one of the partners in the firm hinting (on the eve of issuing the seventh number) that the condition was likely to be enforced, Dickens became wroth, and, conceiving that his publishers (who had secured certain shares in the venture) were attempting to take an unfair advantage, he intimated that all business transactions with them would close with the conclusion of "Chuzzlewit." The parting thus becoming inevitable, negotiations were presently opened with the printing firm of Bradbury & Evans, with whom an agreement was drawn up covenanting that, in consideration of an advance to Dickens of £2800, he would assign to them a fourth share of whatever he might write during the ensuing eight years. The incident well illustrates the fact that even from the days when—as a young and unknown writer—he essayed the "Sketches by Boz," the Author directed keen attention to the financial side of his labours, in the legal aspect of which he had the valuable advice of his friends Mitton and Forster, the latter occasionally acting as mediator between him and his publishers.

In June 1843 Dickens took the chair at a complimentary dinner given to his friend Macready, on the occasion of the famous actor's retirement from the management of Drury Lane Theatre, and to wish him good-speed on his way to America. The dinner, which took place at the "Star and Garter," Richmond, was preceded by the presentation of a testimonial to Macready from his friends and fellow actors, and a few days later, the Novelist, with Stanfield, Maclise, and Forster, accompanied him to Liverpool to say goodbye. During this year, too, Charles Dickens (ever ready to assist in the cause of charity) presided at a dinner for the Printers' Pension Fund, and it was mainly due to his unremitting exertions that ample provision was made for the many children of Elton the actor, who lost his life at sea through a terrible accident. August found him again at Broadstairs, whence he wrote to Forster: "I performed an insane match against time of eighteen miles by the milestones in four hours and a half, under a burning sun the whole way. I could get no sleep at night, and really began to be afraid I was going to have a fever. You may judge in what kind of authorship training I am today. I could as soon eat the cliffs as write about anything." In a letter to Professor Felton he gave the following amusing account of his daily life at this favourite watering place: "In a bay window in a one-pair sits, from nine o'clock to one, a gentleman with rather long hair and no neckcloth, who writes and grins as if he thought he were very funny indeed. His name is Boz. At one he disappears, and presently emerges from a bathing machine, and may be seen—a kind of salmon-coloured porpoise—splashing about in the ocean. After that he may be seen in another bay window on the ground floor, eating a strong lunch; after that, walking a dozen miles or so, or lying on his back in the sand reading a book. Nobody bothers him unless they know he is disposed to be talked to; and I am told he is very comfortable indeed. He's as brown as a berry, and they *do* say is a small fortune to the innkeeper who sells beer and cold punch. But this is mere rumour. Sometimes he goes up to London (eighty miles, or so, away), and then I'm told there is a sound in Lincoln's Inn Fields" [Forster's residence] "at night, as of men laughing, together with a clinking of knives and forks and wine-glasses."[1] From Broadstairs he wrote to Macvey Napier, of the *Edinburgh Review*, suggesting a paper on Religious Education as the subject of an article by himself, for publication in the *Review*. "I should like to show," he said, "why such a thing as the Church Catechism is wholly inapplicable to the state of ignorance that now prevails; and why no system, but one, so general in great religious principles as to include all creeds, can meet the wants and understandings of the dangerous classes of society." He proposed to include in this paper "a description of certain voluntary places of instruction, called 'the ragged schools,' now existing in London, and of the schools in jails, and of the ignorance presented in such places," by which he hoped to demonstrate that the very nature of these miserable and neglected people rebelled against the simplest religion, and that "to convey to them the faintest outlines of any system of distinction between right and wrong is in itself a giant's task, before which mysteries and squabbles for forms *must* give way."[2] The article in question was declined by the editor as unsuitable for the pages of the *Review*, and a similar result attended the Novelist's proposal to supply the same journal with a paper on Capital Punishment, as then carried out, the notoriety accorded to condemned criminals acting (in his opinion) as an incentive to crime in others possessing vicious tendencies, and public executions having a brutalising effect upon the crowds that witnessed them. These important social questions formed the theme of letters

[1] "The Letters of Charles Dickens."
[2] Ibid.

contributed by him to the *Daily News* during 1846, and they indicate the strong bent of his mind in the direction of Social Reform.

Early in October 1843 Dickens returned to town "for good"; but before many days had elapsed he again left home for the purpose of presiding at the opening of the Manchester Athenaeum, at which ceremony both Cobden and Disraeli "assisted," and this afforded him the opportunity of referring in his speech to the education of the very poor—a matter which (as Forster reminds us) lay always nearest his heart, in proof thereof he had but recently sent Miss Coutts (now the Baroness Burdett-Coutts, ever a cherished friend) what he described as "a sledgehammer" account of the Ragged Schools, taking pains to show her that "religious mysteries and difficult creeds wouldn't do for such pupils," and pointing out "that it was of immense importance they should be *washed*."

## CHAPTER 6

# "A CHRISTMAS CAROL"
# AND "THE CHIMES"

In a letter to Professor Felton in May 1843 Dickens said: "I am writing a little history of England for my boy" [Charles, then about seven years of age], "which I will send you when it is printed for him, though your boys are too old to profit by it. It is curious that I have tried to impress upon him . . . the exact spirit of your paper, for I don't know what I should do if he were to get hold of any Conservative or High Church notions; and the best way of guarding against any such horrible result, is, I take it, to wring the parrot's neck in his very cradle." This "little history," however, was destined not to appear, although a similar production was launched by him at a later date. The same year marks the publication of a work from the Novelist's pen which has proved to be the most popular, perhaps, of his minor writings; this was "A Christmas Carol"— the first of that remarkable series of Yuletide stories by which he succeeded so admirably in pleasing the public taste. It has been claimed for Charles Dickens that, by virtue of this fascinating little allegory, he was the actual pioneer of the Christmas story; certain it is that ever since the "Carol" was given to the world, there has been an enormous demand for such publications, with the result that at the approach of the festive season no home was considered complete without its complement of Christmas books and Christmas numbers.

The fancy for his "memorable 'Christmas Carol'" occurred to Dickens during his brief stay at Manchester in the beginning of October, and before the end of November he had quite finished the writing of it. The Author himself declared that he "excited himself in a most extraordinary manner in the composition," and described himself as alternately laughing and weeping over it, and, while thinking of it, he "walked about the black streets of London, fifteen and twenty miles, many a night when all the sober folks had gone to bed." "To keep the Chuzzlewit going," he said to Felton, "and do this little book, the Carol, in the odd times between two parts of it, was, as you may suppose, pretty tight work. But when it was done I broke out like a madman!' To Sir E. Bulwer Lytton he confessed that the subject seized him with a strange mastery, and described how, for many weeks, he was so closely occupied with his "little Carol" (as he affectionately called it) that he never left home before the owls went out, and led quite a solitary life. "The small crimson covered volume was published at Christmas time 1843, with coloured etchings, and woodcuts by John Leech, the humorous and talented artist who had vainly competed for the post of illustrator of "Pickwick." Never had such a book so brilliant a send-off; its popularity was extraordinary, and by every post the delighted Author received letters from complete strangers, telling him about their homes and hearths, and how this same "Carol" was read aloud there, and kept on a little shelf by itself. "Indeed," he observed to Felton, "it is the greatest success, as I am told, that this ruffian and rascal has ever achieved." Concerning it Thackeray essayed one of the most genial criticisms ever penned: "Who can listen," he queries, "to objections regarding such a book as this? It seems to me a national benefit, and to every man or woman who reads it a personal kindness. The last two people I heard speak of it were women; neither knew the other, or the author, and both said by way of criticism, 'God bless him!' . . . What a feeling is this for a writer to be able to inspire, and what a reward to reap!" Lord Jeffrey,[1] in a letter of enthusiastic praise, said: "You should he happy yourself, for you may be sure you have done more good by this little publication, fostered more kindly feelings, and prompted more positive acts of beneficence than can be traced to all the pulpits and confessionals in Christendom since Christmas 1842." Dickens, naturally gratified by such applause, affirmed in a letter to Thomas Mitton that he knew he meant a good thing, "and when I see the effect of such a little *whole* as that, on those for whom I care, I have a strong sense of the immense effect I could produce with an entire book. . . . I am sure it will do me a great deal of good; and I hope it will sell well." That wish was amply realised, for the first edition of six thousand copies was disposed of in twenty-four hours, and within a week or so no less than two thousand of the three printed for second and third editions had been secured by the trade. The proceeds, however, proved sadly disconcerting, for Dickens had set "his heart and soul upon a thousand clear whereas he received, from a sale of fifteen thousand copies, less than three-fourths of that sum, the deficiency having originated (says

[1] *See* page 505.

Forster) in "a want of judgment in adjusting the expenses of production with a more equable regard to the selling price." This disappointment, and the soreness occasioned by a certain clause in the "Chuzzlewit" agreement (to which an allusion has been made), caused a temporary severance of Dickens's connection with Chapman & Hall. Upon the publication of the "Carol," the Author presented the manuscript to Thomas Mitton, since when it has changed hands several times, its ultimate destination being America, and the purchase price £2000.[1]

That Dickens thoroughly appreciated not only the religious aspect of Christmastide, but also cordially approved of the social festivities which mark that joyous season, is evidenced in his own observance of them. No man entered more heartily into the spirit of fun and frolic which characterised what is now usually termed the "old-fashioned Christmas." "Such dinings, such dancings, such conjurings, such blindman-buffings, such theatre-goings, such kissings-out of old years and kissings-in of new ones, never took place in these parts before." Thus, in a sprightly note, he referred to the particular Yuletide which brought forth the "Carol." "If you could have seen me," he wrote to a friend at this date, "at a children's party at Macready's the other night, going down a country dance with Mrs. M., you would have thought I was a country gentleman of independent

[1] It is interesting to note that the Novelist's son, Mr. Henry Fielding Dickens, K.C., reads the "Carol" aloud to his family every Christmas Day. That the little story still maintains its hold upon the public is testified by the fact that during the last three or four years Sir Squire Bancroft has on several occasions read it (gratuitously) before large audiences in town and country, thereby raising large sums of money in aid of charitable projects.

property, residing on a tip-top farm, with the wind blowing straight in my face every day." The occasion was a birthday celebration of one of Macready's children, and, in a letter to the famous actor himself, he described how he and Forster amused the juvenile guests with wonderful conjuring tricks; how "a plum pudding was produced from an empty saucepan, held over a blazing fire kindled in Stanfield's hat without damage to the lining"; how "a box of bran was changed into a live guinea pig," and so forth, the successful performance of these and similar feats of skill exciting "the unspeakable admiration of the whole assembly."

It seems evident that Charles Dickens did not permit business worries to affect his enjoyment of these social frivolities; for we are told that the year 1843, when, at its close, he threw himself with such *abandon* into Christmas festivities, was a time "of much anxiety and strange disappointments." Strange to relate, the results of the sale of "Chuzzlewit" and the "Carol" brought him financial embarrassment; his labours and successes thus far had enriched others more than himself, and the Novelist's own view of the situation is given in a letter to Forster, dated November 1, 1843. He was afraid (as he expressed it) of putting himself before the town "as writing tooth and nail for bread, headlong, after the close of a book taking so much out of one as 'Chuzzlewit.'" He doubted the advisability of projecting a new magazine, or of issuing a cheap edition of his stories at this juncture, and the thought occurred to him of enlarging his stock of description and observation by seeing countries new to him, "and which with an increasing family I

can scarcely hope to see at all, unless I see them now."
He had for some time previously encouraged a hope
and desire to travel again, and this he now resolved to
do, not merely for the purpose of profiting by an
extended knowledge of the world, but that, by residing
abroad for a little while, he might be in a better
position to face the money difficulties, which were
unquestionable; for, besides his own domestic
expenses, there were many unreasonable family
claims upon his purse. His first intention was to settle
down, with family and servants, in some quiet town in
Normandy or Brittany where the cost of living was
likely to be small, and, travelling in advance of the
rest, to walk through Switzerland, cross the Alps, and
thence through France and Italy, seeing everything
there is to be seen, and describing from time to time,
in letters to Forster, everything of interest, as he did
during his American visit, with the view, possibly, to
subsequent publication of his notes and observations.
"I am quite serious and sober," he presently observed,
"when I say, that I have very grave thoughts of
keeping my whole menagerie in Italy, three years."

Early in January 1844 a third son (the fifth child)
was born to him, receiving the baptismal names
Francis Jeffrey, from his godfather, Lord Jeffrey;[1] in
honour of the event, the Novelist's friends Maclise,
Stanfield, and Forster pressed him to dine with them at
Richmond—an invitation to which he responded by a
letter addressed to his "Fellow Countrymen," such as
might have been penned by Micawber himself, so
high-flown is its eloquent phraseology. Before his
departure for Italy in the summer there was much work
to be done, and many social engagements to fulfil.
For the beautiful Countess of Blessington, who

[1] *See* page 505.

numbered Dickens among a host of admirers, he had
written a thoughtful little poem entitled "A Word in
Season," and it was published in the *Keepsake* early in
the year. To Lady Blessington, too, he appealed for
advice regarding a favourable place abroad in which to
settle down for a time, informing her that he had made
up his mind to "see the world," and meant to "decamp,
bag and baggage, for a twelve-month," establishing
his family in some convenient spot whence he could
make "personal ravages on the neighbouring country."
In February he occupied the chair at two great
meetings, the first at the Liverpool Mechanics'
Institution, and the second at the Birmingham
Polytechnic Institution, the speeches on the subject of
Education which he then delivered being highly
eulogised. In a letter to his wife, dashed off
immediately after the event, he jocosely described the
Liverpool oration as "a vigorous, brilliant, humorous,
pathetic, eloquent, fervid, and impassioned speech,"
adding that "the said speech was enlivened by thirteen
hundred persons, with frequent, vehement, uproarious,
and deafening cheers," while he himself believed that
he "did speak up like a man." The immense hall was
hung round with artificial flowers, and on the front of
the great gallery were the words (also in artificial
flowers) "Welcome Boz," in letters six feet high, while
about the great organ were large transparencies
representing several Fames crowning a corresponding
number of portraits of the Novelist.

The day of departure for Italy now rapidly
approached. To one of his particular friends, Mr.
T. J. Thompson (father of Lady Butler, the battle
painter), Dickens expressed a hope that he would join
the expedition. "Think of Italy," he said in

March. "Don't give that up. . . . My last number of
'Chuzzlewit' comes out in June; and the first week, if
not the first day in July, sees me, God willing,
steaming off towards the sun. Yes. We must have a few
books, and everything that is idle, sauntering, and
enjoyable. We must lie down at the bottom of those
boats, and devise all kinds of engines for improving on
that gallant holiday. I see myself in a striped shirt,
moustache, blouse, red sash, straw hat, and white
trousers, sitting astride a mule, and not caring for the
clock, the day of the month, or the week. Tinkling
bells upon the mule, I hope. I look forward to it day
and night, and wish the time were come. Don't *you*
give it up. That's all."[1] Again, a little later: "D'Orsay,
who knows Italy very well indeed, strenuously insists
there is no such place for headquarters as Pisa. Lady
Blessington says so also. What do you say? On the
first of July! The first of July! Dick[2] turns his head
towards the orange groves."[3]

In June we find him taking the chair at a dinner
at the London Tavern, the object of which was to
provide a fund for the benefit of the Sanatorium, or
sick-house for students, governesses, young artists,
and so forth, who were above hospitals, and unable to
afford the expense of home-nursing in their own
lodgings. He had let his house in Devonshire Terrace
to a widow lady, who agreed to occupy it during his
absence; she took possession, however, a week or two
before he left England, thus compelling him to seek
temporary quarters elsewhere. The Novelist had
previously determined to invite a number of

[1] "The Letters of Charles Dickens."
[2] The name which the Novelist sometimes bestowed upon himself.
[3] "The Letters of Charles Dickens."

cherished friends to a farewell dinner, but the accommodation at 9 Osnaburgh Terrace, New (now Euston) Road, which he rented during the brief interval prior to his departure, proved so limited that he found himself placed in the "preposterous situation" of being obliged to postpone the dinner party, the house having no convenience (as he explained to an invited guest) "for the production of any other banquet than a cold collation of plate and linen, the only comforts we have not left behind us." Eventually the matter was arranged and the function went off very pleasantly, to be followed shortly afterwards by a farewell dinner to Dickens himself at Greenwich, which was also designed to celebrate the completion of "Martin Chuzzlewit"; Lord Normanby presided, and among the guests was Turner, the famous painter. Carlyle, who could not be present, sent the following delightful and characteristic letter to Forster:—

"I truly love Dickens; and discern in the inner man of him a tone of real Music which struggles to express itself as it may, in these bewildered, stupefied, and indeed very crusty and distracted days—better or worse! This which makes him in my estimation one of a thousand, I could with great joy and freedom testify to all persons, to himself first of all, in any good way. But by dinner—at Greenwich—in the dog days— under Lord Mahogany—by leg-of-mutton eloquence; alas, my soul dies away at the idea; exclaims, '*Quae nunc abibis in loca*'? I pray you have me excused—

"The Lord love you.
"Yours very truly,
"T. Carlyle."

Mention must here be made of one of the many gracious deeds performed by Charles Dickens. It relates to a thoughtful and graceful act on his part in aiding a poor carpenter named John Overs, who was dying of consumption. During his leisure moments this intelligent, but unfortunate, man had composed several poems and verses, hoping by their publication to leave some small provision for wife and children. Dickens's friend, Dr. Elliotson, who had shown extraordinary kindness to the sick man, informed the Novelist that Overs could not return to his old work, whereupon he took an especial interest in the case, and was induced to assist him in publishing several of his verses. When, at last, Overs became too ill for his ordinary occupation, he further aided him in his literary labours by putting a few books in his way, giving him an occasional word of advice, and reading his compositions with him whenever opportunity offered. It was presently decided to issue, in volume form, a selection from Overs' stories, and Dickens not only promised to edit them but to write an introduction as well—a promise which he fulfilled shortly before he left England for Italy. The book, entitled "Evenings of a Working Man," was published in June 1844. The author, however, did not long survive the event, and it is related that, when at the point of death, he suddenly demanded writing materials and made up a parcel containing a copy of his little production, in which he had previously inscribed the Novelist's name, with the intimation that the author presented it "With his devotion"—a simple and unassuming incident that considerably affected the recipient of the gift.

Dickens and his family departed for the Continent at the beginning of July 1844. Travelling in

those days was much more expensive than now—
"what with distance, caravan, sightseeing, and
everything," two hundred pounds were nearly
swallowed up, even before the destination was
reached. An amusing reminiscence is recorded of the
Novelist's first experience of a foreign tongue. On
landing at Boulogne he went to the bank for money,
delivering in his best French a rather long address to
the clerk behind the counter, and was much
disconcerted by that official inquiring in "the native-
born Lombard Street manner—'How would you like
to take it, sir?'" Dickens, by the way, had an aptitude
for acquiring a knowledge of languages, and
succeeded, after a month's application, in making
himself so familiar with Italian that he was enabled not
only to read it fairly well, but to ask for anything he
required in any shop or coffee-house. "The audacity
with which one begins to speak when there is no help
for it," he observed, "is quite astonishing." In the
midst of an entirely new environment, he informed
Forster that he felt as if he had a new head on side by
side with his old one. The sixteenth of the month
found him in Villa di Bagnarello at Albaro, a suburb of
Genoa, which had been taken for him by his whimsical
friend Angus Fletcher, who then lived near at hand.
The Novelist described the Villa as an unpicturesque
and uninteresting dwelling, resembling "a pink jail"—
"the most perfectly lonely, rusty, stagnant old
staggerer of a domain that you can possibly imagine .
. . the stable is so full of 'vermin and swarmers' that I
always expect to see the carriage going out bodily,
with legions of industrious fleas harnessed to
and drawing it off, on their own account." He
desired to occupy Lord Byron's house, but it had

fallen into neglect and become a third-rate wine shop. To Maclise, on the 22nd of July, he wrote : "I address you with something of the lofty spirit of an exile—a banished commoner—a sort of Anglo-Pole. I don't exactly know what I have done for my country in coming away from it; but I feel it is something—something great—something virtuous and heroic. Lofty emotions rise within me, when I see the sun set on the blue Mediterranean." He was, indeed, immensely struck by the beauty of the natural scenery of Italy, and in his letters home recorded his impressions with his customary power in descriptive writing, heightened here and there with those humorous touches so characteristic of the man. Forster received from week to week the story of his travels — the "first sprightly runnings" of those "Pictures from Italy" to which special reference will presently be made.

The Novelist soon concentrated his attention upon his literary labours, and on the receipt of a certain box from Osnaburgh Terrace he announced to Forster that he had now got his "paper and inkstand and figures[1] . . . and can think . . . with a business-like air, of the Christmas book.[2] My paper is arranged, and my pens are spread out, in the usual form." But the opportunity for writing had hardly yet arrived. The eager, active, youthful figure of the Author soon became familiar in the streets of Genoa, and he lost no time in making himself acquainted with the characteristics and peculiarities appertaining to the people and their mode of life in the old Italian city, instinctively making mental notes of everything curious and quaint that attracted his attention. On

[1] The little models which always stood on his writing-table.
[2] "The Chimes."

one occasion he attended a great reception given by
the Marquis di Negri, to celebrate the birthday of the
daughter of that Genoese magnate, and this led to a
misadventure. Beginning to tire of the insipid character of the entertainment—"ices and variegated
lamps"—he determined just before midnight to make
his escape. Running quickly to reach the town gate
before it closed, he came to a pole fastened across the
street, and, the said pole being invisible in the dark-
ness, he went over headlong with considerable force,
the accident bringing on a short but sharp attack of
illness—an agonising pain in the side—which recalled
to his mind the "blacking-bottle period," when he
suffered in a similar way and was patiently attended by
his colleague Bob Fagin, who successfully applied hot
bottles to alleviate the pain. Recovering from his indisposition, he went in the second week of September to
meet his brother Frederick at Marseilles, and after four
days' travelling they arrived at Albaro, The next
morning the two brothers went for a swim in the bay,
and Frederick, who found himself in too strong a
current, was very nearly drowned. "It was a world of
horror and anguish to me," said Dickens, "crowded
into four or five minutes of dreadful agitation"—by
good fortune, a fishing boat arrived on the scene in
time to effect a rescue. A change in the Novelist's
personal appearance, by-the-bye, now became notice-
able, which quite altered the aspect of his face. "The
moustaches are glorious, glorious. I have cut them
shorter, and trimmed them a little at the ends to
improve their shape. They are charming, charming.
Without them, life would be a blank."

Early in August he had rented rooms in the

Palazzo Peschiere for his winter residence; it being the largest palace in Genoa let on hire, standing on elevated ground in the outskirts of the town and surrounded by its own gardens, and to this "Palace of the Fishponds" he transferred himself and his belongings at the end of September. He described it as a wonderful place, with stately old terraces flanked by antique sculptured figures, stone balconies, fountains, with their gold fish, groves of camellias and orange trees; the interior walls and ceilings were painted with frescoes by Michael Angelo, and, although three centuries old, were "as fresh as if the colours had been laid on yesterday." He was fond of expatiating upon the attractions of this picturesque residence and its environment, the view over into Genoa on clear days, with the blue Mediterranean beyond, being a source of never failing enjoyment. He declared that "no custom can impair, and no description enhance, the beauty of the scene." But, delightful as the situation might be, it did not prove conducive to literary composition. He craved for the London streets, and so missed those long night walks which he had been accustomed to take before embarking upon fresh labours that he seemed dumfounded without them. "Never did I stagger so upon a threshold before," he remarked to Forster. "I seem as if I had plucked myself out of my proper soil when I left Devonshire Terrace; and could take root no more until I return to it. . . . Did I tell you how many fountains we have here? No matter. If they played nectar they wouldn't please me half so well as the West Middlesex waterworks at Devonshire Terrace." His mind had been occupied with his second Christmas story, the subject of which he had already chosen, but the title remained stubbornly in abeyance, until it came to him suddenly one morning when, as he sat at his table resolute for work, a maddening peal of chimes rose from the city of Genoa which lay beneath him—such a terrific clang and clash of all its steeples that made his ideas "spin round and round till they lost themselves in a whirl of vexation and giddiness, and dropped down dead." The distressing discord really proved a blessing in disguise, inasmuch as it suggested the very thing he needed—a title for his little book. Two days later Forster received from him a brief but significant epistle containing merely the Shakespearian quotation, "We have heard THE CHIMES at midnight, Master Shallow"—thereby implying that "The Chimes" was to be the designation of the forthcoming Christmas story. "It's a great thing to have my title," he said on the 8th of October, "and see my way how to work the bells. Let them clash upon me now from all the churches and convents in Genoa, I see nothing but the old London belfry I have set them in. In my mind's eye, Horatio, I like more and more my notion of making, in this little book, a great blow for the poor. Something powerful, I think I can do, but I want to be tender too, and cheerful; as like the 'Carol' in that respect as may be, and as unlike it as such a thing can be. The duration of the action will resemble it a little, but I trust to the novelty of the machinery to carry that off; and if my design be anything at all, it has a grip upon the very throat of the time." In writing "The Chimes" he was determined (as intimated by him) to champion the cause of the poor, and it may truly be said that the helpless and poverty-stricken section of the community were ever in his thoughts, and it was his desire to ameliorate, if possible, their distress by means of his powerful pen. As time progressed, this admirable trait in the Novelist's character became more pronounced, and even prior to the events now recorded he had begun to realise that the solution of either political or social problems by ordinary Parliamentary methods was hopeless—a fact startlingly presented to him in Carlyle's writings. In "The Chimes" his main, if not sole, object was to convert society, as he had converted Scrooge in the "Carol," by showing "that its happiness rested on the same foundations as those of the individual; which are mercy and charity not less than justice. The hero of "The Chimes" was to be a seedy London ticket porter or messenger, who, in his anxiety not to distrust or think hardly of the rich, has fallen into the opposite extreme of distrusting the poor, from which distrust he was to he reclaimed. Dickens, just before leaving England, felt greatly disgusted by the action of a certain London Alderman, Sir Peter Laurie, who made himself conspicuous by his expressed determination to "put down" suicide, and in the garrulous Alderman Cute he has perpetuated the objectionable idiosyncrasies of Sir Peter, who became so highly incensed at this direct attack upon him that he soon afterwards availed himself of the opportunity afforded him for retaliation by publicly ridiculing the Novelist's description of Jacob's Island and the Folly Ditch in "Oliver Twist," which he declared to be grossly and wilfully exaggerated. The Author, alluding to this incident in the preface to the first cheap edition of that story, treated his judicial critic as one whose impertinent observations were unworthy of attention.

One of Dickens's idiosyncrasies at this time was

his fancy for confiding in his intimate friends respecting his books and their preparation. During his stay in Italy he sadly missed the opportunities of doing this, and in its stead wrote frequently to Forster when fairly at work, to inform him of the progress he had made. A trouble that arose to hinder his labours was the absence of "a crowded street to plunge into at night," for he wanted to be "on the spot," as it were, in order to derive inspiration from the living masses of humanity that thronged the thoroughfares of London. Presently he was enabled to write: "I am in regular, ferocious excitement with the 'Chimes'; get up at seven; have a cold bath before breakfast; and blaze away, wrathful and red-hot, until three o'clock or so; when I usually knock off (unless it rains) for the day. . . . I am fierce to finish in a spirit bearing some affinity to those of truth and mercy, and to shame the cruel and the canting. . . . "He declared that the story had a great hold of him. "It has affected me, in the doing, in divers strong ways, deeply, forcibly." He considered, too, that the tale was "well-timed, and a good thought. . . . It has great possession of me every moment in the day, and drags me where it will. . . ." The manuscript of each section (or "Quarter") he forwarded to Forster as soon as finished. The strain was evidently great, for in a note accompanying the third instalment he said: "This book . . . has made my face white in a foreign land. My cheeks, which were beginning to fill out, have sunk again; my eyes have grown immensely large; my hair is very lank; and the head inside the hair is hot and giddy. Read the scene at the end of the third part, twice. I wouldn't write it twice, for something. . . . Tomorrow I shall begin afresh (starting the next part with a broad grin, and ending it with the very soul of jollity and happiness. . . ."). As indicating how substantial to him were the fictions of his brain, he said: "Since I conceived, at the beginning of the second part, what must happen in the third, I have undergone as much sorrow and agitation as if the thing were real; and have wakened up with it at night." He felt obliged to lock himself in when he had concluded the story, as his face "was swollen for the time to twice its proper size, and was hugely ridiculous." On November 3rd he joyfully announced to Forster that the tale was completed, "Thank God!"—adding that he had thereupon indulged in "what women call 'a real good cry'!" thus showing how earnest he was, and how great the mental caused the highly-strung nerves to tension which cause relax directly the strain ceased. Two days later, writing to Thomas Mitton, he said: "I have worn myself to death in the month I have been at work. None of my usual reliefs have been at hand; I have not been able to divest myself of the story—have suffered very much in my sleep in consequence—and am so shaken by such work in this trying climate, that I am as nervous as a man who is dying of drink, and as haggard as a murderer. I believe I have written a tremendous book, and knocked the 'Carol' out of the field. It will make a great uproar, I have no doubt."[1]

The Christmas Book finished, Dickens indulged in a well-earned holiday—to rest the brain rather than the body and on the sixth of November he started on a travelling tour, leaving Genoa for Venice and many other places. From Cremona, ten days later, he wrote to Douglas Jerrold saying that he very

---

[1] "The Letters of Charles Dickens."

much wished him to hear him read aloud "The Chimes," for the Novelist was 'eager thus to try the effect of it upon his friends. A meeting was arranged at Forster's residence, Lincoln's Inn Fields, for December 3. Before this private reading took place, however, Forster read the story (for dramatic purposes) to A'Beckett, who "cried so much and so painfully that Forster didn't know whether to go on or to stop." Meanwhile Dickens continued his holiday excursion, Journeying to Milan in severe wintry weather, visiting Mantua and Cremona on the way, and then through Switzerland and France *en route* for England, leaving his wife "shut up in her palace like a baron's lady in the time of the Crusades." He had already notified to Forster his intention to reach Milan by the 18th of November. "Now, you know my punctuality. Frost, ice, flooded rivers, steamers, horses, passports, and customhouses may damage it. But my design is, to walk into Cuttris's coffee room [then the Piazza Hotel, Covent Garden] on Sunday the 1st of December, in good time for dinner. . . . I will not fail to write to you on my travels. . . . And when I meet you—oh Heaven! What a week we will have." This journey through Italy afforded him his first real experience of the wonders of that country—of its cities and peoples, its picture galleries, churches, and other public institutions. Arriving in London on the 30th of the month, he at once rushed into the arms of Maclise and Forster. The latter speaks of the eager face and figure of the Novelist as they flashed upon him suddenly that wintry Saturday night—so suddenly, that almost before he became conscious of his friend's presence he felt the grasp of his hand.

Three days subsequently the memorable reading took place, an event immortalized by Maclise in a sketch of the scene. Besides Dickens and his host, there were present Carlyle, Stanfield, Laman Blanchard, Douglas Jerrold, Frederick Dickens (the Novelist's brother), Fox, Rev. Alexander Dyce, Rev. William Harness, and, of course, Maclise; all the actors in this historic scene have passed away—indeed, only two had survived when described by Forster in 1872, Viz., Carlyle and himself. On December 5th a second reading was given, on the pressing intercession of the Rev. H. Barham (Thomas Ingoldsby), who recorded in his diary under that date that "Dickens read with remarkable effect his Christmas story 'The Chimes' from the proofs." This pleasurable interlude over, Dickens made his way back to Genoa, stopping at Paris to see Macready, who was then fulfilling a professional engagement in the "gay city"; they went to the Odéon together and to the Italian opera to hear Grisi sing. After witnessing the rehearsal by Macready of a scene in "Othello," in which play the famous tragedian was about to take part, Dickens left Paris to resume, on the 22nd of December, his ordinary Genoa life. It must be confessed that "The Chimes," when published, hardly created the excitement which the Author anticipated. Nevertheless, the profits greatly exceeded those of the "Carol," for they amounted to nearly £1500 on the sale of the first twenty thousand copies. Lord Jeffrey[1] believed that Dickens had entirely succeeded in his object, and that therefore "all the tribe of selfishness, and cowardice, and cant" would hate him and accuse him of wicked exaggeration; declaring, too that the good and the brave were with its Author, and the truth also. John

[1] *See* page 505.

Leech, in one of his illustrations for the story, made a curious mistake; instead of drawing Richard "with matted hair," he depicted a figure entirely different from what Dickens intended—an oversight which the artist promptly rectified.

The opening days of 1845 found Dickens and his family still living at the Palazzo Peschiere. In February he and his wife went to Rome for the Carnival, and again for the Holy Week—then to Florence, and so back to Genoa in April, where he remained until June. His first impression of Rome was disappointing. "It is no more my Rome, degraded and fallen and lying asleep in the sun among a heap of ruins, than Lincoln's Inn Fields is." Florence, Venice, and Genoa he regarded as the three great Italian cities, and the Bay of Genoa the "most lovely thing" he had ever seen, while Herculaneum and Pompeii were, for him, "more full of interest and wonder than it is possible to imagine." In February he favoured Thomas Mitton with a realistic description of an ascent (by himself in a small party of six) of Mount Vesuvius, with saddle horses, litters, and twenty-two guides; he and another venturesome spirit, with the head guide, resolved, "like jackasses," to peep into the crater. "We looked down into the flaming bowels of the mountain and came back again, alight in half-a-dozen places, and burnt from head to foot. You never saw such devils. And I never saw anything so awful and terrible." When returning down the precipitous and slippery mountain side, three of the attendants lost their footing and plunged into the dark depths below—not killed, but—badly injured as the result of the terrible fall. "A pretty unusual trip for a pleasure expedition," was the Novelist's just comment upon this exciting experience.[1]

His residence in Italy now drew to a close. Once more in my old quarters," he wrote to Lady Blessington from Genoa on the 9th of May, "and with rather a tired sole to my foot from having found such an immense number of different resting places for it since I went away. I write you my last Italian letter, for this boat, designing to leave here, please God, on the ninth of next month and to be in London again by the end of June." Although he had formed a real liking for Genoa, he was rapidly becoming homesick and eagerly anticipated a renewal of the "happy old walks and old talks" with Forster and others in the "dear old home." He returned by the Great St. Gothard and through Switzerland. "Oh God! What a beautiful country it is! How poor and shrunken beside it is Italy in its brightest aspect." Such was his opinion of the land of mountains and glaciers. Maclise, Douglas Jerrold, and Forster met the Dickens party at Brussels, and they passed a delightful week in Flanders together before embarking for England.

[1] "The Letters of Charles Dickens."

CHAPTER 7

## "PICTURES FROM ITALY" AND
## "DOMBEY AND SON"

After a year's sojourn abroad, Dickens gladly settled down again in Devonshire Terrace, amidst familiar home surroundings. Before many days had elapsed, a hope which he had sometime previously entertained was revived, viz., that of establishing a periodical. "I really think I have an idea," he wrote to Forster, "and not a bad one, for the periodical. I have turned it over, the last two days, very much in my mind: and think it positively good. I incline, still to weekly; price three half-pence, if possible; partly original, partly select; notices of books, notices of theatres, notices of all good things, notices of all bad ones; 'Carol' philosophy, cheerful views, sharp anatomisation of humbug, jolly good temper; papers always in season, pat to the time of year; and a vein of glowing, hearty, mirthful, beaming reference in everything to Home, and Fireside. And I would call it, sir—

'THE CRICKET. A cheerful creature that chirrups on the Hearth.—*Natural History*.'"

His aim was that the "Cricket" should "put everybody in a good temper, and make a dash at people's fenders and armchairs as hasn't been made for many a long day," and that he would "chirp, chirp away in every number" until he "chirped it up to—well, you shall say how many hundred thousand!" While he himself had great confidence in the probable success of the project, he felt anxious to know Forster's opinion, and this proved to be not altogether favourable. The proposal, however, was nipped in the bud by a larger venture, nothing less than the founding of a daily paper, a scheme that seemed "in its extent and danger more suitable to the wild and hazardous enterprises of that prodigious year [1845] of excitement and disaster," for at that period the country had become involved in the great Free Trade struggle and stirred by the principles advocated by the Anti-Corn Law League. In the meantime, the idea of the "Cricket" developed in another direction. "What do you think," wrote Dickens to Forster, about halfway through the summer of 1845, "of a notion that has occurred to me in connection with our abandoned little weekly? It would be a delicate and beautiful fancy for a Christmas book, making the "Cricket" a little household god—silent in the wrong and sorrow of the tale, and loud again when all went well and happy." Thus originated the little story—the third of the series of Christmas Books—which appeared in December of that year; but before the Author began to work at it, he and his friends diverted themselves by getting up a play. On the 27th of August Dickens informed his artist friend, George Cattermole, that "a little party of us" had taken Miss Kelly's theatre for a night, and they were going to act there, "with correct and pretty costume, good orchestra, &c. &c." The affair was strictly private, the play selected being Ben Jonson's "Every Man in his Humour." The Novelist's exceptional ability as an actor is fully dealt with in a subsequent chapter; it will therefore suffice

now to remark that he often thought he would
certainly have been as successful "on the boards as he
had been between them" (meaning the bindings of his
books), and when performing on the stage at Montreal
in 1842 he was much astonished at the reality and ease
(as it seemed to himself) of his impersonations. In less
than three weeks after his return to Devonshire
Terrace, all the preliminaries of the play had been
arranged, and the cast included such notable names as
Douglas Jerrold, John Leech, Mark Lemon, Gilbert
A'Beckett, Percival Leigh, Dudley Costello, Frank
Stone, in addition to Forster and Dickens himself,
Stanfield's office being that of scene-painter. The
Novelist also assumed the heavy responsibilities of
stage-manager, and it is no exaggeration to say that he
greatly distinguished himself in that capacity, a
consensus of opinion inclining to the belief that there
never had been such an energetic, persevering,
enthusiastic, and withal temperate and diplomatic
stage-manager as Charles Dickens; on similar
occasions he often combined in a marvellous manner
the duties of that position with those of stage
carpenter, scene arranger, property man, prompter, and
bandmaster! The first performance of "Every Man in
his Humour" took place on the 21st of September with
a success that exceeded all expectation, whereupon the
amateur company yielded to a pressing demand for a
second performance in a larger theatre, to which the
public were admitted, the proceeds being devoted to a
charitable object.

A brief autumn holiday was spent at Broadstairs,
prior to the play, and on the 28th of October a sixth
child, and fourth son, was born to him, christened
Alfred Tennyson after his godfathers, Count D'Orsay
and the late Poet Laureate. The third Christmas

Book, already referred to as "The Cricket on the Hearth," called for his attention at this time, but the writing of it did not run so smoothly as could have been desired. The fact is (as Forster explains), he was then actively assisting in the preparation for the proposed daily newspaper, and doubtless the manifold details worried him not a little. We are not surprised, therefore, that his literary labours were hindered; indeed, he came to a deadlock in his Christmas story, and informed Forster on October 31st that he was "sick, bothered, and depressed," with "visions of Brighton" upon him, and had a great mind to finish the second part there or at Hampstead. "I never was in such bad writing cue," he declared, "as I am this week, in all my life." He suffered, too, from giddiness, and could hardly see—a state of things attributed by him mainly to the absence of his usual walking exercise, in which his multifarious occupations just then prevented him from indulging. In due course "The Cricket on the Hearth" was printed and published, and so great was the demand for the book that the sale doubled that of its predecessors.

In the early 'forties Dickens found an occasional vent for his political views, not only by composing squib verses for the *Examiner*, but also by writing articles for his old acquaintance, the *Morning Chronicle*. The proprietor of that paper, Sir John Easthope, made certain proposals to him respecting a continuance of those articles, or of a weekly letter *apropos* of his travelling experiences on the Continent—the journey to Italy being then contemplated. The attempt thus to secure his services proved ineffectual, as he did not care to become a regular contributor to a daily paper; but the subject is worthy of attention here because in the consultation held to decide the momentous question lay the germ of that newspaper enterprise which was now to be developed. Forster had great misgivings regarding this enterprise and advised its abandonment, fully realising what it would mean to a man of Dickens's health and temperament, and in appealing against the project he placed before the Novelist, "in the strongest form, all the considerations drawn from his genius and fame that should deter him from the labour and responsibility of a daily paper." But he would not be dissuaded. Accordingly, a prospectus was drawn up and an advertisement inserted in *Punch* on the 27th of December 1845, announcing the "New Morning Paper" (Price Fivepence), to be called the *Daily News*, that successful journal which claims to be the oldest Liberal daily paper in London, and which recently celebrated its jubilee. The prospectus, in briefly setting forth its leading features, significantly stated that the literary department would be "under the direction of Mr. Charles Dickens," a notification which excited great public interest, for it really meant that the whole of the political and literary matter would be personally superintended by the most popular author of the day. Directly it was settled that Dickens should undertake the conduct of the new paper, Forster (ever loyal to his friend) consented to hold a place on the staff— and a powerful staff it soon became, including as it did such influential and practical men as W. J. Fox (afterwards M.P. for Oldham), Douglas Jerrold, Mark Lemon, Dudley Costello, George Hogarth, Scott Russell, &c., and among the outside contributors were many other writers of distinction. John Dickens, the Novelist's father, had the management of the reporting staff, while the father of John Leech, the artist, acted as a kind of assistant secretary. Sir Joseph Crowe, who was a member of the *Daily News* staff at this time, remembers John Dickens as "short, portly, obese, fond of a glass of grog, full of fun, never given to much locomotion, but sitting as chairman, and looking carefully to the regular marking and orderly despatch to the printers of the numerous manuscripts thrown off at lightning speed by the men from the 'gallery.' It was his habit to come down to the office about eight at night, and he invariably in all weathers walked down Fleet Street and turned into the passage leading into Whitefriars. Every night as regularly as clockwork he was relieved of his silk pocket-handkerchief by the thieves of the great neighbouring thoroughfare, and he would deplore the loss in feeling terms when he tried to wipe the perspiration from his brow; for it was a peculiarity of his nature that he was always hot, whatever the weather might be. He maintained that he knew when his pocket was picked, but that he could not help himself, because the thief was too nimble and he too stout.

Among the original proprietors of the new daily journal were Sir William Jackson, Sir Joshua Walmsley, and Sir Joseph Paxton, who had at their back a capital of £100,000, paid-up and underwritten. Dickens, with a salary of £2000 a year, flung himself into the work with characteristic energy, sparing no pains in order to ensure perfection, or something approaching it, and for months he was to be found, morning, noon, and night, at the offices. A writer on

---

[1] "Reminiscences of Thirty-Five Years of My Life," by Sir Joseph Crowe, K.C.M.G., C.B., 1895.

the subject remarks: "It was no light matter to attempt in 1846 to set up a newspaper in rivalry to old established prints, and to announce that while adopting and impressing opinions not in accordance with those of the more powerful part of the community in general, the journal would also undertake to be better worth the buying of the ordinary man in the streets than any of its long established and well paying rivals. Dickens was just the man to become the inspiring force to such an idea. It had a positive fascination for him. He threw his own soul into it. His very manner and voice had something encouraging and inspiriting. Younger people who did not know Charles Dickens, who perhaps never saw him, can have little idea of the moving power of his words, his appeals, his very presence over men. The mere thrill of his wonderful voice had a magic of persuasion in it. There was no more strenuous and commanding figure in the England of Queen Victoria's reign. He was just the man to start such a venture as the *Daily News*."[1]

The first number (the printing of which proved unsatisfactory) appeared on January 21, 1846, and it is said that specimen copies were despatched to almost every house in the kingdom. The year that ushered in the new paper was a time of great political disquietude; indeed, the very day which saw its advent immediately followed that on which Sir Robert Peel delivered his remarkable speech for the repeal of the corn laws—a subject that the *Daily News* lost no time in concentrating its activity upon.[2]

[1] "The *Daily News* Jubilee," by Justin McCarthy, M.P., and Sir John R. Robinson, 1896.

[2] "He [Dickens] was a thorough Liberal, and the tradition he established has remained with the *Daily News* unbroken to this day. We were, indeed, born fighting, and Dickens began by leading a desperate onslaught on Protectionism."—See the *Daily News*, February 7, 1902.

It will be remembered that during his sojourn abroad during the previous year Dickens wrote to Forster, at frequent intervals, letters describing his Italian experiences, with a view to their publication. In one of his epistles he expressed himself as gratified in finding that his friend was really pleased with these "shadows in the water," and that he thought them worth looking at. "Writing in such odd places," he said, "and in such odd seasons, I have been half savage with myself, very often, for not doing better." He admitted, however, his inability at that time to devise a plan of using them to his own satisfaction; but the launching of the *Daily News* afforded the opportunity he had been seeking, and the initial number contains the first of a series of "Travelling Sketches—Written on the Road, by Charles Dickens," these "Sketches," which appeared at irregular intervals until March 2nd, constituting a marked innovation in, journalism, and, as such, were doubtless considered in many quarters as an experiment of doubtful propriety. Dickens, as his friends anticipated, quickly discovered that the editing of a daily political paper, with the incessant labour and worry it involved, proved for him impossible; he sickened of the mechanical drudgery, and at the expiration of a few weeks (being "tired to death and quite worn out") he resigned his editorial functions, abiding in office, however, for a short time longer, when Forster reluctantly assumed the editorial reins for the rest of the year. Owing to the series of "Travelling Letters" having begun, Dickens's name could not at once be withdrawn, and while they continued to appear he contributed letters on such important social questions as Crime and Education (urging the claims of Ragged

Schools) and Capital Punishment; some verses, entitled "The Hymn of the Wiltshire Labourers" also bear
his signature. The Novelist always regarded this experience in journalism with a tinge of regret; but it may
be said of him, as of Thackeray when he abandoned
Art for Literature, that the world profited by the act of
renunciation, for had Dickens consented to remain in
the editorial chair, conscientiously devoting the whole
of his mind and the greater part of his time to the
supervision of the work of others, he would necessarily have sacrificed the best portion of a superb
literary career. During the year of his resignation the
"Travelling Sketches" were reprinted in book form as
"Pictures from Italy," with five additional chapters and
illustrations by Samuel Palmer. The "Brave C.," who
figures so constantly in his letters and "Pictures," was
Louis Roche, a native of Avignon and the prince of
couriers, whose services in that capacity played an
important part in rendering the Italian tour both pleasurable and delightful.

In the preface to "Pictures from Italy," Dickens
avowed that it was a mistake to have disturbed, by
venturing upon this big scheme, the old relations
between himself and his readers. The departure,
however, had been only "for a moment." In January
he again conceived the notion of going abroad to
write another story in shilling numbers, and thus
confided the interesting fact to Lady Blessington:
"Vague thoughts of a new book are rife within me just
now; and I go wandering about at night into the
strangest places, according to my usual propensities at
such a time, seeking rest, and finding none." Craving,
too, for early associations, he and his wife,
accompanied by Miss Hogarth, Maclise, Jerrold, and

Forster, went to Rochester on his birthday, having their quarters for the time at the "Bull" Inn of Pickwickian fame, and visiting favourite places in the neighbourhood. He felt that he could not commence the book in London, because he feared the newspaper business just relinquished would still be too much in his mind to permit him to formulate his ideas. He therefore determined to embark upon the story in Lausanne and in Genoa, and "forget everything else if I can; and by living in Switzerland for the summer, and in Italy or France for the winter, I shall be saving money while I write." Accordingly the house in Devonshire Terrace was let to Sir James Duke for twelve months, and he made his summer residence at Lausanne, in Switzerland. On the eve of his departure he presided at the first dinner of the General Theatrical Fund, in the establishment of which he took a keen interest. Again obtaining the services of the courier Roche, the Novelist and his wife left England on May 31, 1846, arriving at Lausanne on June 11th, where he secured the very first villa he had seen; it was called Rosemont, and he described it as being "quite a doll's house . . . beautifully situated on the hill that rises from the lake," with a little study looking out upon the water and the mountains, while there were roses enough "to smother the whole establishment of the *Daily News* in." At Lausanne he found a small colony of English people with whom an agreeable intercourse ensued, and with particular members of it, including Mr. and Mrs. de Cerjat, and Mr. and Mrs. Watson (of Rockingham Castle, Northamptonshire) he became on very intimate terms. In the midst of these beautiful surroundings he settled down at his desk, and presently announced to Forster that "an odd

shadowy undefined idea" was generating within him,
that he could connect a great battlefield somehow with
his next Yuletide story—for it was the fourth
Christmas volume upon which his thoughts were
centred, as well as upon the longer romance.

A fortnight after his arrival at Lausanne he
commenced his book; he had, in fact, been waiting for
a certain box from London containing not only the
necessary materials, but certain quaint little bronze
figures which customarily stood upon his desk, and
which Forster assures us "were as much needed for the
easy flow of his writing as blue ink or quill pens"—the
Novelist, by the way, favoured blue ink because it
dried rapidly, while the quill pen he used until the last.
On the 28th of June he averred that he had not been
idle during the interval: "I had a good deal to write for
Lord John [Russell] about the Ragged Schools. I set to
work and did that. A good deal for Miss Coutts [after-
wards the Baroness Burdett-Coutts] in reference to her
charitable projects. I set to work and did *that*. Half of
the children's New Testament to write, or pretty
nearly. I set to work and did *that*.[1] . . . and then. . . .

### "BEGAN DOMBEY!

"I performed this feat yesterday," he continues, only
wrote the first slip—but there it is, and it is a plunge
straight over head and ears into the story." *Apropos*
of this, the Novelist said that he took a book from his
box and intimated to the assembled members of
his household that whatever passage his thumb

---

[1] The children's New Testament was an abstract of the narrative of
the Four Gospels for the use of juvenile readers, written exclusively for
his own children and never intended for publication.

rested on in perfunctorily opening the volume he would take as having reference to his projected novel; the book was "Tristram Shandy" (an old favourite), and the words that first caught his eye were, "What a work it is likely to turn out! Let us begin it!" which he regarded as a good omen. Thoughts of the forthcoming Christmas tale, at this time, subjected him to alternate fits of the wildest enthusiasm and of anxious consideration, the "field of battle" notion still being uppermost in his mind; but the fancy was temporarily laid aside, in order that "Dombey and Son" should receive his undivided attention. Dinner parties, whist parties (card games were played "with great dignity and gravity sometimes"), and visits to the theatre, constituted harmless forms of recreation in which he occasionally indulged in the evenings, while the customary long walks at night were kept up, thus affording him opportunities of beholding the beautiful and ever changing aspect of mountain and lake under effects of moonlight or tempest. "Dombey" progressed steadily, but somewhat tardily at first, for, as usual when abroad, he felt the absence of populous streets; this induced an "extraordinary nervousness it would be hardly possible to describe," which would come upon him after he had been busy all day with his pen. On July 5th he expressed a hope that the first number would be finished "in the course of a fortnight at farthest," at the same time intimating that "a great surprise might be looked for in the fourth number"—an allusion to the death of little Paul, delayed, however, until the fifth number. Still cherishing the "battle" conception for his Christmas book, he thought it possible (when the first instalment of "Dombey" was completed) he might run and look for the little, tale in the glaciers at

Chamounix by way of relaxation. Writing presently to
Forster, he referred with a touch of fervour to the
advancement of the main story: "I think 'Dombey'
very strong—with great capacity in its leading idea;
plenty of character that is likely to tell; and some
rollicking facetiousness, to say nothing of pathos."
Again, a few days later: "I think the general idea of
'Dombey' is interesting and new, and has great material in it." Then came a suggestion for the title of the
Christmas tale—"The Battle of Life": "It is not a name
I have conned at all, but has just occurred to me in
connection with that foggy idea. If I can see my way,
I think I will take it next, and clear it off. If you knew
how it hangs about me, I am sure you would say so
too. It would be an immense relief to have it done, and
nothing standing in the way of 'Dombey.'" A little
mountain expedition—to view the wonders of Mont
Blanc, the Valley of Chamounix, and the Mer de
Glace—followed. "I cannot imagine anything in
nature more stupendous or sublime," he said; "if I
were to write about it now, I should quite rave—such
prodigious impressions are rampant within me." From
Dickens's account of his life in Switzerland, as related
to his biographer, we learn that his literary labours
were varied by relaxations of this kind, but such pleasures were never permitted to interfere with the
important duties of life. The many delightful excursions included a trip to the convent of the Great St.
Bernard, concerning which he informed Forster that
"the brother who carved at our supper could speak
some English, and had just had 'Pickwick' given
him!—What a humbug he will think me when
he tries to understand it! If I had had any other book
of mine with me, I would have given it him,

that I might have had some chance of being intelligible."

As, for the space about two years, no serial story by "Boz" had been published, his numerous readers were puzzled to know the reason, and various conjectures were circulated. The public prints, too, commented on the situation, the *Sporting Magazine* indulging in the following amusing epigram:

> "It's so long since Dickens has written a book,
> That all the world's authors consider it rum of him;
> They hint that he's dead, with a wink and a look,
> If he's not, what the Dickens on earth has become of him?"

That the Novelist's mental activities and imaginative powers exhibited no signs of abatement is indicated by the fact that ideas for stories other than those upon which he was then engaged continually floated through his mind, to be utilised thereafter. "Dombey and Son" was paramount, however, although he complained of his extraordinary difficulty in "getting on FAST," and of feeling, at times, "most abominably dull and stupid." "Invention, thank God," he remarked, "seems the easiest thing in the world; and I seem to have such a preposterous sense of the ridiculous . . . as to be constantly requiring to restrain myself from launching into extravagances in the height of my enjoyment." Attributing this difficulty to the absence of crowded streets, he said, "I can't express how much I want these. It seems as if they supplied something to my brain, which it cannot bear, when busy, to lose. For a week or a fortnight I can write prodigiously in a retired place (as at Broadstairs), and a day in London sets me up again and starts me. But the toil and labour of writing day after day, without that magic lantern, is IMMENSE!! . . . My fingers seem disposed to stagnate without crowds about them. I wrote very little in Genoa (only the 'Chimes'), and fancied myself conscious of some such influence there—but Lord! I had two miles of streets at least, lighted at night, to walk about in; and a great theatre to repair to, every night." With "The Battle of Life" and "Dombey" simultaneously engaging his attention, there is no doubt he essayed too much; the former he hoped, by attacking it at once and temporarily turning aside from "Dombey," to complete within a month, for he was eager to get to begin it, and thought it would be all the better, for a change, to make it a simple domestic tale, without the supernatural features. The worry of thus driving in "double harness" distressed him exceedingly, and he described himself as being sick, giddy, and capriciously despondent—as having bad nights, and being full of disquietude and anxiety—symptoms indicative of excessive mental effort. At first making light of Forster's warning against overwork, he now began to realise its wisdom, and almost determined to abandon the idea of issuing a Christmas book this year, fearing to wear himself out. A change of scene became imperative, so he went to Geneva at the end of September to recuperate; but for this, he believed that he would have been prostrated by "some bad low fever." A few days at Geneva set him up again, and he returned to Lausanne, to welcome as guests at Rosemont his friends the Talfourds. On October 10th he sent Forster two-thirds of the manuscript of "The Battle of Life," desiring him to read the first and second parts together. "I made a tremendous day's work of it yesterday," he said, "and was horribly excited—so am going to rush out, as fast as I can: being a little used up, and sick."

The sale of the first number of "Dombey" exceeded that of the first of "Chuzzlewit" by more than twelve thousand copies, an announcement which greatly delighted the Author. On submitting to Forster the concluding pages of the Christmas book, Dickens, in a desponding note, intimated that he really did not know what the story was worth. "I am so floored: wanting sleep, and never having had my head free from it for this month past." On the 20th he declared his determination to start on No. 3 of "Dombey" as soon as he could, but "at present I am the worse for wear," and he again complained of insomnia. A bottle of hock at this juncture did him "a world of good;" "the change comes in the very nick of time," he said, "and I feel in Dombeian spirits already. . . . I dreamed all last week that 'The Battle of Life' was a series of chambers impossible to be got to rights or got out of, through which I wandered drearily all night. . . . The mental distress, quite horrible." In requesting Forster's criticism of "The Battle of Life" before the proofs were passed for press, the Author referred to a certain mannerism of which he was sometimes guilty, namely, the unconscious act of dropping into blank verse. Hain Friswell first noted this peculiarity in "The Old Curiosity Shop," and instances may be discovered in subsequent works. Dickens explained that he could not help the tendency to blank verse when "very much in earnest," and authorised Forster to "knock out a word's brains here and there," in such cases where the versification became objectionably apparent. In one of Leech's drawings for "The Battle" a strange error was committed by the artist, who made the mistake of supposing that Michael Warden had taken part in the elopement of Marion, introducing his figure with that of the bride; this oversight was not discovered until too late for correction, and Dickens (to his honour be it said) preferred to pass it silently rather than hurt the tender susceptibilities of his friend. Lord Jeffrey[1] accorded the highest praise to the little Love Story, and said, "It is better than any other man alive could have written, and has passages as fine as anything that ever came from the man himself. . . ."

"Dombey and Son" proceeded apace. The third number was begun on October 26th, nine days later he was half through it, and by the 9th of November its last chapter had been penned—marvellously rapid work. A week after the completion of the number he and his family left Lausanne, somewhat regretfully, for Paris, travelling post for the space of five days in wintry weather and along bad roads before reaching their destination—an expedition requiring all the skill and ingenuity of the "brave courier," Roche, to bring to a successful issue when the encumbrances are remembered—"several tons of luggage, other tons of servants, and other tons of children." Two days later they were "in the agonies of house-hunting" ("one paroxysm for four mortal days"), the Novelist designing to stay in Paris during three months. Eventually, after a brief but enjoyable residence at the Hotel Brighton, they settled down in the Rue de Courcelles (No. 48), in the "most ridiculous, extraordinary, unparalleled, and preposterous house in the whole world" (as the Novelist described it), containing a suite of rooms such as "the maddest man in Bedlam" would be likely to devise, "supposing

[1] *See* page 505.

his case to be hopeless and quite incurable"; the place partook of the character of a baby-house, a haunted castle, and a mad kind of clock, one room being like a tent, another a grove, a third resembling a theatrical scene, and so forth.

Anxiety respecting the health of his sister Fanny now took possession of him. She had married Henry Burnett, a professional vocalist and teacher of singing, and while singing herself at a party in Manchester she suddenly broke down, a subsequent medical examination disclosing symptoms of consumption; her death, which took place in the summer of 1848, grieved the Novelist exceedingly. Good news concerning his story, however, cheered his spirits. "'Dombey' is doing wonders," he informed M. de Cerjat on November 27th, while to another dear friend he announced that 'Dombey' has passed its thirty thousand already." Meanwhile, Albert Smith had been occupied in dramatising "The Battle of Life" for Mr. and Mrs. Keeley, the first performance taking place at the Lyceum Theatre on December 21st. The Novelist agreed to see the rehearsal of the play, leaving Paris for that special purpose. Writing to his wife from Lincoln's Inn Fields on December 19th, he said: "I really am bothered to death by this confounded *dramatisation* of the Christmas book. They were in a state so horrible at Keeley's yesterday . . . that I was obliged to engage to read the book to them this morning. . . . Unless I had come to London, I do not think there would have been much hope of the version being more than just tolerated, even that doubtful. All the actors bad, all the business frightfully behindhand. The very words of the book confused in the copying into the densest and most insufferable nonsense. I must exempt, however,

from the general slackness both the Keeleys. I hope
they will be very good. I have never seen anything of
its kind better than the manner in which they played
the little supper scene between Clemency and Britain,
yesterday. It was quite perfect, even to me." He
concluded the letter by announcing: "Christmas book
published today—twenty-three thousand copies
already gone!!!"[1] The play proved much more
satisfactory than Dickens anticipated, and, in reporting
the result to Mrs. Dickens, he admitted that it went
with great effect. "There was immense enthusiasm at
its close, and great uproar and shouting for me. . . . I
saw the Keeleys on the stage at eleven o'clock or so,
and they were in prodigious spirits and delight."[2]
Returning to Paris two days later in bitterly cold
weather, he attacked "Dombey" with renewed vigour,
and on completing the fifth number early in the new
year (1847), Forster joined him. The two friends
passed a fortnight together, devoting. most of the time
to sightseeing and in visits to the theatres; they also
paid their respects to famous Frenchmen, including
Victor Hugo, by whom Dickens was received "with
infinite courtesy and grace." The Novelist's stay in
Paris was curtailed by the illness of his eldest son, who
was at school in London; he and his wife at once left
the French capital in order to be present at the bedside
of the invalid, making a temporary abode at the
Victoria Hotel, Euston Square, the house in
Devonshire Terrace being still occupied by Sir James
Duke. But the parents were not allowed immediate
access to their boy, owing to the infectious nature of
the disease from which he was suffering—scarlet

---

[1] "The Letters of Charles Dickens."
[2] Ibid.

fever—and nearly a month elapsed before they were permitted to visit him, at his lodgings in Albany Street. Respecting this affecting interview an amusing incident is recorded, which afforded the Novelist not a little pleasure. An elderly charwoman, on being told by Mrs. Hogarth (the boy's grandmother, who nursed him during sickness) that Mr. Charles Dickens was coming to see the patient, inquired if "the young gentleman was the son of the man that wrote "Dombey"; reassured on that point, the old dame exclaimed, "Lawk, ma'am! I thought that three or four men must have put together 'Dombey'!" It transpired that the 'woman lodged at a snuff shop hard by, and it was the custom of the landlord to read aloud, for the benefit of herself and fellow lodgers, each number as it came out—hence the interest she displayed in the story and its creator.

While the writing of "Dombey and Son" progressed, the trusty Forster received many communications from the Author, explaining from time to time his intentions with regard to it, and desiring his opinion respecting particular points in the story. Forster devotes an entire chapter to the subject of these communications, where we find Dickens exhibiting some uneasiness about the illustrations, and especially fearing that "Phiz" would caricature the face of his merchant hero; so, to prevent the possibility of misconception, he indicated by a living person the type of City gentleman he desired the artist to select. "I do wish he could get a glimpse of A, for he is the very Dombey;" but this not being possible, "Phiz" delineated several types whence the Author could choose the most suitable. Dickens took greater pains than is customary with novelists in furnishing hints to the artists who illustrated his writings, and "Phiz" doubtless considered, sometimes, that his requirements were rather exacting, while his conceptions were not always capable of realisation. Not possessing a practical knowledge of art, he occasionally failed to realise its limitations, with the result that he now and then experienced a sense of disappointment in the pictorial rendering of certain scenes or incidents. In the second number of "Dombey and Son" one of the illustrations was found to be so "dreadfully bad" that it made him "curl his legs up," and he intimated to Forster that he would cheerfully have given a hundred pounds if this particular design could have been omitted. The artist, however, cannot be entirely exempted from misrepresenting his author—the consequence, maybe, of carelessly reading the proofs.

The real anguish that Dickens underwent, when he killed Little Nell (in "The Old Curiosity Shop") was renewed when, in the fifth number of "Dombey," he narrated the death of Paul, and the greater part of the night of January 14, 1847 (the day on which that chapter was written), the Author wandered desolate and sad about the streets of Paris; he told his children that when rehearsing the incident of the boy's demise for the public readings, he could only master his intense emotion by keeping steadily before his eyes the picture of his own youngest child ("Plorn"), who was well, strong, and hearty. The pathetic denouement created a profound impression. "Paul's death has amazed Paris," he wrote. "All sorts of people are open-mouthed with admiration." Lord Jeffrey,[1] who thought it "the best thing past, present, or to come," became greatly excited thereby, and thus addressed the Novelist: "Oh, my dear, dear Dickens! What a No. 5 you have now given us! I have so cried and sobbed over it last night, and again

[1] See page 505.

this morning; and felt my heart purified by those tears, and blessed and loved you for making me shed them; and I never can bless and love you enough. Since the divine Nelly was found dead on her humble couch, beneath the snow and the ivy, there has been nothing like the actual dying of that sweet Paul, in the summer sunshine of that lofty room. And the long vista that leads us so gently and sadly, and yet so gracefully and winningly, to the plain consummation!  . . ." Thackeray, too, on reading the affecting account of the passing away of little Paul, seemed electrified at the thought that there was one man living who could exercise so complete a control over him. Putting No. 5 of "Dombey and Son" in his pocket, he hastened to the printing office of Punch (for the great "Titmarsh" was numbered among the chief contributors to that journal), and entering the editor's room, he dashed it on the table with startling vehemence, exclaiming, "There's no writing against such power as this—one has no chance! Read that chapter describing young Paul's death; it is unsurpassed—it is stupendous!"

The interest of the story was so well maintained that the demand for each number increased month by month. In a letter to his sister on March 31, 1848 (that is, when the story drew near its conclusion), Dickens remarked: "'Dombey' is prodigiously triumphant, and I *believe* the end of that immortal history is tolerably good. I have taken great pains with it, and have been continually crying over the manuscript." The last two numbers were issued together in one wrapper in April of that year. The financial success of the story was immediate, and the profits for the half-year were brilliant; deducting the £100 a month which, for six successive months, the Author received from his publishers (Bradbury & Evans), there was due to him the sum of £2200, Which he thought "pretty tidy." That "Dombey and Son" ranked high in the Author's estimation is indicated by his belief that if any of his books "are read years hence, 'Dombey' will be remembered as among the best of them."

Dickens's presentment of little Paul was inspired by the touching personality of a favourite nephew, Master Harry Burnett, a cripple, who died in his tenth year; notwithstanding his affliction, he was one of the happiest and brightest of children, with a mind marvellously active, and, especially during the latter portion of his short life, full of religious sentiment. The prototype of the scheming Carker is said to have been connected with an eminent London firm of engineers, and to have lived in Oxford Street, where he might frequently be seen prowling about. Mrs. Skewton's original was recognised at the time in a Mrs. Campbell, a lady well known at Leamington, who indulged in such tight lacing that the slightest exertion caused her to pant for breath; her daughter stood for the second Mrs. Dombey. The genial Captain Cuttle (says Dr. Shelton Mackenzie) was one David Mainland, a merchantman, who was introduced to Dickens one day in the City, and it is curious to note that Pepys, as circumstantially recorded in the Diary, once met a Captain Cuttle, a Sea Commander, at the Royal Exchange. Sol Gills found his prototype in Mr. Norie, of the firm of Norie & Wilson, nautical instrument makers, of Leadenhall Street, outside whose shop might be observed the carved sign of the Little Wooden Midshipman; the firm afterwards relocated to the Minories, in close proximity to the Tower of

London, and has since changed hands; quite recently the business was transferred to premises nearer Aldgate, where the celebrated Midshipman is still to be seen upon his bracket surveying the passers-by. Forster tells us that he had himself some knowledge of Miss Cornelia Blimber, and Charles Dickens the younger recalled the interesting fact that at a school in St. John's Wood, where he was a pupil, the master was assisted by his daughter—an amiable young lady and a thorough classical scholar—an arrangement which at that time was regarded as somewhat eccentric and first suggested the Blimber notion, "although in matters of detail there was not the slightest likeness between the two families." Mrs. Pipchin in the flesh was personally known to the Novelist; her name was Roylance, and in his boyhood he lodged with her for a few months.[1] His notes for the number in which Mrs. Pipchin appears contain the various names out of which that finally selected was evolved: "Mrs. Roylance . . . House at the seaside. Mrs. Wrychin, Mrs. Tipchin, Mrs. Alchin, Mrs. Somching, Mrs. Pipchin." Certain critics averred that it was inartistic to introduce Paul Dombey and then. promptly kill him; that it formed part of the original plan of the story, however, is evidenced by the Author's memoranda, thus:—

"Sketch of Dombey.—Mother confined with long expected boy. Boy *born to die*. Neglected girl, Florence—a child.
"Mrs. Chick—common-minded family humbug.
"Wet nurse—Polly Toodle.
"Toodle, a stoker.

[1] See page 18.

"Lots of children.

"Wooden midshipman.

"Uncle—adventurous nephew—Captain Cuttle."

In the preface to the first cheap edition of "Dombey and Son" (1858) the Author says : "I began this book by the Lake of Geneva, and went on with it for some months in France. The association between the writing and the place of writing is so curiously strong in my mind that at this day, although I know every stair in the little midshipman's house, and could swear to every pew in the church in which Florence was married, or to every young gentleman's bedstead in Dr Blimber's establishment, I yet confusedly imagine Captain Cuttle as secluding himself from Mrs. MacStinger among the mountains of Switzerland. Similarly, when I am reminded by any chance of what it was that the waves were always saying, I wander in my fancy for a whole winter night about the streets of Paris—as I really did, with a heavy heart, on the night when my little friend and I parted company for ever."

CHAPTER 8

# "DAVID COPPERFIELD"

As already stated, Dickens returned to England from Paris sooner than he originally contemplated. This unforeseen change of plans forced him to make a temporary home elsewhere than in Devonshire Terrace, which was still occupied by Sir James Duke. A suitable residence was soon discovered in Chester Place, Regent's Park, where, on April 18, 1847, his fifth son (Sydney Smith Haldimand)[1] was born; this son was the smallest in size of all the children, and throughout his infancy was never called by any other name than the "Ocean Spectre" (sometimes corrupted into "Hoshen Peck") from a strange little weird look in his large wondering eyes.[2] This designation had a sad significance, for Sydney Dickens, as a lieutenant in the Royal Navy, died on board the P. and O. steamer *Malta*, and was buried at sea

[1] The boy's godfathers were Mr. H. P. Smith, of the Eagle Life Assurance Office, and Mr. Haldimand, a former Member of Parliament, who lived at Lausanne, where Dickens met him in 1846.

[2] Dickens was fond of bestowing nicknames upon his children, such names being usually suggested by some personal characteristic, as explained by him in a letter addressed to his sister Letitia's husband, Henry Austin, in 1842.

"*P.S.*—The children's present names are as follows:

Katey (from a lurking propensity to fieryness), Lucifer Box.

Mamey (as generally descriptive of her bearing), Mild Glo'ster.

Charley (as a corruption of Master Toby), Flaster Floby.

Walter (suggested by his high cheek-bones), Young Skull.

"Each is pronounced with a peculiar howl, which I shall have great pleasure in illustrating."

on May 2, 1872. For some weeks Dickens had lodgings in Brighton, to hasten the recovery of his wife's health. Here the writing of "Dombey" was continued, in the intervals of which he directed his attention to a project having for its object the raising of a fund for the benefit of Leigh Hunt, then in financial difficulties, and of John Poole, author of "Paul Pry," &c., whose literary career and resources had simultaneously come to an end. It was proposed to give two representations of Ben Jonson's "Every Man in His Humour," with accompanying farces, and among the artists and authors associated with the enterprise were Frank Stone, A.R.A., Augustus Egg, A.R.A., John Leech, George Cruikshank, Douglas Jerrold, Mark Lemon, Dudley Costello, and George Henry Lewes—with Dickens himself as general manager. The Novelist, as was his nature in everything he undertook, threw himself heart and soul into the rehearsals and general business, fighting through his managerial troubles with such success that this amateur company gave an excellent account of themselves on the boards. Maclise described the actors as "splendid strollers," and Forster avers that they richly deserved the term. The performances took place at Manchester on July 26th, and at Liverpool two days later, the total receipts being about £900. Dickens, with his usual consideration in a charitable cause, earnestly desired to supplement the fund by writing a history of the trip à la Mrs. Gamp, to be illustrated by the artist members of this benevolent fraternity; but, after a few pages had been penned, the matter dropped, owing mainly to the artists failing to carry out their share of the undertaking.

Early in the summer Dickens relocated from

Brighton to Broadstairs, which remained his headquarters until the autumn, and his own home at Devonshire Terrace being then available, he joyfully took possession of it. We are told that his portmanteau fell off the cart during conveyance from the railway station; but happily the manuscript of an unfinished chapter of "Dombey" was not in it: "Whenever I travel," he said, "and have anything of that valuable article [i.e., unpublished manuscript], I always carry it in my pocket." The bag, however, contained "on a moderate calculation £70 worth of clothes," so that he had "no shirt to put on," and was obliged to send out for a barber to shave him! Before leaving Broadstairs he commenced to write a fifth Christmas book; finding, however, the interest of his novel too engrossing as it neared completion, he put aside the shorter tale, and allowed that Yuletide season to pass without a Christmas volume, although very loath to lose the money—and still more so "to leave any gap at Christmas firesides" which he felt he ought to fill. There were certain obstacles, too, at the hitherto quiet seaside town, which began to make themselves apparent, and proved a serious hindrance to writing. "Vagrant music is getting to that height here," he informed Forster, "and is so impossible to be escaped from, that I fear Broadstairs and I must part company in time to come. Unless it pours of rain, I cannot write half-an-hour without the most excruciating organs, fiddles, bells, or glee-singers. There is a violin of the most torturing kind under the window now (time, ten in the morning) and an Italian box of music on the steps—both in full blast."

On the 1st of December the Novelist occupied the chair at a meeting of the Leeds Mechanics'

Institute, and on the 28th he performed the ceremony
of opening the Glasgow Athenaeum, on each occasion
delivering a powerful speech. Briefly referring to the
latter event, in a letter to Forster the next day, he said:
"A most brilliant demonstration last night, and I think
I never did better. Newspaper reports bad"; and to
Miss Hogarth on the 30th he confided the fact that the
meeting was the it most stupendous" thing as to
numbers, and the most beautiful as to colours and
decorations he ever saw." The Inimitable[1] did
wonders. His grace, elegance, and eloquence
enchanted all beholders."[2] The cordial, hospitable, and
enthusiastic reception accorded to Dickens during this
visit to Scotland afforded him unbounded satisfaction.
Before closing these references to the events of 1847,
mention must be made of an extremely pleasant
incident in the life of the Novelist, namely, his
introduction to Hans Christian Andersen, for whom he
entertained the greatest admiration, and whose
charming fairy tales are familiar all the world over.
This memorable meeting, which took place at Gore
House, proved the beginning of a lasting friendship
between the two great writers. Andersen, in "The
Story of my Life," has printed a letter (probably the
first he received from Dickens) which belongs to this
period, and in which the Novelist conveys to the
Dane "a thousand thanks" for his "kind and very
valuable recollection" of him in his Christmas book. "I
am very proud of it," he added, "and feel deeply
honoured by it: I cannot tell you how much I value
such a token of acknowledgment from a man with the

---

[1] See page 8.
[2] "The Letters of Charles Dickens," where this letter is incorrectly
dated the *thirteenth*.

genius which you are possessed of. . . . Come again to England, soon! But whatever you do, do not stop writing, because we cannot bear to lose a single one of your thoughts. They are too true and simply beautiful to be kept safe only in your own head. . . ." That Andersen heartily reciprocated this amiable and genial attitude towards himself is testified in a letter addressed by him to a friend in London at this time: "If you see Dickens or write to him, please to tell him how glad I am to find him just as I pictured him to myself. I was so delighted to meet him that I quite forgot to deliver him a message from the Dutch author Van der Vliet."

From Glasgow Dickens proceeded to Edinburgh, where he spent the first day of 1848. During this year he took a very active part in a scheme for the purchase and preservation of Shakespeare's house at Stratford-on-Avon, throwing himself into the project with his wonted energy and enthusiasm. The plan for raising the necessary capital assumed the form of theatricals by the goodly company of distinguished Amateurs, of whom Dickens was the guiding star. Performances were given in Manchester, Liverpool, Glasgow, and other great provincial towns, and the gross receipts from nine representations (between April. 15th and July 20th) amounted to, £2551; owing to the fact of Stratford and its Town Council taking charge of the house, and providing an endowment fund, the profits were handed over to Sheridan Knowles, who had just signed a declaration of bankruptcy, and who was recommended to the Government as the first curator of Shakespeare's house. It should be noted that at one of these performances, in the Haymarket Theatre, London, both Queen Victoria and the Prince Consort were present. In speaking of Dickens as the leading figure in connection with these Thespian amenabilities and delights, Forster observes: "His, animal spirits, unresting and supreme, were the attraction of rehearsal at morning, and of the stage at night. At the quiet early dinner, and the more jovial unrestrained supper, where all engaged were assembled daily, his was the brightest face, the lightest step, the pleasantest word. There seemed to be no rest needed for that wonderful vitality."

In March 1848 Dickens and his wife stayed two or three weeks at Brighton. Finishing "Dombey and Son" early in the year, the Novelist had sufficient leisure to superintend rehearsals for the amateur plays. After this he enjoyed a summer idleness, having no important writing in hand until the autumn, which he spent at Broadstairs. At this watering place, not yet entirely deserted by him, he wrote the greater portion of "The Haunted Man," begun the previous year and laid aside. Among the holiday incidents he recorded an accident to Mrs. Dickens, who, while being driven in a chaise to meet her husband, was thrown out of the vehicle by the bolting of the pony, but happily escaped injury. In a letter that closed this period of relaxation, he said: "At last I am a mentally matooring of the Christmas book—or, as poor Macrone [the publisher of "Sketches by Boz"] used to write, 'booke,' 'boke,' 'buke,' &c." The task was rapidly consummated in London, and the little crimson-covered volume duly appeared at the proper season, the sale beginning with a subscription of twenty thousand copies. Mark Lemon immediately adapted it for the Adelphi Theatre, where, in its dramatised form, the story achieved considerable success. On the 3rd of January following there was a "christening" dinner to celebrate the completion of "The Haunted Man," the guests including a host of the Author's intimate friends, the only survivor of the merry party being the venerable Sir John Tenniel, who collaborated as illustrator of the story.[1] The original manuscripts of all the Christmas books can be traced with the exception of that of "The Haunted Man and the Ghost's Bargain,"[2] which has mysteriously disappeared; members of the Dickens family were under the impression that it remained with other manuscripts in Forster's possession, and were therefore much surprised when, at his death, this particular autograph was not among those bequeathed to the Nation.

In the late months of 1848 Dickens's thoughts were concentrated upon another serial story, and he pondered a good deal as to the form it should assume. Forster proposed that it might, for a change, be written in the first person, and the Novelist regarded the hint with favour, although he did not at first contemplate introducing his own personal and private recollections. In fact, the autobiographical touches in "David Copperfield" (as the new story was destined to be called) were an afterthought, inspired by Forster's suggestion. In order to obtain local colouring for the opening chapters, Dickens journeyed into Norfolk early in the New Year (1849), then for the first time beholding the quaint fishing town of Great Yarmouth and its interesting environment. Yarmouth, sir," he presently informed Forster, ". . . . is the strangest place in the wide world one hundred and

---

[1] In addition to Sir John Tenniel, the following artists contributed designs to the series of Christmas books: John Leech, Richard Doyle, Clarkson Stanfield, R.A., D. Maclise, R.A., Sir Edwin Landseer, RA, and Frank Stone, A.R.A.

[2] Forster gives the title incorrectly as "The Haunted Man, *or* the Ghost's Bargain."

forty-six miles of hill-less marsh between it and London. . . . I shall certainly try my hand at it." It is said that Dickens actually saw the old boat, high and dry on the open Denes, which he made the home of Little Eml'y; as intimated in the story, Peggotty's Hut stood upon its keel, and therefore was not an *inverted* boat, as depicted in "Phiz's" illustrations. It is curious, therefore, that Dickens should have accepted the artist's version without a protest.

The 16th of January, 1849, marked the birth of his eighth child, whom at first he meant to christen Oliver Goldsmith, probably because he had recently been reading, with great interest, Forster's biography of the author of "The Vicar of Wakefield"; but he changed his mind and called the boy Henry Fielding. In the following month the Novelist (with members of his family) again went to Brighton for a seaside holiday, where Mr. and Mrs. John Leech joined him. He had not been in his rooms many days when a strange incident happened—both the landlord and the landlord's daughter went raving mad! This awkward predicament constraining the lodgers to seek refuge at the Bedford Hotel. In a characteristic letter to Forster describing the adventure, the Novelist asserted that he was then thinking of his next story and of a suitable title for it. "My mind running, like a high sea, on names—not satisfied yet, though." The end of the month again found him at Devonshire Terrace, where he began energetically to work upon the new tale, that most attractive of all his novels—"David Copperfield"—the writing of which engaged his attention during the whole of the year. The selection of a title for this masterpiece of fiction caused the usual trouble. "I should like to know how the enclosed strikes you," he said to Forster on February 23rd, "on a first acquaintance with it. It is odd, I think, and new; but it may have A.'s difficulty of being 'too comic, my boy.' I suppose I should have to add, though, by way of motto, 'And in short it led to the very Mag's Diversions.—*Old Saying.*' Or would it be better, there being equal authority for either, 'And in short they all played Mag's Diversions.—*Old Saying?*' The following was then suggested:—

"*Mag's Diversions,*
Being the Personal History of
MR. THOMAS MAG THE YOUNGER,
Of Blunderstone House."

Dickens, however, felt dissatisfied, and composed three alternative titles. The first of these was "Mag's Diversions, being the Personal History, Adventures, Experience, and Observation of Mr. David Mag the Younger, of Blunderstone House"; the second omitted "Adventures," and "Blunderstone House" was changed to "Copperfield House"; while the third approached more nearly the ultimate choice, "Mr. David Mag" being altered to "Mr. David Copperfield the Younger and his great-aunt Margaret," but still retaining "Mag's Diversions" as its leading line. In addition to these, no less than seven tentative titles were considered, in all of which the surname, Copperfield, prominently appeared; the following, however, eventually became the designation: "The Personal History, Adventures, Experience, and Observation of David Copperfield the Younger, of Blunderstone Rookery, which he never meant to be Published on any Account." The cognomen of the hero was arrived at by a process of evolution, thus—

Trotfield   Trotbury,   Copperboy,   Copperstone, Copperfield. In a similar way Dickens devised other names for his characters; Maidstone first stood as Harden, Murdle, Murden, and Littimer as Lorrimer; Mr. Dick originally appeared in the manuscript as Mr. Robert, while in the draft of the title we find the names of Wellbury, Flowerbury, Magbury, and Topflower, which were discarded. Dickens was much startled, and not displeased, when Forster pointed out to him something which had escaped his notice, viz., that David's initials, "D. C.," were the Novelist's own, reversed; he protested that such a coincidence was just in keeping with the fates and chances which were always befalling him. "Why else," he wished to know, "should I so obstinately have kept to that name when once it turned up?" Although the question of title was disposed of, the Novelist underwent some tribulation at the beginning of his task. That he lacked the necessary inspiration is evidenced by a letter addressed to Forster on April 19th, in which he remarked with a sense of distress: "My hand is out in the matter of 'Copperfield.' Today and yesterday I have done nothing, though I know what I want to do. I am lumbering on like a stage wagon . . . and the long Copperfieldian perspective looks snowy and thick, this fine morning." Once fairly launched, however, the tale proceeded rapidly and pleasantly, and more smoothly than any other of his books. On June 6th he said: "I feel, thank God, quite confident in the story. I have a move in it ready for this month; another for the next; and another for the next." On the 25th he wrote to Mark Lemon, advising him to "get a clean pocket handkerchief ready for the close of 'Copperfield' No. 3; 'Simple and quiet, but very natural and touching.—*Evening Bore*.'" The number in question contains the affecting account of the death and burial of David's mother.

At the period which witnessed the birth of David Copperfield, Charles Dickens had attained the very pinnacle of fame. His powerful and versatile pen, ever wielded in the cause of the helpless and oppressed, had gained for him a multitude of friends, among them being the most distinguished representatives of the learned professions. Prominent members of the aristocracy, too, deemed it a privilege to be invited to his table as the guests of the great writer, who, by the way, never disguised his radical tendencies, nor bent the knee to those who wore "purple and fine linen." In recounting the incidents appertaining to the year 1849—the "Copperfield" year—Forster alludes to certain dinners given by Dickens at Devonshire Terrace, and mentions that among those who assembled under the Novelist's roof on such occasions were Lord and Lady Lovelace, Milner Gibson, Mowbray Morris, Horace Twiss, Lady Molesworth, Charles Babbage, John Delane, Isambard Brunel, Thomas Longman, Lord Mulgrave, Lord Carlisle, the Tagarts, the Denmans, and the Pollocks, Tom Taylor, Charles Kemble, Monckton Milnes, Captain Marryat, Bulwer Lytton, Talfourd, &c. &c., with all of whom his intercourse was intimate and frequent. To this list must be added the equally honoured names of Thomas Carlyle and his wife, Thackeray, Samuel Rogers, Mrs. Gaskell, and Douglas Jerrold. At Devonshire Terrace there were also musical evenings and dances, and *apropos* of the latter Dickens confided in Forster the noteworthy incident of his youthful daughters, Mary and Kate, having taken much pains to teach him the polka that he might dance it

with them at their brother's birthday festivity, and that
the fear had fallen on him suddenly in the small hours
of the morning of the eventful day that he had
forgotten the step, whereupon he leaped out of bed
and, in the cold winter's night, practised it in the dark.
"Remember that for my biography!" was his strict
injunction to Forster, and it was remembered
accordingly.

Such sociable diversions formed agreeable interludes between severe and exacting spells of literary
work. "Copperfield" had now made its public appearance, the first of its twenty monthly numbers being
issued in May 1849. The writing of the story
progressed satisfactorily, and was continued during a
long summer holiday in the Isle of Wight, where, at
Bonchurch, he took "a most delightful and beautiful
house . . . cool, airy, private bathing, everything delicious. . . . *P.S.*—A waterfall on the grounds, which I
have arranged with a carpenter to convert into a
perpetual shower bath." Here, in this attractive retreat,
the months of July, August, and September were
passed, his labours relieved by occasional picnics and
other festivities, into which he entered with customary
zest. He made it a rule, however, to devote the earlier
portion of each day to writing—"the Inimitable [he
said] is invisible until two every day." I have not
worked quickly here yet," he added, "but I don't know
what I *may* do. Divers cogitations have occupied my
mind at intervals respecting the dim design." The "dim
design" has reference to a project of which an explanation will presently be tendered. Doubts as to the
state of his health now supervened, and it transpired
that the utter prostration and kindred symptoms which
induced so marked a change in his physical

condition were mainly, if not entirely, due to the ener-
vating climate of Bonchurch. "It's a mortal
mistake!—that's the plain fact," was his comment
upon this inconvenient position of affairs. "Of all the
places I have ever been in, I have never been in one
so difficult to exist in, pleasantly. Naples is hot and
dirty, New York feverish, Washington bilious, Genoa
exciting, Paris rainy—but Bonchurch, smashing. I am
quite convinced that I should die here in a year." His
wife and sister-in-law and the Leeches were similarly
indisposed, though not to the same extent, and the
Novelist determined to leave Bonchurch at the end of
September and "go down to some cold place."
Meanwhile, he completed the fifth number of
"Copperfield," after which, during the remainder of
the holiday, he and his party (by way of relaxation)
indulged in such amusements as "great games of
rounders every afternoon, with all Bonchurch looking
on." But a disagreeable interruption to these revels
took place in a grave accident to John Leech, who
was knocked over by an immense wave while bathing
in a rough sea, this resulting in congestion of the
brain and necessitating first the placing of "twenty of
his namesakes on his temples," and then, as the
illness developed, the continuous application of
ice to the head, with blood-letting from the arm.
The artist becoming seriously worse, Dickens
essayed the effect of mesmerism, and in the middle of
the night commenced the experiment, the invalid
being thus put to sleep for an hour and thirty-five
minutes. "I talked to the astounded little Mrs. Leech
across him, when he was asleep, as if he had been a
truss of hay. . . . What do you think," queried
Dickens, for a moment in a frivolous mood, "of my
setting up in the magnetic line with a large

brass plate?—'Terms, twenty-five guineas per nap.'"
The health of the patient improved, and by the end of
the month he had nearly recovered, when Dickens
decided to leave Bonchurch for Broadstairs—a change
by which his health benefited—and here he remained
until the completion of No. 7 of "Copperfield."

The "dim design," to which allusion has just
been made, had reference to an idea (long entertained)
of launching a cheap weekly journal, with original and
selected matter, and possibly some poetry. At
Broadstairs the notion began to assume a more
tangible form, and, after recounting to Forster a
number of subjects suitable for such a popular
periodical, he adds: "Now to bind all this together, and
to get a character established as it were which any of
the writers may maintain without difficulty, I want to
suppose a certain SHADOW, which may go into any
place by sunlight, moonlight, starlight, firelight,
candlelight, and he in all houses and all nooks and
corners, and be supposed to be cognisant of
everything, and go everywhere, without the least
difficulty . . . . ." Ultimately the scheme took a
different shape, that of a weekly miscellany of general
literature, comprising short stories by himself and
others, papers upon important social questions, and
articles upon subjects of general public interest. The
proposed publication had been so far determined upon
that at the close of the year a preliminary
announcement of the venture was made. The title
primarily suggested by him—*The Shadow*—did not
sufficiently "express the notion of its being a cheerful,
useful, and always welcome Shadow," so he thought
of *The Robin*, *Mankind*, and (strange to say) his
own name—"*Charles Dickens*—a weekly journal

designed for the instruction and entertainment of all classes of readers—'conducted by himself.'" Many other titles, more or less suitable, occurred to him; presently came *Household Words* ("a very pretty name," he thought), of which the final choice was made, supplemented by an apt quotation from Shakespeare's "Henry V," in the King's St. Crispin day's speech: "Familiar in their mouths as Household Words."[1]

While formulating this scheme and endeavouring to secure the services of promising young writers of both sexes for the forthcoming periodical, the Novelist made steady progress with "Copperfield," the monthly parts appearing with unfailing regularity. In November he witnessed the execution of the notorious Mrs. Manning at Horsemonger Lane gaol, with the intention of observing the crowd there assembled to witness the carrying out of the extreme penalty of the law, and he had excellent opportunities of so doing, while regarding the multitude of human beings at intervals throughout the previous night and continuously from daybreak until the dreadful spectacle was over. The whole scene, inexpressibly odious and ghastly in its details, impressed him so strongly by its absolute offensiveness that he was induced to offer, in a letter to *The Times*, his opinions respecting public executions and their demoralising effect upon the minds of callous observers. "I am solemnly convinced," he said, "that nothing that ingenuity could devise to be done in this city, in the same compass of time, could work such ruin as one public

---

[1] The quotation is inaccurate, the correct reading being: "Familiar in *his mouth* as household words." In the new series of *Household Words* (1902), under the editorship of Mr. Gordon Hall Caine, it is properly rendered.

execution, and I stand astounded and appalled by the wickedness it exhibits." This letter was followed, a few days later, by another on the same subject, in which the Novelist explained in greater detail his attitude in reference to the degrading character of public executions. He contended (first) that they chiefly attracted as spectators the lowest, the most depraved, the most abandoned of mankind, in whom they inspired no wholesome emotions whatever; and (second) that "the public infliction of a violent death is not a salutary spectacle for any class of people, but that it is in the nature of things that on the class by whom it is generally witnessed it should have a debasing and hardening influence." To obviate these palpable objections, it seemed to him necessary that the awful sentence of death should be carried out within prison walls, and he quoted Fielding in support of that view; although opposed on principle to capital punishment, he acknowledged the existence of public sentiment which regarded it as essential in extreme cases. It is, therefore, interesting to note that the very suggestions offered by the Novelist in his second communication to *The Times* have been adopted almost exactly as he prescribed, the extreme penalty being now enacted in as private a manner as possible—an improved condition of affairs with the initiation of which Dickens may justly be credited, for, as he informed M. de Cerjat a month later, his letters made "a great to-do, and led to a great agitation of the subject."

The first few weeks of the New Year, 1850, found him still at Devonshire Terrace, busy with "David Copperfield," his thoughts somewhat divided between the story and the periodical to be styled

*Household Words.* Among the authors whose services he at once sought to enlist for the "new cheap weekly journal of general literature" (as it was described in the press announcements) were Mrs. Gaskell, Mrs. William Howitt, and the Rev. James White. He intended to print no names of contributors, either in his own case or any other, and would give established writers the power of reclaiming their papers after a certain time. An outline of the scheme presented to Mrs. Howitt on February 23rd, contained an intimation that the kind of papers of which he stood most in need were short stories, while all social evils, and all home affections and associations, he expressed himself as being particularly anxious to deal with. In the early spring he went to Brighton for a short time, probably in order that he might, without interruption, frame his plans regarding the projected journal, to the immediate production of which he had now become pledged. Dickens himself assumed the responsibilities of editor-in-chief, and he appointed W. H. Wills as subeditor and manager. No. 16, Wellington Street, Strand, was rented as the office of the paper, the building with a large bow window facing the portico of the Lyceum Theatre,—still standing, but soon to be demolished, to make way for the new Holborn-Strand thoroughfare.[1] The first number of *Household Words* made its appearance, according to promise, on

[1] The building acquired as the office of *Household Words* stood on the site of a very old tenement, with which (according to W. H. Wills) there was bound up a very weird London legend, setting forth how the room on the first floor front was the identical apartment which had served Hogarth as the locality of the final tableau in "The Harlot's Progress." Dickens used to tell his contributors that he had often sat in that first floor front conjuring up mind pictures of Kate Hackabout lying dead in her coffin, and wept over by drunken beldames.

Charles Dickens

*From the painting by S. Drummond, A. R. A., circa 1850. Through the courtesy of the Baroness Burdett-Coutts, the owner of the picture, this portrait of the Novelist is now engraved for the first time*

Charles Dickens

*From a daguerreotype by Henri Claudet, 1852*

Saturday March 30, 1850, price two-pence, with an introduction, or "preliminary word," by the Editor. Besides Dickens and Wills, the only regular staff-contributor of original articles, at the period of its inauguration, was R. H. Horne, author of "Orion" (known as "the farthing epic"), but the energetic "Chief" (as his contributors affectionately termed him) soon secured many of the best writers of the day, the younger scribes imitating, more or less, his literary style, thus imparting to their articles and stories (unconsciously perhaps) a Dickensian feeling which was apt to mislead the uninitiated. That the authorship of particular papers has been wrongly attributed to Dickens, even by bibliographers, may be explained by the fact that he exercised the editorial prerogative in an exceptionally liberal manner, for he not only freely touched up the proofs, but frequently interpolated entire paragraphs, thereby improving very considerably the author's treatment of his subject. Sala has pointed out that the strict preservation of the anonymity in *Household Words* (coupled, of course, with the effect of the Editor's manipulation of proofs) had certain evil consequences to the young writers, not the least of which was that many of the contributions were not only ascribed to Dickens, but were sometimes actually reprinted with his name. At the outset, the printing firm of Bradbury and Evans (according to the Agreement of 1844) had an ownership in *Household Words*, jointly with Wills, Forster, and Dickens himself, and it was stipulated that the Novelist (who held the largest share of this property) should receive £500 per annum as editor, with additional payments for any literary articles he might contribute, as well as participating in any profits that might accrue to him as part proprietor.[1]

[1] Edmund Yates, in *Town Talk*, April 9, 1859.

It speedily became apparent that in *Household Words* Dickens had struck the right vein, and in the course of a few months its reputation was made, the Editor thus achieving a success which may be considered as unique in the history of journalism. A paper in the second number, entitled "A Child's Dream of a Star," written by Dickens himself, was based upon a reminiscence of his boyhood, when he and his sister Fanny used to wander at night about a churchyard near their house at Chatham, looking at the stars, and making friends of one particular star; when travelling to Brighton, thinking of his second number and revolving in his mind a little idea about the stars, at which he gazed from the carriage window, the sad loss he had then recently sustained in the death of that sister (Mrs. Burnett) revived the early associations which made her memory dear to him.

Returning to Devonshire Terrace from Brighton refreshed by his seaside residence, Dickens wrote to Macready on June 11th, "Between 'Copperfield' and *Household Words*, I am as busy as a bee. May the former be as good a book as I hope it will be for your children's children to read." Towards the end of June the Novelist made a trip to Paris with Maclise, then to Rouen and other towns, afterwards settling down at Devonshire Terrace for a while; when abroad, his thoughts continued to revert to *Household Words*, and writing to Wills, he said: "I hope we are doing pretty well in Wellington Street. My anxiety makes me feel as if I had been away a year." About a month later he informed the Rev. James White that he had taken a house at Broadstairs, from early in August until the end of October, "as I don't want to come back to London until I shall have finished 'Copperfield.'. . .

I am glad to say," he added, "as I know you will be glad to hear, that there seems a bright unanimity about 'Copperfield.' I am very much interested in it and pleased with it myself. I have carefully planned out the story, for some time past, to the end, and am making out my purposes with great care. . . . *Household Words* goes on *thoroughly well.* It is expensive, of course, and demands a large circulation; but it is taking a great and steady stand, and I have no doubt already yields a good round profit." The Novelist succeeded, for the first time, in obtaining possession of Fort House, Broadstairs, on which he had always set his affections; it is known locally as "Bleak House," and erroneously believed by some persons to be the original of Mr. Jarndyce's residence, in the story of that name.[1] Dickens's old friend Edmund Yates thus described Fort House as it appeared in his day: "It stands at the eastern extremity of the little town, perched on the edge of a small cliff immediately overlooking the harbour. . . . It is a small house without any large rooms, but such a place as a man of moderate means, with an immoderate family of small children, might choose for a summer retreat. The sands immediately below afford a splendid playground; there is abundant supply of never failing ozone; there is a good lawn, surrounded by borders well stocked with delicious smelling common English flowers; and there is, or was in those days, I imagine, ample opportunity for necessary seclusion. The room in which Dickens worked is on the first floor—a small three-cornered slip, 'about the size of a warm bath' as he would have said, but with a large expansive

---

[1] An article by Dickens, entitled "Our Watering-Place," descriptive of Broadstairs at that period, appeared in *Household Words* on August 2, 1851.

window commanding a magnificent sea view. His love for the place, and his gratitude for the good it always did him, are recorded in a hundred letters. 'For the last two or three days I have been rather slack in point of work, not being in the vein. Today I had not written twenty lines before I rushed out (the weather being gorgeous) to bathe. And when I have done that, it is all up with me in the way of authorship until tomorrow.' Again: 'It is more delightful here than I can express. Corn growing, larks singing, garden full of flowers, fresh air on the sea—Oh, it is wonderful!'"

This was penned on the first day of June, and in the following week there was a banquet at the "Star and Garter," Richmond, in honour of "Copperfield," with Thackeray and Alfred Tennyson among the guests; Forster tells us that he had rarely seen Dickens happier than he was "amid the sunshine of that day," the generous giver of the feast being in his best vein. In July, the Novelist and his family journeyed to Broadstairs; Mrs. Dickens, however, remained for a time in London, for the birth of a third daughter was imminent, this domestic event taking place on the 16th of August, shortly after the fate of David Copperfield's child-wife, Dora, had been decided (but before she breathed her last), and upon the newly-born daughter he bestowed the heroine's name, with the addition of Annie. On the 20th of August he told Forster that he had been very hard at work for three days, and had still Dora (David's Dora) to "kill"—"but with good luck, I may do it tomorrow." We are assured that, once fairly in it, the story bore him irresistibly along, and that he was probably never less harassed by interruptions or

breaks in his invention. On October 21st he announced
that the close was at hand—"I am within three pages
of the shore, and am strangely divided, as usual in such
cases, between sorrow and joy. Oh, my dear Forster, if
I were to say half what 'Copperfield' makes me feel
tonight, how strangely, even to you, I should be turned
inside out! I seem to be sending some part of myself
into the Shadowy World." In a week or so, he wrote (in
his "airy nest" at Broadstairs) the concluding lines of
what he himself considered the best of all his books,
for the reason that (he supposed) so many of the
experiences related in it were based upon actualities in
his own life. The fact that "David Copperfield" (like
Thackeray's "Pendennis" and Daudet's "Le Petit
Chose") is largely autobiographical, was never fully
realised by his innumerable readers until the Author
had passed away. To particularly intimate friends he
had confided the interesting intelligence, as, for
example, in a letter addressed to Mrs. Howitt in 1859,
where he says that he had worked "many childish
experiences and many young struggles" into the story.
Reading between the lines, we are enabled to picture
to ourselves the uncongenial environment and the
mental distress of his boyhood's days, and, later, the
difficulties he encountered when mastering the
mystery of shorthand, coupled with his first attempts
at authorship. Forster considered it necessary,
however, to warn us against assuming too much with
respect to the identity of David Copperfield with his
creator, assuring us that "the language of fiction
reflects only faintly the narrative of the actual fact."
The fragment of autobiography which he prints in the
"Life" had been written before "Copperfield" was
contemplated, and not until several months later,

when the idea of that story was entertained, did the Novelist abandon his first intention of writing his own life, deciding, in its stead, to incorporate with the story a description of his juvenile troubles. When Forster's biography appeared, containing these personal reminiscences, Mrs. Charles Dickens desired her eldest son to make the fact public if, after her death, an opportunity should arise, that "David Copperfield" was read to her in strict confidence by her husband, who notified his inclination to print it by-and-by as a portion of his autobiography. "From this purpose," writes Charles Dickens the younger, "she endeavoured to dissuade him: on the ground that he had spoken with undue harshness of his father, and, especially, of his mother: and with so much success that he eventually decided he would be satisfied with working it into 'David Copperfield,' and would give up the idea of publishing it as it stood." This being the case, the younger Dickens failed to understand how it happened that Forster committed what he regarded as an indiscretion in printing those autobiographical details, but supposed that the biographer was ignorant of what had passed between the Novelist and his wife on the subject.

As Charles Dickens's mother unconsciously posed for Mrs. Nickleby, so did his father inspire the presentment of Mr. Micawber, whom he resembled physically, and in whom are shadowed forth certain peculiarities of action and speech that appertained to John Dickens. This is current belief, and so much is asserted by Forster; but the Novelist's eldest son (whom we must surely accept as an authority) has declared it to be absolutely without foundation, "except within the limits of the description given in the autobiographical sketch, and except as to certain odd phrases and turns of expression in speech and letter writing."[1] The Novelist (he reminds us) acknowledged his father to be "as kind-hearted and generous a man as ever lived in the world," while his conduct "to wife, or children, or friends, in sickness or affliction, is beyond all praise. . . . He never undertook any business, charge, or trust, that he did not zealously, conscientiously, punctually, honourably discharge. The longer I live, the better man I think him." Within certain limits, doubtless, Charles Dickens portrayed Micawber from his father; but it is said that he also availed himself of the idiosyncrasies

---

[1] The following characteristic letter by John Dickens to his son's publishers was printed in the *Illustrated London News*, April 1, 1893. As Mr. Percy Fitzgerald observes, "it has the true Micawberian flavour":—

"34 Edwards Street, Portman Square,
14th February 1837.

"Gentlemen,—It has occurred to me that *at a moment of some difficulty* you may be willing to extend to me your *obliging assistance.* If not inconvenient, or inconsistent with your arrangements, will you *do me the favour to deduct the Four Pounds I owe you from the enclosed bill for* £20 due 7th April, with four shillings, the amount of the interest, and let me have the balance, £15, 15s.? Do not suppose I ask this on any other footing than that of *an act of obligation conferred on me,* and I assure you, though small in amount, *its effects* to me are *matters of grave consideration,* because anything that should occasion my absence from my duties in the Gallery *would be productive of fatal effects.*

"You may consider it an intrusion that I should apply to you *in a moment of difficulty:* and I feel it to be so; but, recollecting how your interests are bound up with those of my son, I flatter myself if you can confer a favour upon the father without transgressing any rule that you have laid down, and without inconvenience, you may feel disposed to do so.

"I do not enhance it when I say that the favour, though small in amount, yet under the circumstances *would be signal obligation conferred on,*

"Gentlemen, your obliged and obedient servant,

"JOHN DICKENS.

"MESSRS. CHAPMAN & HALL."

of Thomas Powell, "a so-called 'literary man,'" of America, many of whose personal traits were set forth, years ago, in a story published in the *Boston Index*. Like Micawber, Powell had a trick of becoming very confidential on small or no provocation, and possessed a perfect mania for writing letters, even to persons in the same room.[1] It is not, perhaps, generally known that another alleged prototype of Micawber actually lived in York about the time the story was written, concerning whom the following particulars were recorded in the Leeds Mercury, January 21, 1899. The individual in question rejoiced in the name of Richard Chicken—an eccentric person, described in 1843 as a teacher of elocution—who resembled Micawber in many points, notably in regard to pecuniary difficulties, gloomy forebodings, sanguine anticipations of something "turning up," flourishes of speech, epistolary effusions, &c. He held a subordinate position in the office of an engineer (J. C. Birkinshaw), where, curiously enough, Alfred Dickens (a brother of the Novelist) was employed for several years. Chicken had a shabby genteel appearance, was always attired in an old swallow-tailed coat, and his appeals to the clerks for pecuniary assistance were frequent. It is of course possible that Dickens's attention may have been called by his brother to his strange colleague during one of his visits to York, and thus found further material for his portrait.[2]

[1] Powell was the author of "Pictures of the Living Authors of Britain" (1851), which included a biographical sketch of Dickens.

[2] Another coincidence is the fact that the name Wilkins, during the early part of the last century, was a slang name, common in York, applied to impecunious or shabby persons; it seems that in the eighteenth century a Major Wilkins suffered imprisonment in York Castle for a period of fifty years, his name becoming a byword in the city for persons in similar

*Apropos* of other characters in "Copperfield," we are assured by Forster that the prototype of the good-natured but eccentric Miss Mowcher was a neighbour of Dickens, who followed the same occupation as the "volatile" lady. Detecting the portraiture, she seriously remonstrated with the Author, who, while regarding the protest as "serio-comic," admitted that it was wrong to use such a power as he was enabled to exercise at the expense of living personages; he undoubtedly erred in portraying too exactly (as in the case of Squeers) the physical peculiarities of the original. He experienced much distress on learning that he had unwittingly caused pain to a really worthy person, and the result of the protest was that he altered altogether his intentions as to Miss Mowcher's connection with the plot, and to her advantage. A letter from Dickens to his biographer proves that David's child-wife was founded on an actual Dora whom the Novelist knew very early in his career,[1] and we are also told that the description of Flora Finching in "Little Dorrit" was derived from the same source. The Author's favourite people in the story were the Peggotty group, and it is not in the least improbable that certain characteristics appertaining to Clara Peggotty were suggested by the personal attributes of the amiable woman, Mary Weller, who nursed Charles Dickens when a child. Forster is responsible for the assertion that

straits. For these notes I am indebted to Mr. Thomas P. Cooper, of York, who contributed them to the Leeds newspaper.

[1] The identity of the living prototype of Dora has never been divulged. It is, however, fair to surmise that she was one of two sisters, named Beadnell, whom Dickens met at the house of a mutual friend, a Mr. W. H. Kolle, then engaged in a banking house in the City of London. The period referred to is 1830, before the first of the "Sketches by Boz" appeared.

the portrait of Rosa Dartle was partly drawn from one of the Novelist's familiar acquaintances, whose identity, however, has not been disclosed; while Thomas Traddles, referred to in one of the concluding chapters as the next Judge, is said to have been intended (in a restricted sense) for Serjeant Talfourd, who was promoted to the Bench in 1849, shortly after the publication of the first number of "Copperfield." It will be remembered that David Copperfield, during his bachelor days, occupied apartments at Mrs. Crupp's, in Buckingham Street, Adelphi; we learn, on the authority of Charles Dickens the younger, that the Author actually rented rooms here before he lived in Furnival's Inn (a fact not alluded to by Forster), and that these rooms were (as described in the story) at the top of one of the end houses, overlooking the Thames. "Charles Dickens," writes the Novelist's son, "if he lived in David Copperfield's rooms—as I have no doubt he did—must have kept house on the top floor of No. 15 on the east side, the house which displays a tablet commemorating its onetime tenancy by Peter the Great, Czar of all the Russias."[1] William Black, the novelist, and that devoted Dickensian, William Burges, A.R.A., also resided in this house (known as York House); it is worth mentioning, too, that in 1684 Samuel Pepys lived opposite, and Henry Fielding took up his abode here in 1735.

The final instalment of "David Copperfield" was launched in November 1850. Strange to relate, the circulation of this typical English novel did not nearly attain to that of previous works, although the book subsequently became the most popular of all his writings with the single exception of "Pickwick."

[1] *Pall Mall Magazine*, July 1896.

Wilkie Collins attributed this decline in the sale to the disappointment created in the public mind by "Dombey and Son," which apparently did not realise the high expectations formed of it. Dickens, in his preface to the later editions, candidly confessed that of all his books he liked it the best: "It will be easily believed," he says, "that I am a fond parent of every child of my fancy, and that no one can ever love that family as dearly as I love them. But, like many fond parents, I have in my heart of hearts a favourite child, and his name is 'David Copperfield.'" To Miss Mary Boyle he wrote: "I am not quite sure that I ever did like, or ever shall like, anything quite so well as 'Copperfield.'" Among those of his contemporaries who praised without stint the story which the present Vice Chancellor of Cambridge University (Dr. A. W. Ward) describes as "a pearl without a peer among the later fictions of our English school," was William Makepeace Thackeray. The night after the Oxford election (1857), in which the author of "Vanity Fair" suffered defeat, he gave some readings on behalf of a fund then being raised to the memory of Douglas Jerrold, in the course of which he thus alluded to the novels of Dickens: "I think of these past writers [Sterne and his "school"], and of one who lives amongst us now, and am grateful for the innocent laughter, and the sweet and unsullied pages, which the author of 'David Copperfield' gives to my children." Again, in "Sketches and Travels in London," 1856, he places this fine eulogium of the story in the mouth of one of his characters: "How beautiful it is—how charmingly fresh and simple! In those admirable touches of tender humour, a mixture of love and wit— who can equal this great genius?"

CHAPTER 9

## "BLEAK HOUSE"

No sooner had Dickens completed the concluding chapters of "David Copperfield," coming out of the story "into a condition of temporary and partial consciousness," than he plunged into histrionic duties in the shape of certain private theatricals at Knebworth. This "great dramatic festival," as the Novelist termed it, took place during the month of November 1850, at the Hertfordshire mansion of Sir Edward Bulwer Lytton (afterwards Lord Lytton), who received as guests the members of the distinguished amateur company of which Dickens was commander-in-chief. The play was "Every Man in his Humour," with farces, varied each night, and Sir Edward invited all his county neighbours to witness the entertainment. Referring to the incident, Forster says: "All the circumstances and surroundings were very brilliant; some of the gentlemen of the county played both in the comedy and farces; our generous host was profuse of all noble encouragement." Mrs. Dickens, with other ladies, had arranged to take a part in these, but was unfortunately prevented by an accident; while rehearsing at a theatre she fell through a trapdoor, spraining her ankle so badly as to become temporarily incapacitated. The performances went off (as Dickens expressed it) "in a whirl of triumph, and fired

the whole length and breadth of the county of
Hertfordshire."[1] Before the close of the year he made
preparations for a private play at Rockingham Castle
(the seat of the Watsons), and his published correspondence at this time indicates the zest with which he
threw himself into the hundred-and-one details
involved. With the help of the country carpenter he
constructed at the Castle a "very elegant; little
theatre," of which he constituted himself manager. The
first representation took place on the 15th of January
1851, and after the performance there was a country-
dance which lasted until far into the morning. On the
next evening the Novelist travelled by rail to London
(a distance of more than a hundred and twenty miles)
to dine with the Prime Minister, Lord John Russell—
so it is not surprising that Forster should characterise
such continued exertion as an attempt on the part of
Dickens to do too much.

The year 1851 began with domestic anxieties,
for both Mrs. Dickens and the youngest daughter were
attacked by severe illness. "Little Dora is getting on
bravely, thank God!" was his bulletin to Forster when
the child rallied early in February, and presently it was
decided to make trial of Great Malvern for the mother,
Dickens dividing his time between that well known
health resort and Devonshire Terrace. In February he
made a short bachelor excursion to Paris with John
Leech and the Hon. Spencer Lyttleton, lodging at the
Hotel Wagram, whence he wrote to his wife: "We had
D'Orsay to dinner yesterday, and I am hurried to dress
now in order to pay a promised visit to his *atelier*. . . .

---

[1] "The Letters of Charles Dickens." He should have written "the
county of Hertford."

Tomorrow at noon we leave Paris for Calais. . . . Leech and I had a charming country walk before breakfast this morning at Poissy, and enjoyed it very much. The rime was on the grass and trees, and the country most delicious. . . ."[1] On his return to London he was busily occupied in superintending the arrangements for Macready's last appearance on the stage at Drury Lane, and for a public dinner in honour of the famous actor-manager, at which presided Sir Edward Bulwer Lytton, whose health was proposed in a striking speech by the Novelist. The dinner was given on the 1st of March, and later in the month he took an active part in the business connected with a home of refuge for women, established by Miss (afterwards the Baroness) Burdett-Coutts.

At this time another very important scheme monopolised much of his attention, namely, the Guild of Literature and Art, the object of which was to create a provident fund whereby impecunious authors and artists might spend the closing days of an honourable and industrious career in comfort and repose. This admirable idea originated during the theatrical performances at Knebworth, and Bulwer Lytton eagerly associated himself with Dickens in the inauguration and realisation of the excellently devised Guild. The Novelist secured the goodwill and approbation of the Duke of Devonshire[2] towards the new endowment, his Grace not only subscribing to the fund but offering his services and the use of his fine mansion in Piccadilly for theatrical representations in aid of the design, for it was proposed to raise money by such means. The performance at Devonshire House

[1] "The Letters of Charles Dickens."
[2] William George Spencer, the sixth Duke,—a sincere friend of Art and Letters.

of "Not so Bad as we Seem"[1] took place on May 16th, in the presence of Queen Victoria, the Prince Consort, and a large audience. Probably there is no event more notable in the annals of the Stage (certainly not as regards amateur theatricals) than the splendid achievement of the little band of actors and actresses who laboured so indefatigably and disinterestedly on behalf of the admirable cause which Dickens and Bulwer Lytton had so much at heart. Those eminent Royal Academicians, Clarkson Stanfield, Sir Edwin Landseer, and David Roberts were enrolled as scene painters, together with Louis Haghe, and with such a galaxy of talent, dramatic and artistic, supreme success might be reasonably anticipated. In spite of all this excitement, the conduct of *Household Words* obtained a share of attention at the hands of the Editor, who never failed in his official duties, such as suggesting subjects for articles and revising the manuscripts and proofs of contributors, much of the actual drudgery naturally falling to his able coadjutor, W. H. Wills.

The illness of his father, John Dickens, now occasioned him much distress; grave symptoms supervened, and at Malvern the end came suddenly and unexpectedly. "My poor father died this morning," he wrote to Forster on the last day of March 1851. "He did not know me, nor anyone. He began to sink at about noon yesterday, and never rallied afterwards. I remained there until he died—Oh so quietly." He breathed his last at the age of sixty-six, and his remains were interred at Highgate Cemetery. The Novelist had pledged himself to take

---

[1] Sir Edward Bulwer Lytton wrote the comedy, for that special purpose, to be played in London and the provinces.

the chair at the annual dinner to he held at the London Tavern a few days later, in aid of the General Theatrical Fund, which so sorely needed help and relied upon his presence and stimulating speech to give it a fillip. The promise was duly fulfilled, family affliction notwithstanding, and his oration proved worthy of the occasion. Half-an-hour before he rose to speak a servant arrived from Devonshire Terrace, with the intelligence, imparted quietly to Forster, that Dickens's little daughter, Dora, with whom the father had been playing before he went to the dinner, had just passed away; but the sad truth was not disclosed to him until his part of the proceedings had concluded. The child also lies in a grave at Highgate, near that of Mr. and Mrs. John Dickens. At the death of her little girl, the mother returned to London from Malvern, but as she had not yet recovered from her malady, and London being extremely full of visitors for the Great Exhibition in Hyde Park, the Novelist decided to let Devonshire Terrace again for a few months, and rent Fort House (now called "Bleak House"), Broadstairs, where they stayed from the beginning of May until November. This, by the way, was Charles Dickens's last sojourn at Broadstairs; owing to the fact that it had become too noisy for him, he never resided again in that hitherto favourite watering place, although always retaining an affectionate interest in it. Writing to Lord Carlisle in July, he said: "The general character of Broadstairs as to size and accommodation was happily expressed by Miss Eden, when she wrote to the Duke of Devonshire (as he told me), saying how grateful she felt to a certain sailor, who asked leave to see her garden, for not plucking it bodily up, and sticking it in his buttonhole. . . . It is a very rough little place, but a very pleasant one."[1]

It will be remembered that, in a letter to Douglas Jerrold (1843), Dickens stated that he was writing a little history of England for his boy. This was never finished, but during the early part of 1851 he revived the notion by printing, as a serial in *Household Words*, "A Child's History of England," which was published in the pages of that journal during this and two following years, and eventually appeared in book form, three volumes (dated respectively 1852, 1853, and 1854), with frontispieces by F. W. Topham. With the exception of two chapters (the second and the sixth) the Novelist dictated the whole of this work to Miss Hogarth, it being probably the only instance of the employment by him of an amanuensis; he was excessively busy at the time with "Bleak House," and it proved a great relief to him, after sitting for hours at his desk, to dictate this "History" while walking about the room. The Author availed himself of Keightley's "History of England" as the groundwork of his own book, which he dedicated "To my own dear children, whom I hope it will help, by-and-by, to read with interest larger and better books upon the same subject." Regarding this production—a theme altogether outside his usual range of authorship—it may be remarked that he compiled it obviously with the view of bringing such matters within the comprehension of youth, as the dedication proves; but Forster says that he "cannot be said to have quite hit the mark with it."

There is no doubt that, by reason of his little Christmas Books, Dickens had distinctly identified himself with the festive season, to which he thus

[1] "The Letters of Charles Dickens."

imparted a touch of joviality and good feeling of the
old fashioned English kind, so much so that the
omission of a Yuletide story, around which his magic
pen could weave such delightful fancies, was regarded
as a real public loss. Nearly two years had now elapsed
since the publication of "The Haunted Man," and it
happily occurred to him that an Extra Christmas
Number might be made an annually recurring feature
of *Household Words*. This Christmas Number,
however, was not to be written entirely by himself; he
sought assistance in collaboration, but at the same time
had in view the desirability that his own contributions
should express and explain themselves when
republished apart from their environment. Mr. Percy
Fitzgerald records that "the time when 'the Christmas
Number' had to be got ready was always one of
pleasant expectancy and alacrity. It was an object for
all to have a seat in a 'vehicle' which travelled every
road, and reached the houses of a quarter of a million
persons. With his usual conscientious feeling of duty
to the public, Dickens laboured hard, first, to secure a
good and telling idea; and second, to work it out on the
small but effective scale with which he had latterly
grown unfamiliar, owing to his habit of dealing with
large canvases." The first Christmas Number of
*Household Words* (1850), which had no distinctive
title, consisted of a series of nine separate stories, for
he had not yet devised the excellent plan
(subsequently adopted) of making each story more or
less dependent upon, and to hold some relationship
with, the rest of the number, thus cementing together
the various contributions under one general
designation. His own share of this issue of the
periodical is called "A Christmas Tree"—the opening
story—which, needless to add, has the true flavour, the

imaginations as well as kindly thoughts that rightly belong to the ever popular festival.

The year 1851 marks an important residential change. It was the year in which he relinquished the tenancy of No. 1 Devonshire Terrace, because the house did not afford sufficient accommodation for his growing family. This had been his home since 1839, the Novelist's occupation of it being for a longer period than that of any other of his London residences. He, therefore, was very partial to Devonshire Terrace, and confessed to a considerable reluctance in quitting it. To Forster he said, after the change had been effected: "I seem as if I had plucked myself out of my proper soil when I left Devonshire Terrace, and could take root no more until I return to it."[1] He elected to purchase Tavistock House, Tavistock Square, then (and for many years previously) the residence of his friend Frank Stone, A.R.A., and quite recently demolished.[2] In the autumn an exchange of houses was made, Mr. Stone taking possession of Devonshire Terrace "as a temporary encampment," while getting his new domicile into order, thus allowing the Novelist an opportunity of carrying out necessary repairs at

[1] It is interesting, by the way, to note that No. 1 Devonshire Terrace was the first English home of the late George Du Maurier, the well-known *Punch* artist. About four years ago the house underwent considerable structural alterations, the owner having raised the roof and inserted another storey. Miss Dickens recalled her father's study as "a pretty room, with steps leading directly into the garden from it, and with one extra baize door to keep out all sounds and noise."

[2] Tavistock House was for many years in the occupation of James Perry, editor of the *Morning Chronicle* in its best days. Eliza Cook, the well-known poetess, also lived here, and in more recent times it was the home of Mrs. Georgina Weldon and her husband, with whom Gounod resided for some time, holding singing classes in the drawing room. Eventually the building was converted into a Jewish College.

Tavistock House before his return to town. This reparation was superintended by his brother-in-law, Henry Austin, an architect, to whom Dickens (harassed by the delay in the work) wrote the following characteristic letter:

"Broadstairs,
Sunday, *Seventh September*, 1851.

"My Dear Henry,—I am in that state of mind which you may (once) have seen described in the newspapers as 'bordering on distraction'; the house given up to me, the fine weather going on (soon to break, I daresay), the painting season oozing away, my new book waiting to be born, and

"NO WORKMEN ON THE PREMISES,

along of my not hearing from you!! I have torn all my hair off, and constantly beat my unoffending family. Wild notions have occurred to me of sending in my own plumber to do the drains. Then I remember that you have probably written to propose *your* man, and restrain my audacious hand. Then Stone presents himself, with a most exasperatingly mysterious visage, and says that a rat has appeared in the kitchen, and it's his opinion (Stone's, not the rat's) that the drains want 'compo-ing'; for the use of which explicit language I could fell him without remorse. In my horrible desire to 'compo' everything, the very postman becomes my enemy because he brings no letter from you; and, in short, I don't see what's to become of me unless I hear from you tomorrow, which I have not the least expectation of doing.

"Going over the house again, I have materially altered the plans—abandoned conservatory and front balcony—decided to make Stone's painting-room the drawing room (it is nearly six inches higher than the room below), to carry the entrance passage right through the house to a back door leading to the garden, and to reduce the once intended drawing room—now schoolroom—to a manageable size, making a door of communication between the new drawing room and the study. Curtains and carpets, on a scale of awful splendour and magnitude, are already in preparation, and still—still—

"NO WORKMEN ON THE PREMISES.

"To pursue this theme is madness. Where are you? When are you coming home? Where is THE man who is to do the work? Does he know that an army of artificers must be turned in at once, and the whole thing finished out of hand? Oh rescue me from my present condition. Come up to the scratch, I entreat and implore you!

I send this to Laetitia to forward,

> "Being, a you well know why,
> Completely floored by N. W., [1] I
> *Sleep.*

"I hope you may be able to read this. My state of mind does not admit of coherence.—Ever affectionately          CHARLES DICKENS

"*P.S.*—NO WORKMEN ON THE PREMISES!
"Ha! Ha! Ha! (I am laughing demoniacally.)"[2]

Other letters followed, all testifying to the

---

[1] *I.e.* No Workmen.

[2] "The Letters of Charles Dickens." This illustrates the manner in which Dickens mastered all details of the proposed alterations. Similar instances are given in W. R. Hughes's "A Week's Tramp in Dickens-Land," 1891.

apparently agitated condition of the writer relative to the alterations. In one of them he said: "I am perpetually wandering (in fancy) up and down the house [Tavistock House] and tumbling over the workmen; when I feel that they are gone to dinner I become low, when I look forward to their total abstinence on Sundays, I am wretched. The gravy at dinner has a taste of glue in it. I smell paint in the sea. Phantom lime attends me all the day long. I dream that I am a carpenter and can't partition off the hall. I frequently dance (with a distinguished company) in the drawing room, and fall in the kitchen for want of a pillar. . . . I dream, also, of the workmen every night. They make faces at me, and won't do anything . . . "Oh! If this were to last long; the distraction of the new book, the whirling of the story through one's mind, escorted by workmen, the imbecility, the wild necessity of beginning to write, the not being able to do so, the, Oh! I should go——Oh!"[1]

The "new book" was his next long story, "Bleak House," of which a beginning was made as soon as he and his family were established in their new abode. The theatrical performances in aid of the Guild were already in full swing, and he was enabled to announce to Macready that they were "getting in a good heap of money" for the cause. A provincial tour of the Company was arranged during the autumn of this year, and, writing from Clifton to his wife concerning the performance there, the Novelist said: "We had a noble night last night. The room (which is the largest but one in England) was crammed in every part. The effect of from thirteen to fourteen hundred people, all well

---

[1] "The Letters of Charles Dickens."

dressed, and all seated in one unbroken chamber, except that the floor rose high towards the end of the hall, was most splendid, and we never played to a better audience. The enthusiasm was prodigious. . . . We were all thoroughly pleased, I think, with the whole thing, and it was a very great and striking success. . . . I am tired enough, and shall be glad when tomorrow night is over."[1]

During the excitement attendant on the Guild performances the earlier chapters of "Bleak House" were planned in the Author's mind. The actual writing of this romance was begun at the end of November 1851, but the first number did not appear until the following March, the date of publication thus synchronising with the birth of the Novelist's youngest child, named after Sir Edward Bulwer Lytton, his godfather, whom Dickens ever regarded with sincere affection and respect. The Author originally intended to open the book in that pretty bit of English landscape, Strood Valley, between Gad's Hill and Rochester, which always reminded him of a Swiss scene; but he altered his plans, the initial chapter describing a very different locality—namely, the neighbourhood of Chancery Lane on a foggy day in November. As was not unusual with him when commencing a novel, he experienced an intolerable restlessness. "I sit down between whiles," he wrote from Broadstairs when turning the subject over in his mind, "to think of a new story, and, as it begins to grow, such a torment of a desire to be anywhere but where I am, and to be going I don't know where, I don't know why, takes hold of me, that it is like being *driven away*." This disquietude was occasioned to a great extent (as we have seen) by

---

[1] "The Letters of Charles Dickens."

the troubles and delays in regard to his new residence, Tavistock House; directly he had settled down there he was enabled to direct his thoughts upon the tale; and as generally happened, accidentally, with the more important incidents of his life, it was on a Friday (usually believed by the superstitious to be an unlucky day) when the first words were penned. A dozen tentative titles were proposed before he adopted that of "Bleak House," eight of which indicated that the Author intended to make a very prominent feature of a certain low neighbourhood, which, however, afterwards took a subservient place. The trial titles were: 1. "Tom-all-Alone's. The Ruined House." 2. "Tom-all-Alone's. The Solitary House that was always shut up." 3. "Bleak House Academy." 4. "The East Wind." 5. "Tom-all-Alone's. The Ruined [House, Building, Factory, Mill] that got into Chancery and never got out." 6. "Tom-all-Alone's. The Solitary House where the Grass grew." 7. "Tom-all-Alone's. The Solitary House that was always shut up and never Lighted." 8. "Tom-all-Alone's. The Ruined Mill that got into Chancery and never got out." 9. "Tom-all-Alone's. The Solitary House where the Wind howled." 10. "Tom-all-Alone's. The Ruined House that got into Chancery and never got out." 11. "Bleak House and the East Wind. How they both got into Chancery and never got out." 12. "Bleak House."

In this work Dickens determined to assail the Court of Chancery by drawing public attention to the enormous waste of time and money which usually characterises its proceedings. He was encouraged in this design by receiving (after two numbers had been written and the first one published) a pamphlet dealing with this very subject,[1] and the instances of Chancery abuses quoted by the author were so apposite that the Novelist borrowed from them (without change in any material point) the remarkable case of Gridley, as related in the fifteenth chapter of the story. This was a suit affecting a single farm valued at not more than £1200—all that the owner possessed in the world—against which a bill had been filed for a £300 legacy left in the will bequeathing the farm. In reality there was only one defendant, but in the bill, by the rule of the Court, there were seventeen; and, after two years had been occupied over the seventeen answers, everything had to begin over again because an eighteenth had been accidentally omitted, the costs thus incurred amounting to three times the amount of the legacy. As the writer observed: "What a mockery of justice this is!" In "Bleak House," Dickens found an opportunity of thoroughly exposing what he rightly regarded as a serious public grievance, illustrating it by the supposititious case of Jarndyce *v.* Jarndyce, based upon the notorious Jennens suit, which has been before the Court so many times during the last century. In the notorious Jennens action the vast estates of Earl Howe are still involved; the property in litigation (comprising, it is believed, about one-half of the ground on which Birmingham is built) belonged to William Jennens (or Jennings, as the name is sometimes spelt), who died in 1798, at the age of ninety-seven, and respecting which the decisions of the Court have been invariably in favour of the Curzon family, the defendants, who took the earldom in

[1] "The Court of Chancery: its Inherent Defects," &c., by W. Challinor, A.B., London: Stevens & Norton, 1849. 2nd ed.

1821. It seems that William Jennens, an old miser who lived at Acton in Suffolk, made a will, and that neither this instrument nor the executors could be discovered; eventually the heir-at-law was traced in the person of the great-great-grandson of C. Jennings of Gopsal, the eldest uncle of the deceased, who then entered into possession of the property, since when there has been constant litigation concerning it. In consequence of certain criticisms upon his presentment of the Jarndyce case, Dickens (in his preface to the story) thought proper to defend his assertions, declaring that everything set forth in "Bleak House" concerning the Court of Chancery is "substantially true, and within the truth," and further asserting that if he wanted other authorities than that cited he could "rain them on these pages, to the shame of a parsimonious public."

The year 1851 was not allowed to pass without a Christmas Story, for he decided to make the Extra Christmas Number of *Household Words* an annual feature. As in the previous year, this issue bore no distinctive title, his own contribution, "What Christmas is as we Grow Older," leading off the number.

Hans Andersen, who visited Charles Dickens at this date, has given a pleasant picture of the Novelist and his home surroundings: "In Tavistock Square stands Tavistock House. This and the strip of garden in front of it are shut out from the thoroughfare by an iron railing. A large garden with a grass plot and high trees stretches behind the house, and gives it a countrified look in the midst of this coal and gas steaming London. In the passage from street to garden hung pictures and engravings. Here stood a marble bust of Dickens, so like him, so

Tavistock House, Tavistock Square

Residence of Charles Dickens, 1851-1857

*Photographed by Catharine Weed Ward*

Charles Dickens

*From the painting by Ary Scheffer, 1856*

youthful and handsome; and over a bedroom door and a dining room door were inserted the bas-reliefs of Night and Day, after Thorwaldsen. On the first floor was a rich library with a fireplace and a writing table, looking out on the garden; and here it was that in winter Dickens and his friends acted plays to the satisfaction of all parties. The kitchen was underground, and at the top of the house were the bedrooms. I had a snug room looking out on the garden; and over the treetops I saw the London towers and spires appear and disappear as the weather cleared or thickened."

Charles Dickens was occupied with "Bleak House" all through 1852. Prior to the launching of the first instalment in March, there were Guild performances in the provinces, with their accompanying responsibilities, of which he bore the brunt. In a letter to Sir Edward Bulwer Lytton (dated from Tavistock House on the 15th February) the Novelist said: "I left Liverpool at four o'clock this morning, and am so blinded by excitement, gas, and waving hats and handkerchiefs, that I can hardly see to write, but I cannot go to bed without telling you what a triumph we have had. Allowing for the necessarily heavy expenses of all kinds, I believe we can hardly fund less than a Thousand Pounds out of this trip alone. And, more than that, the extraordinary interest taken in the idea of the Guild by 'this grand people of England' down in these vast hives, and the enthusiastic welcome they gave it, assure me that we may do what we will if we will only be true and faithful to our design. . . ."[1] Thus we see that, fatigued as he was with his efforts—for he "had been at it almost incessantly, day and night, for a

---

[1] "The Letters of Charles Dickens."

week"—he could not refrain from describing to Sir Edward, without loss of time, the grand reception accorded to the Amateurs by the people of Lancashire. "Believe me," he said, "we may carry a perfect fiery cross through the North of England, and over the Border, in this cause, if need be—not only to the enrichment of the cause, but to the lasting enlistment of the people's sympathy."

The activity of the Novelist, now in the prime of life, was truly astounding. This "splendid strolling" must have severely tried his constitution and told upon his health and strength. It should be remembered that, in addition, there were the editorial supervision of *Household Words* and the writing of "Bleak House." Dickens, therefore, could not fail to realise before many months had elapsed that he was attempting too much, and an illness, in the shape of a severe inflammatory pain in the side, from which he began to suffer at this time, must undoubtedly be attributed principally to his extraordinary exertions. As soon as the first number of "Bleak House" appeared he exhibited signs of mental distress, and complained of being unable to make satisfactory progress with his story. "Wild ideas are upon me," he wrote, "of going to Paris—Rouen—Switzerland—somewhere—and writing the remaining two-thirds of the next number aloft in some queer inn room. I have been hanging over it, and have got restless. Want a change I think." He dreaded, too, the possibility "of not being able to come up to time," that is, of not completing the manuscript of each number punctually. This inability to "grind sparks out of his dull blade" continued to harass him, and he thought of going to Switzerland, but went to Dover instead, where at length he contrived to settle down at his desk. In July matters looked more promising, judging from a letter addressed to Miss Mary Boyle. "I foresee, I think, some very good things in 'Bleak House.' . . . I behold them in the months ahead and weep." Renting a house at No. 10 Camden Crescent, Dover, he and his family remained there for three months, at the expiration of which he sent his children and servants back to Tavistock House, and, accompanied by his wife and her sister, crossed over to Boulogne to inspect that town and its neighbourhood, with a view to making it his summer quarters in the following year. He was very sorely distressed by the unexpected death, in July, of the Hon. Richard Watson of Rockingham Castle, to whom and Mrs. Watson he had dedicated "David Copperfield"; to the widow he sent a tenderly sympathetic letter such as he, of all men, knew how to write, and offered to compose an inscription for her husband's memorial in the village church. The death of Mr. Watson was soon followed by the demise of other familiar acquaintances, Count D'Orsay and Mrs. Macready. "It is a tremendous consideration," he commented figuratively, "that friends should fall around us in such awful numbers as we attain middle life. What a field of battle it is! . . . Ah me! Ah me! This tremendous sickle does cut deep into the surrounding corn, when one's own blade has ripened. . . ."

Rockingham Castle, where he frequently stayed as an honoured guest, had peculiar attractions for him, so much so that he introduced it in "Bleak House" as Chesney Wold, the home of Sir Leicester Dedlock. In a subsequent letter to Mrs. Watson (November 22nd) he said: "You ask a question about 'Bleak House.' Its circulation is half as large again as 'Copperfield'!"— a fact which seemed, by the note of exclamation, to surprise him. In the same epistle he mentioned that he had written for *Household Words* an article[1] showing why he considered it a mistake to accord a state funeral to the great Duke of Wellington then recently deceased—that such a ceremony ought to be "temperately but firmly objected to—which I daresay will make a good many of the admirers of such things highly indignant."[2] He admitted that it might have right and reason on its side, nevertheless.

In October we find the Novelist at Boulogne, preparing for his next Christmas number. It was to assume the form which eventually characterised these annual publications, and which he described in a letter to his friend the Rev. James White, whom he had invited to contribute: "I propose to give the number some fireside name, and to make it consist entirely of short stories, supposed to be told by a family sitting round the fire." Strange as it may appear, he intimated to Mr. White that he did not care about these stories referring to Christmas at all, nor did he, in this instance, design to connect them together otherwise than by their names. The general designation given to the number was "A Round of Stories by the Christmas Fire," and the Novelist furnished two of the ten short tales therein contained, viz. "The Poor Relation's Story" and "The Child's Story." Other contributors to this number included Mrs. Gaskell and Harriet Martineau.

It is natural to suppose that the works of so popular a writer as Charles Dickens were occasionally subjected to private as well as public criticism. In

[1] "Trading in Death" (*Household Words*, Nov. 27, 1852).
[2] "The Letters of Charles Dickens."

July of this year (1852), he became the recipient of a
letter from a stranger, who addressed him as follows:
"I venture to trespass on your attention with one
serious query, touching a sentence in the last number
of 'Bleak House.' Do the supporters of Christian
missions to the heathen really deserve the attack that is
conveyed in the sentence about Jo seated in his
anguish on the doorstep of the Society for the
Propagation of the Gospel in Foreign Parts? The
allusion is severe, but is it just? Are such boys as Jo
neglected? What are ragged schools, town missions,
and many of those societies I regret to see sneered at
in the last number of *Household Words?*" In his
defence, the Novelist said: "There was a long time
during which benevolent societies were spending
immense sums on missions abroad, when there was no
such thing as a ragged school in England, or any kind
of associated endeavour to penetrate to those horrible
domestic depths in which such schools are now to be
found, and where they were, to my most certain
knowledge, neither placed nor discovered by the
Society for the Propagation of the Gospel in Foreign
Parts. If you think the balance between the home
mission and the foreign mission justly held in the
present time, I do not. I abstain from drawing the
strange comparison that might be drawn between the
sums even now expended in endeavours to remove the
darkest ignorance and degradation from our very
doors, because I have some respect for mistakes that
may be founded in a sincere wish to do good. But I
present a general suggestion of the still existing
anomaly (in such a paragraph as that which offends
you), in the hope of inducing some people to reflect
on this matter, and to adjust the balance more
correctly. I am decidedly of opinion that the two

works, the home and the foreign, are *not* conducted with an equal hand, and that the home claim is by far the stronger and the more pressing of the two. Indeed, I have very grave doubts whether a great commercial country, holding communication with all parts of the world, can better Christianise the benighted portions of it than by the bestowal of its wealth and energy on the making of good Christians at home, and on the utter removal of neglected and untaught childhood from its streets, before it wanders elsewhere. For, if it steadily persists in this work, working downwards to the lowest, the travellers of all grades whom it sends abroad will be good, exemplary, practical missionaries; instead of undoers of what the best professed missionaries can do. These are my opinions, founded, I believe, on some knowledge of facts and some observation. If I could be scared out of them, let me add in all good humour, by such easily impressed words as 'antichristian' or 'irreligious,' I should think that I deserved them in their real signification."[1]

With these sentiments every broadminded person must agree. At the same time it should be remembered that the methods of dealing with such wretched outcasts as those exemplified in poor Jo have vastly improved since "Bleak House" was written, and it is fair to assume that the story, directly or indirectly, had much to do with the mitigation of their distressful condition.

The year 1853 opened with "Bleak House" well in hand—in fact, more than half the story had then been written. The excessive strain of endeavouring to accomplish too much began seriously to affect Dickens's health, and he complained that

---

[1] "The Letters of Charles Dickens."

"hypochondriacal whisperings" told him he was "rather overworked." Early in the year he was accorded a tremendous ovation at Birmingham. Of the kind intentions of his friends in that great midland town he had already received an inkling, as, during the previous December, a letter reached him from Mr. G. Linnaeus Banks on the subject of a proposed public dinner to be given in honour of the Novelist, the originators of this festive demonstration being Mr. Banks and Mr. J. C. Walker, an artist. The great banquet, which took place on Twelfth Night, was designed by the people of Birmingham to mark not only their appreciation of the eloquent service rendered by him to the new Midland Institute, but as a testimony of their admiration for his literary acquirements and high moral teaching. The function was preceded by the presentation, at the rooms of the Birmingham Fine Arts Association, of a diamond ring and silver gilt salver, and at the banquet Dickens offered to give a couple of readings from his books at the following Christmas, in aid of the Midland Institute. This was his first formal undertaking to read in public; "there would be some novelty in the thing," he wrote the next day to Mr. Arthur Ryland, of Birmingham, "as I have never done it in public, though I have in private, and (if I may say so) with a great effect on the hearers."

The sale of "Bleak House" continued to increase, and had risen to nearly forty thousand copies per month, this success doubtless serving to cheer him during this period of lapsing health. He could, however, no longer bear easily what he carried so lightly of old, and found that social enjoyments, in conjunction with literary undertakings, taxed his strength too severely. "What with 'Bleak House' and

*Household Words*, and 'Child's History,' and Miss Coutts's Home, and the invitations to feasts and festivals, I really feel as if my head would split like a fired shell if I remained here,"—i.e., in London. It is surprising, by the way, how he suppressed references to his ailments in letters to friends. Indeed, to Clarkson Stanfield, on the 2nd of January, he wrote quite jocularly, in nautical parlance, from "H.M.S. *Tavistock*,"—*apropos* of the artist's previous experience as a sailor:—

"Yoho, old salt! Neptun' ahoy! You don't forget, messmet, as you was to meet Dick Sparkler and Mark Porpuss[1] on the fok'sle of the good ship *Owssel Words*, Wednesday night, half-past four? Not you; for when did Stanfell ever pass his word to go anywheers and not come? Well. Belay, my heart of oak, belay! Come alongside the *Tavistock* same day and hour, 'stead of *Owssel Words*. Hail your shipmets, and they'll drop over the side and join you, like two new shillings a-droppin' into the purser's pocket. Damn all lubberly boys and swabs, and give *me* the lad with the tarry trousers, which shines to me like di'mings bright!"[2]

On April 19th the Duke of Devonshire entertained at dinner at Devonshire House, Sir E. L. Bulwer Lytton, and about thirty of the gentlemen who interested themselves in the Guild of Literature and Art, the dinner being succeeded by an evening party, at which a selection of music was performed by his Grace's private band.[3] The incident is not mentioned by Forster, but there can be no doubt that Dickens was present. In May the Novelist suffered considerably

---

[1] Nicknames bestowed by Dickens upon himself and Mark Lemon. The latter was extremely corpulent, hence the designation.

[2] "The Letters of Charles Dickens."

[3] "Dramatic Register for 1853."

from a return of the inflammatory pain in his side—an unusually sharp attack—and on his recovery early in the following month he tried Brighton for a change, but, deriving no benefit therefrom, he promptly decided that, as soon as he was sufficiently strong for the journey, he would take up his quarters, for a summer sojourn, at Boulogne, where he, with his wife and sister-in-law, arrived on the 13th of June, after a delightful passage, thankful for having escaped from an absolute breakdown in health and work. "If I had substituted anybody's knowledge of myself for my own," he confessed to Forster, "and lingered in London, I never could have got through." At this seaside watering-place, to which he became much attached,[1] he discovered the Château des Moulineaux, and this pretty little villa with its excellent landlord, M. Beaucourt, at once took his fancy as a place of residence. He described the house as "not a large one, but stands in the middle of a great garden, with what the landlord calls a 'forest' at the back, and is now surrounded by flowers, vegetables, and all manner of growth. A queer, odd, French place, but extremely well supplied with all table and other conveniences, and strongly recommended. . . ." Directly he had installed himself here, he felt inspired to begin his next number of "Bleak House," and was able to announce, five days later (June 18th), that satisfactory progress had been made: "Thank God I have done half the number with great care. . . . Oh how thankful I feel to be able to have done it, and what a relief to get the number out,"—an observation which justifies the conclusion that the story did not flow from

[1] See an article by him in *Household Words*, November 4, 1854, under the title of "Our French Watering-Place."

his pen with the customary ease and fluency. Happily, his health rapidly improved amidst the new environment, so much so that ten days after his arrival he reported himself as being "brown, well, robust, vigorous, open to fight any man in England of my own weight, and growing a moustache. Any person of undoubted pluck, in want of a customer, may hear of me at the bar of Bleak House, where my money is down." During the summer he supplemented the writing of his serial story by dictating further instalments of "A Child's History of England" then course of publication, chapter by chapter, in *Household Words*, his arduous labours being agreeably lightened by visits of friends from England, including Frank Stone and family, Mr. and Mrs. John Leech, and Wilkie Collins. Leech declared that when he stepped from the boat after a stormy passage, he was received by the congregated spectators with a distinct round of applause—a welcome not inspired (as might be conjectured) by the popularity and fame which the genial *Punch* artist had achieved, but because he was by far the most intensely and unutterably miserable looking object that had yet appeared among the *voyageurs*. The laughter which greeted him was tumultuous, and the artist (said Dickens) wished his friends to know that altogether "he made an immense hit."

In August the final chapters of "Bleak House" were penned, the two concluding numbers (Parts 19 and 20) being issued simultaneously in September. At the same time the complete story was published in volume form, and dedicated, "as a Remembrance of our Friendly Union," to his companions in the Guild of Literature and Art. In a letter to the Hon. Mrs. Watson on August 27th he acknowledged his own satisfaction with the conclusion of the tale, which he thought *"very pretty indeed."* "The story has taken extraordinarily," he added, especially during the last five or six months, when its purpose has been gradually working itself out. It has retained its immense circulation from the first, beating dear old 'Copperfield' by a round ten thousand or more. I have never had so many readers."[1]

Dickens's extraordinary method of disposing of one of the characters in his novel—the death of Krook by spontaneous combustion—excited considerable controversy, one of his critics, the eminent scientist George Henry Lewes, being strongly opposed to the validity of the theory regarding the possibility of such an anomaly. Whereupon the Novelist, in his preface, cited some notable instances of death thus effected, and made especial reference to that of the Countess Cornelia de Bandi Cesenate, which had apparently borne the test of minute investigation. It will be remembered that about twenty years previously another writer of repute, Captain Marryat, had resorted to a similar device in "Jacob Faithful," although he admitted that such cases present themselves but once in a century; this being so, it is fair to argue that phenomena so rare become improbable and incongruous in fiction.

The portraiture of two of the prominent characters in "Bleak House" was undoubtedly inspired by living personages. The Novelist's friend, Walter Savage Landor, is admitted to be the original of Lawrence Boythorne. Thomas Carlyle called Landor "the unsubduable Roman," and the late Mrs. Lynn Linton, who knew him intimately, records that he was irascible and obstinate, rash in speech and action,

---

[1] "The Letters of Charles Dickens."

but that his nature was a noble one, for he was faithful,
upright, and most generous. Dickens himself, in one of
his letters, speaks of him as "a true gentleman in his
manner, so chivalrously polite;" adding that "there
was a sterling quality in his laugh, and in his vigorous,
healthy voice, and in the roundness and fullness with
which he uttered every word he spoke, and in the very
fury of his superlatives, which seemed to go off like
blank cannons and hurt nothing;" while sitting at
dinner, he would smilingly converse, and be
occasionally led into "some great volley of
superlatives," now and then throwing up his head "like
a bloodhound," and give vent to a tremendous "Ha!
Ha! Ha!" Landor was fond of animals, and had several
domestic pets, so that the presentment of him in
"Bleak House" is fairly accurate and recognisable.
Although by no means an unpleasing portrait, he
apparently did not relish the liberty which
Dickens had taken with his personality—at least, that
is Mrs. Linton's statement; Dickens, on the other
hand, affirmed that the poet seemed rather proud
of the picture than otherwise. With regard to
the second portrait, that of Harold Skimpole, in
whom are embodied the more pronounced
idiosyncrasies of Leigh Hunt, the consequences were
more lamentable, inasmuch as grave offence was
unintentionally given to the author of "Rimini," whose
friends, by the way, were the first to detect a similarity
between the impecunious and unworldly Skimpole
and his alleged prototype; left to himself, Hunt would
probably never have guessed that he had anything in
common with that character. Dickens, on being
accused of thus plagiarising Hunt, emphatically
averred that "he no more thought that the admired

original could be charged with the imaginary vices of the fictitious creature than he has himself ever thought of charging the blood of Desdemona and Othello on the innocent Academy model who sat for Iago's leg in the picture." Leigh Hunt, in his "Autobiography" (1850), confessed to certain peculiarities—such as incapacity for figures and business—which, three or four years later, became distinguishing traits of Harold Skimpole, whose airy qualities were similarly grounded on Hunt's avowed "gay and ostentatious wilfulness."[1] Dickens naturally felt exceedingly vexed on learning that Hunt and his familiars regarded the presentment of Skimpole as a serious portrait, and subsequently made ample amends by writing a most amiable paper about Leigh Hunt in *Household Words*,[2] as well as by a fine tribute to his genius in *All the Year Round*.[3] The Novelist, who erred from thoughtlessness only, also conveyed to Hunt personally his regret at the Skimpole mistake.

Notwithstanding careful inquiry and research, the identity of Bleak House (the residence of Mr. Jarndyce, which Dickens places near St. Albans) is still a matter for conjecture. There are many habitations so called, but none of them satisfactorily answers to the description, the nearest to resemble it being,

---

[1] For his stinging diatribe in the *Examiner* upon the Prince Regent, in 1813, Leigh Hunt suffered two years' incarceration in the Surrey Jail, and on recording the trifling cost of decorating with a gay wallpaper his prison home he pathetically lamented his incapacity for computation in money matters. "I had not then learned to think about money," he remarked regretfully. To repeat the query propounded by an anonymous writer in the *Cornhill Magazine* (May 1892): "Poor poet! Did he ever in truth master that dreary lesson so hard for a man who lives in a world of dreams and fancies to acquire?"

[2] "By Rail to Parnassus" (*Household Words*, June 16, 1855).

[3] "Leigh Hunt: A Remonstrance" (*All the Year Round*, December 24. 1859).

perhaps, the fine old Georgian mansion standing in its own grounds, on the confines of St. Albans, which the owner has recently re-christened "Bleak House." There once existed a colony of brickmakers in the immediate neighbourhood—a fact which seems to support the theory that Dickens may have seen this identical residence during his visit to St. Albans at the time the story was proceeding, and made it the home of Mr. Jarndyce. One thing is certain—the substantial looking domicile standing prominently on the cliff at Broadstairs, and locally known as "Bleak House," is not the building thus immortalised by the Novelist; originally called "Fort House," it by no means tallies with the account given in the sixth chapter of the book.[1] Another point of topographical interest is the identity of the pauper graveyard usually referred to as "Jo's burial-ground." When "Bleak House" was written, quite a number of these unsanitary and neglected graveyards existed in London, several being within the radius of a mile from Chancery Lane, and any one of them compared fairly well with the Novelist's forcible picture of the scene of "Nemo's" interment. The general belief is that the particular burial ground which Dickens had in his mind was that adjoining Russell Court, Drury Lane—a belief which found acceptance even in the Novelist's lifetime and is strengthened by the assurance of Mr. Percy Fitzgerald that Dickens used often to wander round and (like Jo) look in at the graves through the bars of the

---

[1] One regrets to learn that, owing to the fact that Fort House (otherwise "Bleak House") has been tenantless for a number of years, it is now in such a bad state of repair as to necessitate considerable restoration, by which, it is feared, certain features that were familiar to Charles Dickens will disappear. The garden, so replete with interesting memories, had been allowed to become a wilderness.

iron gate at the end of a tunnelled passage such as that depicted in "Phiz's" illustration. The place was closed as a burial ground in 1853 (just before the conclusion of the story), and thirty years later was converted into a recreation ground for children living in Drury Lane and the neighbouring streets and alleys; this locality, however, has undergone considerable transformation, a new thoroughfare having recently been constructed at the south side of Drury Lane Theatre, which entirely obliterates what remained of Jo's burial ground. The iron gate, however, is preserved as a Dickens relic.

The description of Tom-all-Alone's is said to have been suggested by a similar "slum" in the neighbourhood of Chatham, which must have been familiar to Dickens during the days of his boyhood there. This has also been swept away, and the modern portion of the Royal Marine barracks stands upon the site. Such "rookeries" were common enough in London prior to the passing of Lord Shaftesbury's Common Lodging-houses Act in 1851, and one of them, situated near Cursitor Street, Chancery Lane, bore a strong similitude to Tom-all-Alone's. With respect to the name given by Dickens to the noisome alley which Jo regarded as his home, it is easy to believe that it was derived from that of a lonely house which once stood on waste ground in Chatham, at a spot near the present Government offices; according to Mr. Robert Langton, this tenement was the abode of one Thomas Clark, who lived there in solitary state for twenty-five years (1747-1772), and whose custom it was, when returning home of an evening, to cry, "Tom's all alone!"

Many of the localities delineated in "Bleak House" are still in existance, although altered somewhat in their general aspect. Staple Inn, Thavies Inn, Quality Court, and, of course, Lincoln's Inn, have changed but little. On the other hand, the "Sol's Arms" (otherwise the "Old Ship" tavern) in Chichester Rents, Chancery Lane, has been pulled down, together with the fine old Queen Anne building in Took's Court (otherwise Cook's Court), which is believed to have been Snagsby's. No. 58 Lincoln's Inn Fields, assigned by the Novelist as Mr. Tulkinghorn's chambers, is doomed, alas! By the "improvement" scheme projected by the London County Council; this mansion is of peculiar interest, inasmuch as it was for some time the residence of John Forster, where (in the room with the painted allegory, long since obliterated) Dickens and his friends frequently foregathered, notably on that memorable occasion of the reading of "The Chimes" prior to publication.

The sale of "Bleak House" in numbers attained (as already stated) to nearly forty thousand copies, and from the very beginning it won the approval of the public, which is attributed partly to the fact that "Copperfield" had become so endeared to innumerable admirers that it paved the way for its successor. Concerning the story, Dean Ramsay wrote to Forster: "We have been reading 'Bleak House' 'aloud.' Surely it is one of the most powerful and successful! What a triumph is Jo! Uncultured nature is *there* indeed: the intimations of true heart feeling, the glimmerings of higher feeling, all are there but everything still consistent and in harmony. . . To my mind, nothing in the field of fiction is to be found in English literature surpassing the death of Jo!"

CHAPTER 10

## "HARD TIMES"
## AND "LITTLE DORRIT"

In October 1853 Charles Dickens, with Wilkie Collins
and Augustus Egg, started from Boulogne on a two-
months' excursion through Switzerland and Italy. This
was to celebrate the completion of the story, and the
Novelist described the interval previous to their
departure as a fearful "reaction and prostration of
laziness." At the end of September he had written the
concluding chapters of the "Child's History of
England." and notified that he was "trying to think of
something for the Christmas Number of *Household
Words*—after which I shall knock off, having had quite
enough to do, small as it would have seemed to me at
any other time, since I finished 'Bleak House.'" A
week before leaving Boulogne he announced to
Forster that he had recovered his Italian, which he had
all but forgotten, and "am one entire and perfect
chrysolite of idleness." According to a synopsis of the
projected tour, based on the assumption of a fine
autumn, it was Dickens's intention to go first by Paris
and Geneva to Lausanne—thence by Chamounix and
Martigny, over the Simplon to Milan, thence to Genoa,
Leghorn, Pisa, Naples, and Sicily; returning by
Bologna, Florence, Rome, Verona, Mantua, &c., to
Venice, and so home through Germany, arriving in
good time for Christmas Day. Almost at the outset

an accident happened which nearly proved fatal to a member of the party; while travelling to the Mer de Glace, along a narrow path at a great height ("like a chimneypiece"), with sheer precipice below, a huge block of stone, probably loosened by the heavy rains, rolled down the mountain side from above, and, missing Egg by barely a yard, tumbled into the valley. Dickens, in letters to friends, amusingly describes the adventures of himself and his boon companions during this delightful holiday expedition.

Although journeying for recreation and to obtain temporary relief from literary worries, the Novelist's faithful henchman, W. H. Wills, kept him in touch with *Household Words*, the editorial liabilities of which he could never entirely escape. On November 17th he sent Wills the MS. of a "little paper" for the Christmas Number, "in a character that nobody else is likely to hit, and which is pretty sure to be considered pleasant." It was "The Schoolboy's Story," which, with "The Nurse's Story," constituted his share of the number entitled "Another Round of Stories by the Christmas Fire," published in December of this year. The name of the hero of "The Schoolboy's Story," Old Cheeseman, was that of one of his own schoolfellows at Chatham. "KEEP 'HOUSEHOLD WORDS' IMAGINATIVE!" was his solemn and continual editorial injunction, emphasized in his letters by vigorous underlining. It is desirable, perhaps, to mention here that the Novelist's eldest son had left Eton to complete his education at Leipsic, and was to leave Germany at the end of the year; so that, early in December, when the travellers returned to London after their Continental tour, they were accompanied by this young man, soon to be engaged in business life.

[BIRMINGHAM 1853]

It will be remembered that in January of this year Dickens had promised to give, in Birmingham, a couple of readings from his Christmas books in aid of the new Midland Institute. That promise was faithfully fulfilled on his return from the continent, the readings (from the "Carol" and the "Cricket") taking place in the Town Hall on 27th and 28th December, with the result that the fund was augmented by nearly five hundred pounds; a flower basket in silver, presented to Mrs. Dickens, commemorated these readings ("to nearly six thousand people") and the design they had generously helped. On the occasion of the second reading, Dickens stipulated for the admission of working men at moderate prices, and in a letter to the Hon. Mrs. Watson, written a few days afterwards, he said: "I never saw, nor do I suppose anybody ever did [see], such an interesting sight as the working people's night. There were two thousand five hundred of them there, and a more delicately observant audience it is impossible to imagine. They lost nothing, misinterpreted nothing, followed everything closely, laughed and cried with the most delightful earnestness, and animated me to that extent that I felt as if we were all bodily going up into the clouds together. It is an enormous place for the purpose; but I had considered all that carefully, and I believe made the most distant person hear as well as if I had been reading in my own room. I was a little doubtful before I began on the first night whether it was quite practicable to conceal, the requisite effort, but I soon had the satisfaction of finding that it was, and that we were all going on together, in the first page, as easily, to all appearance, as if we had been sitting round the fire."[1] This is

[1] "The Letters of Charles Dickens."

specially interesting in view of the fact that they were absolutely the first of those public readings by which he was soon destined to make a stir in the world.

The work that next engaged the Novelist's attention was "Hard Times, for these Times," which he prepared as a serial in *Household Words*, where it appeared from 1st April to 12th August 1854. As explained to Charles Knight, his satire was directed against those "who see figures and averages, and nothing else—the representatives of the wickedest and most enormous vice of this time—the men who, through long years to come, will do more to damage the real useful truths of political economy than I could do (if I tried) in my whole life. . . ."[1] Many titles were thought of for the work, three being selected by Forster and three by Dickens, both finally making an independent choice of the same title, which was accordingly adopted. Invariably harassed by anxiety through publishing his extended narratives by instalments, the Novelist, curiously enough, found the weekly portion less trying to prepare than the customary monthly one, for the reason that its comparative brevity made it easier for him to come up to time, although he admitted it to be more perplexing to get sufficient interest within the, exceptionally limited space at his disposal. This problem presented itself in regard to "Hard Times," and, after a few weeks' trial, he said: "The difficulty of the space is CRUSHING. Nobody can have an idea of it who has not had an experience of patient fiction writing with some elbowroom always, and open places in prospective." He derived amusement and entertainment from children's theatricals, which began on the, first Twelfth Night at Tavistock House with a

---

[1] "The Letters of Charles Dickens."

performance of Fielding's burlesque, "Tom Thumb," Dickens and Mark Lemon ("Uncle Mark," as the juvenile members affectionately called him) taking parts in the representation, the names by which they were res-pectively enrolled being "The Infant Phenomenon" and "The Modern Garrick." In the auditorium was seen the already grizzled head of Thackeray, who, during the singing of the ballad of Miss Villikins, rolled off his seat in a burst of laughter at the humorous absurdity of the thing. Dickens's dear friend, Miss Mary Boyle, had pleasant recollections of Tavistock House. "The very sound of the name," she says, "is replete to me with memories of innumerable evenings passed in the most congenial and delightful intercourse: dinners, where the guests vied with each other in brilliant conversation, whether intellectual, witty, or sparkling—evenings devoted to music or theatricals. First and foremost of that magic circle was the host himself, always 'one of us,' who invariably drew out what was best and most characteristic in others. . . . I can never forget one evening, shortly after the arrival at Tavistock House, when we danced in the New Year. It seemed like a page cut out of the 'Christmas Carol,' as far, at least, as fun and frolic went."[1]

The summer of 1854 was spent at Boulogne as in the previous year, and he again became the tenant of M. Beaucourt, but occupied another château placed on the very summit of a hill, called the Villa du Camp de Droite; here he stayed until the eve of his winter residence in Paris, and here he continued at work upon "Hard Times." It is interesting to know that, anxious to verify (for the purposes of this story) the principal details of a strike in a

[1] "Mary Boyle—Her Book," 1901.

manufacturing town, he took train to Preston in Lancashire, where a trouble of that kind was then proceeding. He was somewhat disappointed, however, and thus wrote from Preston to Forster: "I am afraid I shall not be able to get much here. Except the crowds at the street corners reading the placards *pro* and *con*; and the cold absence of smoke from the mill chimneys; there is very little in the streets to make the town remarkable. I am told that the people 'sit at home and mope.' The delegates with the money from the neighbouring places came in today to report the amounts they bring; and tomorrow the people are paid. When I have seen both these ceremonies I shall return." Coketown, by the way—the scene of the principal incidents in the tale—was intended as a representation of Manchester. At Boulogne, in July, the final chapter of "Hard Times" was written, and in a note penned just before the close of the tale the Author said: "I am three-parts mad and the fourth delirious, with perpetual rushing at 'Hard Times.' I have done what I hope is a good thing with Stephen,[1] taking his story as a whole . . . I have been looking forward through so many weeks and sides of paper to this Stephen business, that now—as usual—it being over, I feel as if nothing in the world, in the way of intense and violent rushing hither and thither, could quite restore my balance." The inclusion of "Hard Times" in the pages of *Household Words* nearly doubled the circulation of that journal. Immediately after publication as a serial it was launched in volume form, with a

[1] Stephen Blackpool, the power-loom weaver in Mr. Bounderby's factory. Mrs. Oliphant regarded the episode of Stephen and Rachel as one of the best pieces of serious writing Dickens ever did.

dedication to Thomas Carlyle. Among those who were most emphatic in praising the book was Ruskin, and his opinion is decidedly worth quoting:—

"Allowing for his manner of telling them, the things he tells us are always true. I wish that he could think it right to limit his brilliant exaggeration to works written only for public amusement; and when he takes up a subject of high national importance, such as that which he handled in 'Hard Times,' that he would use severer and more accurate analyses. . . . He is entirely right in his main drift and purpose in every book he has written; and all of them, but especially 'Hard Times,' should be studied with close and earnest care by persons interested in social questions. They will find much that is partial, and, because partial, apparently unjust; but if they examine all the evidence on the other side, which Dickens seems to overlook, it will appear, after all their trouble, that his view was the finally right one, grossly and sharply told."[1]

On completing his "socialistic romance" (as it has been termed), Dickens journeyed to London for a brief spell, proposing to pass that interval (as he previously notified to Wilkie Collins) "in a career of amiable dissipation and unbounded license in the metropolis." "If you will come and breakfast with me about midnight," he added—"anywhere— any day, and go to bed no more until we fly to these pastoral retreats, I shall be delighted to have so vicious an associate." After a "blaze of dissipation," he returned to his hilltop residence at Boulogne, which he described as like being up in a balloon—"lionising Englishmen and Germans

[1] "Unto this Last," by John Ruskin, 1862.

start to call, and are found lying imbecile in the road half-way up. Ha! Ha! Ha!"

In October 1854 Dickens returned to Tavistock House for the winter months. Earlier in the year, owing to the pronounced success of his public readings at Birmingham during the previous December, he was inundated with applications to give similar readings for various charitable purposes. Certain of these he favourably entertained, and the idea conceived at Lausanne in 1846 (after he had made a marked impression upon a private audience by a reading from "Dombey") recurred to him of the possibility of paid public lecturing proving highly remunerative. The objection raised by Forster did not appeal to him with much force, and further experience as a reader of his own works justified the Novelist's anticipation. On the 19th of December he read the "Carol" at Reading, where he assumed the presidency of the Literary Institute on the death of Talfourd, and a day or two later (at Macready's wish) he appeared in a similar capacity for the benefit of another Institution "in the busy town of Sherborne, in Dorset." With reference to the latter he wrote to Macready, whose interest in that particular organisation was one of the few remaining pleasures of his old age:—

"I wonder what accommodation there is for reading! Because our illustrious countryman likes to stand at a desk breast high, with plenty of room about him, a sloping top, and a ledge to keep his book from tumbling off. If such a thing should not be there, however, on his arrival, I suppose even a Sherborne carpenter could knock it up out of a deal board. *Is* there a deal board in Sherborne though? . . . ."

The Novelist, with his wife and sister-in-law, remained as guests of the veteran actor until the 23rd, when they journeyed home to spend Christmas.

The extra Yuletide number of *Household Words* for this year is entitled "The Seven Poor Travellers," to which Dickens contributed "The First [Poor Traveller]" and the concluding chapter, "The Road." The former opens with an account of the celebrated Charity at Rochester, founded in the sixteenth century by Richard Watts (a Rochester celebrity, who represented that ancient city in Parliament from 1563 to 1571) for Six Poor Travellers, "who, not being Rogues or Proctors,[1] may receive gratis for one Night, Lodging, Entertainment, and Fourpence each." Thus runs the inscription on the front of the quaint building in the High Street of Rochester, which remains today exactly as Dickens saw it when, accompanied by Mark Lemon, he visited the place on May 11, 1854, in order to learn something of the administration of the ancient bequest. It is supposed by many that the Novelist's account of the festivities here on Christmas Eve was founded on fact, whereas it is wholly imaginary. The pathetic narrative of Richard Doubledick moved the Author not a little in the writing. "The idea of that little story," he observed to a Birmingham friend, "obtained such strong possession of me when it came into my head, that it cost me more time and tears than most people would consider likely." It is

---

[1] According to Steerforth ("David Copperfield," chap. 23) a Proctor is, in a legal sense, "a sort of monkish attorney." The late Sir Francis Palgrave explained, however, that the word "proctor" in the above inscription refers to those who had letters of procuration from some hospital or lazar-house to beg on behalf of the inmates. These men, who were exempted from the laws against sturdy beggars, seem generally to have borne a bad character, and are several times referred to in the literature of the sixteenth century.

gratifying to learn that within recent years a lady in Rochester, doubtless inspired by Dickens's description of the revels in the opening chapter, gave a Christmas feast to the Poor Travellers who sought the hospitality afforded by Master Richard Watts, and it is recorded that on the night of Christmas Day, 1888, the fortunate half-dozen travellers were indulged (through the kindly action of an anonymous benefactor) with a hot dinner of roast beef and plum pudding, and beer, each man being also the recipient of a seasonable card, a pair of cuffs, a full tobacco pouch, a pipe, a box of matches, and a sixpenny piece! Some of the reforms that have been effected in the management of the now munificent revenues of Richard Watts's Charity were instigated as a sequence to the appearance of "The Seven Poor Travellers."[1]

In 1855 Dickens's first public engagement was a reading at Bradford—"to a little fireside party of four thousand," as he humorously observed in a letter to Mrs. Watson. To his friend, M. de Cerjat, he gave the number more exactly as three thousand seven hundred—"and yet but for the noise of their laughing and cheering, they 'went' like one man." The subject of this reading was the "Carol," always a favourite with his audiences. On his return to London he speedily became immersed in preparations for a children's play to be acted on the 6th of January (his eldest son's birthday) at his own little theatre, "Tavistock Theatre," described in the bills as the smallest in the world. The piece selected was Planché's "gorgeous" fairy extravaganza, "Fortunio and his Seven Gifted Servants," the parts being filled by all his own children and some of their young

---

[1] "A Week's Tramp in Dickens-Land," by W. R. Hughes, F.L.S., 1891.

friends, with Mark Lemon, Wilkie Collins, and Charles Dickens as the adult members of the company. He at first thought of getting up for this purpose a new little version of "The Children in the Wood" ("yet to be written, by-the-bye," he intimated on the first of the previous November, presumably by himself), but the intention was not realised. Prior to the event the house was "full of spangles, gas, Jew theatrical tailors, and pantomime carpenters," while the distinguished head of the establishment revelled in the general excitement which all these preliminaries induced. In the play Dickens assumed the role of the testy old Baron, and availed himself of the public resentment against the Czar (it was the, time of the Crimean War) to denounce him, in a song, as no other than own cousin to the very Bear that Fortunio had gone forth to subdue. The bill, which attributed such interpolations to "the Dramatic Poet of the Establishment" (i.e., himself) humorously proclaimed, in large type, the "Re-engagement of that irresistible comedian, Mr. Ainger! Reappearance of Mr. H. [Henry Fielding Dickens, then not four years of age], who created so powerful an impression last year! Return of Mr. Charles Dickens, junior, from his German engagements! Engagement of Miss Kate [the Novelist's younger daughter], 'who declined the munificent offers of the management last season!' Mr. Passé [his own pseudonym], Mr. Mudperiod, Mr. Measly Servile, and Mr. Wilkini Collini! First appearance on any stage of Mr. Plornishmaroontigoonter (who has been kept out of bed at a vast expense)." The latter was the Novelist's youngest son, Edward Bulwer Lytton, then not quite three years old, and with quite a reputation as a comedian.

[PARIS 1855]

The year 1855 was a period of much unsettled discontent with Dickens, and just for a change he indulged in a week's holiday, departing for Paris with Wilkie Collins (who then suffered from ill-health), and stopping at Boulogne on the way to see two of his sons at school there. He announced to his friend, Monsieur Regnier, that during his stay in the French capital he wished to be "pleasant and gay," and to throw himself "*en garçon* on the festive *diableries de Paris*." He lodged at the Hotel Meurice, whence he wrote: "We breakfast at ten, read and write till two, and then I go out walking all over Paris, while the invalid sits by the fire or is deposited in a café. We dine at five, in a different restaurant every day, and at seven or so go to the theatre—sometimes to two theatres, sometimes to three. We get home about twelve, light the fire, and drink lemonade, to which *I* add rum. We go to bed between one and two. I live in peace, like an elderly gentleman, and regard myself as in a negative state of virtue and respectability. . . ."[1] Again, to Wills, he said: I am living like Gil Blas and doing nothing. . . . Paris is finer than ever, and I go wandering about it all day. I suppose, as an old farmer said of Scott, I am 'makin' mysel' ' all the time; but I seem to be rather a free-and-easy sort of superior vagabond."[2] Owing to the continuance of wintry weather, deep snow abounding everywhere, he abandoned his purpose of going on to Bordeaux; this state of things, however, proved but little better when he arrived in London, where he found "everything weeping," in consequence of the rapid thaw. "All the buildings have severe

[1] "The Letters of Charles Dickens."
[2] Ibid.

colds in the heads, all the windowsills are in the first stage of measles, all the water pipes are bursting, all the streets are great black heaps of mud . . . Five hundred thousand pairs of pattens are now going to church [it was Sunday], and the bells are making such an intolerable uproar that I can't hear myself think."[1]

A delightful incident, connecting the names of Dickens and Thackeray, occurred at this time. On the 22nd of March (1855) a lecture was given by Thackeray, in the course of which he made graceful mention of "Boz." A report of the lecture duly appeared in *The Times* on the following day, and its perusal by Dickens afforded him such infinite pleasure that he felt impelled to send a letter of grateful thanks to the famous "Titmarsh." "I cannot refrain from assuring you," he said, "in all truth and earnestness that I am profoundly touched by your generous reference to me. I do not know how to tell you what a glow it spread over my heart. Out of its fullness I do entreat you to believe that I shall never forget your words of commendation. If you could wholly know at once how you have moved me, and how you have animated me, you would be the happier I am very certain."

The Novelist, whose mind continued in a condition of unrest, felt unable for the moment to renew his writing, and inclined to go off somewhere, to wander about in his "old wild way." "Sometimes," he remarked, on the 3rd of April, "I am half in the mood to set off for France, sometimes I think I will go and walk about on the seashore for three or four months, sometimes I look towards the Pyrenees, sometimes Switzerland. I made a compact with a

[1] "The Letters of Charles Dickens."

great Spanish authority last week, and vowed I would go to Spain. Two days afterwards Laylard[1] and I agreed to go to Constantinople when Parliament rises. Tomorrow I shall probably discuss with somebody else the idea of going to Greenland or the North Pole. The end of all this, most likely, will be, that I shall shut myself up in some out-of-the-way place I have not yet thought of, and go desperately to work there."[2] To Leigh Hunt he wrote on the 4th of May: "I am now, to boot, in the wandering—unsettled—restless—uncontrollable state of being about to begin a new book. At such a time I am as infirm of purpose as Macbeth, as errant as Mad Tom, and as rugged as Timon. I sit down to work, do nothing, get up and walk a dozen miles, come back and sit down again next day, again do nothing and get up, go down a Railroad, find a place where I resolve to stay for a month, come home next morning, go strolling about for hours and hours, reject all engagements to have my time to myself, get tired of myself, and yet can't come out of myself to be pleasant to anybody else."[3]

We cannot help wondering what could have been the cause of such unusual restlessness? To a correspondent Dickens admitted that "once upon a time" he was not troubled in this way; but for several years past he had been addicted to roaming, and such peregrinations had developed into a part of his very life. The present perturbation of his mind, however, was so extraordinary that one must assume the existence of some unprecedented reason for it, and

---

[1] Austen Henry Layard, M.P., subsequently knighted.
[2] "The Letters of Charles Dickens."
[3] *Cornhill Magazine*, May 1892. This letter indicates that the Skimpole portrait did not seriously affect the friendship subsisting between the two writers.

the explanation is doubtless to be found in a certain domestic trouble then impending, to which a more direct reference must presently be made.

Finding it impossible, just then, to resume his pen, the Novelist flung himself rather hotly into politics, and in June 1855 he made a speech at a great meeting at Drury Lane Theatre on the subject of Administrative Reform, which produced a marked effect upon his hearers. "The whole speech," said a London journalist who attended in the capacity of reporter, "was at once a masterpiece of raillery and of rebuke to a I how-not-to-do-it' Government, and it was relished immensely by the audience, who repeatedly rose in spontaneous admiration of the brilliancy of the effort. Mr. Dickens apologised for having been led away from his 'trade and calling,' and declared that as it was his first political speech, so it would be his last. He kept his word. It was the only occasion, as far as I can learn, upon which Dickens adventured a political harangue. At the time I considered it an extraordinary manifestation of the *ars celare artem*, for I was confident that the whole thing had been carefully prepared at home, but in its conception and in its delivery it was alike inimitable."

The Novelist eagerly welcomed the proposal to prepare another play for performance at Tavistock House Theatre, securing the services of "Mr. Crummles" (thus he styled himself) as lessee and manager; the poet for the occasion was Wilkie Collins, and the scene-painter, Clarkson Stanfield, R.A. The title of the play was "The Lighthouse," of which Collins was the author, and which he described to Stanfield as "a regular old style melodrama." "I am going to act in it," wrote Dickens to the artist, "as an experiment, in the children's theatre here—I, Mark, Collins, Egg, and my daughter Mary, the whole *dram. pers.;* our families and yours the whole audience. . . . We mean to burst on an astonished world with the melodrama, without any note of preparation. So don't say a syllable to Forster if you should happen to see him."[1] For the play he composed "The Song of the Wreck" (five verses), and it was sung to the music of "Little Nell," a ballad of which the Novelist was very fond, and which his eldest daughter used frequently to sing to him.[2] "The Lighthouse," was acted with "brilliant success" for three nights in June,[3] followed by "Mr. Nightingale's Diary" and "Animal Magnetism" as farces.

These cheerful distractions well over, the Novelist felt in a better mood for commencing his next important work of fiction. Upon it he had conferred the title, "Nobody's Fault," and by this designation he continued to call it until the eve of publication—that is, after four numbers had been written—when it was changed to that of "Little Dorrit." We are told that the story derived its origin from the notion he had of a leading man who should bring about all the mischief in the tale, attribute it all to Providence, and observe at

[1] "The Letters of Charles Dickens."
[2] The words by Charlotte Young, and the music by George Linley.
[3] One of the scenes represented the Eddystone Lighthouse, the painting of which occupied the artist only one or two mornings. It was afterwards framed and placed in the hall at Gad's Hill, and at the sale of Dickens's effects in 1870 the picture realised a thousand guineas! The purchaser was Mr. Richard Attenborough, in whose office (at 33 Piccadilly) the picture was placed; he subsequently disposed of it to the notorious Baron Grant, whose effects were sold in 1897 by Messrs. Christie, Manson, & Woods, when the painting was acquired by Messrs. T. Agnew & Sons, acting on behalf of Lord Iveagh, its present owner.

every fresh calamity, "Well, it's a mercy, however, nobody was to blame you know!"—an idea that was evidently abandoned as the plot developed. Six months before the first chapter was written, the Novelist recorded in a notebook certain memoranda for possible use in his work, jotting down in a haphazard manner any hints or suggestions that occurred to him—such as a mere piece of imagery, the outline of a subject or character, a bit of description or dialogue. Among these entries are some fancies for "Little Dorrit," as, for example, the following, appertaining to the home of the Barnacle family:—

"Our House. Whatever it is, it is in a first-rate situation, and a fashionable neighbourhood. (Auctioneer calls it 'a gentlemanly residence.') A series of little closets squeezed up into the corner of a dark street—but a Duke's Mansion round the corner. The whole house just large enough to hold a vile, smell. The air breathed in it, at the best of times, a kind of Distillation of Mews."

There are notes, too which led up to the Author's final treatment of such incidents as the close of old Dorrit's life, Clennam's reverse of fortune, Mrs. Clennam's personality, &c. The actual writing of the story was begun at Tavistock House in May, but, owing to the unsettled state of his mind, the Author found it difficult to make a good start. As was not unusual under such circumstances, when the brain refused to supply the necessary conceits, he would address a letter to some particular friend, and expatiate upon his dilemma. So to Wilkie Collins he said: "The restless condition in which I wander up and down my room with the first page of my new book before me defies all description. I feel as if nothing would do but setting up in a balloon. It might be inflated in the garden in front, but I am afraid of its scarcely clearing those little houses." Presently he was able to announce that the story was "breaking out" all around him, and that he intended "going off down the railroad to humour it," hence a visit to Folkestone, which he hoped would help his sluggish thoughts, making his quarters at No. 3 Albion Villas, in "a very pleasant attic house, overlooking the sea." Here he spent the month of July, and in this quiet retreat, at a distance from the distractions of London, he soon became thoroughly absorbed in his book. On reaching the second number he felt dissatisfied with what he had written, and believed that he had missed an effect, this inclining him to begin all over again. From such intimations we may infer that (as Forster surmised) "the old, unstinted, irrepressible flow of fancy had received a temporary check," for the Novelist experienced exceptional trouble and labour in regard to the story. In August, while still at Folkestone, he wrote: "I am just now getting to work on No. 3: sometimes enthusiastic, more often dull enough. There is an enormous outlay in the Father of the Marshalsea chapter, in the way of getting a great lot of matter into a small space. I am not quite resolved, but I have a great idea of overwhelming that family with wealth. Their condition would be very curious. I can make Dorrit very strong in the story, I hope." With the number just referred to he made but slow progress, for we find him writing to W. H. Wills on September 16th that he was in the "hideous state of mind" resulting from "getting to work on No. 3 of the new book," rising and, falling by turns into enthusiasm and depression. In another letter of the same date he said: "You know my state of mind as well as I do. . . . How

I work, how I walk, how I shut myself up, how I roll down hills and climb up cliffs; how the new story is everywhere—heaving in the sea, flying with the clouds, blowing in the wind; how I settle to nothing, and wonder (in the old way) at my own incomprehensibility. . . ."[1] On the last day of the month he announced to Wilkie Collins that he had almost finished the number which had proved so very irksome. "Sticking at it day after day, I am the *in*completest letter writer imaginable—seem to have no idea of holding a pen for any other purpose than that book."[2] Indeed, he confessed to Macready that he had a horrible temptation, when laying down his "book-pen," to "run out on the breezy downs here, tear up the hills, slide down the same, and conduct myself in a frenzied manner, for the relief that only exercise gives me."[3]

An irresistible engagement recalled the Novelist to London in October of this year, namely, to preside at a dinner to Thackeray prior to his departure for America on a lecturing tour. More than sixty admirers of the eminent author assembled to do him honour, and Dickens, in a speech which gave happy expression to the spirit that animated all, told the guest of the evening how much they prized his friendship and how proud they were of his genius, offering him, "in the name of the tens of thousands absent who had never touched his hand or seen his face, lifelong thanks for the treasures of mirth, wit, and wisdom within the yellow-covered numbers of 'Pendennis' and 'Vanity Fair.'" Dickens had decided to spend the winter in Paris, and directly after

[1] "The Letters of Charles Dickens."
[2] Ibid.
[3] Ibid.

the send-off dinner to Thackeray he set out for the "gay city," which was so full that he had the greatest difficulty in meeting with suitable accommodation. "However," he wrote to his wife on the 16th of October, "we have found two apartments . . . at No. 49, Avenue des Champs Elysées . . . the front apartments all look upon the main street . . . and the view is delightfully cheerful. . . . I think the situation itself almost the finest in Paris; and the children will have a window from which to look on the busy life outside."[1] He acknowledged a sense of pride in finding himself generally known and liked in Paris, for whenever he entered a shop the proprietor brightened up and addressed him as "the celebrated writer, with the distinguished name—'*Monsieur Dick-in.*'" The sudden death of a friend again brought him to London before the close of the month, and one wet November night, prior to his return to France, he sallied out for a walk in the London streets, full of thoughts of "Little Dorrit," when a strange sight outside the door of a Whitechapel Workhouse arrested his attention. Against the dreary enclosure he saw what looked like heaps of rags, but which proved to he homeless girls— dumb, wet, silent horrors," as he described them, sphinxes set up against that dead wall, and no one likely to be at the pains of solving them until the General Overthrow." His kind heart saddened by the pathetic spectacle, he sent in his card to the master of the Workhouse who at once gave personal attention to the outcasts, but the casual ward being already full he was helpless; whereupon the Novelist gave a shilling to each of the wretched creatures, one of whom declared she had been without food for

[1] "The Letters of Charles Dickens."

four-and-twenty hours. This incident confirmed his views concerning the inefficient manner in which laws, meant to be most humane, are too often administered in England. A day or two later he again left for Paris, to resume his labours on "Little Dorrit."

Since his first public reading given at Birmingham two years before, Dickens had been besieged with requests for similar favours from various towns in England, Scotland, and Ireland in aid of public objects. In September of this year (1855) he told Forster that during the previous fortnight he had answered thirty applications of this nature, the majority of which he was compelled to reject. He stood pledged, however, to give a reading of the "Carol" at Sheffield in December following, in aid of the funds of the Mechanics' Institute, which still required help; this took place in the Mechanics' Hall on December 22nd, and at its conclusion the Mayor (on behalf of a few fellow townsmen) presented to the Novelist some useful items of Sheffield manufacture in the shape of a handsome service of table cutlery, a pair of razors, and a pair of fish carvers, offered for his acceptance as a proof of their gratitude—a gift which the recipient promised should be retained as an heirloom in his family.

Dickens made his home in Paris until the ensuing May. His absence abroad did not prevent him from taking his share of the editing of *Household Words*, and with such a faithful and trustworthy henchman as W. H. Wills, the purely mechanical portion of those responsibilities were minimised. Wills, of course, kept his "Chief" in touch with the more important details, and sought by letter his advice on particular matters. The preparation and planning of the Extra Christmas Number invariably constituted a subject for anxious consideration, and sometimes occasioned vexation. The Christmas Number for 1855 was entitled "The Holly-Tree Inn," to which Dickens contributed three chapters—The Guest, The Boots, and The Bill—the remainder being by Wilkie Collins. We must infer, from the following letter to Collins, that Dickens had enlisted the services of a third author, whose contribution did not meet with approval: "The botheration of that No. has been prodigious. The general matter was so disappointing, and so impossible to be fitted together or got into the frame, that after I had done the Guest and the Bill, and thought myself free for a little Dorrit again, I had to go back once more (feeling the thing too weak), and do the Boots. Look at said Boots; because I think it's an odd idea, and gets something of the effect of a Fairy Story out of the most unlikely materials." The story has reference to the elopement of two little children, boy and girl, of the mature ages of eight and seven respectively, who were determined to get married at Gretna Green; that such an apparently unlikely incident is within the bounds of probability is evidenced by the fact that a similar thing actually took place in Flintshire in 1884, when two children (a boy aged seven and a girl three years his junior) eloped in the selfsame fashion; the young gentleman arranged to meet the young lady at a distance from their respective homes, and, driving together to Wrexham, they proceeded to Liverpool. The distracted parents, obtaining a clue to their whereabouts, hurriedly followed them, and, after some exhortation and remonstrance, induced them to return home!

Dickens, during his residence in Paris, passed much of his leisure time in the company of artists and literary men, actors and musicians, while, as a relief from mental tension, he occasionally spent an evening at a theatre—a place of entertainment which ever attracted him—being vividly impressed by the fine performances of Frédérick Lemaitre and other distinguished thespians. As a sincere lover of good music, the opera also claimed a share of his attention, and at the house of that famous artiste, Madame Viardot (whom he held in the highest esteem), he had the fortune to meet Georges Sand, who proved to be singularly unlike his preconceptions of that illustrious writer. Shortly afterwards, Emile de Girardin gave a banquet in his honour, carried out with Oriental magnificence. To Ary Scheffer he sat for his portrait. "Conceive this, if you please (he said, addressing Wilkie Collins), with No. 5 [of "Little Dorrit"], upon my soul—four hours!! I am so addle headed and bored, that if you were here, I should propose an instantaneous rush to the Trois Frères. Under existing circumstances I have no consolation." The artist's brother, Henri, also attempted a portrait, and they both "pegged away" at him simultaneously, the sittings being varied by a special entertainment in the *atelier*, where Ary Scheffer received some sixty people, to whom, by urgent entreaty, Dickens read his "Cricket on the Hearth."

In December 1855 the first number of "Little Dorrit" duly appeared, and on January 22, 1856, Forster became the recipient of an exultant note from the Author stating that the sale of the initial instalment of the new story had beaten even 'Bleak House' out of the field." "It is a most tremendous start," he added, "and I am overjoyed at it." The demand for the second number proved equally satisfactory, no less than thirty-five thousand copies being sold on New Year's Day. On the eve of the publication of No. 3, the Novelist expressed himself as having a grim pleasure in wondering what effect it would make in certain quarters. This, it will be remembered, was the number which caused him infinite trouble in the composition, and concerning which, when nearing completion, he wrote to Wilkie Collins that in it he had relieved his indignant soul "with a scarifier," and to Macready that he "had been blowing off a little of indignant steam which would otherwise blow me up. . . ." It contained his famous attack upon the dilatory system of conducting public business by Government officials— a system which he aptly designated by the word "Circumlocution." Dr. A. W. Ward considers that "the mere name of the Circumlocution Office was a stroke of genius, one of those phrases of Dickens which Professor Masson justly describes as, whether exaggerated or not, 'efficacious for social reform.'" By this time the Novelist had obtained a thorough grip of the story: "My head really stings with the visions of the book," he wrote on January 30th, "and I am going, as the French say, to disembarrass it by plunging out into some of the strange places I glide into of nights in these latitudes." Throughout the year the publication continued in regular monthly instalments. That the Author was not always in a mood for work, however, is indicated by a letter written in April to Wilkie Collins: "The first blank page of 'Little Dorrit,' No. 8, now eyes me on the desk with a pressing curiosity. It will get nothing out of me today, I distinctly perceive."

During the winter the Novelist travelled

frequently from Paris to London on *Household Words* business, and a letter (dated the 14th of March 1856) written to Miss Hogarth from the office of that journal, on the occasion of one of these flying visits, is memorable for the reason that it notifies the completion of negotiations for the purchase of Gad's Hill Place, at Higham, near Rochester—negotiations which had been pending for some months. We are told that when quite a lad, living with his parents at Chatham, he frequently accompanied his father in walks to Rochester, Strood, Cobham, &c., and the "queer small boy" took quite a fancy to this homely, dignified looking residence standing near the Dover Road, on the summit of a hill about two miles from the western boundary of Strood; whereupon his father, seeing him so fond of it, often told him that if he were very persevering and worked hard, he might some day come to live in it![1] The redbrick building, with its bay windows, porch, dormers, and bell turret, is a familiar object to all travellers by road between Gravesend and Rochester. It was erected in 1779 by a then well-known character in those parts, a wealthy brewer named Thomas Stevens, whose daughter became the wife of John Prentis Henslow (father of the Cambridge Professor of Botany).[2] After Stevens had relinquished the brewery business he retired to his country seat at Gad's Hill, which subsequently was tenanted by the Rev. James Lynn, who, like Dickens, had fallen in love with the place when a youth, and resolved to buy it (if

[1] The story receives authentic confirmation in one of Dickens's minor writings, entitled Travelling Abroad, in "The Uncommercial Traveller."

[2] Memoir of Professor Henslow, by the Rev. L. Jenyns, M.A. Forster incorrectly states that Stevens was the *Father-in-law* of the Professor.

ever he could) when a man. The worthy clergyman, with his daughter (afterwards Mrs. Lynn Linton, the authoress), resided here for twenty-six years. Dickens had notified to his particular friends his desire to acquire this property and to make his home there. His long cherished dream was now to come true. Shortly after the death of the rector, in 1855, W. H. Wills (as one of the guests at a dinner party) sat next to Miss Lynn, when, in the course of a desultory conversation, he spoke to her about Gad's Hill Place, giving her to understand that he wished to buy it; the result was that, as the only unmarried daughter and the executrix under her father's will, she placed the matter in the hands of the family solicitor—her co-executor. Dickens was naturally informed of what had transpired, and business negotiations were at once commenced, so that, before many months had elapsed, he became the owner of this interesting and attractive domicile.[1] In the previously mentioned letter to Miss Hogarth, he said: "This day [March 14, 1856] I have paid the purchase money for Gad's Hill Place. After drawing the cheque, I turned round to give it to Wills (£1790), and said: 'Now, isn't it an extraordinary thing—look at the day—Friday! I have been nearly drawing it half-a-dozen times, when the lawyers have not been ready, and here it comes round upon a Friday, as a matter of course.'" He frequently remarked that all the important events of his life had happened to him on a Friday, which he and his family (contrary to the usual superstition) had come to regard as his

[1] ". . . I have always in passing looked to see if it was to be sold or let, and it has never been to me like any other house, and it has never changed at all." See "Letters of Charles Dickens" (M. de Cerjat, Jan. 17, 1857).

"lucky" day. He did not, however, obtain possession of the coveted house until the following February.

Leaving Paris at the beginning of May, in advance of his family, Dickens returned to Tavistock House, whence, on the fifth of that month, he wrote that he had not yet begun No. 8 of "Little Dorrit," having only just settled down in a corner of the schoolroom: "The extent to which John and I wallowed in dust for four hours yesterday morning, getting things neat and comfortable about us, you may faintly imagine."[1] His mind was a little distracted just now by thoughts of another play, and the subject having been broached to Stanfield, that artist called to discuss it with Dickens immediately on his arrival home. No sooner had the Novelist divulged his intention to the painter than the latter (who became immensely excited thereby) "immediately upset all my new arrangements by making a proscenium of chairs, and planning the scenery with walking-sticks." But the proposed play remained for the present in abeyance. In June Dickens again left London, paying a third visit to Boulogne, where the summer months were passed. Not a word of the ninth number of the new story had then been written, nor did he expect for another month to "see land from the running sea of 'Little Dorrit.'" He became once more the tenant of the kind-hearted Beaucourt, occupying the Villa des Moulineaux, and after industriously spending a few days in garden operations, donning the garb of a French farmer (blue blouse, leathern belt, and military cap)—the only costume (he averred) which ensured complete comfort for the wearer—he announced to Forster that

[1] "The Letters of Charles Dickens."

he was getting into harness again. "To work! The story lies before me, I hope, strong and clear. Not to be easily told; but nothing of that sort *is* to be easily done that *I* know of." It became customary, for him, during his literary labours here, to sit late at his desk, and then, postponing his usual walking exercise until night, to lie down among the roses reading until after tea ("middle-aged Love in a blouse and belt," as he humorously described himself), when he went down to the pier. Wilkie Collins was again his companion, and Douglas Jerrold stayed with him for a time. "It was here," says his eldest daughter, "that the Plorn [his youngest child, then about four years of age] would be carried about in his father's arms to admire the flowers, or as he got older trot along by his side. The remembrance of these two, hand in hand, the boy in his white frock and blue sash, walking down the avenue, always in deep conversation, is a memory inseparable from those summers at Boulogne." The Crimean War had just concluded, and referring to the subject generally the Novelist remarked: "Nobody at home has yet any adequate idea, I am deplorably sure, of what the Barnacles and the Circumlocution Office have done for us. But whenever we get into war again, the people will begin to find out." As a change from graver occupations, he and Wilkie Collins turned their attention at intervals to the development of the private theatrical project then in contemplation, and the task of preparing the new drama fell to Wilkie Collins, Dickens undertaking to sketch a farce for Mark Lemon to fill in. Unhappily, this congenial employment was suddenly interrupted by the breaking out of an epidemic in the town, necessitating a speedy flight on the part of Dickens, his family and friends, who left the disconsolate Beaucourt in grief at their premature departure.

The Christmas Number of *Household Words* for this year was planned by Dickens and Collins during the summer holiday. The number is entitled "The Wreck of the Golden Mary," Dickens being responsible for the first of the three chapters of which it consists—"The Wreck"—and Collins for the remainder. The prototype of "Golden Lucy" in this little romance was Lucy Stroughill, the daughter of a neighbour of the Dickens family in the Chatham days, the golden-haired child being the little sweetheart of the then youthful Charles.[1]

As soon as Dickens and his family had settled down in Tavistock House for the winter, the Novelist's thoughts were divided between his book and the forthcoming theatricals. He informed Mrs. Watson that, owing to the exacting nature of his literary work, he sometimes fancied he had "a digestion, or a head, or nerves, or some odd encumbrance of that kind,"[2] and this obliged him to rush at some other object of relief, which he found in these dramatic entertainments. "The preparations for the play are already beginning," he wrote to his daughter Mamie on 4th October, "and it is christened (this is a dramatic secret, which I suppose you know already) 'The Frozen Deep.'"[3] It was to be produced on Twelfth Night, his son Charles's birthday, and he described how, three months beforehand, the transformation of the schoolroom was being effected, in view of the performances, by a posse of carpenters, and how "men

[1] "The Childhood and Youth of Charles Dickens," by Robert Langton.
[2] "The Letters of Charles Dickens."
[3] Ibid.

from underground habitations in theatres, who looked as if they lived entirely upon smoke and gas," met him at unheard of hours. "Mr. Stanfield is perpetually measuring the boards with a chalked piece of string and an umbrella, and all the elder children are wildly punctual and businesslike to attract managerial commendation."[1] As the time for the performances drew near, excitement at Tavistock House increased, and it is not surprising to learn that Dickens began to feel the effect of the numerous responsibilities and distractions now crowding upon him. "You may faintly imagine, my venerable friend," he wrote to Macready on December 13th, "the occupation of these also grey hairs, between 'Golden Marys,' 'Little Dorrits,' 'Household Wordses,' four stage-carpenters entirely boarding on the premises, a carpenter's shop erected in the back garden, size always boiling over on all the lower fires, Stanfield perpetually elevated on planks and splashing himself from head to foot, Telbin requiring impossibilities of smart gasmen, and a legion of prowling nondescripts for ever shrinking in and out. Calm amidst the wreck, your aged friend glides away on the 'Dorrit' stream, forgetting the uproar for a stretch of hours, refreshing himself with a ten or twelve miles' walk, pitches headforemost into foaming rehearsals, placidly emerges for editorial purposes, smokes over buckets of distemper with Mr. Stanfield aforesaid, again calmly floats upon the 'Dorrit' waters."[2] Thus we see that, notwithstanding the topsy-turveydom of the general domestic arrangements —with "a painter's shop in the schoolroom; a gasfitter's shop all over the basement; a dressmaker's

---

[1] "The Letters of Charles Dickens."
[2] Ibid.

shop at the top of the house; a tailor's shop in my dressing-room"—the writing of 'Little Dorrit' perforce continued, in order that the public might receive the usual monthly number, the Author meanwhile being compelled to ensconce himself in sundry available corners of his establishment, "like the Sultan's groom, who was turned upside-down by the genie."[1] The babel of noise continued for weeks, during which period the house was in a state of siege. No trouble or expense was spared in overcoming difficulties which presented themselves, as testified when, a certain contingency having arisen, the services of Mr. Cooke (from Astley's Amphitheatre) had been requisitioned by Dickens. One morning that gentleman—a man of much resource—drove up to the Novelist's house in an open phaeton drawn by two white ponies with black spots all over them (evidently stencilled), and the striking cavalcade went in at the gate of Tavistock Square with a little jolt and a rattle exactly as if they were entering the ring at the theatre, "and went round and round the centre bed of the front court, apparently looking for the clown, much to the delight of the youthful crowd that swarmed over the railings." The Novelist required advice as to obtaining more space both for audience and actors, but Mr. Cooke proved unequal to the occasion, and "might just as well have been the popular minister from the Tabernacle in Tottenham Court Road."

The New Year (1857) opened with the theatrical business still in full swing. Special invitations were despatched to friends to witness the performances, and the pressure for admittance to the

---

[1] Dickens was fond of quoting from "The Arabian Nights' Entertainments."

miniature auditorium became so great that the difficulty of providing the requisite accommodation severely taxed the resources of even such a tactful manager as Dickens. "My audience is now 93," he wrote to Forster in despair, "and at least 10 will neither hear nor see"; so there was no alternative but to increase the number of nights. The eventful day at length arrived, and the excellence of the performances became the talk of all London; indeed, the result was so remarkable that Dickens doubted if anything so complete as that play would ever be seen again. The rhyming prologue to "The Frozen Deep" was composed by him and recited by Forster; at the public performances a little later, Dickens himself recited the prologue. As to the play, the Novelist confessed (in an interesting letter to Sir James Emerson Tennant) that he "derived a strange feeling out of it, like writing a book in company; a satisfaction of a most singular kind, which has no exact parallel in my life; a something that I suppose to belong to a labourer in art alone, and which has to me a conviction of its being actual truth without its pain, that I never could adequately state if I were to try never so hard." He also opined that its preparation constituted a remarkable lesson for the young members of the company "in patience, perseverance, punctuality, and order; and, best of all, in that kind of humility which is got from the earnest knowledge that whatever the right hand finds to do must be done with the heart in it, and in a desperate earnest."[1] The performances over, it became necessary to restore the house to its normal state, and immediate measures were taken to remove the stage and other paraphernalia. On the 17th of January the

---

[1] "The Letters of Charles Dickens."

place had become "a mere chaos of scaffolding, ladders, beams, canvases, paint pots, sawdust, artificial snow, gas pipes, and ghastliness," and the prime instigator of all, after devoting the leisure time of ten weeks to rehearsals, &c., felt as though he were shipwrecked. By the 28th the little theatre and its appurtenances had entirely disappeared; whereupon he was enabled to announce to Macready the satisfactory intelligence that "the house is restored to its usual conditions of order, the family are tranquil and domestic, dove-eyed peace is enthroned in this study, fire-eyed radicalism in its master's breast. . . . Your friend and servant is as calm as Pecksniff, saving for his knitted brows now turning into cordage over 'Little Dorrit.'"[1]

In April the Novelist stayed, with his wife and sister-in-law, for a week or two at Wate's Hotel, Gravesend, to be at hand to superintend the beginning of his alterations at Gad's Hill Place, whither he relocated as a summer residence in June. One of the first visitors to his ever-delightful Kentish abode was Hans Christian Andersen, and a host of beloved friends whom he then invited thither ("where cigars and lemons grew on all the trees") included Sir Joseph Paxton, the famous landscape gardener and designer of the Crystal Palace. Hans Andersen, in recalling his most pleasing impressions of Gad's Hill Place and its distinguished occupant, contributed to *Temple Bar* (December 1870) some interesting reminiscences of this time: "As I was stepping into the house," he says, "Dickens came out to meet me, with bright looks and a hearty greeting . . . His eyes were bright as ever; the smile on his lips was the same; his frank

[1] "The Letters of Charles Dickens."

voice was just as friendly—ay, and if possible, more
winning still. He was now in the prime of manhood, in
his forty-fifth year; full of youth and life and
eloquence, and rich in a rare humour that glowed with
kindliness. I know not how to describe him better than
in the words of one of my first letters home: 'Take the
best out of all Dickens's writings, combine them into
the picture of a man, and there thou hast Charles
Dickens.' And such as in the first hour he stood before
me, the very same he remained all the time of my visit;
ever genuine, and cheerful, and sympathetic. The
room in which we and some of the children sat down
to breakfast was a model of comfort and holiday
brightness. The windows were overhung, outside, with
a profusion of blooming roses; and one looked out
over the garden to green fields and the hills beyond
Rochester.'"

At Gad's Hill "Little Dorrit" was completed, and
Dickens thus joyfully disclosed the important fact to
Wilkie Collins: "Thank God, I *have* finished. On
Sunday last I wrote the two little words of three letters
each." The story contained forty etched illustrations by
H. K. Browne, and a Dedication to Clarkson Stanfield,
R.A. Although meeting with an excellent reception,
the book cannot justly be placed on an equality with
his most successful efforts, and even Forster considered that, on the whole, it made no material addition to
the Author's reputation. The Circumlocution Office
passages, however, call forth our sincere admiration,
while the chapters appertaining to the Marshalsea are
in the true Dickensian vein, as might be expected from
one who had so accurate a knowledge of that debtors'
prison, in depicting which he relied upon a
marvellous memory, this enabling him to recall
some experiences of his childhood for his

pictures of life within that gloomy structure. In the preface he tells us that after the last chapter had been written he decided to renew acquaintance with the place which possessed so many depressing associations, for the purpose of ascertaining whether any part of the building remained, and, although it had undergone considerable change, he could identify the portion in which was preserved the chamber he had in his mind's eye when he became Little Dorrit's biographer. Writing half jocosely to Forster, he said: "There is a room there—still standing, to my amazement—that I think of taking! It is the room through which the ever-memorable signers of Captain Porter's petition filed off in my boyhood. The spikes are gone, and the wall is lowered, and anybody can go out now who likes to go, and is not bedridden." The Marshalsea, the smallest of the debtors' prisons, ceased to be used as such in 1849, and was partly demolished some years before Dickens's preface appeared; a fragment of the old building may still be seen on the north side of St. George's Church, Southwark, and to this surviving wall are attached large enamelled tablets recording the fact that it "marks the site of the old Marshalsea Prison, made famous by Charles Dickens in his well-known 'Little Dorrit.'" The remains of the gaol, with the exception of this wall, were pulled down in 1887, and a clearance has recently been made close by, as an open space for public recreation, which the local authorities have appropriately christened "Little Dorrit's playground," in memory of the Novelist's heroine.

The portrait of Flora Finching, in "Little Dorrit," was derived from the same living original as the Dora of "David Copperfield," although it finds an entirely different development in the later story. Dickens, besides highly enjoying his conception of Mr. F.'s Aunt, was very partial to Flora and her surroundings. As a further proof of the reality with which he viewed the creatures of his imagination, he wrote to Forster: "There are some things in Flora in No. 7 that seem to me to be extraordinarily droll, with something serious at the bottom of them after all . . . Nothing in Flora made me laugh so much as the confusion of ideas between gout flying upwards, and its soaring with Mr. F—— to another sphere." Forster, in a spirit of fun, used to tell Dickens that he (Forster) had no belief in any but the fictitious Dora, until the incident of a sudden reappearance of the real one in the Novelist's life, nearly six years after he had written "Copperfield," and when "Little Dorrit" was just begun: this convinced him that there had been a more actual foundation for those chapters in his former story than his biographer previously imagined.[1] "I am so glad you like Flora," wrote Dickens to the Duke of Devonshire. "It came into my head one day that we have all had our Floras, and that it was a half serious, half ridiculous truth which had never been told. It is a wonderful gratification to me to find that everybody knows her. Indeed, some people seem to think I have done them a personal injury, and that their individual Floras (God knows where they are, or who!) are each and all Little Dorrit's."[2] In his preface, the Novelist confides to us the interesting fact that the "extravagant conception of Mr. Merdle originated after the Railroad share epoch, in the times of a certain Irish bank, and of one or two other equally laudable enterprises."

[1] *See* footnote, p. 191.
[2] "The Letters of Charles Dickens."

He informed Forster that he "shaped" Mr. Merdle himself from "that precious rascality," John Sadleir, an Irish banker, who, in consequence of financial difficulties, committed suicide on Hampstead Heath.[1] Although Dickens usually disregarded anonymous criticisms in the public press, he could not well ignore an attack made upon him by a writer in the *Edinburgh Review*, who, in a caustic article, accused him of selecting "one or two popular cries of the day, to serve as seasoning to the dish which he sets before his readers," and reproached him for his "unjust" and "cruel" imputations against the Government, the judges, and private individuals; he further suggested that the catastrophe in the thirty-first chapter was "evidently borrowed from the recent fall of houses in Tottenham Court Road [Messrs. Maple's], which happens to have appeared in the newspapers at a convenient moment."[2] Needless to observe, Dickens had no difficulty in defending himself against this skilful diatribe, and inserted a spirited rejoinder in *Household Words*, refuting the critic's various misstatements, pointing out that, so far as the fall of houses in Tottenham Court Road was concerned, the disaster referred to in the tale was "carefully prepared for from the very first presentation of the old house in the story . . . that the catastrophe was written, was engraven on steel, was printed, had passed through the hands of compositors, readers for the press, and pressmen, and was in type and in proof . . . before the accident in Tottenham Court Road occurred."[1]

[1] Mr. Percy Fitzgerald points out that there is a slight confusion of dates here, as the Railroad share epoch occurred long before the days of the Tipperary bank with which Sadleir was connected.

[2] "The License of Modern Novelists," in *Edinburgh Review*, July 1857.

A reply so convincing brought forth a semi-apologetic "Note" in the succeeding number of the *Edinburgh Review*, thus proving the unassailability of the Author's vindication.

[1] Curious Misprint in the *Edinburgh Review* (*Household Words*, August 1, 1857).

# CHAPTER 11

# "A TALE OF TWO CITIES"

That the year 1857 was replete with activities is fully shown in Dickens's published letters. Besides his literary work, the Novelist devoted much of his time and attention this year to alterations and improvements at Gad's Hill Place, of which he took possession in February, subscribing himself in a letter announcing the fact as "the Kentish Freeholder on his native heath, his name Protection." He relocated his family here for a summer residence early in June, and it was then that a great shock befell him in the unexpected death of Douglas Jerrold. He at once proposed a memorial tribute to his dear friend, and organised a series of entertainments, consisting mainly of theatrical performances both in London and the provinces, in which he and some of Jerrold's colleagues on *Punch* took part, the amateur company being strengthened by professional talent, including that of Mrs. Compton and T. P. Cooke. Dickens also gave three readings of the "Christmas Carol" at St. Martin's Hall, in aid of the Jerrold fund, and so successful were these that the idea of giving public readings for his own benefit then first occurred to him.[1] Both Thackeray and Dr. W. H.

[1] "The St. Martin's Hall audience was, I must confess, a very extraordinary thing. The two thousand and odd people were like one, and their enthusiasm was something awful."—*Letter from Dickens to Macready*, July 13, 1857.

Russell (the well-known war correspondent) lectured in support of this project. The fund was still further augmented by a special performance of "The Frozen Deep" at the Gallery of Illustration in July, by express desire of her late Majesty Queen Victoria (who, with the Prince Consort, attended the representation), the financial result of the enterprise, which was carried to a close with commendable vigour and promptitude, fully realising Dickens's expectations, the money thus procured being invested ultimately for Jerrold's unmarried daughter. "My gracious Sovereign," wrote Dickens, directly after the performance, "was so pleased that she sent round begging me to go and see her and accept her thanks. I replied that I was in my farce dress, and must beg to be excused, whereupon she sent again, saying that the dress 'could not be so ridiculous as that,' and repeating the request. I sent my duty in reply, but again hoped that her Majesty would have the goodness to excuse my presenting myself in a costume and appearance that were not my own." The objection to making himself "a motley to the view" of Queen Victoria was natural enough, and her Majesty, with her usual tact and consideration, yielded to his reluctance; but thirteen years elapsed before the Queen had another opportunity of personally, expressing her thanks.

Thus passed the greater part of the summer. In July, the Novelist's second son, Walter Landor, went to India as a cadet in the East India Company's service (from which he was afterwards transferred to the 42nd Royal Highlanders), and the youth was accompanied by his father and elder brother to Southampton, where they wished him Godspeed. Dickens felt the parting sorely, and, *apropos* of this family incident, thus wrote from Southampton to his friend Edmund Yates: "I have come here on an errand which will grow familiar to you before you know that Time has flapped his wings over your head. Like me, you will find those babies grow to be young men before you are quite sure they are born. Like me, you will have great teeth drawn with a wrench, and will only then know that you ever cut them. I am here to send Walter away over what they call, in Green Bush melodramas, I 'the Big Drink,' and I don't at all know this day how he comes to be mine, or I his."[1]

In September Dickens went away for a week or so with Wilkie Collins, on a "tour in search of an article" for *Household Words*. At the end of August he broached the subject to Collins in the following letter: "Partly in the grim despair and restlessness of this subsidence from excitement, and partly for *Household Words*, I want to cast about whether you and I can go anywhere—take any tour—see anything—whereon we could write something together. Have you any idea tending to any place in the world? Will you rattle your head and see if there is any pebble in it which we could wander away and play at marbles with? We want something for *Household Words*, and I want to escape from myself. For, when I *do* start up and stare myself seedily in the face, as happens to be my case at present, my blankness is inconceivable—indescribable—my misery amazing. . . ." "We have not the least idea where we are going; but *he* says, 'Lets look at the Norfolk coast,' and *I* say, 'Let's look at the back of the Atlantic.' I don't quite know what I mean by that; but have a general

[1] "The Letters of Charles Dickens."

impression that I mean something knowing." As intimated by the Novelist, this little expedition with
Wilkie Collins was to be partly regarded as a holiday
trip, by which he hoped for a brief respite from his
literary labours and to enjoy a little repose now that the
theatricals and readings were over. He confessed that
he was "horribly used up after the Jerrold business:
low spirits, low pulse, low voice, intense reaction." "If
I were not like Mr. Micawber, 'falling back for a
spring' on Monday," he added, "I think I should slink
into a corner and cry."[1] A day or two later he
announced the intention to Forster of indulging in an
excursion to "out-of-the-way places, to do (in inns and
coast corners) a little tour in search of an article and in
avoidance of railroads. I must get a good name for it,
and I propose it in five articles, one for the beginning
of every number in the October part." The decision
arrived at was "for a foray upon the fells of
Cumberland," Dickens having discovered in the
guidebooks "some promising moors and bleak places
thereabout." For the lake-country the two friends
departed accordingly, in September, and during the
peregrination they had some whimsical experiences,
the relation of which formed the subject of letters
home. Among other adventures they (with the landlord
of the little inn) climbed Carrick Fell in a downpour of
rain accompanied by a black mist, and on the return
journey (not devoid of danger) Wilkie Collins fell into
a rivulet and seriously sprained his ankle, which accident considerably increased the difficulty of the
descent, for it necessitated getting the sufferer
painfully on, shoving, shouldering, carrying alternately, till *terra firma* was reached. They arrived at last

---

[1] "The Letters of Charles Dickens."

in a wild, outlandish place, and, the landlord being despatched for a dogcart, so got back to the inn. "Shoe or stocking on the bad foot, out of the question. Foot tumbled up in a flannel waistcoat. C. D. carrying C. melodramatically . . . everywhere; into and out of carriages; up and down stairs; to bed; every step. And so to Wigton, got doctor, and here we are!! A pretty business, we flatter ourselves!" Wherever the Novelist went he was recognised and honoured, and, writing to Miss Hogarth from Lancaster, he said that she would hardly be prepared for the proportions which such homage to the "Inimitable" assumed in the North. "Stationmasters assist him to alight from carriages, deputations await him in hotel entries, innkeepers bow down before him and put him into regal rooms, the town goes down to the platform to see him off, and Collins's ankle goes into the newspapers!!!"[1] On their way home the friends stayed at the "Angel" Hotel, Doncaster; it was race-week and the noise and tumult and general vagabondage which such events bring forth impressed Dickens by no means favourably. Here, a "wonderful, paralysing, coincidence" (as he termed it) befell him. On the St. Leger day he purchased a race card, facetiously wrote down three names for the winners of the three chief races (never in his life having heard of any of the horses, except that one—a Derby winner, which proved to be a "rank outsider" in this instance—had been mentioned to him) "and, if you can believe it without your hair standing on end, those three races were won, one after the other, by those three horses!!!" The circumstances attending this horseracing business were so repellent that Dickens felt convinced that "if a boy with any

[1] "The Letters of Charles Dickens."

good in him, but with a dawning propensity to sporting and betting, were but brought to the Doncaster races soon enough, it would cure him."

The narrative of their expedition appeared in *Household Words* during the month of October, under the title of "The Lazy Tour of Two Idle Apprentices." To four out of the five chapters of which the record consists Dickens contributed a considerable portion, while Wilkie Collins was responsible for the remainder of those chapters, and (according to Forster) for the whole of the fifth, although it is certain that portions of the latter (such as the description of Doncaster and the races) indicate the master hand of "Boz." They similarly collaborated in producing the Extra Christmas Number of *Household Words* for this year, entitled "The Perils of Certain English Prisoners, and Their Treasure in Women, Children, Silver, and Jewels"—a simple narrative, in three chapters, suggested by the Cawnpore and Lucknow tragedies, then engrossing public attention. The first and third instalments—viz., The Island of Silver Store and The Rafts on the River—were written by Dickens, and the rest by Collins, who sketched the plot with the aid of hints and suggestions from his coadjutor. At the conclusion of the "lazy" tour, the Novelist returned to Gad's Hill for a brief spell, and then spent the winter months at Tavistock House.

In recounting the incidents appertaining to Dickens's life at this period, Forster makes a marked reference to that restlessness of spirit which, for some time, had been obvious to his friends, and to which, indeed, the Novelist himself called attention in certain of his letters. In 1857, this mental perturbation had become almost habitual. He failed to find in his

own domestic circle the satisfactions which home
should have supplied, and, disliking what is called
"Society," often took as much pains to keep out of the
houses of fashionable people as other folk take in
order to gain access to them. Certain misgivings
respecting his powers of invention, first felt during the
composition of "Little Dorrit," tended to increase the
trouble from which he evidently suffered, and he now
realised the necessity, for the first and only time in his
life, of making notes as memoranda for characters or
incidents to aid him when writing, his usually teeming
fancy now seeming to require such help. "He could no
longer fill a widespread canvas with the same facility
and certainty as of old; and he had frequently a
quite unfounded apprehension of some possible
breakdown, of which the end might be at any moment
beginning." Besides those intervals of unusual
impatience and strange restlessness, he greatly
surprised his intimates by relinquishing old pursuits in
favour of other forms of excitement, such as politics
and theatricals; into the latter he again entered with a
vigour so indomitable and sustained that even
experienced actors could not but behold with
astonishment the energy he displayed. Remonstrance,
as yet, was unavailing. "Too late to say, put the curb
on," was his pathetic response to an urgent appeal to
conserve himself; "I have now no relief but in action.
I am become incapable of rest. I am quite confident I
should rust, break, and die if I spared myself.
Much better to die, doing. What I am in that
way, nature made me first, and my way of life has
of late, alas, confirmed. I must accept the
drawback—since it is one—with the powers I
have; and I must hold upon the tenure prescribed

to me." He desired intensely to get away somewhere altogether by himself—to spend half a year or so in all sorts of inaccessible places, and opening a new book therein; a "floating idea" hovered about him of living in some convent above the snowline in Switzerland— in fact, if *Household Words* could be got into a goods train he did not know in what strange place he might resume work. "*Restlessness*, you will say. Whatever it is, it is always driving me, and I cannot help it. . . . If I couldn't walk fast and far, I should just explode and perish." On another occasion he said: "It is much better to go on and fret than to stop and fret. As to repose—for some men there's no such thing in this life." Then came the mournful aspiration: "The old days—the old days! Shall I ever, I wonder, get the frame of mind back as it used to be then? Something of it perhaps—but never quite as it used to be. I find that the skeleton in my domestic closet is becoming a pretty big one!" Here, then, we have an inkling as to the reason of this restlessness and impatience, the origin of which was not fully revealed until after his return to England in 1857, when he relieved his mind by confiding to Forster the truth of the matter over which he had so long been brooding. No biographer of Dickens can entirely avoid referring to the cause of the unhappiness which overshadowed the last few years of his marvellous career, and which startled the world at large as much as it grieved those who were near and dear to him. After twenty years of wedded life, Charles Dickens concluded that he and his wife—the mother of his children—were "not made for each other." "It is not only that she makes me uneasy and unhappy," he explained, "but that I make her so too—and much more so. . . . Her temperament will not go with mine. It mattered not so much when we had only ourselves to consider, but reasons have been growing since which makes it all but hopeless that we should even try to struggle on. . . ."[1] He claimed no immunity from blame. "There is plenty of fault on my side, I daresay, in the way of a thousand uncertainties, caprices, and difficulties of disposition; but only one thing will alter all that, and that is, the end which alters everything." Attempts were made by his friends to adjust the unfortunate difference that had arisen, but their efforts proved fruitless, circumstances being unfavourable to such a course. In May of the following year (1858) Dickens and his wife mutually agreed to separate, the eldest son going to live with his mother at her express wish, and the other children remaining with their father. Forster alludes but slightly to the painful theme, for he regarded it as an arrangement of a strictly private nature, and so it would doubtless have remained but for the appearance in the *New York Tribune* of a confidential communication addressed by Dickens to Mr. Arthur Smith, authorising him to correct certain false rumours and scandals. The publication of what the Novelist afterwards referred to as the "violated letter" naturally attracted much attention and gave rise to so many untruthful statements, that the Novelist, exasperated by some miserable gossip

[1] "The happiness I had vaguely anticipated once, was not the happiness I enjoyed, and there was always something wanting . . . what I missed, I still regarded—I always regarded—as something that had been a dream of my youthful fancy; that was capable of realisation; that I was now discovering it to be so, with some natural pain, as all men did."— *See* "David Copperfield," chp. 68.

which he ought to have treated with contempt, decided
to send forth a statement respecting this unfortunate
conjugal incompatibility,[1] which naturally gave it a far
wider publicity than would otherwise have been the
case.[2]

That there were intermutual mistakes is probable
enough, and this assumption will account for the fact
that some of Dickens's friends remained loyal to him,
while others considered his wife the aggrieved party.
Edmund Yates, when referring to the subject in his
reminiscences, says: "It had been obvious to those
visiting at Tavistock House that, for some time, the
relations between host and hostess had been somewhat
strained; but this state of affairs was generally ascribed
to the irritability of the literary temperament on
Dickens's part, and on Mrs. Dickens's side to a little
love of indolence and ease, such as, however
provoking to their husbands, is not uncommon among
middle-aged matrons with large families. But it was
never imagined that the affair would assume the
dimensions of a public scandal. . . . Dickens had the
faults, as well as the virtues, of the literary character. .
. . He was full of the irritability, the sensitiveness, and
the intolerance of dullness which might have been
expected. If his temperament had been more rigid,
more severe; if he had not given such prominence
in his thoughts to the link which bound him to the
public whom he served so splendidly, he would

---

[1] In "David Copperfield," seven years previously, Dickens had
significantly written: "There can be no disparity in marriage like unsuit-
ability of mind and purpose" (Chp. 45.). "It would have been better for
me if my wife could have helped me more, and shared the many thoughts
in which I had no partner . . ." (Chp. 68.).

[2] The article, headed "Personal," occupied the front page of
*Household Words*, June 12, 1858. Mrs. Dickens died in November 1879,
thus surviving her husband nearly nine and a-half years.

not, in this particular affair, have acted as he did." The unhappy subject may be justly dismissed in these words of Mr. Yates: "The two leading personages in this little drama are dead, and I fail to see the necessity or expediency of recalling various details."[1]

For Dickens to concentrate his mind upon the writing of a book under such harassing circumstances would have been impossible, and we can understand why he welcomed the opportunity of opening up another field of labour and of resuscitating an old project. Writing to Forster from Gad's Hill, before the close of 1857, he said "What do you think of my paying for this place [not yet his permanent home] "by reviving that old idea of some readings from my books. I am very strongly tempted. Think of it." As on the previous occasion when the scheme respecting public readings was submitted, Forster would not countenance it, for he regarded it as "a substitution of lower for higher aims—a change to commonplace from more elevated pursuits;" in short, he considered it derogatory, and that the realisation of such a project would militate against Dickens's dignity as a writer— an opinion in the communication of which he did not stand alone. It is conceivable that Dickens believed that the excitement he would derive from public readings might act as a palliative in causing him to forget, for the nonce, his domestic troubles. Before committing himself to the venture, he sought the advice of intimate friends, some of whom raised objections, but, as will presently be seen, these were overruled by force of circumstances, and the Novelist had his way.

Early in 1858 Dickens performed a particularly

[1] "Edmund Yates: His Recollections and Experiences," 1885.

kind act. Funds were sorely needed for the maintenance of a Hospital for Sick Children in Great Ormond Street, London; whereupon it was resolved to make a public dinner the excuse for a charitable appeal, at which the Novelist was elected to preside. The dinner accordingly took place on February 9th, and, with characteristic energy, he entered heart and soul into the service, the speech which he delivered from the chair proving to be one of the most impressive ever uttered by him, and so persuasive and convincing that the funds were augmented that night by the handsome sum of three thousand pounds. To crown the good work, he gave (on April 15th) another reading of the "Carol," in aid of this admirable institution, thus placing it in a firm financial position. On March 26th he read aloud the same little allegory in Edinburgh, before the members and subscribers of the Philosophical Institution, and at its conclusion the Lord Provost presented him with a massive silver wassail cup—a tribute appropriately acknowledged by him in a few words. The extraordinary success of this reading, and of that which followed it in aid of the Children's Hospital, bore down all opposition to the suggestion of his engaging publicly in such readings for himself, and determined him to embark upon the enterprise he had so long looked upon with approbation. Exactly a fortnight after the hospital reading came the first reading for his own benefit, at St. Martin's Hall, and in a short prefatory address he said that, among other reasons which led him to adopt this course, he considered it a good thing for a public man like himself to be brought face to face with the public, on terms of mutual confidence and respect. The experiment was followed by fifteen

Gad's Hill Place, Near Rochester

From the Garden at the rear.  Residence of Charles Dickens, 1857-1870

*Photographed by Catharine Weed Ward*

Gad's Hill Place

The Tunnel under Dover Road — One of Charles
Dickens's important improvement

*Photographed by Catharine Weed Ward*

other readings in the same building, the last on July 22nd, and the entire series met with marked approbation.

Meanwhile improvements were being effected at Gad's Hill Place, of which continued ownership brought increased liking. In an interesting letter written to M. de Cerjat on July 7th, he said: "At this present moment I am on my little Kentish freehold . . . looking on as pretty a view out of my study window as you will find in a long day's English ride. My little place is a grave red-brick house, which I have added to and stuck bits upon in all manner of ways, so that it is as pleasantly irregular, and as violently opposed to all architectural ideas, as the most hopeful man could possibly desire. The robbery was committed before the door, on the man with the treasure, and Falstaff ran away from the identical spot of ground now covered by the room in which I write.[1] A little rustic alehouse, called the Sir John Falstaff, is over the way—has been over the way, ever since, in honour of the event. Cobham, Woods and Park are behind the house; the distant Thames in front; the Medway, with Rochester, and its old castle and cathedral, on one side. The whole stupendous property is on then old Dover Road.

"The blessed woods and fields have done me a

[1] Gad's Hill (Shakespeare's Gad's Hill) was notorious for robbers in the poet's time. The allusion here is to the incident recorded in Shakespeare's "King Henry the Fourth," Act 1. scene 2, where Poins says (addressing Falstaff, Prince Henry, and others): "But, my lads, my lads, tomorrow morning by four o'clock early at Gad's Hill. There are pilgrims going to Canterbury with rich offerings, and traders riding to London with fat purses; I have vizards for you all; you have horses for yourselves." At Dickens's request, this quotation was handsomely illuminated by Owen Jones, and placed in the entrance hall at Gad's Hill, where it may still be seen.

world of good, and I am quite myself again. The children are all as happy as children can be. My eldest daughter, Mary, keeps house, with a state and gravity becoming that high condition; wherein she is assisted by her sister Katie, and by her aunt Georgina, who is, and always has been, like another sister. Two big dogs, a bloodhound and a St. Bernard, direct from a convent of that name . . . are their principal attendants in the green lanes."[1]

During this year, from the end of April (when the public readings commenced), Dickens was constantly travelling from place to place, the reading tours covering England, Scotland, and Ireland. He informed M. de Cerjat that he would read at least four or five times a week; "it will be sharp work, but probably a certain musical clinking will come of it, which will mitigate the hardship."[2] There were, in all, four series of readings; the first took place in 1858-59, under Mr. Arthur Smith's management; the second in 1861-63, under that of Mr. Headland; the third and fourth in 1866-67 and 1868-70 respectively, these being organised by Mr. George Dolby on behalf of Messrs. Chappell. The first provincial tour comprised eighty-seven readings, beginning at Clifton on August 2nd, and concluding at Brighton on November 13th, to which were added three Christmas readings in December. Forster gives the following synopsis of a single day's work (quoted from one of the letters written in August of that year), thus clearly indicating the amount of fatigue involved, which must have been enormous: "On Friday we came from Shrewsbury

[1] "The Letters of Charles Dickens."
[2] Ibid.

to Chester; saw all right for the evening; and then went to Liverpool. Came back from Liverpool and read at Chester. Left Chester at 11 at night, after the reading, and went to London. Got to Tavistock House at 5 a.m. on Saturday, left it at a quarter-past 10 that morning, and came down here [Gad's Hill]." The numerous epistles addressed to members of his home circle and to his friends when on tour amply testify to the marked enthusiasm, as well as personal affection and respect, which greeted him wherever he went. In the early days of the readings his voice often partly failed him, for he had not then acquired the art of husbanding it, and in attempting to recover the lost power, he would test it by singing Irish melodies to himself as he walked about. The story of the public readings has been amply recorded by Forster and George Dolby, as well as by the Novelist himself in his correspondence, all these sources of information affording most interesting matter for perusal. The subjects of the readings were specially condensed by himself from his books, and the first series included "A Christmas Carol," "The Chimes," "The Trial from 'Pickwick,'" "The Story of Paul Dombey," "Boots at the Holly-Tree Inn," "The Poor Traveller," and "Mrs. Gamp," the most popular of all being the "Carol."[1] The net profits which accrued to him were substantial enough, varying from three hundred to five hundred pounds weekly, while he had the satisfaction of knowing that, contrary to

[1] The adaptations were printed and published, and the sale of the little green covered volumes yielded Dickens a good profit. When reading at Manchester, he said that the city "became green with the little tracts, in every bookshop, outside every omnibus, and passing along every street."

Forster's anticipations, the readings materially
increased the sale of his books,

With the greater part of the year 1858
monopolised by the readings, it is not surprising that
the Novelist had but little opportunity for literary
work. *Household Words* naturally required the usual
amount of attention, and in September the subject for
the Extra Christmas Number began to engage his
thoughts. He conceived the idea of publishing it in the
form of a collection of stories under the general title of
"A House to Let," one of which, called "Going into
Society," emanated from his pen, it being practically
his only contribution to literature during this year.
Certain social obligations, which so prominent a man
as he could not avoid, also demanded a share of his
leisure time. In addition to presiding at the anniversary
festival of the Hospital for Sick Children (as already
recorded), he attended the dinner held on the thirteenth
anniversary of the General Theatrical Fund, and on
that occasion the chair was occupied by Thackeray, to
whom the Novelist, in a stimulating speech, paid a
warm public tribute. After declaring that the Fund
never had, and never could have, a greater lustre cast
upon it than by the imposing presence of that
"noble English writer," Dickens thus continued: "It is
not for me at this time, and in this place, to take on
myself to flutter before you the well thumbed pages of
Mr. Thackeray's books, and to tell you to observe
how full they are of wit and wisdom, how out
speaking, and how devoid of fear and favour; but I will
take leave to remark, in paying my due homage and
respect to them, that it is fitting that such a writer and
such an institution should be brought together. Every
writer of fiction, although he may not adopt the

dramatic form, writes in effect for the stage. He may never write plays; but the truth and passion which are in him must be more or less reflected in the great mirror which he holds up to nature. Actors, managers, and authors are all represented in this company, and it may be supposed that they all have studied the deep wants of the human heart in many theatres; but none of them could have studied its mysterious workings in any theatre to greater advantage than in the bright and airy pages of 'Vanity Fair.' To this skilful showman, who has so often delighted us, and who has charmed us again tonight, we have now to wish Godspeed, and that he may continue for many years to exercise his potent art. To him fill a bumper toast, and fervently utter, God bless him!" It may be here observed that Dickens always spoke of his brother novelist with undisguised admiration and affectionate regard, and deplored Lord Lytton's attitude towards him. "Boz" once said to a lady acquaintance: "We shall not see another Thackeray this century." In the correspondence of Thackeray which has been brought to light the name of Dickens is invariably mentioned with profound respect.

On May 1st the Novelist attended the banquet of the Royal Academy, and eloquently returned thanks, after the health of Thackeray and himself had been proposed by the President, Sir Charles Eastlake. A week later he presided at the forty-eighth anniversary of the Artists' Benevolent Fund, and, in a striking oration, warmly appealed for the support of that excellent charity. In July, at a public meeting held for the purpose of establishing the now famous Royal Dramatic College (Charles Kean in the chair), Dickens, in submitting the resolution, entrusted to him, delivered a stirring speech advocating schools for actors' children. At Manchester, on December 3rd, he presided at the annual meeting of the Institutional Association of Lancashire and Cheshire, when he congratulated the Association upon the progress which "real mutual improvement societies" were then making in that neighbourhood "through the noble agency of individual employers and their families," and urged the desirability of encouraging, in this age of mechanical devices, the fancy and the imagination. "Let the child have its fables; let the man or woman into which it changes always remember those fables tenderly. Let numerous graces and ornaments that cannot be weighed and measured, and that seem at first sight idle enough, continue to have their places about us, be we never so wise." The following day found the Novelist at Coventry, where, at the Castle Hotel, a public dinner was held on the occasion of the presentation to him of a gold repeater watch, specially constructed by local watchmakers, as a mark of gratitude for the reading of his "Christmas Carol" twelve months previously, in aid of the funds of the Coventry Institute; in acknowledging the kind gift he assured the donors that the watch would be his company in hours of sedentary labour at home and in wanderings abroad—that it would never be absent from his side—and that when he had done "with time and its measurement" it should belong to his children.

In 1858 Dickens was nominated by some of the students for election as Lord Rector of Glasgow University, a fact not recorded by Forster; he received, however, a very small vote indeed, the Glasgow *Morning Journal* asserting that it had seen a letter from the Novelist in which he repudiated strongly his nomination to the rectorship, adding that the movement of a section of the students was not only without his sanction, but was expressly opposed by him. During the winter of 1858-59 he took up his residence at Tavistock House, the lease of which had not yet expired. Owing to a break in the continuity of the public readings, he was enabled, with the opening of 1859, to direct his thoughts upon a fresh work of fiction. A year prior to this date he told Forster that "growing inclinations of a fitful and undefined sort" were upon him sometimes to fall to work upon a new book. At one moment he thought it better not to worry himself for a while; at another he considered it would be useless if he did, in his then disturbed mental condition. Yet a little later he said: "If I can discipline my thoughts into the channel of a story, I have made up my mind to get to work on one: always supposing that I find myself, on the trial, able to do well. Nothing whatever will do me the least 'good' in the way of shaking the one strong possession of change impending over us that every day makes stronger; but if I could work on with some approach to steadiness, through the summer, the anxious toil of a new book would have its neck well broken before beginning to publish, next October or November. Sometimes I think I may continue to work; sometimes, I think not." This was written in January 1858, and (as we have seen) the intention to begin the new tale was to be frustrated by the decision (soon after arrived at) to give public readings.

Dickens at first favoured the idea of writing his next romance upon a plan proposed in his manuscript-book: "How as to a story in two periods—with a lapse of time between, like a French Drama?" He follows the query with a list of titles suitable for such a notion, such as "Time," "Scattered Leaves," "Long Ago," "Rolling Years," "Memory Carton," "Rolling Stones," "Two Generations," &c. Before the plot was effectually grasped he suggested to Forster other titles: "What do you think of *this* name for my story— BURIED ALIVE? Does it seem too grim? Or, THE THREAD OF GOLD? Or, THE DOCTOR OF BEAUVAIS?" At length, on March 11, 1859, he certified that he had "got exactly the name for the story that is wanted; exactly what will fit the opening to a T. A TALE OF TWO CITIES." He had set himself "the little task of making *a picturesque story*, rising in every chapter, with characters true to nature, but whom the story should express more than they should express themselves by dialogue;" in other words, he "fancied a story of incident might be written (in place of the odious stuff that *is* written under that pretence), pounding the characters in his own mortar, and beating their interest out of them." In the preface he says that he desires to offer something to "the popular and picturesque means of understanding that terrible time"—the French Revolution—although admitting the impossibility of adding anything to the philosophy of Carlyle's wonderful work, the book of all others which he read perpetually, and of which he never tired; indeed, it is said that he carried a copy of it about with him wherever he went.[1]

Concerning his preparation for this historical

[1] An interesting photograph was taken in 1865, representing Charles Dickens reading to his daughters on the lawn in front of Gad's Hill Place; the book which engages their attention is Carlyle's "French Revolution."

novel, a somewhat amusing incident is recorded. Anxious to be accurate regarding facts and dates, he begged Carlyle to lend him some of the authorities quoted in his own history—whereupon "the Sage," grimly enjoying the jest, despatched to Gad's Hill *all* his reference volumes, comprising about two cartloads of books! We are assured, too, that Dickens read them faithfully, thus testifying to the earnestness with which he regarded his task, and indicating that thoughtful deliberation of which Forster gives many instances. One of the tentative titles for "A Tale of Two Cities" (viz., "Memory Carton") points to the conclusion that its leading personage was uppermost in his mind from the beginning. The Author decided to publish the story not only in the customary monthly parts, but to issue it also as a serial in *Household Words*, which, however, ceased to exist before the opening chapters were ready. The journal was the joint property of Dickens, Messrs. Bradbury & Evans, Forster, and W. H. Wills, the latter officiating as subeditor. On June 17, 1858, Messrs. Bradbury & Evans (the printers of *Household Words*, as well as of certain of Dickens's books) were informed that the Novelist had resolved to sever his connection with them because his "Personal" statement (denying the unfounded rumours concerning the separation from his wife) had not been reprinted in *Punch*, of which they were the proprietors. It is difficult to understand Dickens's attitude in this matter, for it seems that he expected a humorous periodical to give unsolicited publicity to his private affairs, and so strongly resented the firm's refusal to interfere in this grave concern that he determined to dissolve partnership. The result of that decision was the sale by auction of *Household Words* (with all rights) on May 16, 1859, under a decree in Chancery, when it was purchased for £3500 by Mr. Arthur Smith, acting on Dickens's behalf. Unhappily, this seemingly arbitrary proceeding brought about an estrangement between Dickens and Mark Lemon, then the editor of *Punch*—an estrangement which continued for years, until Clarkson Stanfield, on his deathbed, besought the Novelist to resume the friendship so regretfully interrupted; whereupon he relented, and when Stanfield was buried the two men clasped hands over his open grave.[1]

The final issue of *Household Words* appeared on May 28, 1859. A month previously Dickens had launched a new periodical, at the same price and of a similar character, which was destined to take the place of its predecessor; it may, in fact, be said that the younger journal was identical therewith except in name. Many titles were suggested for the new weekly publication. At length a suitable one was found in *All the Year Round*, which, with the quotation from Shakespeare preceding it, "The story of our lives from year to year," was immediately adopted; on the appearance of the last number of *Household Words*, the title of *All the Year Round* included the line, "with which is incorporated *Household Words*."[2] The first number of *All the Year Round*, dated April 30, 1859, contained the initial weekly instalment of "A Tale of Two Cities," the concluding chapter being printed in the number dated November 26th following.

[1] "The History of *Punch*," by M. H. Spielmann.

[2] The office of *All the Year Round* was No. 26 Wellington Street, Strand, at the south corner of Tavistock Street. In 1872 the lessee of the property was unavailingly approached by emissaries from Chicago, with the view of purchasing and transporting the building to the World's Fair!

The story was also issued in the customary monthly parts by Chapman & Hall (from June to December in the same year), with sixteen etched illustrations by Hablot K. Browne ("Phiz"). These designs, by the way, were the last which that artist prepared for Dickens, after more than twenty years' collaboration, and he naturally felt aggrieved by "Dickens's strangely silent manner of breaking the connection," surmising that it was to be attributed to the Novelist's determination to try the effect of a new hand, that "would give his old puppets a fresh look;" or it might be that he resented "Phiz" illustrating Trollope simultaneously. "Confound all authors and publishers, say I," observed the artist in a letter to his coadjutor, Robert Young, written at this time. "There is no pleasing one or t'other. I wish I never had anything to do with the lot." The famous and versatile "Phiz," who ever entertained a tender regard for "Boz," survived him twelve years; he died in 1882, after a long period of ill health, by which his fanciful imagination and power of invention were sadly affected.

Dickens grasped the main idea of "A Tale of Two Cities" while acting in Wilkie Collins's drama of "The Frozen Deep." In his preface to the story he says: "A strong desire was upon me then to embody it in my own person; and I traced out in my fancy the state of mind of which it would necessitate the presentation to an observant spectator, with particular care and interest. As the idea became familiar to me, it gradually shaped itself into its present form. Throughout its execution, it has had complete possession of me: I have so far verified what is done and suffered in these pages as that I have certainly done and suffered it all myself." The writing of the narrative did not continue under very auspicious circumstances, for during the summer the Author became seriously handicapped by a sharp attack of illness; but in July his health had so far improved that he was able to make some progress with the story. "I have been getting on in health very slowly and through irksome botheration enough. But I think I am round the corner. This cause—and the heat—has tended to my doing no more than hold my ground, my old month's advance, with the 'Tale of Two Cities.' The small portions thereof drive me frantic." In order that his mind should be thoroughly imbued with the subject of his romance, he read no books while engaged upon it but such as had the air of the time in which the scenes are laid. *Apropos* of the story, "Phiz" pointed out a rather curious thing that happened. It seems that Watts Phillips, the dramatist, hit upon exactly the same plot, which justified the conclusion that both had gone to the same source for the idea. Phillips's play was performed with considerable success simultaneously with the appearance of Dickens's sixth number, and the public at once detected the resemblance; whereupon Dickens (according to "Phiz") decided to wind up at the eighth number instead of going on to the twentieth, as hitherto. This, however, must be purely conjectural.

"A Tale of Two Cities" deservedly met with a cordial reception at the hands of its readers, and its publication in *All the Year Round* undoubtedly increased the circulation of that journal materially. In July the Author announced to Forster that the run upon the monthly parts was extraordinary, and that during the previous month the publishers sold thirty-five thousand back numbers. Dickens's American publisher paid him a thousand pounds for the first year for the privilege of republishing the story one day after its appearance in London. "Not bad?" queried the Author, who asserted, however, that nothing in the way of mere money could repay the time and trouble of the incessant condensation requisite for the particular method of publication; that it was the interest of the subject, and the pleasure of striving with the difficulty of the form of treatment, which really compensated him. On the completion of the tale he intimated to M. Regnier that he hoped it was the best he had produced, while to Wilkie Collins he said that it had greatly moved and excited him in the writing, "and Heaven knows I have done my best and believed in it." The Novelist had a particular liking for his conception of Sydney Carton, concerning whom the distinguished American writer, Richard Grant White, averred that there is not a grander and lovelier figure in literature or history. Of all the criticisms showered upon the book none afforded the Author greater pleasure than that contained in a note addressed to him by Carlyle.

In January 1859 a proposal had reached him from New York, suggesting that he should give a series of readings in America, but, after serious and careful consideration, the matter was temporarily abandoned; indeed, he declared that he would never comply unless a small fortune be first paid down in money on this side of the Atlantic.[1] His daughter, Kate, was at this time engaged to be married to Charles Allston Collins, brother of Wilkie Collins, and such an interesting family event he thought would induce M. de Cerjat to pay him a long promised

[1] "The Letters of Charles Dickens."

visit. "You shall have a bed here [Tavistock House]
and a bed at Gad's Hill, and we will go and see strange
sights together. When I was in Ireland I ordered the
brightest jaunting-car that ever was seen. It has just
this minute arrived per steamer from Belfast. Say you
are coming, and you shall be the, first man turned over
by it. . . . They turned the basket-phaeton over, last
summer, on a byroad, Mary and the other two—and
had to get it up again; which they did, and came home
as if nothing had happened."[1] Early in June Dickens
and his household relocated to Gad's Hill, where they
spent the summer. In September he went to
Broadstairs to recuperate after a short attack of illness,
returning to Gad's Hill about a fortnight later. In
October the second portion of the first series of his
public readings commenced in the provinces; these
were fourteen in number, the first taking place at
Ipswich and the last at Cheltenham—the series
comprising altogether a hundred and twenty-five
readings when it ended on the 27th of that month.

In the course of this year Dickens was
approached by the late Robert Bonner of the *New York
Ledger* with regard to the writing of a short story for
that enterprising journal. Although the proffered
honorarium was a thousand pounds, the Novelist at
first refused to accede to the request, but, his
objections being overcome by such generous terms, he
eventually consented. "I thought," he wrote to
Bonner, "that I could not be tempted at this time to
engage in any undertaking, however short, but the
literary project which will come into active

---

[1] "The Letters of Charles Dickens."

existence next month.[1] . . . I will endeavour to be at work upon the tale while this note is on its way to you across the water." It bore the title "Hunted Down," and took the form of "a romance of the real world," narrating the history of an assurance effected on the life of Mr. Alfred Becksmith by Julius Slinkton of the Middle Temple, whom he (Slinkton) attempts to poison, but, foiled in his object, destroys himself. The prototype of Slinkton was the notorious Thomas Griffiths Wainewright, surgeon, essayist, artist, and critic—the "Janus Weathercock" of the *London Magazine*, the *confrere* of Northcote, Campbell, and Lamb, the friend of Talfourd, Bulwer, and Dickens himself.[2] In a little memorandum-book which the Novelist used for jotting down hints for future stories we find the following entry:—

"Devoted to the Destruction of a man. Revenge built up on love. The secretary in the Wainewright case, who had fallen in love (or supposed he had) with the murdered girl."

Then comes a hint of the villain in the story:—

"The man with his hair parted straight up the front of his head, like an aggravating gravel-walk. Always presenting it to you. 'Up here, if you please. Neither to the right nor left. Take me exactly in this direction. Straight up here. Come off the grass——'"

"Hunted Down" was published in the *New York Ledger* on August 20th and 27th and September 3,

---

[1] "A Tale of Two Cities."

[2] Wainewright, for his detestable crimes, was transported to New South Wales, and, after being liberated, died at Sydney in abject misery. Besides figuring as Julius Slinkton in "Hunted Down," he is the *primum mobile* of Bulwer Lytton's novel, "Lucretia."

1859, with illustrations; and in *All the Year Round* twelve months later.

The first Extra Christmas Number of *All the Year Round* was published this year, entitled "The Haunted House," and it is fair to surmise that the theme may have been suggested by a work (then recently issued) called "A Night in a Haunted House: a Tale of Facts," which was dedicated to Charles Dickens. To William Howitt, who had a pronounced *penchant* for the supernatural, the Novelist expressed his doubts on the subject of ghosts, and requested him to point out certain houses supposed to be haunted. This he did, whereupon Dickens, accompanied by Wilkie Collins, W. H. Wills, and John Hollingshead, went to one of them (in Cheshunt, Hertfordshire) and then reported to Howitt that the domicile which he alleged to be peopled by spirits had been greatly enlarged, commanded a high rent, "and is no more disturbed than this house of mine." To the Christmas Number Dickens contributed three chapters—namely, "The Mortals in the House," "The Ghost in Master B.'s Room," and "The Ghost in the Corner Room." In the second chapter he incidentally mentions an actual occurrence relating to his own boyhood—the sale of his little bed during a time of dire distress, to which reference is made in the first chapter of this biography. Respecting these Christmas Numbers, Dickens often experienced much difficulty in putting within a framework by himself several fictions by other writers. The "Haunted House" Number proved no exception to the rule, and writing to Forster on November 25th (that is, about a month before it became due), he said: "As yet not a story has come to me in the least belonging to the idea (the simplest in the world; which I myself described in writing, in the most elaborate manner); and every one of them turns, by a strange fatality, on a criminal trial!" It had all to be set right by him.

The winter of 1859-60 was the last spent at Tavistock House. The Novelist had for some time favoured the notion of making his quarters altogether at Gad's Hill, giving up his London home, and taking a furnished residence for the sake of his daughters for a few months of the London season. He now resolved to carry out this intention, and accordingly disposed of Tavistock House, of which he relinquished possession in the September following. Until this date Gad's Hill Place had been furnished merely as a temporary summer abode, so that the preparations necessary for making it comfortable and cheerful demanded much of the Novelist's attention during 1860. He also furnished, as bachelor apartments, a sitting room and one or two bedrooms at the office of *All the Year Round* in Wellington Street, Strand, for occasional use as town quarters.[1]

A letter written by Dickens in May 1860 makes interesting reference to his sons. After announcing the impending marriage of his younger daughter, and alluding to the possibility of the elder following her sister's example, he says: "My eldest boy, Charley, has been in Barings' house for three or four years, and is now going to Hong Kong, strongly backed up by Barings, to buy tea on his own account, as a means

[1] A recent sale at Sotheby's included the office table, two chairs, and a looking-glass, which for many years were in daily use by Charles Dickens at the office of *All the Year Round*. These mementoes, vouched for as authentic, realised £85.

of forming a connection, and seeing more of the practical part of a merchant's calling, before starting in London for himself. His brother Frank (Jeffrey's godson) I have just recalled from France and Germany, to come and learn business, and qualify himself to join his brother on his return from the Celestial Empire. The next boy, Sidney Smith, is designed for the navy, and is in training at Portsmouth, awaiting his nomination. He is about three feet high, with the biggest eyes ever seen, and is known in the Portsmouth parts as 'Young Dickens, who can do everything.' Another boy is at school in France; the youngest of all has a private tutor at home. I have forgotten the second in order, who is in India. He went out as ensign of the non-existent native regiment, got attached to the Forty-Second Highlanders, one of the finest regiments in the Queen's service; has remained with them ever since, and got made a lieutenant by the chances of the rebellious campaign, before he was eighteen. Miss Hogarth, always Miss Hogarth, is the guide philosopher, and friend of all the party, and a very close affection exists between her and the girls."[1]

During 1860, Dickens's literary output was limited to a series of detached papers written for *All the Year Round*, and published under the general title of "The Uncommercial Traveller." They were seventeen in number, the first appearing on January 28th, and the last on October 13th, and in them the Author makes many pointed allusions to his early days and to well remembered places. He suffered so much at this time from insomnia that it was not unusual for him to rise from his bed directly after lying down, go out, and return home thoroughly tired at sunrise.

[1] "The Letters of Charles Dickens."

"My last special feat," he said on one occasion, "was turning out of bed at two, after a hard day, pedestrian and otherwise, and walking thirty miles into the country to breakfast." Addressing an audience interested (like himself) in the welfare of the Commercial Travellers' Schools, he assumed for the nonce "the character and title of a Traveller Uncommercial." "I am both a town traveller and a country traveller," he said, "and am always on the road. Figuratively speaking, I travel from the great house of Human-interest Brothers, and have rather a large connection in the fancy-goods way. Literally speaking, I am always wandering here and there from my rooms in Covent Garden, London: now about the city streets, now about the country byroads, seeing many little things, and some great things, which, because they interest me, I think may interest others." Hence, many of the adventures and impressions received during his nightly perambulations are duly recorded in "The Uncommercial Traveller," papers which, in some respects, are reminiscent of his "Sketches by Boz."

The marriage of his daughter, Kate, in the summer of 1860, created no little excitement in Gad's Hill and the neighbourhood. All the villagers turned out in honour of the event, and a number of triumphal arches were erected en route to the church; the local blacksmith, too, imparted a dramatic effect to the joyful incident by firing a couple of small cannon as the wedding party returned after the ceremony— an ovation for which the Novelist was entirely unprepared, and which he rightly regarded as a tribute of respect to himself. There are many of the labouring class still living in the locality who recall with evident pleasure the presence in their midst of the genial, kind-hearted Charles Dickens, whose death they sincerely deplore. To name the principal guests at the wedding festivities will indicate who were the most familiar visitors at Gad's Hill during these later years. They included Mary Boyle, Marguerite Power, Fechter (the actor), Charles Kent, Edmund Yates, Percy Fitzgerald, Marcus Stone, Henry Fothergill Chorley, Frederic Lehmann, W. H. Wills, and Wilkie Collins (who was accompanied by Mr. Holman Hunt); not the least welcome among them was the Novelist's old and cherished friend, Thomas Beard, one of his colleagues in the parliamentary reporting days, who (it will be remembered) acted as "best man" at the Novelist's own wedding. The bridegroom, Charles Collins, as a son of a Royal Academician, was bred as a painter, but is best recalled through his efforts in literature; he occasionally contributed to *All the Year Round*, and was the author of the "New Sentimental Journey" and the "Cruise on Wheels," both of these productions being characterised by a delicate and refined humour. His premature death in 1873, after years of patient suffering, sorely grieved all who enjoyed the privilege of his acquaintance. The widow, herself a prominent figure in artistic circles, subsequently married the well-known painter, Mr. C. E. Perugini.

CHAPTER 12

## "GREAT EXPECTATIONS" AND "OUR MUTUAL FRIEND"

About a month after the marriage of his daughter, Dickens received from Manchester the intelligence of the demise of his brother Alfred, and all that this death invoked, together with the little worries caused by the impending change of residence, seriously handicapped him in his literary undertakings. He was busily engaged with a new story for *All the Year Round.* "Tomorrow," he wrote, directly after his brother's funeral, "I have to work against time and tide and everything else, to fill up a No. keeping open for me, and the stereotype plates of which must go to America on Friday." The title selected for the tale was "Great Expectations"—"I think a good name?" he queried. It had been suggested that, instead of utilising his time by writing detached papers, he should "let himself loose" upon some single humorous conception in the vein of his youthful achievements. Fortunately, at this moment he happened to hit upon a novel and grotesque idea which opened upon him in a little piece then nearly completed; whereupon he determined to cancel the brief paper and reserve for an extended story the notion which he so vividly realised that he could "see the whole of a serial revolving on it, in a most singular and comic manner." This was the germ of Pip and Magwitch. Originally the intention was to make it the groundwork of a tale in the old twenty-number form; but the sale and prospects of *All the Year Round* had recently been somewhat prejudicially affected by the publication therein of "A Day's Ride; a Life's Romance," by Charles Lever, which had disappointed expectation, and Dickens perceived the advisability of strengthening the journal by another serial from his own pen. "It was perfectly clear," he wrote to Forster on October 4th, after calling a council of war at the Office, "that the one thing to be done was, for me to strike in. I have therefore decided to begin the story as of the length of the 'Tale of Two Cities' on the first of December—begin publishing, that is. I must make the most I can out of the book." Again, a little later: "The sacrifice of 'Great Expectations' is really and truly made for myself. The property of *All the Year Round* is far too valuable, in every way, to be much endangered. Our fall is not large, but we have a considerable advance in hand of the story we are now publishing, and there is no vitality in it, and no chance whatever of stopping the fall; which on the contrary would be certain to increase. Now, if I went into a twenty-number serial, I should cut off my power of doing anything serial here for two good years—and that would be a most perilous thing. On the other hand, by dashing in now, I come in when most wanted." During the latter part of September the writing of the story began, and in a few days Forster received the manuscript of the initial chapters, with a forecast of the plot: "The book will be written in the first person throughout, and during these first three weekly numbers you will find the hero to be a boy child, like David [Copperfield].

Then he will be an apprentice. You will not have to complain of the want of humour, as in the 'Tale of Two Cities.' I have made the opening, I hope, in its general effect exceedingly droll. I have put a child and a good-natured foolish man, in relations that seem to me very funny. Of course I have got in the pivot on which the story will turn, too—and which, indeed, as you remember, was the grotesque tragicomic conception that first encouraged me." To prevent the possibility of repeating himself, he read "David Copperfield" again, and assured Forster that he "was affected by it to a degree you would hardly believe."

In the interval that elapsed between the writing of the early chapters of "Great Expectations" and their publication in December, the Novelist had transferred his domestic paraphernalia from Tavistock House (of which he delivered up possession early in September) to Gad's Hill, where one of his first acts was to burn, in an adjoining field, the accumulated letters and papers of twenty years. "They sent up a smoke like the genie when he got out of the casket on the seashore; and as it was an exquisite day when I began, and rained heavily when I finished, I suspect my correspondence of having overcast the face of the heavens."[1] This is probably the most valuable bonfire on record as regards the nature of its constituents; it is difficult to conceive what sum could be obtained at the present time by the disposal of such an extensive collection of autographs, which must have had a remarkable literary value as well as a pecuniary one. Many will regard such a holocaust as inexcusable; but Dickens, who held very strong views on the subject, thus defended his action in

[1] "The Letters of Charles Dickens."

a letter addressed to Macready in 1865: "Daily seeing improper uses made of confidential letters, on addressing them to a public audience that has no business with them, I made, not long ago, a great fire in my field at Gad's Hill, and burnt every letter I possessed. And now I destroy every letter I receive not on absolute business, and my mind is so far at ease."[1] Once fairly established in his permanent abode, the beautifying and altering of Gad's Hill Place afforded him continual amusement and recreation; so extensive, indeed, were the improvements he effected here during a few years that the reserved price placed upon the estate after his death more than quadrupled what he had paid in 1856 for the house, shrubbery, and twenty years' lease of a meadow field. Not only did he enlarge the house and improve the grounds, but he acquired an extended area of the adjoining land, where several quick growing trees were subsequently planted. A considerable expenditure was also incurred in boring for water, "at the rate of two pounds per day for wages." "Here are six men," he wrote characteristically to Forster, "perpetually going up and down the well . . . in the course of fitting a pump, which is quite a railway terminus—it is so iron, and so big. The process is much more like putting Oxford Street endwise, and laying gas along it, than anything else. By the time it is finished, the cost of this water will be something absolutely frightful. But of course it proportionately increases the value of the property, and that's my only comfort." The exterior of the building underwent but little alteration, presenting until the last much the same appearance as when he knew it in the days of his boyhood, its red-brick

[1] "The Letters of Charles Dickens."

front becoming gradually more and more hidden from view by clustering masses of ivy and Virginia creeper. Among the later additions to the house were a new drawing room and a conservatory opening into it— "brilliant but expensive, with foundations as of an ancient Roman work of horrible solidity." The conservatory had long been an object of desire with him, and on its completion a few days before his death he said to his younger daughter, "Well, Katey, now you see POSITIVELY the last improvement at Gad's Hill," and every one laughed at the asseveration, regarding it as a joke against himself, for each alteration he declared would be "really, truly, and positively the last." One of the bedrooms he had transformed into a study, which he lined with books and sometimes wrote in. But the study proper, called by him the library, was the front room on the ground floor, on the right as one enters the house—a room of which the general aspect, as seen at the time of Dickens's death, has been cleverly depicted in the admirable drawing executed by Mr. Luke Fildes, R.A., for publication in the *Graphic*, where it appeared with the appropriate title of "The Empty Chair." An interesting description of the study, written by Charles Allston Collins, is worthy of quotation, as it brings clearly to the mental retina the surroundings so familiar to the Novelist during the final years of his life. "Ranged in front of and round him were always a variety of objects for his eye to rest on in the intervals of actual writing, and any one of which he would have instantly missed had it been removed. There was a French bronze group representing a duel with swords, fought by a couple of very fat toads, one of them (characterised by that particular buoyancy which belongs to corpulence) in the act of making a prodigious lunge forward, which the other receives in the very middle of his digestive apparatus, and under the influence of which it seems likely that he will satisfy the wounded honour of his opponent by promptly expiring. There was another bronze figure which always stood near the toads, also of French manufacture, and also full of comic suggestion. It was a statuette of a dog fancier, such a one as you used to see on the bridges or quays of Paris with a profusion of little dogs stuck under his arms and into his pockets. . . . There was the long gilt leaf with the rabbit sitting erect upon its haunches, the huge paperknife often held in his hand during his public readings, and the little fresh green cup ornamented with the leaves and blossoms of the cowslip, in which a few fresh flowers were always placed every morning—for Dickens invariably worked with flowers on his writing table. There was also the register of the day of the week and of the month which stood always before him. . . ." A remarkable feature of the library or study is the door, the interior surface of which the Novelist disguised by means of imitation book-backs (the majority brought from Tavistock House), so that the door when closed continued the effect imparted to the room by the rows of books with which the walls were covered. Humorous titles had been invented for these pseudo volumes by Dickens and his friends, such as the following:—

| | |
|---|---|
| Five Minutes in China. | 3 vols. |
| Forty Winks at the Pyramids. | 2 vols. |
| Captain Cook's Life of Savage. | 2 vols. |
| A Carpenter's Bench of Bishops. | 2 vols. |
| Jonah's Account of the Whale. | |

| The Quarrelly Review. | 4 vols. |
| The Gunpowder Magazine. | 4 vols. |
| Noah's Arkitecture. | 2 Vols. |
| Cats' Lives. | 9 vols. |
| Drowsy's Recollections of Nothing. | 3 vols. |
| Morrison's Pills Progress. | 2 vols. |
| Miss Biffin on Deportment. | |
| Lady Godiva on the Horse. | |
| Munchausen's Modern Miracles. | 4 vols. |
| History of a Short Chancery Suit. | 21 vols. |
| Hansard's Guide to | |
| Refreshing Sleep. | In many volumes.[1] |

At the side of the main road opposite the house is a shrubbery, with two magnificent cedars overhanging the footpath, which formed part of the Gad's Hill property, and one of Dickens's numerous alterations was to make this "wilderness" easy of access by tunnelling under the Dover Road, thus obviating the necessity of crossing the highway itself. The entrance to the tunnel is by a flight of stone steps leading from the garden, while a corresponding flight leads upwards into the shrubbery. Here stood the pretty Swiss Chalet presented to him in 1865 by his friend Fechter, which became a favourite retreat in summer months, much of his work being carried on within its wooden walls. A sundial in the garden possessed a certain historical interest in the fact that the pedestal previously formed part of old Rochester Bridge, demolished in 1856, to make way for the existing iron structure. In 1859 one of the balustrades of the destroyed bridge had been given to him by the contractors, and he caused it to be duly "stonemasoned" and set up on the lawn behind

[1] It is probable that Dickens had seen, or heard of, a similar device of dummy book-backs at Chatsworth, where, in the library, a blank door is thus treated.

the house. "I have ordered a sundial for the top of it, and it will be a very good object indeed."[1]

Of Dickens's life at Gad's Hill a most fascinating chapter might be written. From day to day he divided his time for the most part between working and walking, and, endowed as he was with exceptional powers as a pedestrian, soon made himself acquainted with every detail of the country within a twelve mile radius of his home. The visits of cherished friends offered agreeable interludes, and on these occasions (ever memorable to his guests) he entirely devoted himself to such projects as seemed likely to afford them the greatest pleasure; he never tired of introducing to their notice the beauties of the surrounding scenery, the charm of Cobham Woods, and the archaeological features of the old City of Rochester, including Restoration House (the "Satis House" of "Great Expectations"), these expeditions being varied by drives to Canterbury, Maidstone, &c. To the country folks round about Higham and Rochester one of the most interesting figures was Charles Dickens, who, with a vigorous stride, might be seen any day taking his customary constitutional, sometimes with Miss Hogarth as a companion, but more frequently accompanied by his big dogs, which were not only an enjoyment to him but a necessity on a road traversed probably more than any other in the kingdom by the *genus* tramp. One of his favourite walks (indeed *the* favourite) was round Cobham, skirting the park and village—another, by Rochester and the Medway to the

---

[1] The sundial, unfortunately, has been removed, and was recently offered for sale by a London dealer at a very substantial price. Like Owen Jones's illuminated Shakesperian quotation, such a *souvenir* of Charles Dickens should have been regarded as a fixture, to go with the house.

Chatham Lines. Or he would sometimes direct his steps to Gravesend, through the dreary marshes so vividly portrayed in "Great Expectations," and return homewards by the village of Chalk, where his honeymoon was spent. The marsh country about Cooling attracted him by reason of its weird strangeness, and it was his delight to take particular friends to the desolate churchyard there and show them the row of lozenge shaped tombstones (marking the graves of the Comport family "of Cowling Court, 1771"), which are referred to in the opening chapter of "Great Expectations."

The later months of 1860 were chiefly occupied with "Great Expectations" and with preparations for the forthcoming Christmas Number of *All the Year Round*. It was decided that this number should be written conjointly by himself and Wilkie Collins, and for the purpose of obtaining the necessary local colour the two authors travelled together at the beginning of November into Devonshire and Cornwall. Reporting their safe arrival at Bideford, Dickens referred to their temporary resting place as a "beastly hotel," where they had "stinking fish for dinner, and have been able to drink nothing, though we have ordered wine, beer, and brandy-and-water. There is nothing in the house but two tarts and a pair of snuffers."[1] The title of the Christmas Number is "A Message from the Sea," the scene being laid in Clovelly; Dickens contributed nearly all the first and the whole of the second and concluding chapters, while certain detached passages in the remaining portions are obviously from his pen. One of the characters, Captain Jorgan, was drawn from an American seaman, Captain Morgan, to

[1] "The Letters of Charles Dickens."

whom the Novelist wrote: "Here and there, in the description of the sea-going hero, I have given a touch or two of remembrance of somebody you know; very heartily desiring that thousands of people may have some faint reflection of the pleasure I have for many years derived from the contemplation of a most amiable nature and most remarkable man."[1] The 4th of December found him at Gad's Hill, whither he had just returned "to work so many hours every day for so many days" upon "Great Expectations." The intensely cold Christmas of 1860 was spent in his Kentish home.

The year 1861 was again a very unsettled time with Charles Dickens, and there can be no doubt that the separation from his wife continued to seriously disturb his thoughts and to induce this condition of unrest. The anxiety consequent upon his various undertakings, literary and social, was also greatly responsible for much of this perturbation of spirit, compelling him to resort to physical exertion as an antidote to mental fatigue and disquietude. In February he elected to take a house in London until midsummer. This, the Novelist explained, was on his unmarried daughter's account, for he himself had very good and cheerful bachelor rooms at the office of *All the Year Round*, with an old and tried servant in charge, who "is the cleverest man of his kind in the world, and can do anything, from excellent carpentry to excellent cookery." The house rented by him in town was a pretty furnished residence, No. 3 Hanover Square, Regent's Park, and here, in March, we find him comfortably established with members of his family,

---

[1] "The Letters of Charles Dickens."

and busy with "Great Expectations." "This Journal
[*All the Year Round*] is doing gloriously," he wrote to
M. de Cerjat at this time, "and 'Great Expectations' is
a great success. I have taken my third boy, Frank
(Jeffrey's godson), into this office. If I am not
mistaken, he has a natural literary taste and capacity,
and may do very well with a chance so congenial to his
mind, and being also entered at the Bar."[1] In the same
letter an interesting allusion is made to the new
Thames Embankment, which, with the great alteration
in the western portion of London consequent upon the
construction thereof, he then saw for the first time. "I
walked out from here in the afternoon," he says, "and
thought I would go down by the Houses of Parliament.
When I got there, the day was so beautifully bright and
warm, that I thought I would walk on by Millbank, to
see the river. I walked straight on *for three miles* on a
splendid broad esplanade overhanging the Thames,
with immense factories, railway works, and what not
erected on it, and with the strangest beginnings and
ends of wealthy streets pushing themselves into the
very Thames. When I was a rower on that river, it was
all broken ground and ditch, with here and there a
public house or two, an old mill, and a tall chimney. I
have never seen it in any state of transition, though I
suppose myself to know this rather large city as well
as anyone in it."[2]

In March the second series of paid readings
began. The first six of this series were given at St.
James's Hall (the scene of his former triumphs, St.
Martin's Hall, having been burnt), the last taking place
(as he purposed on April 18th; they were attended by

[1] "The Letters of Charles Dickens."
[2] Ibid.

"perfectly astounding audiences," the upshot being that, after paying expenses and replacing everything destroyed in the fire at St. Martin's Hall, he gained £500 clear profit. "A very great result," he opined. He believed that the readings might have continued through the season with equal prosperity, but, feeling that his story had a prior claim to attention, he resisted the temptation to proceed with them. In June 1861 he finished "Great Expectations"[1] (the final chapter being published in August), and he then declared himself to be "the worse for wear." "Neuralgic pains in the face have troubled me a good deal," he wrote to Macready, "and the work has been pretty close. But I hope that the book is a good book, and I have no doubt of very soon throwing off the little damage it has done me."[2] He told Forster he felt so desperately lazy now that the story was done that he thought of offering himself to the village school as a live example of that vice for the edification of youth. "'Great Expectations' seems universally liked," he wrote to Miss Mary Boyle in December, "I suppose because it opens funnily, and with an interest too." Even Carlyle was among those who admired the story, and used to ask in his characteristic manner for "that Pip nonsense" whenever the new number became due. For this work Dickens received from America (as in the case of "A Tale of Two Cities") the sum of £1000 for early proofs. Directly after its conclusion in *All the Year Round*, it was published by Chapman & Hall in three volumes

---

[1] At Sir Edward Bulwer Lytton's earnest suggestion, Dickens subsequently changed the end of the story, and believed that the alteration constituted a great improvement, an opinion, however, with which Forster did not concur.

[2] "The Letters of Charles Dickens."

as a circulating library book, but without illustrations, and no less than five editions were sold in this form. That strange personage in the tale, Miss Havisham, is believed to have been drawn from a lady who lived near Hyde Park, and who was burnt to death in her house. It is further conjectured that, for purposes of the story, the Novelist partly availed himself of the wedding breakfast incident related in *Household Words* in connection with an old and historic London tavern known as "Dirty Dick's," in Bishopsgate Street Without; the real name of "Dirty Dick" was Nathaniel Bentley, whose bride died suddenly on the morning of the projected wedding, whereupon the room containing the banquet was ordered to be closed and sealed, never to be reopened during his lifetime—a wish that was duly respected.

His literary labours over for a while, Dickens indulged in a brief spell of idleness. "The subsidence of those distressing pains in my face the moment I had done my work, made me resolve to do nothing in that way for some time if I could help it." Such expressed determination his friends regarded as a mere figure of speech, absolute abstention from work, even for a moderately extended period, being a luxury to which Dickens was a stranger. The present instance proved no exception, for, almost immediately, he began to practise daily for two or three hours some new adaptations from his books with a view to future readings. These preparations occurred during July and August, by which time he and his household had returned to Gad's Hill, where the Novelist remained until his travels recommenced in October, in connection with the reading tour in the provinces. In September the business manager of the readings (Arthur Smith) became prostrated by an illness which took unexpectedly a dangerous turn, and ended fatally in the following month. On the day after attending the funeral, Dickens heard of the death of his brother-in-law, Henry Austin—for whom he entertained great respect—and these sorrowful partings, occurring almost simultaneously, saddened and depressed him. It was therefore with a heavy heart that he set out upon his provincial readings, "which," he said, "must be fought out like all the rest of life." Under the management of Mr. Headland, the readings opened at Norwich on October 28th, and continued (with an interval at Christmas) until January 30, 1862, when at Chester this portion of the series closed. At Berwick-on-Tweed a very alarming accident occurred during the progress of the reading, and in describing it to Forster the Novelist said: "The room was tremendously crowded and my gas apparatus fell down. There was a terrible wave among the people for an instant, and God knows what destruction of life a rush to the stairs would have caused. Fortunately a lady in the front of the stalls ran out towards me, exactly in a place where I knew that the whole hall could see her. So I addressed her, laughing, and half asked and half ordered her to sit down again; and, in a moment, it was all over. But the men in attendance had such a fearful sense of what might have happened (besides the real danger of fire) that they positively shook the boards I stood on, with their trembling, when they came up to put things right. I am proud to record that the gasman's sentiment, as delivered afterwards, was, 'The more you want of the master, the more you'll find in him.'" At Glasgow, owing to an over issue of tickets, the most remarkable incident was witnessed of well dressed people pouring into a hall already crowded to excess; even the platform was crammed with people lying down upon it the whole evening, the scene resembling "some impossible tableau or gigantic picnic." This course of readings came to a somewhat sudden termination in December by the death of the Prince Consort. The Novelist had pledged himself to appear at Liverpool when the intelligence arrived, and he consulted W. H. Wills as to the propriety of abandoning that engagement. He said: "I feel personally that the Queen has always been very considerate and gracious to me, and I would on no account do anything that might seem unfeeling or disrespectful." The Mayor and Town Clerk of Liverpool advocated merely a brief postponement, but Dickens had a misgiving that they hardly understood what the public general sympathy with the widowed Queen would be, and, his own views on the subject deriving support from the advice of his subeditor, the readings were withheld. This enabled him, much to his delight, to return to Gad's Hill earlier than he anticipated, to enjoy a well-earned rest.

The death of Arthur Smith distressed the Novelist exceedingly, for, apart from personal friendship, the services rendered by him as manager of the readings were almost indispensable. "It is as if my right arm were gone," Dickens observed to Forster in October. "It is only just now that I am able to open one of the [reading] books, and screw the text out of myself in a flat dull way." The same letter announced that he had reserved ten days in November for the preparation of the Christmas Number of *All the Year Round*. This was entitled "Tom Tiddler's Ground," and, with a view to obtaining the material necessary for his own contributions to the number, he spent a week during the previous summer with Sir E. Bulwer Lytton at Knebworth; for at Redcoats Green, near by, there lived a remarkable miser, locally known as "The Hertfordshire Hermit," and it was the Novelist's desire to see this strange individual. His name was James Lucas—a well-educated man and the son of a prosperous West India merchant; but, notwithstanding these advantages, he persisted (after the death of his wife) to lead the life of a recluse, dressing in an old blanket fastened with a skewer and sleeping on a bed of ashes. Owing to such eccentric habits, Lucas obtained an unenviable notoriety, strangers arriving from all parts to catch a glimpse of him and his uncomfortable surroundings. One day Lucas was honoured with a visit from Dickens, who was accompanied by Mr. (afterwards Sir) Arthur Helps and Lord Orford, and presently the Hermit became immortalised as Mr. Mopes in "Tom Tiddler's Ground," much to his disgust. Lucas died of apoplexy in 1874, and was buried in Hackney churchyard. The chapters written by Dickens for this Christmas Number were: I. Picking up Soot and Cinders; VI. Picking up Miss Kimmeens; VII. Picking up the Tinker.

Before the year closed, Dickens's eldest son, Charles (then in business as an Eastern merchant in the City), married the daughter of Mr. Evans, junior partner in the printing firm of Bradbury & Evans, whose imprint appears on many of the Novelist's works.

At the beginning of 1862 Dickens resumed his public readings the remaining portion of the second

Charles Dickens at his desk

*From a photograph by C. Watkins, 1858, in the*
*possession of the Author*

Charles Dickens

*From a photograph by C. Watkins, 1861*

series—commencing in the south of England
(Torquay, Plymouth, Exeter, &c.), and concluding the
provincial engagements at Liverpool and Chester at
the end of January. Notwithstanding his powers of
endurance, the fatigue caused by the constant strain of
work and travel taxed him severely; he complained of
sleeplessness, and of feeling "dazed and worn by gas
and heat." Rest, therefore, became an absolute
necessity before the London readings in March. The
financial results, however, seem to have compensated
him for these disadvantages. "The money returns have
been quite astounding. Think of £190 a night!" This
was in April, and on June 28th he said: "I finished my
readings on Friday night to an enormous hall—nearly
£200." The success of the tours, both in London and
the provinces, was throughout complete, and, as
regards the Metropolis, he thought it almost suicidal to
discontinue with the town so full. He had an offer, too,
from Australia to read there for eight months, for a
sum of £10,000, which tempted him sorely; he tried to
familiarise himself with the fancy that a visit to the
Antipodes would offer a new field of observation, and
even thought of planning, for *All the Year Round*
during his absence, "The Uncommercial Traveller
Upside Down"—but it was not to be.

In February, the Novelist effected an exchange
of houses with friends for three months, they going to
Gad's Hill, and he, with his family, to No. 16 Hyde
Park Gate, South Kensington. This proved a
convenient arrangement for the London readings at
St. James's Hall, at the termination of which (in
the middle of June) he gladly returned to his country
home. At the end of October the Novelist, with
his daughter and sister-in-law, went to reside for

a couple of months in Paris, whence he returned to Gad's Hill just before Christmas. Meanwhile the usual Christmas Number demanded his attention, his contributions thereto being written in the character of a waiter, which he thought "exceedingly droll." The title bestowed upon the Number was "Somebody's Luggage," and the thread on which the stories hang is spun by this waiter, whose account of himself "includes, I hope, everything you know about waiters, presented humorously." The chapters for which Dickens was responsible are: I. His Leaving it till Called for; II. His Boots; VII. His Brown-paper Parcel; X. His Wonderful End. He made the tale of little Bebelle (which has a small French corporal for a hero) a *camera lucida* of French places and styles of people, having founded it on something he had noticed in a French soldier.

His stay in England, where he spent Christmas, was brief, for he had promised to return to Paris at the beginning of the new year (1863) to give at the English Embassy, at the end of January, four Readings in aid of a British Charitable Fund. Writing to his daughter, Mamie, on February 1st, he said: "I cannot give you any idea of the success of the readings here, because no one can imagine the scene of last Friday night at the Embassy. Such audiences and such enthusiasm I have never seen, but the thing culminated on Friday night in a two hours' storm of excitement and pleasure. They actually recommenced and applauded right away into their carriages and down the street. You know your parent's horror of being lionised, and will not be surprised to hear that I am half dead of it."[1] He was in London again by the middle of February, in good time

---

[1] "The Letters of Charles Dickens."

to prepare for the thirteen readings to complete the second series in June, these being given in the Hanover Square Rooms instead of St. James's Hall, for the sake of obtaining finer effects. "I am reading in London every Friday just now," he informed M. de Cerjat on May 24th. "Great crams and great enthusiasm."

For some time Dickens had indulged in the prospect of preparing a new story, but experienced unaccustomed difficulties in formulating ideas on the subject. His powers of invention had begun to show signs of flagging, and, indeed, it was mainly on this account that he tentatively regarded with approbation the proposal to arrange a reading tour in Australia, doubting, for the moment, his ability to "force an original book" out of himself. The terrible exhaustion, mental and physical, induced by the readings and consequent travelling obviously took too much out of him, and rendered him incapable of settling down at his desk. The second series over, he resolutely determined to devote attention to the next story, endeavouring to make a beginning while occupying his friend's residence in Hyde Park Place; unfortunately he could think of no fresh plot, notwithstanding repeated attempts to conceive something suitably striking and novel, and this he attributed to living in the "odious little house" at Kensington, which "seems to have stifled and darkened my invention." However, in the autumn of 1863, amidst the more congenial environment of Gad's Hill, he described himself as being "full of notions for the new twenty numbers," and hoping, when his Christmas work on *All the Year Round* was done, to "dash into it on the grander journey." Being exceedingly anxious about his book, he even ventured to shirk much of his editorial responsibilities in order that he might be better able to concentrate his thoughts upon the tale in the quietude of his Gad's Hill retreat. Presently he wrote: "I see my opening perfectly, with the one main line on which the story is to turn; and if I don't strike while the iron (meaning myself) is hot, I shall drift off again, and have to go all through this uneasiness once more." His desire was to prepare it for the following spring, and to begin publishing with not less than five numbers completed. The title had been decided upon some months previously; of several designations for forthcoming works entered in his notebook, the following had reference to the story now under consideration: "Rokesmith's Forge," "The Cinder Heap," "Broken Crockery," and "Dust." The name eventually selected was "Our Mutual Friend," which gave rise to considerable controversy at the time, many arguing that the adjective "mutual" was incorrect. In the notebook, too, the Novelist had jotted down some studies of Silas Wegg and his patron, even more comical in conception than he subsequently rendered them; these, together with hints regarding Podsnap's tracts and the idiosyncrasies of other personages, he found invaluable when filling in the details. In his letters at this time the Author mentioned three leading notions on which he founded the story, the most worthy of remark being that which was the outcome of the many handbills he had seen posted up during his riverside wanderings, containing dreary descriptions of persons drowned in the Thames, these suggesting to his mind the long-shore men and their ghastly calling, as graphically sketched in Hexam and Rogue Riderhood. Respecting the germ of an idea for another character in the tale, he said: "I think a man, young and perhaps eccentric, feigning to be dead, and being dead to all intents and purposes, external to himself, and for years retaining the singular view of life and character so imparted, would be a good leading incident for a story"—and the conception was partly carried out in Rokesmith. For other personages he had in view "a poor impostor of a man marrying a woman for her money; she marrying *him* for *his* money; after marriage both finding out their mistake, and entering into a league and covenant against folks in general." With these he proposed to connect some "perfectly new" people, who should have everything new about them; "if they presented a father and mother, it seemed as if THEY must be brand-new, like the furniture and the carriages—shining with varnish, and just home from the manufacturers." This, of course, is fulfilled in the Lammles and Veneerings; while Charley Hexam and his father were suggested by "the uneducated father in fustian, and educated boy in spectacles," whom Dickens and John Leech had one day actually seen in Chatham.

Thus we find the imaginative faculty reinstated, and new fancies freshly flowing. During the remainder of the year, he worked steadily at his book, the course of which was slightly interrupted by the Christmas "stone," as he regarded the Christmas Number of *All the Year Round* for this year (1863), such a heavy impediment did that undertaking prove. "Mrs. Lirriper's Lodgings" was the title thereof, and concerning the number Forster observes: "The triumph of Dickens's achievements in these days was Mrs. Lirriper. She took her place at once among people known to everybody; and all the world talked of

Major Jemmy Jackman and his friend the poor elderly lodging house keeper of the Strand, with her miserable cares, and rivalries and worries, as if they had both been as long in London and as well-known as Norfolk Street itself. A dozen volumes could not have told more than those dozen pages did." The "dozen pages" represent Dickens's share in the production, these comprising two of the seven chapters, viz.: "How Mrs. Lirriper carried on the Business," and "How the Parlours added a few Words." The Novelist's own comment on the number was: "Mrs. Lirriper is indeed a most brilliant old lady. God bless her!" He had evidently heard from his assistant editor a good account of the sales, and we learn (from a letter written to Wilkie Collins) that the number "had been the greatest success of all; has shot ahead of last year; has sold about two hundred and twenty thousand; and has made the name of Mrs. Lirriper so swiftly and domestically famous as never was." Dickens confessed that he had a very strong belief in her, finding that she made a great effect upon him in the writing; but her popularity exceeded his hopes and expectations.

Apart from anxiety respecting his own health, Dickens suffered a personal bereavement at this time, in the death of his mother in September, at the age of seventy-three. On Christmas Eve, too, sad news reached him at Gad's Hill, brought there by friends arriving from London—the sudden death of Thackeray, which affected him exceedingly. There had been, unhappily, a break in the friendship previously subsisting between these literary giants, caused by an incident in connection with the Garrick Club. In 1858, a small weekly periodical called *Town Talk* published a descriptive sketch of Thackeray from the pen of Edmund Yates, who, had already supplied a similar sketch of Dickens (printed for an earlier issue), and Yates thus briefly related the facts to an interviewer: "I had written my matter [for the ensuing number] —enough to fill up, as I thought—when I received a message saying that Mr. Watts Phillips [the editor] had gone and there was a big deficit of copy. I must make it up. I rushed over to the printers in Aldersgate Street, threw off my coat . . . sat down, and without the slightest reflection turned out that article. I was not twenty-seven then, and had but small notion of how little causes often come home to bitterly revisit you."[1] Thackeray was very wroth, and regarded Yates's sketch (especially that portion of it purporting to delineate his personal appearance) as an unwarrantable liberty on the part of a fellow member of the Garrick Club. The author of "Vanity Fair" considered it due to the interests of the Club and to his own self-respect that the offending member should be expelled therefrom, whereupon the matter was placed before the committee, who decided in Thackeray's favour. Dickens, being likewise a member of the Garrick, interposed to avert that extremity, because he thought the penalty too severe, and thus incurred the resentment of Thackeray. The sketch is certainly not all that can be desired from the point of view of good taste, and, in particular passages, sails dangerously near the possibilities of an action for libel: but Yates excused himself on the score of youthful

[1] *Strand Magazine*, Illustrated Interviews, No. 24. In a very scarce pamphlet, entitled "Mr. Thackeray, Mr. Yates, and the Garrick Club," a detailed account is given of the proceedings.

thoughtlessness, and declared that no personal feeling whatever prompted him to write what he did. He met Thackeray but once afterwards, and made several unsuccessful attempts to put the matter right. The most regrettable consequence of the quarrel, however, was the estrangement wrought between Thackeray and Dickens; by a fortunate circumstance, however, the two men accidentally met face to face in the hall of the Athenaeum Club, and a reconciliation took place. This occurred in December 1863, and a week later the great "Titmarsh" had joined the majority. "No one can be surer than I of the greatness and goodness of his heart," said Dickens of his famous contemporary, in the just tribute to his memory which he composed, at the solicitation of some of his friends, for Thackeray's own magazine.[1]

Charles Dickens, with his family and a party of friends, was at Gad's Hill at the opening of 1864. Besides his duties as host, he had much to do in arranging various details preparatory to his son Frank's departure for India at the end of January, to join his brother Walter, then a lieutenant in the 42nd Royal Highlanders. Alas! Before he arrived at his destination, Walter died quite suddenly at Calcutta, on the last night of the previous year, at the age of twenty-three, the mournful announcement being received by his father on February 7th—his own birthday. Although grievously distressed by the intelligence, the Novelist succeeded in making satisfactory progress with the new story, and announced on January 24th that he had then begun the third number. "It is a combination of drollery with romance," he explained

---

[1] "In Memoriam" (*Cornhill Magazine*, February 1864).

to Wilkie Collins, "which requires a great deal of pains and a perfect throwing away of points that might be amplified; but I hope it is *very good.* I confess, in short, that I think it is. Strange to say, I felt at first quite dazed in getting back to the large canvas and the big brushes. . . ."[1] The illustrations for "Our Mutual Friend" constituted a new departure, so far as the serial stories are concerned; not only were they designed by an artist other than "Phiz" (whose collaboration with Dickens ceased on the completion of "A Tale of Two Cities"), but the process of reproduction differed, for the designs were drawn and engraved on wood instead of being etched on steel, as had been. The Novelist, with customary care, superintended the work of illustration, entering into the minutest particulars regarding each and every design, even to the lettering on the monthly wrapper. Mr. Marcus Stone (now the eminent Royal Academician and the son of his old friend Frank Stone, A.R.A.), had been elected to succeed "Phiz"; he was then a promising young artist, and there is no doubt that this association with the most popular author of the day enabled the juvenile draughtsman to make his bow to a pretty large section of the public—an opportunity too seldom afforded to a beginner in the craft.[2] A letter from the Novelist to his *protégé*, regarding his design for the wrapper, sufficiently indicates the solicitude and attention bestowed by the Author upon such details: "The word 'Our' in the title must be out in the open like 'Mutual Friend,' making the title three distinct lines— 'Our' as big as 'Mutual Friend.' This would give you

[1] "The Letters of Charles Dickens."
[2] Mr. Marcus Stone had already supplied the frontispiece for the first cheap edition of "Little Dorrit" (1861).

too much design at the bottom. I would therefore take
out the dustman, and put the Wegg and Boffin
composition (which is capital) in its place. I don't
want Mr. Inspector or the murder reward bill, because
these points are sufficiently indicated in the river at the
top. Therefore you can have an indication of the
dustman in Mr. Inspector's place. Note, that the
dustman's face should be droll, and not horrible.
Twemlow's elbow will still go out of the frame as it
does now, and the same with Lizzie's skirts on the
opposite side. With these changes, work away!"[1] It
was owing to an interesting discovery made by Mr.
Marcus Stone in connection with his art that Dickens
became acquainted with what he described as an
"extraordinary trade" —a discovery which came in the
nick of time, that is to say, when he was endeavouring
to think of a new subject for one of the early chapters
of the story. The "extraordinary trade" was that of a
taxidermist, and the Novelist (veiling his identity)
immediately seized the opportunity of visiting the
proprietor of the curious establishment near Seven
Dials to which Mr. Stone had called his attention, with
the result that we have the inimitable presentment of
Mr. Venus and his queer surroundings.
Notwithstanding the fact that Dickens had an
ample store of material for the story, the actual
writing proceeded laboriously and painfully. At this
juncture he could not afford to spare time for even a
brief holiday at Hastings, whither Forster essayed to
tempt him: "If I were to lose a page of the five
numbers I have purposed to myself to be ready by
the publication day," he said, in reply to the invitation,
"I should feel that I had fallen short. I have

[1] "The Letters of Charles Dickens."

grown hard to satisfy, and write very slowly. . . ." He admitted, too, that it was absolutely essential he should take more care of himself than ever, and this excessive caution may be regarded as indicative of a change, both in body and brain—the consequence of working too hard and of the strain of the public readings, the effects of which now became more apparent. On May 1st, the initial part of "Our Mutual Friend" was launched; two days later the Author gleefully announced that the sale had attained to thirty thousand, "and orders flowing in fast." This success was unfortunately not maintained, there being a distinct abatement in the demand for Part 2; however, before the book closed the original number was again reached. The difference in the extent of the sales of the two first numbers seems to have caused some indecision in the mind of the Author, as on June 10th he wrote: "This leaves me going round and round like a carrier pigeon before swooping on number seven." Worried, too, by an accumulation of engagements, so that hardly a day was left free, he felt that nothing could be done but getting away. "What with public speechifying, private eating and drinking, and perpetual simmering in hot rooms, I have made London too hot to hold me and my work together." He had then but lately presided (May 11th) at a public meeting held at the Adelphi Theatre for the purpose of founding the Shakespeare Schools in connection with the Royal Dramatic College, on which occasion he delivered an address. Incidents of this character were naturally distracting, and increased the difficulty he experienced when busy with a story. In addition there was a return of illness, which explains the sad tone of a letter dated July 29th, when he said:

"Although I have not been wanting in industry, I have been wanting in invention, and have fallen back with the book." He felt, indeed, "out of sorts," and consequently feared that he had "a very mountain to climb" before he would "see the open country."

In the middle of February the Novelist relocated to 57 Gloucester Place, Hyde Park, where he stayed until the middle of June, and where he conscientiously directed his thoughts upon "Our Mutual Friend" and *All the Year Round.* The summer and autumn were spent at Gad's Hill, his literary labours being pleasantly diversified by brief holidays, in receiving visitors, and by occasional trips to the Continent. "My being on the Dover Line, and my being very fond of France, occasion me to cross the Channel perpetually. Whenever I feel that I have worked too much, or am on the eve of overdoing it, and want a change, away I go by the mail train, and turn up in Paris or anywhere else that suits my humour, next morning. So I come back as fresh as a daisy, and preserve as ruddy a face as though I had never leant over a sheet of paper. When I retire from a literary life I think of setting up as a Channel pilot."[1] The death of John Leech, which took place at the end of October, put him out woefully. "Yesterday and the day before," he said, feeling entirely unnerved, "I could do nothing; seemed for the time to have quite lost the power; and am only by slow degrees getting back into the track today." He rallied presently, however, and attacked in earnest his next Christmas Number, which had been "looming large" before him. So great was the interest excited by the

[1] "The Letters of Charles Dickens."

previous Christmas issue that he decided to give a sequel; this he called "Mrs. Lirriper's Legacy," and his contributions were the opening and concluding chapters, which indicate no decline in humour or pathos. *Apropos* of the Lirriper tales, Mr. Percy Fitzgerald recollects the Novelist lamenting that in them he had wasted much that would have been valuable for a serial story.

The writing of "Our Mutual Friend" monopolised a considerable amount of Dickens's attention in 1865, the complete work being published in two volumes in November of that year. During the previous February he suffered from a formidable affection of the foot, which had been frostbitten through walking for hours in the snow, the resulting lameness compelling him to abstain from his favourite exercise—a sad deprivation; this affliction he endured at intervals until the end of his life. For the spring he had taken a furnished house at No. 16 Somers Place, Hyde Park, which he occupied, with his sister-in-law and daughter, from the beginning of March until June. Though the injured foot caused great agony, he continued (at Somers Place) to work "like a dragon" at his book, and was "a terror to the household, likewise to all organs and brass bands in this quarter." Late in April the foot trouble somewhat abated, so much so that he could again walk his ten miles in the morning without inconvenience, "but am absurdly obliged to sit shoeless all the evening," which he considered "a very slight penalty," as it justified him in declining invitations to dine—a dinner party being a function that he had latterly come to regard with detestation. The comparative cessation from pain, however, proved to be but temporary, so that a complete change became necessary for health's sake, and after trying the sea he decided to go abroad, fully understanding that if he did not do this he would break down—"no one knows as I know today how near to it I have been"—for work and worry, without exercise, would (he believed) soon make an end of him. On May 9th he was induced to preside at the Annual Festival of the Newsvendors' Benevolent and Provident Association, when he delivered a characteristic speech in aid of the cause. He also occupied the chair, on May 20th, at the Second Annual Dinner of the Newspaper Press Fund, and proposed the toast of the evening, referring, in the course of his observations, to his early experiences as a reporter.

It was the end of May when he indulged in a short holiday trip into France, and on his way home a few days later (June 9th), a frightful accident overtook the train by which he was travelling, at Staplehurst (a few miles south of Maidstone), from the effects of which his nerves never wholly recovered. The train ran off the rails, and Dickens was in the only carriage that did not go over into the adjoining stream, being caught upon the turn by a portion of the ruined bridge, where it hung in an apparently. impossible manner. Happily, the Novelist was one of the few passengers who escaped injury, and with praiseworthy energy he assisted in the terrible work of getting out the dying and dead; for valuable help thus rendered the directors of the company sent him a resolution of thanks. "No imagination can conceive the ruin of the carriages," he wrote to Thomas Mitton four days afterwards, "or the extraordinary weights under which the people were lying, or the complications into which they were twisted up among iron and wood, and mud and water." Strange to relate, he was not in the least fluttered at the time, and instantly remembering that he had left in the carriage the manuscript of a number of "Our Mutual Friend," he clambered back and recovered it—a fact recorded by him in the "postscript" of the story (dated September 1865), where he says: "I remember with devout thankfulness that I can never be much nearer parting company with my readers forever, than I was then, until there shall be written against my life the two words with which I have this day closed this book—THE END."

One of the passengers whom Dickens rescued from a perilous position, a youth of seventeen named Dickenson (later Major S. Newton Dickenson, of the 19th Regiment), justly believed that he owed his life to the Novelist, whose hospitality he afterwards enjoyed at Gad's Hill. As a slight memento of those days, Major Dickenson cherished some copies of a little newspaper called *The Gad's Hill Gazette*, which was printed and published weekly by Dickens's sons when boys home for the holidays, and established at their father's suggestion as a means of employing their youthful energies. It is a curious specimen of the typographical art, and when matter ran short, it was supplied by humorous letters from the Novelist himself, who would, for instance, write a complaint in one number under a fictitious name, and reply to it in the next. *The Gad's Hill Gazette* (price 2d.) circulated among relatives and friends of the family, and flourished during a period of four years, the final number (as announced in a special circular by the Editor, Henry Fielding Dickens) appearing at Christmas 1866. The pages of this interesting publication are replete with references to incidents occurring at Gad's Hill Place, and the issue dated December 30, 1865, contains the following allusion to Mr. Dickenson: "The latter gentleman has not yet recovered from the effects of a most disastrous railway accident in which he was a sufferer, and had it not been for the courage and intrepidity of Mr. Dickens, he would not now be spending his Christmas at Gad's Hill."

We gather from the Novelist's correspondence that after the fearful Staplehurst experience he could never travel on the railway without great mental anguish, and for a considerable time remained "curiously weak," as though recovering from a long illness, and unable to write half-a-dozen notes without turning faint and sick. The accident caused him to get in arrears with his story. "Alas!" he wrote to Forster at the beginning of July, "for the two numbers you write of! There is only one in existence. I have but just begun the other. . . ." Fancy my having underwritten No, 16 by two and a half pages—a thing I have not done since 'Pickwick'!" (He had forgotten, however, that he committed a similar mistake when writing "Dombey.") With shaken nerves, but with energy unsubdued, the Novelist at length completed the story, some of the final chapters being penned in Paris. It is said that at the last moment, while the manuscript was in the printers' hands, he resolved to rewrite a whole chapter that was then in type, and that this was accordingly done, in the very greatest haste and excitement, while the firm's senior reader waited for it.

Produced under such adverse circumstances, it is hardly surprising that "Our Mutual Friend" should fail to rank with Dickens's higher achievements; even Forster admits that, as a whole, it is wanting in freshness and natural development, and is devoid of the creative power which marked the earlier writings. The prototype of Boffin, the Golden Dustman, was a wealthy philanthropist named Henry Dodd, with whom Dickens had become acquainted; he was a London contractor on a large scale, owning an enormous dust heap in Shepherdess Fields, Islington; being passionately fond of the play, he endowed several dramatic charities, but his pet project of founding a dramatic college unfortunately came to grief by reason of its being based upon a wrong principle. Dodd presented one of the dust heaps to his daughter as a wedding gift, and it afterwards realised £10,000! In a ward at the Children's Hospital, Great Ormond Street, Dickens found a pathetic setting for the deathbed of little Johnny, the adopted orphan, and it must have gratified the Novelist to know that the publication of the story, with its pictures of suffering babyhood, brought a steady flow of subscriptions to the hospital, then badly needing support and interest. The original manuscript of "Our Mutual Friend" was bequeathed by George Washington Childs to the Drexel Institute, Philadelphia, the authorities at the South Kensington Museum having failed to secure it for the sum of £1200.

Dickens had scarcely finished "Our Mutual Friend," his mental powers exhausted by the sustained effort, when the time recurred for the annual Christmas tale. "Tired with 'Our Mutual,'" he said to Forster, "I sat down to cast about for an idea, with a depressing notion that I was, for the moment, overworked. Suddenly, the little character that you will see, and all belonging to it, came flashing up in the most cheerful manner, and I had only to look on and leisurely describe it." The number bore the title, "Doctor Marigold's Prescriptions," and the "little character" was Doctor Marigold himself—a Cheap Jack. "It is wonderfully like the real thing," observed the Author, "of course a little refined and humoured," and he felt that, if people at large understood a Cheap Jack, his own part of the number would certainly prove popular. "I do hope," he said to Forster, "that in the beginning and end of this Christmas Number you will find something that will strike you as being fresh, forcible, and full of spirits." He contributed three out of the eight chapters, viz.: I. To be Taken Immediately; VI. To be Taken with a Grain of Salt (i.e., the portion describing the trial for murder); VII. To be Taken for Life. For his character sketches of Dr. Marigold, Chops the Dwarf, and other similar personages in the tale, Dickens found ample material in the neighbourhood of Gad's Hill, especially on the Dover Road, where travelling caravans may generally be seen slowly wending their way. "Doctor Marigold's Prescriptions" affords a characteristic illustration of the Author's powers, both of humour and pathos, and proved one of the most acceptable of the readings.

CHAPTER 13

PUBLIC READINGS
IN AMERICA

No project in life inspired Charles Dickens with more
practical enthusiasm than the Guild of Literature and
Art. The cause he espoused so warmly was intended to
benefit those literary men and artists who, either
through illness, old age, or misfortune, were prevented
from carrying on their profession, and its promoters
decided to administer the funds in a manner that would
not injure the susceptibilities of the recipients or
prejudice their sense of self-reliance. The idea of such
disinterested philanthropy was originally propounded
by Richard Hengist Horne (the author of "Orion,"
&c.), but it was not until some years had elapsed that
the proposal received substantial recognition, viz., in
the late autumn of 1850, when Dickens and a
distinguished company of amateur actors (including
Mark Lemon, John Leech, Douglas Jerrold, John
Forster, Frank Stone, Augustus Egg, &c.), gave
private performances of Ben Jonson's play, "Every
Man in His Humour," in the great hall of the Lytton
mansion at Knebworth. It was during the presentation
of this comedy that Horne's excellent notion
was eagerly discussed by Dickens and Sir E. Bulwer
Lytton (afterwards Lord Lytton), who forthwith
pledged themselves to mature a scheme for the

formation of a society, the distinguished baronet consenting not only to give a piece of land upon his Hertfordshire estate for the erection of a college, but further agreed to write a comedy in aid of a preliminary fund. As Dickens explained, the objects of the Guild were "to encourage life assurance and other provident habits among authors and artists; to render such assistance to both as shall never compromise their independence; and to found a new institution where honourable rest from arduous labour shall still be associated with the discharge of congenial duties." Several performances were given in London and the provinces by Dickens and his friends in aid of this project, and with the money thus raised it was proposed to establish and endow an institute, having at its disposal certain salaries to which particular duties would be attached, together with a limited number of free residences, completed with due regard to the ordinary habits and necessary comforts of gentlemen, while among other conditions it was stipulated that each member should deliver, either personally or by proxy, three lectures annually on subjects relating to Art or Letters.

Theoretically, the excellence of this object became at once manifest to those who were actively concerned in formulating the design. Dickens himself had implicit confidence in it, so splendidly begun, if only it were carried out with a steadfast energy. "I have a strong conviction," he said to Sir Edward, "that we hold in our hands the peace and honour of men of letters for centuries to come, and that you are destined to be their best and most enduring benefactor." It happened that the singular run of good fortune attendant upon the histrionic efforts of

Dickens and his company of actors failed to keep pace with their hopes and ambition respecting the "Guild" project. The funds, however, enabled the promoters to build three or four houses on the land at Stevenage, presented by Sir E. Bulwer Lytton, and on July 29, 1865, Dickens and other members of the "Guild" Committee journeyed to that pretty Hertfordshire village for the purpose of inspecting the buildings. After the survey the party drove to Knebworth to partake of the baronet's hospitality, and Dickens, in the course of a speech proposing the health of the host, said: "The ladies and gentlemen whom we shall invite to occupy the houses we have built will never be placed under any social disadvantage. They will be invited to occupy them as artists, receiving them as a mark of the high respect in which they are held by their fellow workers. As artists I hope they will often exercise their calling within those walls for the general advantage; and they will always claim, on equal terms, the hospitality of their generous neighbour."

According to the stringent and express prohibition of the Act of Parliament, no pension could be granted until the "Guild" charter was seven years old![1] On discovering this remarkable clause, Dickens immediately recommended that there should be no expenses in connection with the "Guild" affairs—that the interest on the capital should be invested as it accrued, that the "Guild" should have the use of the office of his journal rent free, and the services of W. H. Wills on the same terms—all of which was duly approved and effected. But—alas! For the

---

[1] *Apropos* of this, Dickens observed: "It appears to me that the House of Commons and Parliament altogether is just the dreariest failure and nuisance that has bothered this much-bothered world."

vanity of human wishes and aspirations—the scheme which so abundantly justified the anticipation of success was doomed to end abortively. The very class the "Guild" sought to benefit could not be brought to regard it with favour, and every renewed exertion to secure public appreciation more clearly emphasized the lamentable fact of its failure. It is conjectured that so unfortunate a result was partly attributable to the ridicule poured upon this truly altruistic movement by certain pseudo-facetious newspapers, some of which jocosely anticipated a rush of passengers by rail to Stevenage, to see "the literary lions at feeding time." A more probable cause, however, may be found in the suggestion that such a form of charity militated against the sense of delicacy and refinement usually appertaining to genius; this, coupled with the fact that the "Guild" houses were situated in a locality remote from London, and therefore not easily accessible, suffices to account for a fiasco which proved such a bitter disappointment to Dickens and his coadjutors, who, needless to add, were deeply grieved by the non-realisation of their high expectations. To conclude the story of the famous Guild of Literature and Art, it should be stated that, although its primary objects were not attained, important advantages accrued. The fund raised by means of dramatic performances, supplemented by subscriptions and the rents of the "Guild" houses and land at Stevenage, constituted a not inconsiderable sum, which was invested in Stocks, whence grants were from time to time made to necessitous persons, such grants being carefully and economically administered in conformity with the provisions of the Act of Parliament under which the "Guild" had a corporate existence. The final chapter of its history may be briefly summed up by stating that in 1897, among the private (unopposed) Bills proceeded with in Parliament was that which the Earl of Morley's Committee had ordered to be reported to the House of Lords, the object of which was the winding up and dissolution of the "Guild." The Bill was passed, and power given to transfer the assets to the Royal Literary Fund and the Artists' General Benevolent Institution; by this arrangement the generous and thoughtful movement which Dickens had so much at heart will practically be carried into effect, although in a manner somewhat differing from the founders' intentions.

At the beginning of 1866 Charles Dickens was beset by nervous apprehensions, and feared that the effect upon himself of the Staplehurst accident would gravely impair his powers as a writer of fiction. It came, therefore, as a surprise to those friends who were conscious of his physical condition when he announced his determination to undertake a task involving a supreme effort on his part, and which would make a very considerable demand upon his strength. He decided, at the close of "Our Mutual Friend," to give a third series of public readings, resolving thus to earn the most money in the briefest period, regardless of the fatigue he had already experienced in that direction. He had perhaps become conscious (suggests Forster) that for exertion of this kind the time left him was short, and events proved how totally unfit he had become for so enterprising a venture. Although the opinion of the doctors then consulted by him indicated the existence of a heart trouble, he did not feel disconcerted, and remarked to Forster: "I knew well beforehand that the effect could not possibly be without the one cause at the bottom of it, of some degeneration of some function of the heart. Of course I am not so foolish as to suppose that all my work can have been achieved without *some* penalty, and I have noticed for some time a decided change in my buoyancy and hopefulness. . . ." In spite of this knowledge he accepted an offer, from Messrs. Chappell of Bond Street, of £50 a night for thirty nights to read in "England, Ireland, Scotland, or Paris, in London, the Provinces, or elsewhere," as it might be agreed upon. "All I have to do is, to take my book and read, at the appointed place and hour, and come out again. All the business of every kind is done by Chappells at their own cost, and on their own responsibility." Thus he was relieved from unnecessary anxiety, and for the readings would receive (in three instalments) the sum of £1500 for the entire series.

On St. Valentine's Day the Novelist officiated as chairman at the annual dinner of the Dramatic, Equestrian, and Musical Fund, and advocated the claims of the Fund in most felicitous terms. On March 28th he was present at the annual festival of the Royal General Theatrical Fund, and, as one of the trustees of the Fund, tendered the chairman of the evening (Sir Benjamin Phillips, Lord Mayor of London) his best thanks "for lending the very powerful aid of his presence, his influence, and his personal character" to that very deserving Institution.

In the spring of this year (1866) Dickens rented No. 6 Southwick Place, Hyde Park, where (on March 12th) he wrote to Robert Browning, inviting the poet to join Forster there on the following Sunday and hear him, (Dickens) read "Doctor Marigold," which he was about to include in the public readings. Concerning the readings themselves, George Dolby (his business manager, engaged by Messrs. Chappell) gives a vivid account in "Charles Dickens as I knew Him." Suffice it for the moment to say that the Reader's success proved even more triumphant than on the previous tours, the receipts for one night's work frequently exceeding £300. On April 20th the outlay for the entire venture was covered, so that the rest of the income became actual profit. At Liverpool the police reported officially that three thousand people were turned away from the hall, unable to gain admission. The readings, especially in the larger halls, proved a great strain, and the consequent fatigue induced sleeplessness; but "a dozen oysters and a little champagne between the parts every night" constituted a satisfactory restorative. On May 7th he responded to an invitation to occupy the chair at a dinner of the members of the Metropolitan Rowing Clubs; as President of the Nautilus Rowing Club, he proposed "Prosperity to the Rowing Clubs of London," and, in the course of his speech, referred to the early days of his novitiate as a boatman on the Thames, his tutor being "an anomalous creature called a 'foreman waterman,' who wore an eminently tall hat, and a perfectly unaccountable uniform," the Novelist concluding his remarks by instituting a laughable comparison between the paying off or purification of the National Debt and the purification of the Thames. Three days later, after reading at Birmingham, he complained of a severe pain in the ball of his left eye, which made it difficult for him to do anything after a hundred miles' shaking in the train. He also referred to a trouble in the left hand and faintness of the heart (the latter, alas, a significant symptom), which naturally made him more susceptible to physical exhaustion. The first batch of readings closed in June, when he gladly retired to Gad's Hill to rest "and hear the birds sing." Here he stayed during the remaining part of the year, recuperating, in readiness for a further series of readings, Messrs. Chappell having tempted him (in August) with an offer for fifty more nights to begin at Christmas, for which he meant to ask £70 a night, feeling bound (as he said) to look to himself for the future; the result of the negotiation, however, was an engagement of forty-two nights for £2500. "So I shall now try to discover [the subject for] a Christmas Number," he wrote to Forster, "and shall, please Heaven, be quit of the whole series of readings so as to get to work on a new story for the new series of *All the Year Round*, early in the spring. The readings begin probably in the new year."

In November, replying to a query (propounded by Mr. Percy Fitzgerald) respecting the accuracy of a rumour announcing the appearance of another story in the familiar wrappers, the Novelist said: "Concerning the green covers, I find the leaves to be budding—on questionable newspaper authority; but, upon my soul, I have no other knowledge of this being in embryo! Really, I do not see a chance of my settling myself to such work until after I have accomplished forty-two readings, to which I stand pledged." The truth was that, in consequence of his numerous public engagements, the opportunity did not present itself of contemplating the preparation of a new serial, his only effort in fiction during the year being his contributions to the usual Christmas Number. The title of "Mugby Junction" was bestowed upon this number, in which the names of the various authors were printed for the first time. George Dolby has recorded that the idea of it originated in the following circumstance that happened during one of the reading tours; on arriving at Rugby, the Novelist entered the refreshment room at the railway station (where the appurtenances "were wretched, and the manners of the woman in charge deplorable"), and, extending his hand for sugar and milk for his coffee, the discourteous manageress snatched them away, saying he should not have them until the coffee was paid for—whereat a page in buttons was so amused that he burst out into an uncontrollable fit of laughter. The first four papers in the number fell to Dickens's share, namely, "Barbox Brothers," "Barbox Brothers & Co.," "Main Line. The Boy at Mugby," and "No. 1 Branch Line. The Signal-Man." The Boy at Mugby was of course the hilarious page in buttons, while the prototype of Lamps (another character in the tale) was based upon a lamp foreman at Tilbury railway terminus, named Chipperfield (died in 1889, aged eighty-two), who proudly averred that the Novelist not only had many conversations with him, but presented him with a copy of the number in which he is immortalised. "Mugby Junction" attained high-water mark in respect of sales both in England and America, over seventy thousand copies being disposed of in the latter country within a fortnight after the day of publication. Writing to Macready on December 28th, Dickens said: "'Mugby junction' turned, yesterday afternoon, the extraordinary number of two hundred and fifty thousand!"

In this letter to Macready, the Novelist gives an account of some races and other festivities which he had organised, and which had taken place two days previously. "You will be interested in knowing that, encouraged by the success of summer cricket matches, I got up a quantity of footraces and rustic sports in my field here on the twenty-sixth last past: as I have never yet had a case of drunkenness, the landlord of the Falstaff had a drinking booth on the ground. All the prizes I gave were in money, too. We had two thousand people here. Among the crowd were soldiers, navvies, and labourers of all kinds. Not a stake was pulled up, or a rope slackened, or one farthing's worth of damage done. To every competitor (only) a printed bill of general rules was given, with the concluding words: 'Mr. Dickens puts every man upon his honour to assist in preserving order.' There was not a dispute all day, and they went away at sunset rending the air with cheers, and leaving every flag on a six-hundred yards' course as neat as they found it when the gates were opened at ten in the morning. Surely this is a bright sign in the neighbourhood of such a place as Chatham!"[1] Those who were privileged to enjoy Dickens's hospitality forever retained a delightful impression of their amiable and vivacious host, whose chief care was to provide pleasurable entertainment for, and insure the comfort of, everybody. In summer days at Gad's Hill there were cricket matches, rural sports, walks and drives to places of interest; in the winter all kinds of indoor recreation were indulged in, such as dancing, charades, theatricals, and billiards. When such valued friends as Longfellow, Lowell, Fields, and others from distant countries, visited him at "Gad's" (so the place was familiarly termed), he would compress into a brief space of time a vast amount of sightseeing; castles and cathedrals would be

---

[1] "The Letters of Charles Dickens."

inspected, picnics held among the cherry orchards and hop gardens, excursions to Kits Coty House, Blue Bell Hill, and other beautiful localities in the neighbourhood; and sometimes, when very special occasions warranted such a festive display, he would turn out a couple of postillions "in the old red jackets of the old red royal Dover road" for their drive, these events being reminiscent (as he observed) of a holiday ride in England fifty years ago. Gad's Hill Place was frequently brightened by the presence of his eldest son's children, and writing to Miss Milner Gibson on December 22nd, the Novelist said: "I can never imagine myself grandfather of four. That objectionable relationship is never permitted to be mentioned in my presence. I make the mites suppose that my lawful name is 'Wenerables,' which they piously believe." And "Wenerables" they called him, much to the amusement of his guests. Soon after the building of the Swiss Chalet was completed, in 1865, Dickens transacted a good deal of his literary work there during the summer months, and in a letter to his American friend, James T. Fields, written in his charming retreat, he said: "Divers birds sing here all day, and the nightingales all night. The place is lovely and in perfect order. . . . I have put five mirrors in the chalet where I write, and they reflect and refract, in all kinds of ways, the leaves that are quivering at the windows, and the great fields of waving corn, and the sail dotted river. My room is up among the branches of the trees; and the birds and the butterflies fly in and out, and the green branches shoot in at the open windows, and the lights and shadows of the clouds come and go with the rest of the company. The scent of the flowers, and indeed of everything that is growing for miles and miles, is most delicious." This is justly held to be one of the most pleasing word-pictures ever penned of the Author and his surroundings. At his death the Chalet was taken down and re-erected in the grounds of the Crystal Palace, whence, after remaining there a short time, it was transferred to its present position in Cobham Park, the seat of his esteemed neighbour the Earl of Darnley, to whom this personal relic was presented by the Novelist's family.

Instead of taking a house in London in the spring of 1867, Dickens found it more convenient to make his headquarters at the office of *All the Year Round*, where he lived at intervals while carrying out the next batch of readings. Respecting these readings, here is his first outline of plan: "I start on Wednesday afternoon (the 15th of January) for Liverpool, and then go on to Chester, Derby, Leicester, and Wolverhampton. On Tuesday the 29th, I read in London again, and in February I read at Manchester and then go on into Scotland." The readings began with unabated enthusiasm; but the Reader, alas, speedily discovered his physical unfitness for this arduous and exacting undertaking. Almost at the beginning of the tour he was so overcome by faintness after a reading that he had to be carried out and laid on a sofa for half-an-hour, and he attributed this indisposition to a "distressing inability to sleep at night, and to nothing worse." The climatic conditions, too, were excessively trying, indeed, he thought it was the worst weather he ever experienced; at Chester he read "in a snowstorm and a fall of ice"—at Wolverhampton a thaw had set in and it rained furiously, and touring under such circumstances fairly exhausted him. Writing on January 22nd to his daughter, Mamie, from the

former town, he said: "I have seldom seen a place look
more hopelessly frozen up than this place does. The
hall is like a Methodist chapel in low spirits, and with
a cold in its head. A few blue people shiver at the
corners of the streets. And this house, which is outside
the town, looks like an ornament on an immense
twelfth cake baked for 1847."[1] At the Birmingham
reading two days later an accident happened which,
but for Dickens's presence of mind, might have proved
disastrous. There was an escape of gas from the side of
the top batten, which caught the copper wire and was
within a thread of bringing down the heavy reflector
into the stalls. "It was a very ticklish matter, though
the audience knew nothing about it. I saw it, and the
gasman and Dolby saw it, and stood at that side of the
platform in agonies. We all three calculated that there
would be just time to finish and save it; when the gas
was turned out the instant I had done, the thing was at
its very last and utmost extremity. Whom it would
have tumbled on, or what might have been set on fire,
it is impossible to say."[2] Presently he complained of
feeling "not quite right"; this he believed to be the
effect of the vibration of the train by which he travelled, for it seemed (he said) to tell upon him more and
more after the Staplehurst experience. He referred also
to "a curious feeling of soreness all round the body,"
which he supposed to arise from the great exertion of
voice. On February 19th, graver symptoms prevailed,
caused by an internal malady which, in 1841, necessitated surgical assistance, and was now attended with
the sudden loss of so much blood that he believed it
desirable to write at once for advice to his family

[1] "The Letters of Charles Dickens."
[2] Ibid.

doctor at Gad's Hill. After two days' rest, however, at the Bridge of Allan, he rallied again, although still suffering from insomnia. Happily, everything in connection with the business details of the readings was arranged for him with the utmost liberality and consideration, so that he escaped possible worries of that kind, while he testified to the loyalty of his three men and to the agreeable companionship and good-fellowship of his "excellent manager," George Dolby.

This series of readings included a visit to some of the leading towns in Ireland, to which country (owing to the Fenian excitement) Dickens consented to go with great reluctance. The journey was made on March 13th through an incessant snowstorm, and the train was snowed up among the Welsh mountains in a tremendous gale of wind, the engine having to be dug out of the drift. On arriving at Dublin he found the city in a state of great alarm, and the manager of his hotel very despondent; consequently a breakdown of the readings was expected. There were preparations on all sides in anticipation of riotous proceedings on St. Patrick's Day, a considerable muster of soldiers and police being held in readiness, but kept carefully out of sight. "One would not suppose, walking about the streets, that any disturbance was impending; and yet there is no doubt that the materials of one lie smouldering up and down the city and all over the country. . . . If any riot were to break out, I should immediately stop the readings here."[1] On the other hand, there was feasting going on, and Dickens received invitations to dinner parties from divers civil and military authorities. Notwithstanding the

---

[1] "The Letters of Charles Dickens."

preoccupation of the public mind at this juncture, he was accorded a most hearty reception by the Irish people, who flocked to the readings in large numbers. "You will be surprised to be told that we have done "Wonders!" he wrote to Forster. "Enthusiastic crowds have filled the halls to the roof each night, and hundreds have been turned away. At Belfast the night before last we had £246, 5s. In Dublin tonight everything is sold out, and people are besieging Dolby to put chairs anywhere, in doorways, on my platform, in any sort of hole or corner. In short, the readings are a perfect rage at a time when everything else is beaten down." The Irish engagements concluded, the long journeys ceased, and the third series of readings closed with a tour in the provinces. At Cambridge the colleges assembled in full force, "from the biggest guns to the smallest, and went far beyond even Manchester in the roars of welcome and the rounds of cheers." The Novelist finished the fifty readings on May 14th. He had worked at them very hard, even to the extent of learning them all by heart, so as to have no mechanical drawback in looking after the words. "I have tested," he said, "all the serious passion in them by everything I know; made the humorous points much more humorous; corrected my utterance of certain words; cultivated a self-possession not to be disturbed; and made myself master of the situation." The short intervals between his travels from place to place were utilised by Dickens for his duties in connection with *All the Year Round*. "When I read, I *don't* write," he explained to M. de Cerjat. I only edit, and have the proof-sheets sent me for the purpose."[1] It so happened that there was to

[1] "The Letters of Charles Dickens."

be nothing of special import from his pen for several months to come.

During the period covered by his last readings, the American mails brought him tempting proposals to read in that country, and a committee of private gentlemen at Boston tendered, as a guarantee, the sum of £10,000, to be banked in London. Messrs. Chappell thereupon notified their preparedness to treat for an American series, but he declared that if he went at all he would go on his own account. It being necessary to arrive at a speedy decision, both Forster and Wills were consulted, and, at first, were distinctly adverse to such an undertaking, knowing how much anxiety and fatigue it would involve. Dickens felt, however, that the generous offer from the United States could not be lightly put aside, and after much deliberation it was resolved to ascertain the actual feeling of the States concerning the project. As regards the proposed tour, there were, of course, advantages as well as disadvantages, the former (in Dickens's opinion) outweighing the latter. After experiencing the intense excitement afforded by the readings, he could not now tolerate the notion of dispensing with such a mental stimulant. "I shall never rest much while my faculties last," he observed to Wills, "and (if I know myself) have a certain something in me that would still be active in rusting and corroding me, if I flattered myself that I was in repose. On the other hand, I think that my habit of easy self-abstraction and withdrawal into fancies has always refreshed and strengthened me in short intervals wonderfully. I always seem to myself to have rested far more than I have worked; and I do really believe that I have some exceptional faculty of accumulating young feelings in short pauses, which obliterates a quantity of wear and tear. My worldly circumstances (such a large family considered) are very good. I don't want money. All my possessions are free and in the best order. Still, at fifty-five or fifty-six, the likelihood of making a very great addition to one's capital in half a year is an immense consideration. . . . I repeat the phrase, because there should be something large to set against the objections. . . ."[1] The many conflicting statements, however, with regard to the benefits likely to accrue from a reading tour in America created in his mind much uncertainty, and he clearly saw the impossibility of arriving at any reasonable conclusion "without sending eyes and ears on the actual ground." It was accordingly decided that George Dolby should sail for the States in the following August, to "prospect" for the "Chief," as the Novelist was affectionately termed by the manager of the readings.

Dickens, meanwhile, redeemed a promise to write (for the American publishers, Ticknor & Fields) a short story for insertion in *Our Young Folks, an Illustrated Magazine for Boys and Girls*. This was entitled "Holiday Romance," and concerning it he observed, in a letter to Mr. Fields (dated July 25th): "I hope the Americans will see the joke of 'Holiday Romance.' The writing seems to me so like children's, that dull folks (on *any* side of *any* water) might perhaps rate it accordingly. I should like to be beside you when you read it, and particularly when you read the Pirate's Story. It made me laugh to that extent that my people here thought I was out of my wits, until I gave it to them to read, when they did likewise." The manuscript was entrusted

[1] "The Letters of Charles Dickens."

to Dolby for delivery to Mr. Fields in August, but the story did not appear until the following year, when it was printed simultaneously with another tale which Dickens had consented to compose for the same well-known publishing house. The latter story, bearing the title of "George Silverman's Explanation," was issued by instalments in the *Atlantic Monthly*, and for each tale the Author received an honorarium of £1000—an astounding sum when it is remembered that neither contains more than half the quantity of a shilling number of his ordinary serials. Both productions were subsequently reprinted in *All the Year Round*, and are included in the later editions of the Novelist's works. In its original form, "Holiday Romance" was illustrated by Sir John Gilbert. We learn from Mr. Dolby's book that the writing of "George Silverman's Explanation" occupied but a very few days, and that the scene of the story was laid in a part of Lancashire, between Preston and Blackburn, which had much attracted Dickens. While walking from the one town to the other during the readings, he beheld the picturesque ruins of an old mansion, standing out weird and melancholy on the summit of a precipice, and, on inquiry, learned that the place was called Hoghton Towers: such a building had always a fascination for him, and he obtained permission to roam about the ruin, with the result that he made it the *locale* of the tale which then engaged his thoughts. He confessed to W. H. Wills that "George Silverman's Explanation" made upon himself "the strangest impression of reality and originality." "I feel," he said, "as if I had read something (by somebody else), which I should never get out of my mind!!! The main idea of the narrator's position towards the other people was the idea that I *had* for my next novel in *A.Y.R.* But it is very curious that I did not in the least see how to begin his state of mind until I walked into Hoghton Towers one bright April day."[1]

On June 5th, Dickens presided at the ninth Anniversary Festival of the Railway Benevolent Society and proposed the toast of the evening in an excellent speech. Another interesting oration is placed to his credit this year, namely, the speech delivered by him on the occasion of his occupying the chair at a public meeting of the Printers' Readers, held on September 17th, when, in testifying to the superior intelligence of the correctors of the press, he gratefully acknowledged that he had never gone through the sheets of any book he had written without having his attention called by the printer's reader to something he had overlooked, which indicated that he "had been closely followed through the work by a patient and trained mind, and not merely by a skilful eye."

On the 3rd of August George Dolby sailed for America on his important mission, and Dickens went to Liverpool to see him off. That the Novelist was physically unfit for the exertion which even this short journey necessitated is shown in his letter to Miss Hogarth, dated from the Adelphi Hotel, Liverpool, on the 2nd: "I cannot get a boot on—wear a slipper on my left foot, and consequently am here under difficulties;" he added that, with the view of keeping himself and his foot quiet, he thought of remaining at the hotel for a day or two.[2] On his return home his sufferings increased, erysipelas having supervened, and he was

---

[1] "The Letters of Charles Dickens."
[2] Ibid.

obliged to consult Sir Henry Thompson. "Meantime I am on my back, chafing," was his gloomy comment upon the state of affairs. "I could not walk a quarter of a mile tonight for £500." He tried to believe the cause of the trouble to be gout, but Sir Henry hinted that it originated in something more alarming. A rumour became current (causing great uneasiness among his friends) that the Novelist was in a critical state of health, and that eminent surgeons were sending him across the Atlantic for cessation from literary labour! Whereupon he sent a reassuring line to *The Times*, certifying to the contrary. About the middle of September Dolby returned to England with the result of his careful investigation, and an elaborate report was drawn up by him and Dickens (for consideration by Forster, Wills, and Ouvry), stating that the people were ready to give "Boz" a great reception, and that the prevailing tone of the press and the public was highly favourable to the proposed tour. It was estimated that the suggested eighty readings would yield a profit of £15,500. Forster, however, maintained his objection, protesting that "he had fully made up *his* mind that Dickens *should never go to America again*," one of his contentions being to the effect that the Novelist's "desire to increase his property in such a short space of time, and in such a way, was unworthy of him, or, in fact, of any man of genius, as the business of *reading* was a degrading one."[1] Such a line of argument Dickens regarded as unreasonable, and at length Forster and other friends reluctantly withdrew their opposition, although they still entertained misgivings as to the effect upon his health. On the 30th

---

[1] "Charles Dickens as I knew Him," by George Dolby, 1885.

of September the words "Yes. Go ahead" were cabled to Messrs. Ticknor & Fields, and Dolby was requested to make speedy preparations for returning to the States, to carry out preliminary arrangements. In a letter to his daughter, announcing this decision, the Novelist said: "I begin to feel myself drawn towards America, as Darnay, in the 'Tale of Two Cities,' was attracted to the Loadstone Rock, Paris."

The die was cast, but before the date of Dickens's departure for Transatlantic shores much had to be negotiated, by way of preparation and in other ways. October found him busily at work on the Christmas Number for *All the Year Round*, the title of which he confided to his old friend, Charles Kent— even before the printers were trusted with its name— "No Thoroughfare." It is surmised that this designation was suggested by the notice boards which had been put up at points where private roads or footpaths abut on public roads away from Cobham Park, not far from Gad's Hill. When the time was almost ripe for the number, Dickens wrote to Wilkie Collins (May 1, 1867): "Would you like to do the next Christmas No. with me—we two alone, each taking half? Of course I assume that the money question is satisfactorily disposed of between you and Wills. Equally, of course, I suppose our two names to be appended to the performance. I put this to you, I need hardly say, before having in any way approached the subject in my own mind as to contrivance, character, story, or anything else." The notion proved acceptable to his brother-novelist, and by the 19th of October Dickens had completed the greater part of his share of the composition, which consisted of "The Overture," portions of the First and Fourth Acts, and the whole of

Act III. Wilkie Collins, in subsequently recalling (as far as he was then able) the exact nature of the collaboration, explained that they purposely wrote so as to make discoveries of this kind difficult, if not impossible, each writer inserting passages in the chapters of the other; the story was put together in the Swiss Chalet at Gad's Hill, and the two authors finished the Fourth Act side by side at two desks in Dickens's bedroom. In 1868 the story underwent transformation, Wilkie Collins converting it into a play for Fechter, that being the object for which it had been originally planned. "No Thoroughfare" was the last of a long series of Christmas Numbers.

On the 8th of October the Novelist announced to Forster that he intended sailing for America on Lord Mayor's Day, and had engaged for that "glorious anniversary" an officer's cabin in the *Cuba*. A week prior to his departure, a grand complimentary farewell dinner was given in his honour at the Freemasons' Tavern, when Lord Lytton (who presided) proposed as a toast, "A prosperous voyage, health, and long life to our illustrious guest and countryman, Charles Dickens." In responding to this, the Novelist expressed his sense of the warmth of the reception accorded him by that distinguished assemblage, and, after explaining how the proposal to revisit America had originated and proclaiming his reasons for acceding to it, he thus concluded an oration noteworthy alike for its brilliancy, spontaneity, and dignity:—

"You will readily conceive that I am inspired besides by a natural desire to see for myself the astonishing change and progress of a quarter of a century over there, to grasp the hands of many faithful friends whom I left upon those shores, to see the faces of a multitude of new friends upon whom I have never looked, and last, not least, to use my best endeavour to lay down a third cable of intercommunication and alliance between the old world and the new. Twelve years ago, when, Heaven knows, I little thought I should ever be bound upon the voyage which now lies before me, I wrote in that form of my writings which obtains by far the most extensive circulation, these words of the American nation: 'I know full well, whatever little motes my beamy eyes may have descried in theirs, that they are a kind, large-hearted, generous, and great people.' In. that faith I am going to see them again; in that faith I shall, please God, return from them in the spring; in that same faith to live and to die. I told you in the beginning that I could not thank you enough, and Heaven knows I have most thoroughly kept my word, If I may quote one other short sentence from myself, let it imply all that I have left unsaid, and yet most deeply feel. Let it, putting a girdle round the earth, comprehend both sides of the Atlantic at once in this moment, and so, as Tiny Tim observed, 'God bless us every one.'"

On November 9th, the steamship *Cuba*, with Charles Dickens on board, left Liverpool for Boston, U.S.A. The next day, on arriving at Queenstown Harbour, he informed his daughter by letter that so far the passage had been delightful. "My little cabin is big enough for everything but getting up in and going to bed in. . . . On a writing slab in it, which pulls out when wanted, I now write in a majestic manner. Many of the passengers are American, and I am already on the best terms with nearly all the ship. . . . I am in very good health, thank God, and as well as possible."[1] When five days out the weather changed, and a head wind reminded him of the terrible wretchedness attending his first voyage across the Atlantic five-and-twenty years previously. Happily, so far he did not suffer from sickness, notwithstanding the tremendous rolling and pitching of the vessel. Presently, after a slight but temporary improvement, the weather became worse, with a heavy gale of wind—a state of things which forced him to admit that "these winter crossings are very trying and startling; while the personal discomfort of not being able to wash, and the miseries of getting up and going to bed, with what small means there are all sliding, and sloping, and slopping about, are really in their way distressing. . . . At breakfast time . . . nearly all the passengers in their berths—no possibility of standing on deck—sickness and groans. The sun is shining, but the rolling of the ship surpasses all imagination or description. I write with great difficulty, wedged up in a corner, and having my heels on the paper as often as the pen. . . . My desk and I have just arisen from the floor."[2]

After ten days on the troubled waters—that is to say, on the night of Tuesday the 19th of November— Dickens, with his assistants, landed at Boston Harbour (having remained stuck on a mudbank for some hours), and took up his residence at the Parker House hotel; here a perfect ovation awaited him, for, besides the ordinary crowd to be found in a large American hotel, there had gathered together all the notabilities of Boston to welcome the Novelist, who, escorted by his friends, made the best of

---

[1] "The Letters of Charles Dickens."
[2] Ibid.

his way through this assemblage of excited persons to his own quiet apartments. Mr. Dolby tells us that in arranging the plan for the American tour, provision had been made to enable Dickens to become acclimatised and to recover from the effects of his voyage before commencing the readings; a short interval was allowed for this, during which he renewed acquaintance with old friends, and two days after his arrival he dined with Longfellow, Emerson, Oliver Wendell Holmes, and Agassiz. With this exception, he refused all invitations to great dinners, preferring to pass the time in long walks with Mr. Fields, and in paying brief visits to his more familiar friends, whom he joined at luncheon or family tea.

Writing to his daughter on November 21st, the Novelist stated that his labours would commence on December 2nd, adding that he would be "heartily glad to begin to count the readings off"; again, a little later, he said: "My anxiety to get to work is greater than I can express, because time seems to be making no movement towards home until I shall be reading hard. Then I shall begin to count and count and count the upward steps to May."[1] The formidable enterprise at once presented an encouraging aspect, as all the tickets for the first four readings were sold immediately on their being issued. A serious difficulty arose in keeping tickets out of the hands of speculators, who (as Mr. Dolby records in his entertaining volume) resorted to various ingenious devices in order to procure them at starting prices with a view to realising a handsome profit as the supply ceased; an adventurous individual in New York had actually printed some bogus tickets with the intention of imposing on the public.

[1] "The Letters of Charles Dickens."

Dolby, however, succeeded generally in frustrating such fraudulent designs, and, in consequence, soon discovered that he was the "best abused man in America." So keen was the desire to be present at the readings that the people willingly submitted to great personal inconvenience, and it was not unusual for them to stand in the freezing street for many hours awaiting their turn to purchase tickets. Such enthusiasm both surprised and delighted the Novelist, for he had entertained a suspicion that some of the old grudges against him might still exist; but such doubts were speedily dispelled by the warmth of the greeting accorded to him everywhere. His novels, too, held prominent positions in the booksellers' shops in all the cities of the Union, while his characters and phraseology had become familiar in every house, car, steamboat, and theatre of America. One of the New York newspapers, after averring that even in England Dickens was less known than in that city, said: "Of the millions here who treasure every word he has written, there are tens of thousands who would make a large sacrifice to see and hear the man who has made happy so many hours. Whatever sensitiveness there once was to adverse or sneering criticism, the lapse of a quarter of a century, and the profound significance of a great war, have modified or removed."

Until the date of the initial readings, Charles Dickens passed the time tediously enough, a weariness that would have proved insupportable but for social intercourse with his intimates. At length the eventful evening arrived when the Novelist, as reader of his own works, made his first bow to an American audience. The Tremont Temple at Boston was the

scene of these readings, those selected being the
"Christmas Carol" and the "Trial from Pickwick," the
audience consisting of all the literary and artistic
notabilities in Boston, with a similar contingent from
New York. The effect upon that audience was
electrical—never before had anything in Boston called
forth such intense fervour. Mr. Dolby, however,
records an amusing instance of dissatisfaction on the
part of one who was present, and who, during the
progress of the reading of the Trial scene, suddenly left
the hall in a state of great excitement. Intercepted by
Dolby's query as to whether he had been seized with
illness, this person answered in the negative,
whereupon the following conversation ensued:—

"Say, who's that man on the platform reading?"

"Mr. Charles Dickens."

But that ain't the *real* Charles Dickens, the man
as wrote all them books I've been reading all these
years."

"The same."

After a moment's pause, as if for thought, he
replied, "Wall, all I've got to say about it then is, that
he knows no more about Sam Weller 'n a cow does of
pleatin' a shirt; at all events that ain't *my* idea of Sam
Weller, anyhow." He then clapped on his hat, and left
the building in high dudgeon.

The original design was to give eighty readings
in America, these to include Canada and Nova Scotia,
whence Dickens intended to set sail for England. For
various reasons this plan afterwards underwent
modification, and it was decided to limit the scene of
action as much as possible—not to go further south
than Washington, further west than Chicago, or further
north than Portland, and taking in the New

England cities *en route*. From Boston the Novelist
proceeded to New York, where the success of the readings far exceeded his most sanguine expectations. The
irrepressible speculators were in greater force than
ever; they had taken temporary offices in New York
for the disposal of the tickets at handsome profits, and
some of them attired themselves infancy costumes,
one being made up to resemble George Washington!
The number of persons "in the line" awaiting their turn
to procure tickets for the New York readings exceeded
three thousand, and the queue was over three-quarters
of a mile in length. Dickens estimated that at Boston
he was making a clear profit of £1300 a week, admitting, however, that the work was "rather trying," not
only as regards himself, but also with respect to Dolby,
who experienced great trouble in the manner of
issuing tickets so as to circumvent the speculators;
Dickens described him as "the most unpopular man in
America (and for no reason that I can see except that
he cannot get four thousand people into a room that
holds two thousand), and so he is reviled in print every
day. . . . We always call him P. H. Dolby now, in consequence of one of these graceful specimens of literature
describing him as the 'pudding-headed.'"[1] At New
York, owing to an attack of influenza and the wretched
wintry weather, the Novelist felt "exceedingly
depressed and miserable"; he found the country a bad
one to be unwell and travelling in. "You are one of say
a hundred people in a heated car, with a great stove in
it, and all the little windows closed, and the hurrying
and banging about are indescribable."[2] While

---

[1] "The Letters of Charles Dickens."
[2] Ibid.

staying in this city he elected to hire "a very smart carriage and pair"—"and if you were to behold me driving out [he wrote to his daughter], furred up to the moustache, with furs on the coach-boy and on the driver, and with an immense white, red, and yellow striped rug for a covering, you would suppose me to be of Hungarian or Polish nationality." This vehicle was presently replaced by a comfortable sleigh, in which he and Dolby took long and exhilarating drives every day. The cold and cough from which he suffered (and which he never lost until he left the country) compelled him to seek medical advice. One night at Christmas time, after the reading, he was "laid upon a bed, in a very faint and shady state," indeed, he became quite ill from the effects of a severe catarrh, but fought courageously against it. His kind friend, Mr. Fields, reported, nevertheless, that "his spirit was wonderful, and, although he lost all appetite, and could partake of very little food, he was always cheerful and ready for his work when the evening came round. . . . The strain upon his strength and nerves was very great during all the months he remained, and only a man of iron will could have accomplished what he did." The Novelist feared that the doctor would insist upon a temporary cessation of the readings, but his determination prevailed. Before the year expired he gave four Christmas readings at Boston, which were followed by two more at New York, the railway journey between the two cities being undertaken on Christmas Day, an interval spent somewhat miserably in the train. On the last day of the year he announced that he was getting all right again, and that in a couple of days he would have accomplished a fourth of the entire series of readings.

After a five day vacation, to enable New York to recover from the effects of keeping Christmas and the New Year) and also to give Dickens a little rest, two readings were given in that city on January 2 and 3, 1868. The brief respite from his labours had a most beneficial effect, with the result that these readings passed off as satisfactorily as the others. "The New York reading of 'Doctor Marigold,'" wrote Dickens to Forster, "made really a tremendous hit. The people doubted at first, having evidently not the least idea what could be done with it, and broke out at last into a perfect chorus of delight. At the end they made a great shout, and gave a rush towards the platform as if they were going to carry me off. It puts a strong additional arrow into my quiver." The last New York night yielded £500, but such enormous profits were attained only through excessively hard work in a hard climate. The sale of tickets continued to be enormous, and at Brooklyn the consequent excitement produced an amazing scene, thus graphically described by the Novelist in a letter to his sister-in-law: "The noble army of speculators are now furnished (this is literally true, and I am quite serious), each man with a straw mattress, a little bag of bread and meat, two blankets and a bottle of whisky. With this outfit *they lie down in line on the pavement* the whole night before the tickets are sold, generally taking up their positions at about ten. It being severely cold at Brooklyn, they made an immense bonfire in the street—a narrow street of wooden houses!—Which the police turned out to extinguish. A general fight then took place, out of which the people farthest off in the line rushed bleeding when they saw a chance of displacing others near the door, and put their mattresses in those places, and then held on by the iron rails. At eight in the morning Dolby appeared with the tickets in a portmanteau. . . ."[1]

The influenza attack continued to distress him greatly at times, but was good enough to leave him for the two hours needed for the readings. "I have tried allopathy, homoeopathy, cold things, warm things, sweet things, bitter things, stimulants, narcotics, all with the same result. Nothing will touch it."

On January 13th the real travelling of the tour commenced, with readings at Philadelphia. A newspaper here announced that the pen-portraits of Dickens did not correspond with the descriptions given in the press. "He is not at all foppish in appearance," averred this well-informed journal. "He wears a heavy moustache and a Vandyke beard, and looks like a well-to-do Philadelphian gentleman!"[2] The colour of his eyes was variously reported as "blue, red, grey, white, green, brown, black, hazel, violet, and rainbow coloured"; it was further asserted that he resembled "a well-to-do American gentleman, and the Emperor of the French, with an occasional touch of the Emperor of China, and a decoration from the attributes of our famous townsman, Rufus W. B. D. Dodge Grumsher Pickville." On the 29th the Novelist reported that he was "going on at a great pace and with immense success. Next week, at Washington, I shall, please God, have got through half my readings. . . . It is very hard work, but it is brilliantly paid."[3] At the beginning of February, at Baltimore, an idea occurred to Dolby and Mr. Osgood (who assisted at the

[1] "The Letters of Charles Dickens."
[2] Ibid.
[3] Ibid.

readings), which, if carried into effect, seemed likely to afford much amusement to Dickens, who entered heartily into the arrangements. This was a walking match between the aforesaid gentlemen, to take place on their return to Boston at the end of the month, and Dickens volunteered to draw up the articles of agreement, to act as trainer, and to write a "sporting narrative" of the match after it had taken place. The "articles" were solemnly and formally signed by Massachusetts Jemmy (James T. Fields), the Gad's Hill Gasper (Dickens), and the competitors, respectively named in true sporting parlance the Man of Ross (Dolby) and the Boston Bantam (J. R. Osgood). The "Great International Walking Match" for a distance of twelve miles took place accordingly, and was won by the Boston Bantam, the principal points being duly recorded in Dickens's humorous "Narrative"; at its conclusion, the merry party, with a number of invited guests, dined together at the Parker House, Boston, with Dickens (as giver of the feast) in the chair. The event provided a refreshing interlude in the midst of arduous labours.

Before leaving Baltimore, Dickens met his beloved friend Washington Irving for the last time. Irving went there from New York to pass a day or two with Dickens, and those hours "were made among the most memorable of my life," wrote the Novelist, "by his delightful fancy and genial humour. Some unknown admirer of his books and mine sent to the hotel a most enormous mint julep, wreathed with flowers. We sat, one on either side of it, with great solemnity, but the solemnity was of very short duration. It was quite an enchanted julep, and carried us among innumerable people and places that we both knew. The julep held out far into the night, and my memory never saw him afterward otherwise than as bending over it, with his straw, with an attempted gravity (after some anecdote, involving some wonderful droll and delicate observation of character), and then, as his eyes caught mine, melting into that captivating laugh of his which was the brightest and best I have ever heard."

From Baltimore the Novelist proceeded to Washington, where, by special desire, he visited the President (Andrew Johnston), who engaged a whole row of seats, for himself and family, every night of the readings there. The Washington readings were among the most brilliant of any given in America, the audience including not only the Presidential party but also the English and other ambassadors, with Congressmen and members of the Legislative Assembly. Unfortunately, Dickens's "catarrh" became worse than ever, and in the daytime it quite prostrated him—so much so that on one occasion, when Charles Summer called upon him at the hotel and found him covered with mustard poultices and apparently voiceless, he said to Dolby: "Surely, you are not going to allow Mr. Dickens to read tonight?" Dolby assured him that it was not a question of "allowing," but a question of the Novelist's determination to read if he were alive. "I have told Mr. Dickens," he said, "at least a dozen times today, that it will be impossible for him to read; and but for my knowledge of him and of his wonderful power of changing when he gets to the little table, I should be even more anxious about him than I am." Dolby's conjecture proved correct, for, as usual, Dickens had not faced his audience five minutes before his strength returned to him, and he went through the evening's task as though he were in the most robust health. This extraordinary capacity saved him and his manager considerable anxiety; the great fear was that the Reader's strength would give way, especially as he suffered from sleeplessness and had contracted the habit of taking little or no food.

The first week in March (that is, the week following the walking match) was a period of rest, so far as the readings were concerned, during which he attended a dinner at Longfellow's, when only gentlemen were present, the guests including Agassiz, Lowell, Oliver Wendell Holmes, and Bayard Taylor. This was followed by a dinner party given by Dickens (his last in Boston), and, as the catarrh showed signs of leaving the patient, he was in the best of spirits, the evening being therefore spent most jovially. For some days a heavy snowstorm, with a terrific gale of wind, had been raging, so that the journey to the North-West was effected under disadvantageous conditions. On arriving at Syracuse ("a most out-of-the-way place") a thaw had set in, rendering walking an impossibility; the whole country was under water, and, to make matters worse, Dickens was stranded in "the worst inn that ever was seen." In letters written at this enchanting spot, he said: "I have looked out of window for the people, and I can't find any people. I have tried all the wines in the house, and there are only two wines, for which you pay six shillings a bottle, or fifteen, according as you feel disposed to change the name of the thing you ask for . . . We were so afraid to go to bed last night, the rooms were so close and sour, that we played whist, double dummy, till we couldn't bear each other any longer.

We had an old buffalo for supper, and an old pig for
breakfast, and we are going to have I don't know what
for dinner at six. . . ."[1] He admitted, too, that he was
growing very homesick, and very anxious for the 22nd
of April, "on which day, please God, I embark for
home. I am beginning to be tired, and have been
depressed all the time (except when reading), and have
lost my appetite. . . ." From Syracuse, Dickens
proceeded to Rochester and Buffalo, for readings in
those towns; then came a two day pleasure trip to
Niagara. The Novelist again found great delight (equal
to that afforded by his visit of twenty-five years
previously) in witnessing the Falls from every
available point of view; and after driving up the
country along the sides of the rapids, and passing
through a great cloud of spray, he proceeded to the
Whirlpool, which, with the enormous blocks of ice
and uprooted trees that were tossing about in the
eddying waters, seemed to fascinate him even more
than did the Falls themselves, the latter finally seen
under a most impressive aspect. "Everything in the
magnificent valley—buildings, forest, high banks, air,
water, everything—was *made* of *rainbow*. Turner's
most imaginative drawing in his finest day has nothing
in it so ethereal, so gorgeous in fancy, so celestial. We
said to one another (Dolby and I), 'Let it evermore
remain so,' and shut our eyes and came away."[2]

It was with an unfeigned joy that Dickens,
after the brief holiday at Niagara, turned his back to
the West and faced homewards, for, apart from
his splendid reception everywhere, the life in
America was one of self-denial and misery, owing

[1] "The Letters of Charles Dickens."
[2] Ibid.

to his sufferings from the persistent catarrh. On leaving Niagara for Albany he travelled "through three hundred miles of flood, villages deserted, bridges broken, fences drifting away, nothing but tearing water, floating ice, and absolute wreck and ruin." The train gave in altogether at Utica, and in the morning the journey was resumed through the water, "with a hundred men in seven-league boots pushing the ice from the front of the engine with long poles."[1] A new cause for anxiety now threatened him, not only in the return of the malady in his left foot (which he attributed to walking in the snow), but in similar symptoms presenting themselves in the right foot, causing him to be lame for the remainder of his stay in America. "Still he persevered with the task he had before him," observes Dolby, "and performed it without one word of complaint, all the time; seldom eating and drinking, and scarcely ever sleeping. All his thoughts were of home and of the loved ones there." Five weeks had yet to elapse, however, before the longed for moment of departure arrived, and many were the plans made by the Novelist for the coming summer at Gad's Hill, which he so eagerly anticipated.

Every day the state of Charles Dickens's health became a graver source of alarm. Happily, but little travelling had now to be undertaken prior to the farewell readings in Boston and New York. A repetition of the snowstorms renewed the catarrh trouble, causing sleepless nights, while the suffering induced by the swollen foot rendered its use almost an impossibility; indeed, the change for the worse in his physical condition suggested the impracticability of getting through the final readings in Boston. The

[1] "The Letters of Charles Dickens."

attacks of nervous depression made it necessary that
he should lie down on the sofa in his dressing room for
half-an-hour, in a state of the greatest exhaustion, and
resort to a stimulating glass of champagne, before he
could undergo the fatigue of dressing. Scott, Alison,
and the other assistants would receive Dolby's account
of this serious state of affairs with the remark: "It'll be
all right at night, sir. The gov'nor's sure to come up
smiling when you call time, and the more's wanted out
of him, the more you gets." The nearest approach to
actual collapse occurred at the third reading of the
Boston farewells, for the "Chief" was so ill that his
friends urged him to give in; but he would not, and at
night astonished not only himself but his audience by
his wonderful power of recuperation. "To see me at
my little table at night," he wrote to his daughter at this
time, "you would think me the freshest of the fresh.
And this is the marvel of Fields' life . . . Dolby is as
tender as a woman and as watchful as a doctor. He
never leaves me during the reading now, but sits at the
side of the platform and keeps his eye upon me all the
time."[1] The condition of his health constrained the
Novelist to decline invitations to attend meetings, and
it was with sincere regret that he felt himself unable to
depart from this wise resolution with regard to a public
demonstration, in the form of a farewell banquet,
which had been organised at Boston. In order to
compensate in some measure for the keen
disappointment thus created, he determined to
perform, unostentatiously, an act of charity by which
his second visit to America would be favourably
and agreeably remembered. Having inspected one
of the Blind Asylums in Boston during the early
part of the tour, he had been much struck

[1] "The Letters of Charles Dickens."

with the limited area of literature made available to the afflicted inmates; whereupon he conceived and carried out the happy idea of having one of his own stories, "The Old Curiosity Shop," produced in raised letters for the use of the blind at each asylum in the Union.

On April 8th the farewell reading in Boston took place, and far exceeded, both as regards the success of the reading itself and the effect produced on the audience, the first reading in America four months previously; financially, too, it proved more satisfactory, the receipts amounting to a larger sum than those of any single reading in the series—namely, £690. The subjects chosen for that memorable evening were the same as on the first occasion, viz., the "Christmas Carol" and the "Trial from Pickwick." After concluding the "Carol" with the words, "And so, as Tiny Tim observed, God bless us every one," Dickens was seen to leave the platform, and then the strong, pent-up emotion of his hearers found vent in a vigorous outburst of cheering, which induced him to return and bow his acknowledgments. To the "Trial" scene he imparted, if possible, more humour than usual, and at its termination a storm of applause continued to rend the air until he again came forward, and, with tears rolling down his cheeks, bade farewell in a touching little speech, assuring those present that his gracious and generous welcome in America would never be obliterated from his memory. Immediately after retiring from the platform, the privacy of his dressing room was invaded by a number of sympathetic friends, eager to have another opportunity of saying a parting word.

Then came the farewell readings at New York, beginning on April 13th, and concluding on the

20th On the 18th Dickens was the principal guest at a banquet given to him at Delmonico's Hotel by the Pressmen of America, under the presidency of Horace Greeley, and Mr. George Dolby has recorded that in its arrangements and results it was one of the most magnificent functions of the kind ever held in the Empire City. Owing to an attack of erysipelas in the foot, which had to be carefully bandaged, the Novelist reached Delmonico's an hour late, the delay giving rise to a disheartening rumour that he had succumbed to illness, and would consequently be unable to put in an appearance. When he arrived, therefore, and was escorted to his place at the table by Horace Greeley, the geniality of the welcome accorded him could not have been more marked. Among the two hundred gentlemen present were such representative men as George William Curtis and Charles Eliot Norton. The brilliancy of the scene caused Dickens to forget, for the time, his own sufferings, and replying to the toast of the evening, proposed by Greeley, he earnestly and sincerely thanked the American people, through his kind hosts of that night, for the most friendly behaviour to him throughout his second visit to their remarkable country. The speech was a notable one. After referring to his own early experience of severe newspaper work, to which he constantly ascribed his first successes, he referred to the extraordinary improvements, social and other, which had taken place in America during the twenty-five years that had passed since his previous visit. "I henceforth charge myself, not only here, but on every suitable occasion whatsoever and wheresoever, to express my high and grateful sense of my second reception in America, and to bear my honest testimony to the

[AMERICA 1868]

national generosity and magnanimity. Also, to declare how astounded I have been by the amazing changes that I have seen around me on every side—changes moral, changes physical, changes in the amount of land subdued and peopled, changes in the rise of vast new cities, changes in the growth of older cities almost out of recognition, changes in the graces and amenities of life, changes in the press, without whose advancement no advancement can be made anywhere. Nor am I, believe me, so arrogant as to suppose that in five-and-twenty years there have been no changes in me, and that I had nothing to learn, and no extreme impressions to correct when I was here first. . . . What I resolved upon . . . is, on my return to England, in my own person, to bear, for the behoof of my countrymen, such testimony to the gigantic changes in this country as I have hinted at tonight. Also, to record that wherever I have been, in the smallest places equally with the largest, I have been received with unsurpassable politeness, delicacy, sweet temper, hospitality, consideration, and with unsurpassable respect for the privacy daily enforced upon me by the nature of my avocation here, and the state of my health. This testimony, so long as I live, and so long as my descendants have any legal right in my books, I shall cause to be republished, as an appendix to every copy of those two books of mine in which I have referred to America.[1] And this I will do and cause to be done, not in mere love and thankfulness, but because I regard it as an act of plain justice and honour."

The last reading in America was given at the Steinway Hall, New York, on April 20th, the audience numbering over two thousand persons. The task

[1] "American Notes" and "Martin Chuzzlewit."

finished, the Reader was about to retire, when a tremendous volley of cheering stopped him, and he went forward to make a short speech, bidding his audience farewell, and concluding with the words, "God bless you, and God bless the land in which I leave you." This little *impromptu* oration, listened to with rapt attention, caused immense acclamation and waving of handkerchiefs, amid which Dickens retired from the platform, never to reappear in public in America. Two days later he sailed for England. "Goodbye, Boz," was the final greeting from the host of admirers assembled to witness his departure in the *Russia*. "Goodbye." Then "Boz" put his hat upon his cane and waved it, and the answer came, "Goodbye, and God bless you every one!"

## CHAPTER 14

# FAREWELL READINGS—
# "THE MYSTERY OF EDWIN DROOD"—
# THE END

There could be no mistaking the nature of the feelings with which Charles Dickens was regarded during his second visit to America. That the angry attitude assumed, twenty-five years previously, by a certain section of the American public had practically passed away, and its cause forgotten, was evidenced by the enormous popularity of the readings, as well as by the tributes of affection and respect tendered to the Reader in every part of the States.

The *Russia*, on its departure, was followed for some distance down the bay by several private tugs and launches, and these, by means of miniature cannon, fired a parting salute in honour of the distinguished passenger. Onward sped the Cunarder in the direction of England, and, as the evening closed in, all that could be discerned, by those on board, of the great country they were then leaving was a dim and misty coastline bathed in the light of the setting sun. The first three days of the homeward voyage were passed by Dickens in his cabin, after which the sea-air speedily brought a return of appetite. "I have got on my right boot today for the first time," he wrote on the fourth day to Mr. Fields; "the 'true American [catarrh]' seems to be turning faithless at last; and I made a Gad's Hill breakfast this morning."¹ Before long the weather changed, a heavy gale of wind causing the ship to roll all night, and the sea to break over the decks; nevertheless, excellent progress was made. During the voyage a "deputation" of two persons (of whom only one could get into the Novelist's cabin, while the other looked in at his window) waited upon him to ask him to read to the passengers that evening in the saloon; but he respectfully replied that, sooner than do it, he "would assault the captain, and be put in irons." Notwithstanding that the voyage proved a very rough one, the *Russia* arrived at her destination in nine days from the time of leaving New York.² At Liverpool the fatigued travellers stopped overnight, and journeyed for the south on the following day; on reaching Euston Square terminus, Dickens and his faithful manager parted as though they had just returned together from one of their ordinary English journeys. It was arranged that no friends should be present to welcome them, "and," says Dolby, "it was something ludicrous to see Mr. Dickens walk out of the station, bag in hand, on his way to the Charing Cross Station and Gad's Hill, where of course his arrival had been made known by telegraph to his family." In the event of the Novelist detraining at Higham (the station nearest to Gad's Hill), the villagers had designed to remove the horse from the carriage sent for him and drag him to his own house. Wishing, however, to avoid anything in the nature of a demonstration (of which he had already had a surfeiting), Dickens frustrated the kindly intention by alighting at Gravesend.

¹ "The Letters of Charles Dickens."
² This ship, latterly known as the *Waesland*, was sunk in a collision off Holyhead in March 1902.

The good folks at Higham did not mean to be entirely
deprived of their privileges, so they turned out, on foot
and in market carts and gigs, to meet him on the road,
and, thus escorting him, they gave vent to their
feelings by shouts of welcome. His own servants were
desirous of taking part in the ovation by ringing the
alarm bell in the little turret surmounting the roof of
Gad's Hill Place, but the idea was discouraged. The
following day being Sunday, the bells of his own
church (Higham) rang out a peal after the morning
service in honour of his return.

The fatigue, worry, and responsibility of the
American readings well over, a few days quietly
enjoyed at his beloved Gad's Hill rapidly effected a
marked improvement in Dickens's health and spirits.
Indeed, he presently described himself to his Boston
friends as "brown beyond belief," while his medical
man, Dr. Steele, declared that he looked "seven years
younger," the sea-air and subsequent rest causing him
to appear as though he had never suffered a day's
illness. So great were his recuperative powers that he
was able almost directly to resume his editorial
labours, which then became particularly pressing
owing to an accident having befallen W. H. Wills,
while hunting, this necessitating temporary repose,
and compelling Dickens to assume the entire editorial
burden of *All the Year Round*.

Before the expiration of a month he became
immersed in the business details of a farewell course
of readings, an enterprise that was in hand at the time
of his voyage to America. He had informed the
Chappells of his intention to give this concluding
series on his return to England, "and then read
No More." The terms were settled before the first

Boston readings closed, it being decided that he should give a hundred readings in London and the provinces, for which he would receive from the Chappells a sum of £8000 clear of all expenses. Although a great temptation, it was not solely the financial part of the transaction which attracted him, for (says Forster) "no man could care essentially less for mere money than he did." He was anxious, however, to make necessary provision for many sons, and a certain want of confidence on his part respecting the ability to continue literary work with his customary ease and success induced him to place more reliance upon his readings as a source of income by which his object could be more surely attained. That he thus committed a fatal mistake, from the point of view of his own health, cannot be gainsaid. Forster, who (it will be remembered) consistently opposed the American project, was quick to observe that significant changes had really been wrought thereby in the Novelist's physical condition. "There was manifest abatement of his natural force, the elasticity of his bearing was impaired, and the wonderful brightness of his eye dimmed at times." One day, while walking along the streets of London, he could only read the halves of the letters over the shop doors, and the right foot, as well as the left, continued to trouble him. "But all this disappeared upon any special cause for exertion, and he was never unprepared to lavish freely for others the reserved strength that should have been kept for himself. This, indeed, was the great danger, for it dulled the apprehension of us all to the fact that absolute and pressing danger did positively exist." That the Novelist still suffered from the effects of the Staplehurst accident is testified by a letter written to M. de

Cerjat at this time, in which he says: "My escape . . . is not to be obliterated from my nervous system. To this hour I have sudden vague rushes of terror, even when riding in a hansom cab, which are perfectly unreasonable but quite insurmountable. I used to make nothing of driving a pair of horses habitually through the most crowded parts of London. I cannot now drive, with comfort to myself, on the country roads here; and I doubt if I could ride at all in the saddle. My reading secretary and companion knows so well when one of these odd momentary seizures comes upon me in a railway carriage, that he instantly produces a dram of brandy, which rallies the blood to the heart and generally prevails."[1]

The final readings were appointed to begin in October. During the interval—that is, in the month of June—Dickens went to Paris to superintend the rehearsals, at the Vaudeville Theatre, of a French version of "No Thoroughfare." Then came, as visitors to Gad's Hill, Longfellow and his daughters, and Mr. and Mrs. Charles Eliot Norton, with other friends whose presence there caused him infinite delight. A considerable portion of the summer months was devoted to the uncongenial task of preparing for publication an accumulation of manuscripts representing the "Religious Opinions" of his deceased friend, the Rev. Chauncy Hare Townshend, who had appointed Dickens his literary executor, leaving him a legacy of £1000 as compensation for the trouble involved in carrying out the strange trust; the volume appeared in the following year, with a preface by the Novelist. In September his youngest son, Edward Bulwer Lytton ("Plorn") started for Australia, to join

[1] "The Letters of Charles Dickens."

his brother, Alfred Tennyson, who was already established there as a successful sheep farmer; *apropos* of the parting, the Novelist, writing to his eldest daughter, observed: "These are hard, hard things, but they might have to be done without means or influence, and then they would be far harder;" and to Fechter he said: "He seemed to me to become once more my youngest and favourite little child as the day drew near, and I did not think I could have been so shaken."[1] During the following month his son Henry Fielding entered Trinity Hall, Cambridge, as an undergraduate; a few days later the young man received from his father a letter containing much wholesome advice, and urging the necessity of keeping out of debt. "You know," he said, "how hard I work for what I get, and I think you know that I never had money help from any human creature after I was a child. You know that you are one of many heavy charges on me, and that I trust to your so exercising your abilities and improving the advantages of your past expensive education, as soon to diminish *this* charge. . . . If ever you find yourself on the verge of any perplexity or difficulty, come to me. You will never find me hard with you while you are manly and truthful."[2]

When October came, Charles Dickens started on his last reading tour. Dolby, who again acted as his business manager, assures us that the Novelist looked forward to the approaching campaign with pleasure and interest. The fact that there was a keen demand for tickets even before the titles of the readings had been announced he naturally regarded as a very favourable

[1] "The Letters of Charles Dickens."
[2] Ibid.

augury, and convinced him of the necessity of a novelty in the shape of a new reading which should make a powerful impression upon his audiences, and tend to keep up the receipts. With this object in view he chose as the subject of the new reading that sensational incident in "Oliver Twist"—the murder of Nancy, with which he had no doubt he could petrify his hearers, although he entertained certain misgivings as to the propriety of the selection, fearing that it might prove too horrible a theme for the purpose. It was resolved, therefore, to test the effect upon a small private audience at St. James's Hall, which was accordingly done, with the result that this reading eventually formed part of his repertory, and became one of the most popular. After the commencement of the provincial readings he intimated that he had not been well and felt "heavily tired"—"like Mariana, I am aweary. But think of this," he added, "if all go well, and (like Mr. Dennis[1]) I work off this series triumphantly, I shall have made of these readings £28,000 in a year and a half." Before October closed the renewal of his labours began to tell upon him, and he complained once more of sickness and insomnia, which made it imperative that he should lie on the sofa all day prior to a reading. In Scotland the Novelist met with the greatest cordiality, and at Edinburgh three of his old friends (Peter Fraser, Ballantyne, and John Blackwood, sole survivors of the time when, a quarter of a century before, he received so much kindness and hospitality in that northern city), spent a joyous evening with him in song and recitation, and in recalling early associations. He left Scotland on December 18th, to give one more reading at

---

[1] The hangman in "Barnaby Rudge."

St. James's Hall three days later, previous to a short Christmas vacation; the subject selected was "A Christmas Carol," his little table being appropriately decorated with holly for the occasion.

There was no Christmas Number to be considered this year, for Dickens, observing the extent to which his idea had been poached upon in all directions, concluded that the public palate would be cloyed by such a multiplication of Yuletide stories. Nevertheless he felt exceedingly unwilling to abandon the customary feature of *All the Year Round*, and could not make up his mind to give in without another fight for it. Writing to Wills in July he said: "I offered one hundred pounds reward at Gad's to anybody who could suggest a notion to satisfy me. Charles Collins suggested one yesterday morning, in which there is *something*, though not much. I will turn it over and over, and try a few more starts on my own account."[1] Nothing came of it, however, and the abolition of the popular Christmas Annual caused much comment, the Press emphatically averring that, to the majority of readers, its absence would be a national disappointment. A new series of *All the Year Round* commenced on December 5th, for which Dickens wrote seven papers in the style of "The Uncommercial Traveller;" he called them "New Uncommercial Samples," and hardly any of these sketches are devoid of autobiographical interest.

The second portion of the "Farewell Readings" opened with the New Year, 1869, the country tour beginning in Ireland, and the readings being continued in various parts of England and Scotland until the end of April. The work proved to be harder than ever.

[1] "The Letters of Charles Dickens."

In a letter to M. de Cerjat on January 4th, Dickens said: "Tomorrow night I read in London for the first time the 'Murder' from 'Oliver Twist,' which I have re-arranged for the purpose. Next day I start for Dublin and Belfast. I am just back from Scotland for a few Christmas holidays. I go back there next month; and in the meantime and afterwards go everywhere else." The pain in his foot was always recurring, and occasionally the American catarrh would assert itself, so that it became necessary to exercise the greatest precautions by the strictest observance of a system in prosecuting the task before him. The first public presentation of the "Murder" scene, for which most careful preparations had been made, took place on January 5th, and, both in a financial and an artistic sense, culminated in a complete triumph. "But," says Mr. Dolby, "in the vigour and the earnestness with which it was delivered it was painfully apparent to his intimate friends, and those who knew his state of health best, that a too frequent repetition of it would seriously and permanently affect his constitution. The terrible force with which the actual perpetration of this most foul murder was described was of such a kind as to render Mr. Dickens utterly prostrate for some moments after its delivery, and it was not until he had vanished from the platform that the public had sufficiently recovered their sense of composure to appreciate the circumstance that all the horrors which they had been listening were but a story and not a reality." The usual effect of the "Murder" reading upon Dickens was to raise his temperature dangerously high, but, notwithstanding this disquieting sign, he frequently repeated the effort, and the reading formed part of the published series. The impression it made upon his audiences was remarkable, and at Clifton from a dozen to twenty fainting ladies were removed from the hall during the evening.

On the 15th of February, Dickens returned to London for a reading at St. James's Hall on the succeeding night; but all plans were unhappily frustrated owing to an unusually violent attack of the ailment in his foot confining him to his bed, the doctors, who found their patient in great agony, pronouncing that it would be physically impossible for him to endure the fatigue and pain of standing at his reading desk. There was no alternative, therefore, but to postpone all engagements in London and Scotland until his health was reinstated. "It throws us all back, and will cost me some five hundred pounds," he despairingly wrote to Forster. A few days' rest, however, brought relief sufficient to allow him to resume his labours at Edinburgh, and, although very lame, his spirits were excellent, for he wished to disguise as much as possible the effect of the acute suffering he had undergone. The readings were continued at various towns in the provinces, and at fortnightly intervals in St. James's Hall, until April. On the tenth of that month a public dinner was given him at Liverpool, with the late Lord Dufferin in the chair, and, in the course of a speech acknowledging the toast of the evening, he took occasion to reply to a charge then preferred against him by his old friend Lord Houghton—that he had been "somewhat unconscious of the merits of the House of Lords"—an assumption based upon the portrayal of Lord Verisopht in "Nicholas Nickleby"; he also replied to a remonstrance from Lord Houghton against his (the Novelist's) objection to entering public life, declaring that when he first took literature as his profession in England, he resolved that, whether he succeeded or not, literature should be his sole profession,—that in his person literature should stand, by itself, of itself, and for itself; and that no consideration on earth would induce him to break that compact.

Dickens observed, in a letter to Miss Hogarth, that one of the pleasantest things he experienced in Liverpool at this time was the manner in which he was stopped in the streets by working men, who wanted to shake hands with him and tell him that they knew his books—indeed, he never went out but this happened. Throughout his busy career he was continually receiving tributes from those he had benefited, either by his books or by his friendship, and a story (vouched for as true) is related in illustration of this. During the winter of 1869 he received a letter from a man informing him that he had begun life in the most humble way, and that he attributed his own great success in life entirely to the helpful encouragement and animating influence he had derived from the Novelist's works. This unknown correspondent had just inherited a fortune from his recently deceased partner, and his first desire was to render the Novelist some testimonial of gratitude and veneration; whereupon he sent for his benefactor's acceptance two silver table ornaments of considerable value, bearing this inscription: "To Charles Dickens, from one who has been cheered and stimulated by his writings, and who held the Author amongst his first remembrances when he became prosperous." One of these silver ornaments was supported by a trio of figures, representing three seasons; in the original design there were, of course, four, but the donor, averse to associating the idea of Winter in any sense with Charles Dickens, caused the artist to alter the design and leave only the *cheerful* seasons. No event in the great writer's career was ever more gratifying and delightful to him.[1] Shortly after the Liverpool banquet his friends at home had ill report of him at Blackpool, whither he had gone for brief repose, and whence he wrote that he should require careful attention to get through his readings. "My weakness and deadness are all *on the left side*, and if I don't look at anything I try to touch with my left hand, I don't know where it is."[2] He so far understood the gravity of those symptoms as to telegraph for his London medical man, Mr. F. Carr Beard. Perfect rest was prescribed, but this proved impossible in the face of his various engagements. Presently a consultation was appointed in London with the distinguished physician, Sir Thomas Watson, whose record of the case shows plainly that the Novelist had been on the brink of an attack of paralysis of his left side, and possibly of apoplexy—which the doctors declared to be, "no doubt, the result of extreme hurry, overwork, and excitement, incidental to his readings." There was no help for it—the reading engagements had to be cancelled, and Dickens, relieved of anxiety on this point, retired for a space to Gad's Hill, hoping in the spring to resume his Farewell Readings in London.

On the 26th of May he reported himself to Lord John Russell as "quite well again," and impatiently looked forward to the arrival during the summer of his friends Mr. and Mrs. Fields of Boston and of Mr. and Mrs. Childs of Philadelphia, who were then on their

[1] "Yesterdays with Authors," by James T. Fields, 1872.
[2] "The Letters of Charles Dickens."

way to England. He had written to Mr. Fields on April 9th, saying: "I rather think that when the 12th of June shall have shaken off these shackles [i.e., the readings], there *will* be borage on the lawn at Gad's. Your heart's desire in that matter, and in the minor particulars of Cobham Park, Rochester Castle, and Canterbury shall be fulfilled, please God! The red jackets shall turn out again upon the turnpike road, and picnics among the cherry orchards and hop gardens shall be heard of in Kent."[1] In order that he might be near his London doctor for a while, and, at the same time, be able to avail himself of invitations from innumerable friends, he secured apartments early in May at the St. James's Hotel, Piccadilly, for himself, his daughter, and his sister-in-law; another reason for making a temporary abode in London was that he wished to meet his American friends immediately on their arrival in the Metropolis, and to show them every possible attention, the programme he devised for their entertainment while in England being of colossal proportions—indeed, beyond accomplishment in the time at their disposal. Besides visits to Gad's Hill, excursions were arranged to various strange places in and around London, many of these being nocturnal pilgrimages to the slums, opium dens, and thieves' quarters, effected under the care and skilled guidance of expert detectives. In addition to his American guests there were English friends, to greet the travellers at Gad's Hill Place; the house was full to overflowing, so that some had to be accommodated at the "Sir John Falstaff" across the road. This season of the year, the "leafy month of June," had been most happily chosen, as the Americans could then realise the charms

---

[1] "The Letters of Charles Dickens."

of English scenery at its best, and obtain the most favourable impression of the Novelist's Kentish home and its lovely environment. As for Dickens himself, although he never actually regained his former vigour and elasticity, the presence of so many cherished friends at Gad's seemed to remove all traces of his illness; he was very much sunburnt, and in his light suit of clothes, with the bowler hat carried jauntily, he looked the very embodiment of health and joviality.

In July the Novelist informed Macready that his youngest son, Henry Fielding, had taken the second scholarship (£50 a year) at Trinity Hall, Cambridge, adding that "the bigwigs expect him to do a good deal there." Tidings had reached him, too, of the satisfactory progress made by his two boys in Australia, and induced in him a strong paternal yearning to see them in their distant home.[1] In the land of their adoption he thought it possible to find material for a new book, in addition to which he revived the old idea of giving a series of readings

[1] As I write, the death is announced of Mr. Edward Bulwer Lytton Dickens ("Plorn"). In 1890 he represented Wilcannia in the New South Wales Parliament, and resigned shortly afterwards; he then received an appointment as rabbit inspector for the Government of New South Wales, and latterly had been the officer of the Lands Department in charge of the Moree district, where he died on January 24, 1902, in his fiftieth year, after an illness of some months. Mr. Alfred Tennyson Dickens was associated in business matters with his brother Edward, and is still commercially engaged in Australia. He and Henry Fielding Dickens, K. C. (who took silk in 1892), are the only surviving sons, while Mrs. Perugini is the surviving daughter. It seems fitting to give here a list of the Novelist's ten children, in the order of seniority:—
Charles Culliford Boz, *b.* 1837, d. 1396.
Mary (Mamie), *b.* 1838, *d.* 1896 unmarried).
Kate Macready, *b.* 1839. Married (1) Charles A. Collins in 1860, who died in 1873; then (2) Mr. C. E. Perugini.

[*Continued on next page.*]

there; but many weighty considerations were opposed to such an undertaking, not the least important being the conduct of *All the Year Round*, the sub-editorship of which (owing to the compulsory retirement of W. H. Wills attributable to ill-health) he had recently given into the hands of his eldest son, Charles, who evinced considerable aptitude for the work. His regret at the enforced abandonment of the Australian project was very great, but he found some compensation in the knowledge that he could again devote attention to literary labours. Thoughts of a new book occurred in July, and he thus explained to Forster his first fancy for the tale: "What should you think of the idea of a story beginning in this way?—Two people, boy and girl, or very young, going apart from one another, pledged to be married after many years—at the end of the book. The interest to arise out of the tracing of their separate ways, and the impossibility of telling what will be done with that impending fate." This notion was practically laid aside, and another submitted a month later, when he referred to "a very curious and new idea" for the forthcoming story —"not a communicable idea (or the interest of the book would be gone), but a very strong one, though difficult to work." It was to be the murder of a nephew by his uncle, the originality of

Walter Landor, *b.* 1841, *d.* 1863.
Francis Jeffrey, *b.* 1844, *d.* at Illinois, 1886.
Alfred Tennyson, b. 1845.
Sydney Smith Haldimand, *b.* 1847, *d.* and buried at sea, 1872.
Henry Fielding, b. 1849.
Dora Annie, *b.* 1850, *d.* 1851.
Edward Bulwer Lytton, *b.* 1852 *d.* in New South Wales, 1902.

It is interesting, in this connection, to record that Miss Mary Angela Dickens, one of the Novelist's granddaughters (and a daughter of Charles Dickens the younger), is a successful writer of fiction.

which (as Forster explains) "was to consist in the review of the murderer's career by himself at the close, when its temptations were to be dwelt upon as if not he, the culprit, but some other man, were the tempted. The last chapters were to be written in the condemned cell, to which his wickedness, all elaborately elicited from him as if told of another, had brought him. Discovery by the murderer of the utter needlessness of the murder for its object, was to follow hard upon the commission of the deed; but all discovery of the murderer was to be baffled till towards the close, when, by means of a gold ring which had resisted the corrosive effects of the lime into which he had thrown the body, not only the person murdered was to be identified but the locality of the crime and the man who committed it.[1] So much was told to me," continues Forster, "before any of the book was written; and it will be recollected that the ring, taken by Drood to be given to his betrothed only if their engagement went on, was brought away with him from their last interview. Rosa was to marry Tartar, and Crisparkle, the sister of Landless, who was himself, I think, to have perished in assisting Tartar finally to unmask and seize the murderer." Doubtless during the Novelist's rambles in the east end of London with his American friends, the planning of the story occupied much

---

[1] Such an incident as that narrated really happened in Rochester many years ago. An inhabitant of the town was appointed trustee and guardian of his nephew, who went to sea, and eventually returned to his uncle's house. The young seafarer then mysteriously disappeared, and nothing more was heard of him. The uncle died, and when the house in which he resided underwent certain alterations in order to render it suitable for other purposes, a human skeleton was discovered, supposed to have been that of the missing nephew.

of his thoughts; but the actual writing was to be deferred for a while.

On the 30th of August, the London Rowing Club entertained at dinner, at the Crystal Palace, the crews which had taken part, three days previously, in the International University Boat Race, and it fell to Dickens (as a guest) to propose the health of the crews, and, in a striking speech, he made pleasing allusions to Harvard University. He was induced, also, to deliver the Inaugural Address on the opening of the winter session of the Birmingham and Midland Institute on September 27th, but stipulated that he should first be put in possession of some facts respecting the students, their ways of life, their favourite studies, and kindred information, so that he might be armed with material for his discourse, and thus interest his audience in the advantages of the institution. These rough notes he promised should fall into shape and order in his mind in readiness for the function, and that he had thoroughly digested them we are assured by one who was present, who declares that "no note of any kind" was referred to by the speaker, except a quotation from Sydney Smith; "the address was delivered without a single pause, in Mr. Dickens's best manner, and was a very great success"—a feat rendered the more remarkable by the fact that in the course of his observations he touched upon a number of scientific, educational, and other subjects appropriate to the occasion.

On October 18th, Dickens notified to Macready that he was then in "the preliminary agonies of a new book," which he hoped to begin publishing in the following March, this book, of course, being that which, three months previously, he had mentioned to Forster. He entitled it "The Mystery of Edwin Drood," and its preparation almost monopolised his attention during the remainder of the year, for he was anxious to make as much progress with it as possible before the time arrived for his concluding readings. The composition of the story caused him exceptional trouble and anxiety, and in reply to Mr. Dolby's question as to how he liked returning to the writing of a serial tale he promptly admitted that he "missed the pressure" of former days. His thoughts, too, did not flow so freely as before, with the consequence that he revised and corrected his work continually, sometimes remodelling entire sentences. The plan for the first number was thus briefly indicated: "Mr. Sapsea. Old Tory jackass. Connect Jasper with him. (He will want a solemn donkey by-and-by)"; this was effected by bringing together both Durdles and Jasper, for connection with Sapsea, in the matter of the epitaph on Mrs. Sapsea's tomb. The last of the memoranda, and the final words written by Dickens in the notebook containing them, are these: "Then I'll give up snuff. Brobity.—An alarming sacrifice. Mr. Brobity's snuffbox. The Pawnbroker's account of it?" The Novelist, whose intention here can only be conjectured, completed the manuscript of the first number during October, and we are told that he read it aloud at Forster's house "with great spirit." On December 22nd, he found himself in a dilemma which recalled an earlier experience of a like character, and in this instance was doubtless the result of excessive alteration and interlineation: "When I had written, and, as I thought, disposed of the first two Numbers of my story, Clowes informed me to my horror that they were, together, *twelve printed pages too short!!!* Consequently I had to transpose a chapter from No. 2 to No. 1, and remodel No. 2 altogether." He confided to Mr. Dolby that the price agreed to be paid to him for this book was the largest sum given for any work from his or any other hands, viz., £7500 for the copyright, author and publishers to share equally in the profit of all sales beyond 25,000 copies; in addition to this the Author was to receive £1000 for the advance sheets sent to America. Dickens specially stipulated by deed that the publishers (Chapman & Hall) should be reimbursed for any possible loss that might accrue to them in the event of his being prevented, either by sickness or death, from completing the work—the first time, curiously enough, such a clause had been inserted in one of his agreements, and sadly pertinent in this case, the suggestion probably originating in his nervous fear that a return of his Chester illness (partial paralysis) might permanently incapacitate him.

Christmas Day was spent by the Novelist in the usual way at Gad's Hill, except that he suffered again from an attack of the foot trouble, which quite disabled him on that day, compelling him to keep his bed until the evening, when he managed with difficulty to join the family gathering in the drawing room. Presently his health improved, so much so, that on the 6th of January 1870 he was enabled to fulfil a promise he had made to distribute the prizes and certificates awarded to the most successful students in the first year at the Birmingham and Midland Institute, of which he had been elected the President. One of the prize takers was a Miss Winkle, a cognomen so reminiscent of "Pickwick" that the announcement of it created much laughter and applause; then, after making some remarks to the lady in an undertone, Dickens observed to the audience: "I have recommended Miss Winkle to change her name." The journey to Birmingham, added to the fatigue of delivering the address, had tried his strength so acutely that, on his return to London he again sought medical advice, with the result that his doctor deemed it advisable for him to be present continually at the "Farewell Readings," in order to note carefully their visible effects on his health. These readings were to be given at St. James's Hall during the first three months of the year, and they constituted the concluding portion of the series that had been interrupted by the trying illness which prostrated him nine months previously. For convenience during this London engagement he rented the house of his friends, Mr. and Mrs. Milner Gibson, No. 5 Hyde Park Place (opposite the Marble Arch), where he and his family took up their residence early in January. "I have a large room here," he wrote to Mr. Fields on the fourteenth, "with three fine windows, overlooking the Park unsurpassable for airiness and cheerfulness." In the same letter he thus alluded to his progress with the new story: "There is a curious interest steadily working up to No 5, which requires a great deal of art and self-denial. I think also, apart from character and picturesqueness, that the young people are placed in a very novel situation. So I hope at Nos. 5 and 6, the story will turn upon an interest suspended until the end."[1] Mr. George Dolby informs us that when the title was decided on (and its selection created some difficulty) the Novelist arranged a little dinner party of three persons in honour of the event, at which only one toast was drunk, "Success to

---

[1] "The Letters of Charles Dickens."

'The Mystery of Edwin Drood,'" proposed by Mr. Dolby and humorously responded to by Dickens himself.[1]

The "Farewell Readings" commenced on January 11th, and terminated in the middle of March—twelve readings in all. Three were given (in the morning or afternoon) for the benefit of the theatrical profession whose members could not attend in the evenings, and Dickens succeeded in making manifest how much a single performer could achieve without the aid of the ordinary adjuncts of the stage. The actors and actresses, whose presence greatly enhanced the pleasure of the *matinee* readings, applauded every point; but the strain upon the Reader's nervous system involved by these exceptional efforts was exceedingly intense, as he himself admitted, and as the state of his pulse before and after a reading sufficiently testified. His normal pulsation of seventy-two increased to a hundred and eighteen on the second night of the "Murder" reading—indeed, on one occasion it rose to a hundred and twenty-four—and the after-effects were such as to necessitate his lying on a sofa for fully ten minutes before he could speak a rational or consecutive sentence; when that interval had expired, he would pull himself together, swallow a small quantity of weak brandy and water, and rush on the platform for the concluding reading, his audience little suspecting what had been going on behind the scenes. Charles Dickens the younger remembered that his father, during one of these later readings, found it impossible to pronounce "Pickwick" correctly, calling

[1] "Charles Dickens as I Knew Him." George Dolby died in October 1900, at the Fulham Infirmary, the fact of his utterly destitute condition being quite unknown to his artist son in Paris.

it "Pickswick," and "Picnic," and "Peckwicks," and all
sorts of names except the right, with a comical glance
of surprise at the occupants of the front seats, which
were always reserved for his family and friends.[1] The
final farewell reading took place on March 15th, and
proved to be one of the severest ordeals, but it was
triumphantly accomplished; the knowledge that this
would be absolutely Charles Dickens's last public
appearance caused intense public excitement, and, as
he stepped upon the platform, he faced an enormous
and particularly demonstrative audience. The readings
selected were the "Carol" and the "Trial from
Pickwick," and as soon as the Novelist appeared, book
in hand, and evidently much agitated, the immense
concourse of people rose to greet him with tumultuous
enthusiasm, the ovation continuing several minutes.
The reading over, there came the saddest (and for him
the most dreaded) moment, when, in response to
numerous calls, he returned from his retiring room to
the little table and, with a voice full of emotion, said:
"Ladies and gentlemen, it would be worse than idle—
for it would be hypocritical and unfeeling—if I were
to disguise that I close this episode in my life with
feelings of very considerable pain. For some fifteen
years, in this hall and in many kindred places, I have
had the honour of presenting my own cherished ideas
before you for your recognition, and, in closely
observing your reception of them, have enjoyed an
amount of artistic delight and instruction which,
perhaps, is given to few men to know. In this task, and
in every other I have ever undertaken, as a faithful
servant of the public, always embued with a sense of
duty to them, and always striving to do his best, I have

[1] *North American Review*, May and June 1895.

been uniformly cheered by the readiest response, the most generous sympathy, and the most stimulating support. Nevertheless, I have thought it well, at the full floodtide of your favour, to retire upon those older associations between us, which date from much further back than these, and henceforth to devote myself exclusively to the art that first brought us together. Ladies and gentlemen, in but two short weeks from this time I hope that you may enter, in your own homes, on a new series of readings, at which my assistance will be indispensable; but from these garish lights I vanish now for evermore, with a heartfelt, grateful, respectful, and affectionate farewell." Amidst repeated acclamations on the part of the audience, and while hats and handkerchiefs waved in every part of the hall, Charles Dickens left the platform with quite a mournful gait and tears rolling down his cheeks; but he was impelled to return once again, to be stunned by a still more rapturous outburst of applause.

The full number of readings at home and abroad (omitting those given for charitable or friendly purposes) was four hundred and twenty-three, which yielded Dickens the enormous sum of £45,000—a handsome result, but dearly attained when we remember the great sacrifice of his own health it entailed. That these efforts, so long sustained, curtailed his life cannot for a moment be doubted, and *apropos* of this, the reply of John Ruskin (four years later), in declining an invitation to lecture, may be recalled: "The miserable death of poor Dickens, when he might have been writing blessed books till he was eighty, but for the pestiferous demand of the mob, is a very solemn warning to us all, if we would take it." On another occasion the author of "Modern Painters," after declaring that he thoroughly appreciated "Pickwick," which he knew pretty well by heart, confessed that he loved Dickens with every bit of his mind, and sympathised in everything he thought and tried to do, "except in his effort to make more money by readings, which killed him."[1]

As soon as the grief, mingled with pleasure, of the last reading had passed away, Dickens appreciated greatly the opportunity afforded him of devoting undisturbed attention to his new story, and looked forward with lively satisfaction to the delight of returning to Gad's. The initial number of "Edwin Drood" (hinted at by him, in the just quoted speech, as "a new series of readings") was launched in March 1870, and the demand for it showed unmistakably that the Author had lost nothing of his popularity. "We have been doing wonders with No. 1," he wrote to Mr. Fields on April 18th. "*It has very, very far outstripped every one of its predecessors.*" This number speedily attained to a circulation of fifty thousand. Besides the story, the editing of *All the Year Round* secured a share of his time, as did certain social engagements which he could not well decline. On April 5th he took the chair at a dinner in aid of the funds of the Newsvendors' Benevolent and Provident Institution, when he was supported by the Sheriffs of London and Middlesex; in proposing the toast of the evening, "The Corporation of the City of London," he assured his hearers that he had "never witnessed a Lord Mayor's Show except from the point of view obtained by the other vagabonds upon the pavement." On May 2nd, the Novelist (although far from well) attended the Royal Academy Dinner—his last public appearance of any

[1] *Daily Telegraph*, 6th January 1888.

kind—and to him was assigned the honour and responsibility of responding for "Literature"; in the course of this speech he appropriately adverted to the then recent death of Daniel Maclise, and to the dropping away from his side of other eminent Royal Academicians whom, as in the case of Maclise, he numbered among his most devoted friends. Three days later he was literally "laid by the heels" with the neuralgic affection of the foot, which would "yield to nothing but days of fomentation and horizontal rest," intense suffering preventing him (in his capacity as trustee) from fulfilling an engagement to speak at the annual dinner of the General Theatrical Fund, at which the Prince of Wales presided.

What may be regarded as one of the most important events in the eventful life of Charles Dickens occurred about this time. When entertaining Mr. (afterwards Sir) Arthur Helps (the Clerk of the Privy Council) at dinner, the Novelist showed him a remarkable collection of photographs, depicting scenes on the battlefields in the American Civil War, which had been given to him in Washington. Mr. Helps casually mentioned these photographs to Queen Victoria, who immediately notified a wish to examine them, and the fact being communicated to Dickens, he at once forwarded the collection for her Majesty's inspection. The Queen then desired an opportunity of thanking the Novelist in person, and, in obedience to the royal command, he went to Buckingham Palace, where he was received most graciously; the interview was prolonged for an hour and a half, and he ever remembered with gratitude the Queen's kindness on that auspicious day. After expressing her deep

regret at not having heard one of the readings, and
referring in complimentary terms to the pleasure she
had derived from witnessing his acting in "The Frozen
Deep" in 1857, her Majesty begged his acceptance of
a copy of her "Leaves from the Journal of Our Life in
the Highlands," in which she had written his name,
and said that "the humblest" of writers would be
ashamed to offer it to "one of the greatest," but that
Mr. Helps had suggested that she should give it with
her own hands.[1] Her Majesty then informed the
gratified recipient of her yearning to possess a
complete set of his works; whereupon a specially
bound set was forwarded to Windsor, and placed in the
Queen's private library. A few days after the interview
Dickens received a royal command to attend the next
levee, and an intimation that Miss Dickens should be
presented at the Drawing Room immediately
following, both of which behests (needless to say)
were obeyed.[2] The Prince of Wales, too, coveted a
personal acquaintance with the Novelist, and as His
Royal Highness, together with the King of Belgian,
had just then accepted an invitation to dine with Lord
Houghton (an old and valued friend of Dickens),
"Boz" was bidden at the Prince's special

---

[1] The fly-leaf bore the following inscription, in her Majesty's autograph: "To Charles Dickens, Esq., from Victoria Reg., Buckingham
Palace, March 9, 1870" In November 1899 this interesting volume was
sold at Sotheby's auction rooms, and realised £100, the purchaser being
Mr. Henry F. Dickens, K.C.

[2] Forster quotes the following as illustrating the mirthful side of
Dickens: "Society is unhinged here," wrote the Novelist in 1840, "by her
Majesty's marriage, and I am sorry to add that I have fallen hopelessly
in love with the Queen, and wander up and down with vague and dismal
thoughts of running away to some uninhabited island with a maid of
honour, to be entrapped by conspiracy for that purpose. . . . I have my
eye upon Lady _____, principally because she is very beautiful and has
no strong brothers. . . ."

request to join the party. Up to the last moment it seemed doubtful, owing to the foot trouble, whether he could appear; but, with his usual characteristic determination, he resolved to make the effort, although he found himself unable to ascend the staircase to meet the company, and had to be assisted at once into the dining room. Happily, in the course of the evening, he obtained some relief from pain, and the charm of his conversation contributed in no small measure to the success of the function, the Prince, at parting, heartily expressing a hope for the Novelist's speedy and complete recovery. In consequence of this royal condescension, a rumour became current that Charles Dickens had been desired to accept a place on her Majesty's Privy Council, but it had no foundation in truth; "though all the probabilities [observes Forster] are on the side of his unwillingness to accept any title or place of honour, certainly none was offered to him." Dickens himself was highly amused at the report, and in a letter (dated May 20th) said: "You will probably have read before now that I am going to be everything the Queen can make me. If my authority be worth anything, believe on it that I am going to be nothing but what I am, and that that includes my being as long, as I live, your faithful and heartily obliged, . . ."[1]

The dinner at Lord Houghton's was the last time of his dining out in London. Towards the close of the tenancy of his temporary abode in Hyde Park Place, Dickens gave a delightful series of entertainments, and on the particular occasion of a concert his drawing rooms were crowded with a company

[1] "The Letters of Charles Dickens."

comprising the most prominent people in town—
literary, artistic, and fashionable. Although the host
endured much during these social gatherings, and
looked jaded and worn, he was in good spirits, and, in
spite of pain, appeared at his very best, never relaxing
his efforts in affording pleasure to his guests. At the
end of May he returned to Gad's Hill, hoping to obtain
there that mental rest and refreshment necessary for
the continuation of his work upon "Edwin Drood."
The writing of the story had proceeded meanwhile. On
February 25th he read aloud the third number to
Forster, and a month later he read admirably his fourth
number, shortly after which he felt excessively uneasy
concerning his health, for there was a return of a
disorder (haemorrhage) which troubled him in earlier
life, and had latterly taken an aggravated form. On
May 7th he read to his friends the fifth number, at
which time he felt eager to return to Gad's Hill, but
was prevented by some invitations he was led to
accept. One day he dined with Motley the historian, on
another he met Disraeli at a dinner at Lord Stanhope's,
and on a third he breakfasted with Gladstone. Then on
May 17th came the Queen's ball, to which he and his
eldest daughter had been commanded; but Miss
Dickens went without him, owing to his sudden
disablement, brought about (as he explained) by "the
old preposterous endeavour to dine at preposterous
hours and preposterous places. . . . And serve me
right. . . ."

The end, alas, is drawing near. On May 22nd
Forster dined with the Novelist in Hyde Park Place
—and it was their last meeting. Eight days later he
was at Gad's Hill, and, though suffering severely from
local haemorrhage, he made no complaint of

illness, giving himself wholly to work upon his novel. But "he seemed very weary." He was, however, well enough just for the moment (says Mr. Herman C. Merivale, in correcting Forster's impressions) to attend the rehearsals in London of a play to be privately acted at Cromwell House, the residence of Mr. and Mrs. Freake, of which he undertook the entire management, and, though troubled with lameness, he directed all the rehearsals with his usual boyish spirit. The performance took place on June 2nd, and Dickens was behind the scenes as prompter and stage-manager, "ringing all the bells and working all the lights," and going through the whole thing "with infectious enjoyment."[1] On June 6th he went out with his dogs for the last time, and on the following day drove to Cobham Wood with his sister-in-law; there he dismissed the carriage, and walked round the park, returning home in time to put up in the new conservatory (his latest improvement), some Chinese lanterns, afterwards watching from the dining room their effect when lighted. On the 8th of June he devoted the entire day to writing in the Swiss Chalet, with an interval for luncheon, and did not leave his desk until late in the afternoon. Before the six o'clock dinner, ordered thus early that he might enjoy a stroll afterwards in the country lanes, he wrote a few letters, including one to his friend Charles Kent,[2] making an appointment the next day in London. Dickens had not been long seated at the dinner table when his face assumed a singular expression of trouble and pain, and he then confessed to Miss Hogarth that "for an hour he had been very

[1] *The Times*, February 1883.
[2] This letter, the last written by Dickens, was presented by Mr. Kent to the British Museum.

The Swiss Chalet

In which the last lines of "Edwin Drood" were written. Pictured here in Cobham Park

*Photographed by Catharine Weed Ward*

Charles Dickens's Grave

In Poet's Corner, Westminster Abbey

*Photographed by Catharine Weed Ward*

ill"; but he wished dinner to proceed. These, the only coherent words uttered by him, were followed by disconnected remarks on irrelevant subjects, concluding with a declaration of his intention to depart immediately for London, and, rising from his chair, he would have fallen but for the timely help of his sister-in-law, who endeavoured to get him on the sofa. Her effort, however, was unsuccessful, for, after a slight struggle, he sank heavily on his left side. "On the ground," he said—and they were the last words uttered by "Boz." Medical aid was summoned immediately, and urgent messages despatched to members of the family desiring their speedy presence at Gad's Hill. All human aid was unavailing; an effusion of blood on the brain proved fatal, and, within twenty-four hours from the moment of seizure, the spirit of Charles Dickens had fled.

. . . . . . . . .

Thus, on 9th of June 1870, at the comparatively early age of fifty-eight years and four months, passed away England's greatest Novelist. The sad and unexpected intelligence, flashed by telegraph to all parts of the civilised earth, occasioned sincere tribulation. In his own country it was as if a personal bereavement had befallen every one, and almost the first to express sympathy for the sorrowing family was her Majesty Queen Victoria. Carlyle, in a letter to Forster, said: "I am profoundly sorry for *you*, and indeed for myself and for us all. It is an event world-wide, a *unique* of talents suddenly extinct; and has 'eclipsed,' we too may say, 'the harmless gaiety of nations!' No death since 1866 [Mrs. Carlyle's] has fallen on me with such a stroke. No literary man's hitherto ever did. The good, the gentle, high gifted, ever friendly, noble Dickens—every inch of him an Honest Man." America, too, where the face and figure of the deceased writer had so recently become familiar, yielded touching tokens of keen regret for the deprivation which the world at large had sustained. "The loss of no single man during the present generation, if we except Abraham Lincoln alone," observed Horace Greeley, "has carried mourning into so many families, and been so unaffectedly lamented through all the ranks of Society." Longfellow added his testimony to the universal feeling of disconsolation, and thus wrote to Forster: "The terrible news from England fills us all with inexpressible sadness. Dickens was so full of life that it did not seem possible he would die, and yet he has gone before us, and we are sorrowing for him. . . . I never knew an author's death cause such general mourning. It is no exaggeration to say that this whole country is stricken with grief. Such being the impression abroad, it is easy to conceive that those at home, in England, who knew and loved him—and their name is legion—were heartbroken and depressed by the knowledge that they would never again behold the man whose genius had so long entranced them, and whose amiability, geniality, and sympathy had endeared him to all.

It was Charles Dickens's own desire that he should be interred in the small graveyard of St. Nicholas, under the wall of old Rochester Castle, or in the little Kentish churches of Cobham or Shorne; it transpired, however, that burials were no longer permitted in these places, whereupon the Dean and

Chapter of Rochester preferred a request that the body might repose in their Cathedral. This suggestion was favourably entertained by members of the Dickens family, and the actual spot chosen; meanwhile a wish had been expressed that the mortal remains of him whom the people rightly considered as deserving of a more honoured place of sepulchre should be laid in Westminster Abbey. The Dean of Westminster, therefore, lost no time in giving effect to that wish, and the body was deposited within the precincts of the venerable fane, the last rites being performed, privately, and without pomp or display of any kind, on June 14th. The secrecy thus observed was regarded at the time as one of the strangest events connected with the Abbey during Dean Stanley's rule; but, as Forster says, "the solemnity had not lost by the simplicity—nothing so grand or so touching could have accompanied it as the stillness and silence of the vast Cathedral." After the unpretentious ceremony, crowds of unbidden mourners flocked to the tomb, and "many flowers were strewn upon it by unknown hands, many tears shed from unknown eyes"—significant tributes to which reference was made by the Dean in his impressive funeral discourse at the Abbey on the Sunday following. It is in Poets' Corner—a site hallowed by memories of the most illustrious persons in English history—that we may read upon the stone which marks his grave the simple inscription, "Charles Dickens. Born February the Seventh, 1812. Died June the Ninth, 1870."

"Farewell, our teacher, playfellow, and friend!
Little it matters where thy grave is made,
Whether where England's mightiest dead are laid
Or where the vaulted heavens above thee bend:—

[1870]

Thy resting-place is in the people's heart,
Which throbbed with sorrow when the tidings came
That all now left to England is the *name*
Of him who nobly used a noble art."[1]

· · · · · · · · · ·

The Cathedral at Rochester, too, has its memorial of the Novelist. On the south wall of the south transept, under the mural monument of Master Richard Watts, the executors of Charles Dickens have placed an inscribed tablet of brass, "to connect his memory with the scenes in which his earliest and his latest years were passed, and with the associations of Rochester Cathedral and its neighbourhood which extended over all his life."

· · · · · · · · · ·

As, by the sudden death of William Makepeace Thackeray on the Christmas Eve of 1863, the story of "Denis Duval" was left incomplete, so, by the passing of Charles Dickens, the world is deprived of the latter portion of a novel which promised to be not the least dramatic of the writer's efforts. "It is certainly one of his most beautiful works," said Longfellow, "if not the most beautiful of all" "The Mystery of Edwin Drood" was to have been concluded in twelve (instead of the usual twenty) monthly numbers, in the old form and at the old price; but only six had been written, and three published, when the magic pen dropped from the hand that would never again resume its wonted task. Shortly before his death, Dickens was walking with a dear friend, when the latter observed, speaking of "Edwin Drood": "Well, you, or we, are approaching the mystery——" Whereupon the Novelist, who at the time was all vivacity, extinguished his gaiety, and fell

[1] *Graphic*, June 18, 1870.

into a long and silent reverie, from which he never broke during the remainder of the walk. "Was he pondering," queries Blanchard Jerrold, who records the incident, "another and deeper mystery than any brain could unravel, facile as its mastery was over the hearts and brains of his brethren?"

The wood-engravings in the unfinished story were from the pencil of Mr. Luke Fildes, since elected to the rank of Royal Academician, whose ability as a draughtsman in seizing upon the tragic aspect of humanity became so apparent in a powerful drawing then recently published in the *Graphic*, that Sir John Millais (who had seen the picture) at once informed Dickens that he had discovered the very man for illustrating "Edwin Drood," the health of the Novelist's son-in-law, Charles Collins (who prepared the design for the monthly wrapper), having prevented his acceptance of the post of illustrator. In the final part (issued in August 1870) appeared the following authoritative announcement: "All that was left in manuscript of 'Edwin Drood' is contained in the Number now published—the sixth. Its last entire page had not been written two hours when the event occurred which one very touching passage in it (grave and sad, but also cheerful and assuring)[1] might seem almost to have anticipated. The only notes in reference to the story that have since been found concern that portion of it exclusively which is treated in the earlier Numbers. Beyond the clues therein afforded to its conduct or catastrophe, nothing whatever remains; and

[1] ". . . Changes of glorious light from moving boughs, songs of birds, scents from gardens, woods, and fields—or, rather, from the one great garden of the whole cultivated island in its yielding time penetrate into the Cathedral, subdue its earthly odour, and preach the Resurrection and the Life. . . ."

it is believed that what the author himself would have most desired is done, in placing before the reader without further note or suggestion the fragment of 'The Mystery of Edwin Drood.'"

Notwithstanding this definitive statement, it was rumoured at the time that the novel would be finished by other hands, and in 1882 renewed currency was given to the unfounded report that Wilkie Collins had undertaken to complete the work. The admirers of Dickens also cherished a hope that he had left among his papers some hints that would throw light upon the development of the plot, but nothing could be discovered as to the author's intentions. It was all a blank, although Forster, when engaged upon his "Life of Dickens," believed he had stumbled upon a solution in some pages of nearly illegible manuscript, which, however, proved to be merely a scene where Sapsea was introduced as the principal figure in a group of new characters. Concerning this Forster suggests that Dickens, having become a little nervous about the course of the tale, from a fear that he might have plunged too soon into the episodes leading on to the catastrophe, "conceived the idea of opening some fresh veins of character incidental to the interest of the story." Perhaps no unfinished work of fiction has aroused so much interest, or caused so many attempts to deduce a sequel from the premises, as this fragment of Dickens's last novel.

CHAPTER 14

# DICKENS AS ACTOR, READER, EDITOR, AND PUBLIC SPEAKER

Charles Dickens's life-long predilection for the stage probably originated during his schooldays at Wellington House Academy, although we have his own authority for stating that a taste for theatricals became apparent even prior to this period. When a mere child, he wrote a tragedy called "Misnar, the Sultan of India," founded no doubt on one of the "Tales of the Genii," a book which formed part of his precious library at Chatham, and in after years he said, when alluding to his first attempts at dramatic authorship, "achieved at the mature age of eight or ten," that they were represented "with great applause to over-flowing nurseries." At school, he got up "The Miller and his Men," in a very gorgeous form, and took prominent parts in theatrical representations planned by himself and his fellow pupils, the plays being acted with much solemnity before an audience of boys, and in the presence of the ushers. A little later, after he had finally left school, and had entered an attorney's office at Gray's Inn, he and Potter (a fellow clerk) availed themselves of every opportunity of going to a minor theatre in the neighbourhood, and it is said that they sometimes even engaged to perform there.

In 1833 Dickens wrote a travesty of

Shakespeare's "Othello," entitled "The O'Thello," for private presentation in his own family, and two or three fragments of the original manuscript are still extant. It was at this period that he seriously thought of adopting the stage as a profession, but, under circumstances already related, the project was nipped in the bud. The future Novelist, however, wrote a farce for J. P. Harley in 1836, called "The Strange Gentleman," and about the same time was responsible for the libretto of a comic opera, "The Village Coquettes," produced by Braham at the St. James's Theatre. These were followed, in 1837, by a burletta called, "Is She his Wife? Or, Something Singular," and a farce entitled "The Lamplighter," written for Covent Garden Theatre, but never acted.[1]

In this chapter my object is to descant upon Dickens's powers as an actor rather than as a dramatist; truth to say, he rightly deemed his performances in the latter capacity as unworthy of critical comment. His warm partiality for matters theatrical is evidenced in his books, and in none more conspicuously than "Nicholas Nickleby," where is immortalised the old Portsmouth Theatre—the scene of Mr. Crummles's triumphs with the Infant Phenomenon and the inevitable pump. Mr. Walter Herries Pollock thus writes to me: "It is a legend at the Theatre Royal, Portsmouth—and there may well be truth in it—that Dickens, as a very young man, was for a time a member of the company. This was told me a few years ago by one in authority then who was on most amicable terms with me because of my intimacy with dear old Toole, who was then playing there for a

[1] For further particulars of these plays, see pages 49-52.

week. This personage showed me a playbill which was no doubt the origin of the Crummles bills. He told me that he himself well remembered the original of Folair, hardly caricatured in the novel, and showed me his name in the bill. It was 'Billy Floyer.' My friendly informant spoke of this as a tradition in which he personally believed from putting together the long life of the tradition—and the playbill—and the exact description in 'Nicholas Nickleby' of the old Portsmouth Theatre—the Crummleses, and Folair." The story is also current in Portsmouth that Dickens himself, when visiting that seaport town with Forster at the time the book was in hand, "went on" the stage at this Theatre and asked for a small part; it is, however, at least fair to assume that both he and Forster went behind the scenes and "yarned" with the players, with a view to obtaining "local colour" for the theatrical incidents in a forthcoming number of "Nicholas Nickleby."

As an Actor, Charles Dickens undoubtedly won his first laurels at the Queen's Theatre, Montreal, during his visit to America in 1842, the pieces selected for representation being "A Roland for an Oliver," "Past Two o'Clock in the Morning," and a farce called "Deaf as a Post," Dickens taking a leading character in each play. In addition to this he assumed the arduous duties of stage-manager and prompter (when not acting himself), and he informed Forster that "everybody was told they would have to submit to the most iron despotism; and didn't I come Macready over them? Oh no. By no means. Certainly not. The pains I have expended during the last ten days exceed in amount anything you can imagine, I had regular plots of the scenery made out, and lists of the properties wanted; and had them nailed up by the prompter's chair. Every letter that was to be delivered, was written; every piece of money that had to be given, provided; and not a single thing lost sight of." In learning his lines, he adopted a special system of his own, by which they became familiar almost immediately, and, though he had not acted for years, he astonished both himself and the audience, at the Montreal Theatre, by the reality and ease of his impersonations. "I really do believe that I am very funny," he confessed to Forster; "at least I know that I laughed heartily at myself." Many who subsequently acted with him have testified to the marvellous manner in which he took everything upon himself, for, besides being stage-director, he was very often stage-carpenter, scene-arranger, property-man, and band-master; he invented costumes, devised playbills, wrote out calls, and was ever present, superintending, directing, suggesting, with sleepless activity and vigilance.

More than three years elapsed before Dickens again trod the boards. It was in 1845, on his return from a prolonged sojourn in Italy, that he became actively engaged in preparations for a play, for the production of which he secured the co-operation of his literary and artistic friends, including members of the *Punch* staff. Ben Jonson's comedy, "Every Man in his Humour," was chosen for representation by this distinguished amateur company (of whom, I believe, not one member survives) and the first performance took place at Miss Kelly's Theatre in Soho, a second and more public performance at the St. James's Theatre being promptly acceded to in consequence of the sensation caused by the unusually clever

Charles Dickens giving a reading, 1859

*From a photograph by H. Watkins in the possession
of the Author*

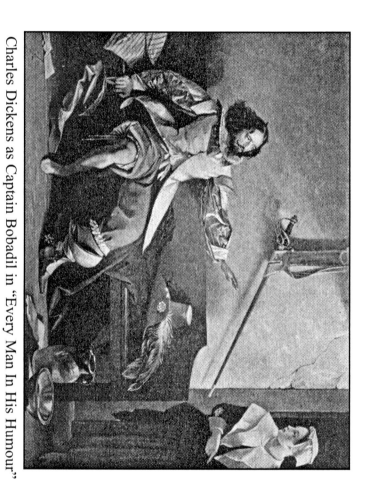

Charles Dickens as Captain Bobadil in "Every Man In His Humour".

*From a painting by C.R. Leslie, R. A.*

rendering of the various characters. Dickens himself assumed the role of Captain Bobadil, and his personification of the arch braggart proved him an actor of exceptional calibre, leaving a sharp and powerful impression upon the minds of his audience; indeed, one of the leading critics of the day declared that "such a Bobadil as that of Mr. Dickens had not been seen within the memory of man." Mrs. Cowden-Clarke, who took part in the play when performed in 1848 (in aid of the fund for the endowment of a Curatorship of Shakespeare's House), describes the acting of Bobadil as a veritable piece of genius, while Leigh Hunt considered that it had "a spirit in it of intellectual apprehension beyond anything the existing stage has shown." Forster, who was also a member of the amateur company, asserts that "though Dickens had the title to he called a born comedian, the turn for it being in his very nature, his strength was rather in the vividness and variety of his assumptions, than in the completeness, finish, or ideality he could give to any part of them;" and, with particular reference to the play in question, he avers that Boz's extraordinary quickness and keenness of insight into character "enabled him to present in Bobadil, after a richly coloured picture of bombastical extravagance and comic exaltation in the earlier scenes, a contrast in the later of tragical humility and abasement, that had a wonderful effect."

In 1848, performances were given by Dickens and his famous company for the benefit of Sheridan Knowles, and, after rehearsing several plays, including "The Alchemist," in which his Sir Epicure Mammon quite equalled anything he had done, choice was eventually made of Shakespeare's "Merry Wives of Windsor," the Novelist securing for himself the part of Justice Shallow. Nine performances took place in London and the provinces, and everywhere Dickens was the leading figure; in the pleasures as well as in the labours connected with the tour he was always foremost—his the brightest face, the lightest step, the cheerfullest word. "The 'makeup' of Dickens as Justice Shallow," says Mrs. Cowden-Clarke, "was so complete that his own identity was almost unrecognisable, when he came on to the stage . . .; but after a moment's breathless pause, the whole house burst forth into a roar of applausive reception, which testified to the boundless delight of the assembled audience in beholding the literary idol of the day actually before them. His impersonation was perfect: the old stiff limbs, the senile stoop of the shoulders, the head bent with age, the feeble step, with a certain attempted smartness of carriage characteristic of the conceited Justice of the Peace, were all assumed and maintained with wonderful accuracy; while the articulation—part lisp, part thickness of utterance, part a kind of impeded sibilation, like that of a voice that 'pipes and whistles in the sound' through loss of teeth—gave consummate effect to his mode of speech."

Towards the close of the year 1850 there were three private performances, by these clever amateurs, of "Every Man in his Humour," in the grand banqueting hall of Lord Lytton's mansion at Knebworth, and, needless to add, all the circumstances and surroundings were most brilliant. The following is a copy of the play bill:—

## KNEBWORTH.

*On Monday, November* 18, 1850
*will be Performed Ben Jonson's Comedy of*
## EVERY MAN IN HIS HUMOUR.

Costumiers.—Messrs. Nathan, of Tichbourne Street.
Perruquier.—Mr. Wilson, of the Strand.

Knowell (*an old gentleman*) . . . . . . . . . . .Mr. Delmé Radcliffe.
Edward Knowell (*his son*) . . . . . . . . . . . .Mr. Henry Hawkins.
Brainworm (*the father's man*) . . . . . . . . . . .Mr. Mark Lemon.
George Downright (*a plain Squire*) . . . . . . . .Mr. Frank Stone.
Wellbred (*his half-brother*) . . . . . . . . . . . . . .Mr. Henry Hale.
Kitely (*a merchant*) . . . . . . . . . . . . . . . . . . . .Mr. John Forster.
Captain Bobadil (*a Paul's man*) . . . . . . . .Mr. Charles Dickens.
Master Stephen (*a country gull*) . . . . . . . .Mr. Douglas Jerrold.
Master Matthew (*the town gull*) . . . . . . . . . . .Mr. John Leech.
Thomas Cash (*Kitely's cashier*) . . . . . . .Mr. Frederick Dickens.
Oliver Cobb (*a water-bearer*) . . . . . . . . . . . .Mr. Augustus Egg.
Justice Clement (*an old merry magistrate*)The Hon. Eliot Yorke.
Roger Formal (*his clerk*) . . . . . . . . . . . . . . . . . . .Mr. Phantom.
Dame Kitely (*Kitely's wife*) . . . . . . . . . . . .Miss Anne Romer.
Mistress Bridget (*her sister*) . . . . . . . . . . . . . . .Miss Hogarth.
Tib (*Cobb's wife*) . . . . . . . . . . . . . . . . . . . . .Mrs. Mark Lemon
(who has kindly consented to act in lieu of Mrs. CHARLES
DICKENS, disabled by an accident).

The Epilogue by Mr. Delmé Radcliffe.

To conclude with Mrs. Inchbald's farce of
## ANIMAL MAGNETISM.
The Doctor . . . . . . . . . . . . . . . . . . . . . . .Mr. Charles Dickens.
La Fleur . . . . . . . . . . . . . . . . . . . . . . . . . . . .Mr. Mark Lemon.
The Marquis de Lancy . . . . . . . . . . . . . . . . .Mr. John Leech.
Jeffery . . . . . . . . . . . . . . . . . . . . . . . . . . . . .Mr. Augustus Egg.
Constance . . . . . . . . . . . . . . . . . . . . . . . . . . . . .Miss Hogarth.
Lisette . . . . . . . . . . . . . . . . . . . . . . . . . . . . .Miss Anne Romer.
stage-manager.—Mr. Charles Dickens.

The theatre will be open at half-past six. The performance will
begin precisely at half-past seven.
GOD SAVE THE QUEEN

As stated in a previous chapter, Sir Edward Lytton wrote a five act comedy, "Not So Bad as We Seem," in aid of the Guild of Literature and Art, which was first performed at Devonshire House on May 16, 1851, before Queen Victoria and Prince Albert, the distinguished audience including the Duke of Wellington, Lord Macaulay, Chevalier Bunsen, and other notabilities. The character assigned to Dickens in the comedy was that of Lord Wilmot, described in the bill as "a young man *at the head of the Mode*, more than a century ago"—a part, by the way, which did not suit him. "His bearing on the stage," says Richard Hengist Horne, "and the tone of his voice, were too rigid, hard, and quarter-deck-like, for such 'rank and fashion,'" while his "make-up" (in three-cornered cocked hat, black curled wig, huge sleeve cuffs, long flapped waistcoat, knee-breeches, &c.) he failed to carry off with the proper air, and caused him to appear more like the captain of a Dutch privateer. At the second performance, on May 27th, the afterpiece was a little farce, in one act, called "Mr. Nightingale's Diary," jointly written by Dickens and Mark Lemon, into which the Novelist introduced a considerable amount of Gampish humour. Here he was inimitable, and Miss Mitford, who witnessed the play, pronounced certain parts of his acting as something wonderful. He impersonated Mr. Gabblewig on the first occasion, but, according to the cast printed on the playbill when the farce was performed at Tavistock House in 1855, he more than doubled the part, for we find that (under the *nom de théâtre* of Mr. Crummles) he personified no less than five individuals besides that of Mr. Gabblewig, one of them being a deaf sexton, and another a Mrs. Gamp-like character, assuming different disguises and changing his dress, voice, and look with a rapidity which the most practised "entertainer" might envy.

"Ah, sir, it's a universal observation in the profession, sir, that it was a great loss to the public when you took to writing books!" Such was the pregnant remark addressed to Dickens by the master carpenter at one of the theatres, while shaking his head with an intensely mournful air. Although complimentary to his dramatic ability, Dickens could hardly be expected to accept this observation as a flattering tribute to his genius as an author, the more especially as "Copperfield" had then been recently published. The deliberate opinion of the master carpenter was the outcome of some "wonderful ideas" that Dickens explained to him respecting certain contrivances which he (the Novelist) had conceived for adapting the difficulties of a comedietta, entitled "Used Up," to a small stage. This play was privately performed at Rockingham Castle early in 1851, with Dickens as Sir Charles Coldstream, and one who saw it spoke of his representation of that character as excellent; the *ennui* of Sir Charles, his mental inanity, the voraciousness of his appetite when he assumed the garb and functions of a ploughboy, were so admirably rendered that his American friend, Mr. J. T. Fields, believed it impossible for even Mathews himself to have surpassed it.

The children's Twelfth Night theatricals at Tavistock House—in "The Smallest Theatre in the World," as the bills described it—were events eagerly anticipated by old and young alike. Plays by adult performers (Dickens and his friends) also took place here, two powerful dramas being specially written by Wilkie Collins, namely, "The Lighthouse" and "The Frozen Deep." "The Lighthouse" was first produced on June 19, 1855, and about a month later it was staged at Campden House, Kensington (the residence of Colonel Waugh), for the benefit of the funds of the Bournemouth Sanatorium for Consumptive Patients. The character assumed by Dickens (which proved to be one of the most realistic and effective in his repertory) was that of Aaron Gurnock, a lighthouse-keeper, this affording scope for a piece of such wonderful acting that even Carlyle (who, with Thackeray and Lord Campbell, attended the play) was fain to acknowledge its merits, and compared Dickens's "wild picturesqueness" to the famous figure in Nicholas Poussin's bacchanalian dance in the National Gallery. "A wonderful impersonation was this," testifies Mrs. Cowden-Clarke; "very imaginative, very original, very wild, very striking; his grandly intelligent eyes were made to assume a wandering look—a sad, scared, lost gaze, as of one whose spirit was away from present objects, and wholly occupied with absent and long past images." *Apropos* of "The Lighthouse," Mr. Walter Herries Pollock favours me with the following reminiscence: "My mother, Juliet Lady Pollock, wife of the second Baronet, congratulating Dickens most enthusiastically after the performance, presently said, 'There is one actor, and only one, I have ever seen of whom you sometimes remind me—that is, Frédérick Lemaître.' Dickens replied, with a twinkle in his eyes, 'Odd you should say that. He is the only actor I have ever tried to take as a model.'" Mrs. Yates (herself a distinguished actress) also compared Dickens, in this part, to Lemaître in his best days. What with consummate acting and beautiful scenery (which included Clarkson Stanfield's remarkable drop scene, portraying the Eddystone Lighthouse), the little piece was unanimously pronounced to be a complete triumph.

Nearly two years later (January 6, 1857) "The Frozen Deep" was first acted, at Tavistock House, and was several times repeated during the year (with an alteration in the cast) in aid of the Douglas Jerrold Fund, one of the representations taking place privately at the Gallery of Illustration, Regent Street, London, in the presence of Queen Victoria and the Royal Family. The important part selected by Dickens for himself was that of Richard Wardour, a young naval officer in love, and we have the opinion of Wilkie Collins himself (he being also in the cast) that "Boz" acted "with a truth, vigour, and pathos never to be forgotten by those who were fortunate enough to witness the performance. . . . He literally electrified the audience." "The character of Wardour," says a writer in a contemporary journal, "afforded the actor opportunity for a fine display of mental struggle and a gradual transition from moodiness to vindictiveness, and finally, under the pressure of suffering, to penitence and resignation,"[1] and Mr. Pemberton points out that although this character was of a kind that bad or even indifferent acting of a melodramatic school would make ridiculous, yet in the hands of Dickens it became "a magnificent human study, and lifted the play, and all concerned in it, into a splendid artistic success."[2]

[1] *Macmillan's Magazine*, January 1871.
[2] "Dickens and the Stage," by T. Edgar Pemberton, 1888.

An eminent critic considered that Dickens's rendering of Wardour might be the beginning of a new era for the stage, so great and well sustained was its excellence. "Mr. Dickens," he affirmed, "shows that he is not only a great novelist, but a great actor also. Both, indeed, proceed from the same intense sympathy with humanity, the same subtle identification of the individual man with the breadth and depth of our general nature. Mr. Dickens has all the technical knowledge and resources of a professed actor; but these, the dry bones of acting, are kindled by that soul of vitality which can only be put into them by the man of genius and the interpreter of the affections." Carlyle often remarked that Dickens's essential faculty was that of a first-rate play-actor, and declared that "had he been born twenty or forty years sooner, we should most probably have had a second and greater Mathews, Incledon, or the like, and no writing Dickens."

As a fitting conclusion to these notes and observations respecting Dickens as an Actor, the following interesting reminiscence may be recorded. In the early summer of 1870, the Novelist and his much loved friend Charles Kent took their last suburban walk together, and just as they were approaching the shadow of the venerable and historic Abbey of Westminster, where the great writer was soon to be laid at rest, Dickens abruptly asked his companion, "What do you think would be the realisation of one of my most cherished daydreams?" adding, instantly, without waiting for an answer, "To settle down now for the remainder of my life within easy distance of a great theatre, in the direction of which I should hold supreme authority,

It should be a house, of course, having a skilled and noble company, and one in every way magnificently appointed. The pieces acted should be dealt with according to my pleasure, and touched up here and there in obedience to my own judgment; the players as well as the plays being absolutely under my command. There," he said laughingly, and in a glow at the mere fancy, "*that's* my daydream!"

.   .   .   .   .   .   .   .   .   .

From the theatrical stage to the reading platform is an easy step. Great as Dickens is acknowledged to have been as an actor, there are some who declare that his abilities as a reader of his own works were even more remarkable. The public readings, which extended over a period of several years, were the means of making his personal appearance known on both sides of the Atlantic to thousands of admirers, who, but for the opportunity thus afforded, might never have enjoyed the privilege of beholding him or hearing his voice. It is no exaggeration to say that, as an example of what can be achieved by genius, Dickens's record remains unique; his unparalleled success in Great Britain and America has never been approached, and the fact that a single individual, by virtue of that genius, could attract vast audiences night after night, winning their applause, and reaping an enormous pecuniary advantage (about forty thousand pounds) justifies the assertion that such an extraordinary instance of the irresistible power of attraction such as Charles Dickens wielded is not likely to be repeated, at least in our time.

Concerning Dickens's merits as a reader, many highly favourable criticisms have been printed. By no means the least interesting is that of Carlyle, who, although not in entire sympathy with such methods of entertaining the public, confessed that "Dickens does do it capitally, such as *it* is." The author of "Sartor Resartus" explained that he *had* to go to Dickens's reading at the Hanover Rooms (April 28, 1863), "to the complete upsetting of my evening habitudes and spiritual composure," so that for *him* to be won over under such circumstances is a sure indication of Dickens's magnetic influence. "Acts better than any Macready in the world," continued the Sage; "a whole tragic, comic, heroic *theatre* visible, performing under one *hat*, and keeping us laughing—in a sorry way, some of us thought the whole night. . . ."[1] Another Scotsman, Dr. Tulloch, heard the Novelist read the "Carol" and considered it a veritable treat. "He has a voice of great compass and play of feeling," observed that eminent divine, "great dramatic gifts altogether, and he maintained unabated interest for upwards of two hours. It was all the better to me, I daresay, as I had pretty well forgot the 'Christmas Carol.' Scrooge, the hero, was his great *forte*; but he gives the Cratchits also—both father and mother and the children—with great effect; and as his voice deepened into the sweetest pathetic tones in reading the death of Tiny Tim, nothing could have been finer. . . ."[2] Sir Frederick Pollock was likewise particularly impressed, and, under date "16th March 1870," made the following entry in his diary: "To reading by Dickens at St. James's Hall. He gave 'Boots at the Holly Tree,' the scene between Bill Sikes and Nancy, and a

[1] "Thomas Carlyle, a History of his Life in London, 1834-81," by J A. Froude (vol. ii., 1884).
[2] "A Memoir of the Life of John Tulloch, D.D.," by Mrs. Oliphant, 1888.

bit of Mrs. Gamp. What an actor he would have made! What a success he must have had if he had gone to the bar! His power of reproducing a scene and bringing it to the very eyes of his audience, its exact features and the relative bearings of its composing parts, has never been equalled. This would have been an invaluable quality in many cases at the bar. He could always at a glance take in the contents and furniture of a room, and in this way was able to astonish his friends by performing some of the feats made famous by Houdin the conjurer. In the scene on the steps of London Bridge from 'Oliver Twist' the whole arrangement of the locality, and the positions of the speakers and listeners, stood out in a kind of reality when accentuated by the voice and gestures of Dickens."[1] In regard to the Novelist's Houdin like power of observation, Mr. Walter Herries Pollock obliges me with a hitherto unrecorded reminiscence: "Dining at my father's house, Dickens took my mother in to dinner. He was deep in conversation all through dinner, and never looked about him; yet, in the drawing room, it came out in some natural way that in the brief time they took going up the dining room and the moment when the men stood up as the ladies went out, Dickens had noted every picture and every item of interest in the room. I am pretty sure that, on my mother expressing surprise, he referred to Houdin's description of how he trained himself and his son to observe and remember every object in the shop windows as they passed down the street. Hence, with a secret code of signals, their astonishing 'second sight' performances.

[1] "Personal Remembrances of Sir Frederick Pollock," 1887.

A realistic description of Dickens as he appeared at his reading desk in 1858 was written at that time by his friend Edmund Yates, and published in *Town Talk*: "He is about forty-five years old, rather above the middle height, and of a slight, lithe figure. If you did not know who he was, you would take him, at first glance, for some remarkable man. His is a decidedly striking face, rather long and thin, with shaved cheeks, a moustache and pointed beard. His hair is light brown, long and silky; his forehead broad and high; but his eyes are his most remarkable feature, dark brown in colour, and flashing, when he is animated, with extraordinary brilliancy. His voice is deep and sonorous, capable of exquisite modulation, and of expressing the deepest feeling. The pathos which he throws into one short line in the 'Carol,' where the Cratchit family are mourning their lost child—'The colour? Ah! Poor tiny Tim!' cannot be described. One slight peculiarity may be noticed, a hissing manner of pronouncing the letter 's.'" In an article which he printed in 1869, Edmund Yates emphasized his preference for Dickens's rendering of Fagin the Jew, which he thought stood out the grandest of all his characters. "Throughout the entire scene of the murder," he says, "from the entrance of Sikes into the house until the catastrophe, the silence was intense—the old phrase 'a pin might have been heard to drop' might have been legitimately employed. It was a great study to watch the faces of the people—eager, excited, intent. . . ." Of the Reader himself, Miss Mary Boyle has left an excellent presentment: "After acknowledging the enthusiastic welcome which always awaited him, he stood for a few moments in silence, beside the little table on the platform, paper cutter in hand, a bright flower in his buttonhole. . . . Then he cast a glance round the hall, and, if ever a look spoke, it was at that moment, when 'he made friends with us all.' His wonderful eyes seemed to have the power of meeting those of every separate individual in the audience, while a smile as eloquent as the words he was about to utter played round his lips."[1]

It has already been hinted that Dickens compiled especially for his readings a series of reading-books, and that he took great pains in thus preparing the subjects for representation. Virtually, the fragmentary portions selected from his stories for this purpose were rewritten and subjected to innumerable alterations and eliminations before he deemed them suitable for the object in view. Even in its printed form, each reading-book underwent at the hands of the Author a further process of revision, with the result that certain pages were cobwebbed over with an intricate network of lines and interlineations, some of the corrections being written in blue ink and entire passages obliterated with a wash of red ink. In order to illustrate the effect of this, the late Mr. Charles Kent, in his valuable work on "Charles Dickens as a Reader," gives a *facsimile* of a page taken from the reading-book of "The Story of Little Dombey." Mr. Kent, who has naturally placed on record his own recollections of the Reader, as well as of the readings themselves, tells us that Dickens conceived everything in his own mind so intently that those who listened to him realised what he spoke of by sympathy. "I can hardly believe," observes Mr. Kent, "but that I was actually present in those scenes; they are impressed upon me with such an astonishing air of fidelity. . . . Attending his readings,

---

[1] "Charles Dickens by Pen and Pencil," 1889-90.

character after character appeared before us, living and breathing, in the flesh, as we looked and listened. It mattered nothing, just simply nothing, that the great Author was there all the while before his audience in his own identity. His evening costume was a matter of no consideration—the flower in his buttonhole, the paperknife in his hand, the book before him, that earnest, animated, mobile, delightful face, that we all knew by heart through his ubiquitous photographs— all were equally of no account whatever. We knew that he alone was there all the time before us, reading, or, to speak more accurately, recreating for us, one and all—while his lips were articulating the familiar words his hand had written so many years previously—the most renowned of the imaginary creatures peopling his books. Watching him, hearkening to him, while he stood there unmistakably before his audience, on the raised platform, in the glare of the gas burners shining down upon him, the pendant screen immediately above his head, his individuality, so to express it, altogether disappeared, and we saw before us instead, just as the case might happen to be, Mr. Pickwick, or Mrs. Gamp, or Dr. Marigold, or Little Paul Dombey, or Mr. Squeers, or Sam Weller, or Mr. Peggotty, or some other of these immortal personages.

Mr. Charles Kent was present on that never-to-be-forgotten occasion, when the Novelist gave his final reading, on the 15th of March 1870: "The manly, cordial voice only faltered once at the very last," he says, "the mournful modulation of it in the utterance of the words, 'From these garish lights I vanish now for evermore,' linger to this moment like a haunting melody in our remembrance . . . .

As he moved from the platform after the utterance of the last words of the address, and, with his head drooping in emotion, passed behind the screen on his way to his retiring room, a cordial hand (my own!) was placed for one moment with a sympathetic grasp upon his shoulder. . . . The prolonged thunder of applause that followed him to his secluded room at the back of the platform, whither he had withdrawn alone, recalled him after the lapse of some minutes for another instant into the presence of his last audience, from whom, with a kiss of the hand, he then indeed parted for evermore."

.   .   .   .   .   .   .   .   .   .

Dickens first held the editorial reins in 1846, when the *Daily News* came into existence, of which journal he was the actual founder. With characteristic energy, he, as conductor of the new Liberal paper, threw himself into the work, and speedily obtained the support of an efficient staff, including such writers as Douglas Jerrold, Mark Lemon, Father Mahony, W. J. Fox, Albany Fonblanque, Charles Mackay, &c. But, as we have already seen, he soon sickened of the mechanical drudgery involved in the production of a daily newspaper, and, after a few weeks' experience, he retired from the editorial chair. Four years later the Novelist, undaunted by that brief and unfortunate experiment, launched the first number of a periodical, the success of which exceeded all expectation, namely, *Household Words*. The speedy popularity achieved by this weekly publication must mainly be attributed to the brightness and originality, combined with an exceptional literary quality, which signalised the contents; for Dickens, the editor, by virtue of his own genius and fame, enjoyed special facilities in securing the services of many of the best writers of the day, to name whom would be to enumerate some of the prominent authors of the 'fifties and 'sixties. Perhaps the most powerful factors in bringing about the success of his venture were the Editor's intuitive knowledge of the public taste, and the means he adopted to supply the particular kind of sound journalistic literature which he believed would meet with general appreciation.

Of Dickens's exceptional qualifications as Editor much is recorded, and by a unanimous verdict he is proclaimed to have been, in every respect, an ideal editor. There are a few (alas! but few) still living who, as contributors to *Household Words* and its offspring, *All the Year Round*, have a lasting recollection of the Editor's genial and amiable relations with themselves and others privileged to write for his periodical—his "literary brethren," as he usually called them. Mr. Percy Fitzgerald, one of the survivors of this rapidly diminishing band of authors, confesses that he is amazed when recalling the extremely amicable relations which subsisted between Dickens and his "young men," and refers to the untiring good humour and modesty of him who was the head, perhaps, of all living writers. "There was ever the same uniform good-nature and ardour, the eagerness to welcome and second any plan, a reluctance to dismiss it, and this done with apologies; all, too, in the strangest contrast to the summary and plainspoken fashion of the ordinary editor." A vast number of manuscripts, from all sorts and conditions of literary aspirants of both sexes, daily poured into the office of *Household Words*;[1] but Mr. Fitzgerald

[1] This house is doomed to demolition, to make way for the new Holborn-Strand thoroughfare, the construction of which will obliterate many other Dickens associations.

believes that every one was seriously glanced at and some estimate formed, while it sometimes happened that discovery was made of hidden talent, which the Editor intuitively recognised. It has been observed that if Dickens, in his editorial capacity, had any fault, it was in the sympathetic nature which prevented him from crushing those who were obviously unfitted for the pursuit of literature, and who were induced to persevere by his misplaced kindness, to their own ultimate sorrow and discomfiture. As one of the old guild says: "Some had written much or little before they came to him, but the fact remains that it was under his leadership that they achieved reputation."

The considerable pains with which Dickens analysed the work of an outside contributor, and the courteous manner with which he sometimes expressed his opinion thereof, is frequently exemplified in his published Letters, where also may be found ample evidence of the minute and careful attention and personal supervision which he bestowed upon articles and stories by members of the regular staff. For his friends he could not take too much trouble or show too much interest, and as an illustration of this Edmund Yates cites the following letter, written by Dickens after reading the manuscript of a story submitted to him for publication:—

"I return the story with pleasure, and I need not tell you that you are not mistaken in the last lines of your note. Excuse me on that ground if I say a word or two as to what I think (I mention it with a view to the future) might be better in the paper. The opening is excellent, but it passes too completely into the Irishman's narrative—does not light it up with the life about it, or the circumstances under which it is delivered, and does not carry through it, as I think it should with a certain indefinable subtlety, the thread with which you begin your weaving. I will tell Wills to send me the proof, and will try and show you what I mean, when I have gone over it carefully."

Mr. Yates and others who speak with authority declare that Dickens was a ruthless "cutter," never hesitating to score out entire passages if he judged that the article or story would thus reap an advantage. "The very last time I saw him at the office," says Mr. Yates, "he laughed immensely as I said, when I noticed him run his blue ink pen through about half a column of the proof before him, 'Poor gentleman! There's fifteen shillings lost to him for ever!'" It sometimes happened that a particular number of *Household Words* required an unusual amount of the Editor's attention, as instanced by a letter to Wills in 1852, where he says: "If my mind could have been materialised, and drawn along the tops of all the spikes on the outside of the Queen's Bench prison, it could not have been more agonised than by the _____, which, for imbecility, carelessness, slovenly composition, relatives without antecedents, universal chaos, and one absorbing whirlpool of jolter-headedness, beats anything in print and paper I have ever 'gone at' in my life."[1] Mr. George Manville Fenn, the well-known novelist, in his "Reminiscences of Dickens," records his own gratifying experience of "Boz" as Editor of *All the Year Round*. To him the young author ventured to write, asking him to say frankly whether he (Mr. Fenn) should "go on hammering patiently" by continuing to

[1] "The Letters of Charles Dickens."
[2] *The Temple Magazine*, July 1901.

send stories to the magazines which so frequently declined them, or give it up at once. "And he answered—never a word. But he did better, for in very few days he had studied up the written evidence I had sent him along with my note, sent it to the printers, and one morning I awoke to find myself, like his own creation, Christopher, in 'Somebody's Luggage,' eagerly examining a long, narrow, bluish envelope, bearing my name and address, and in one corner the magic letters, 'A. Y. R.,' while inside was the proof that my little tale was deemed worthy to go in the pages that at times contained the emanations of his own brain."

Mr. Fenn, whose proof slips escaped the ordeal of editorial supervision tolerably well, admits he has seen proofs that bore evidence of the fact that they had monopolised much of Dickens's attention; these "he had altered to suit his taste, cancelling, transposing, and even rewriting large passages, to make them quite in accordance with his ideas upon the subject under consideration." "Such columns," continues Mr. Fenn, "patched, deleted, erased, and treated in the most terrible manner—from the writer's point of view—are extant, and are dear to the soul of the Dickens collector. . . . He had his own ideas of what the contributions to his periodical should be . . . and his additions were so many that they were doubtless the cause of the vulgar error, common amongst the provincial public, that he wrote the whole of *Household Words* himself; for in many of the articles and stories there is the Dickens touch, often his own, more often, perhaps, the work of his staff, who

¹ "Somebody's Luggage," Chapter 10 ("His wonderful End"), Christmas Number of *All the Year Round*, 1862.

unconsciously imbibed or imitated his style." The public misconception as to the actual authorship had its disadvantages; indeed, George Augustus Sala contended that it was productive of certain evil consequences to the young writers whose anonymity Dickens so strictly preserved, not the least of which was that many of their contributions were, at the time, not only attributed to the "master," but were sometimes reprinted with his name, thus depriving the aggrieved authors of such credit as they deserved.

If further testimony be required of Charles Dickens's amiable characteristics as Editor, it is forthcoming in a series of letters written by the Novelist to an American lady temporarily resident in England during 1863-64.[1] This correspondence "may be taken as representing, faithfully enough," observes Dickens's eldest son, "the pains and attention which were given by my father to a great number of other contributors who had no claims upon him but such as arose from their casual business relations." Charles Dickens the younger, who, by a codicil in his father's will, succeeded to the management of *All the Year Round* (he having acted as assistant editor after the resignation of Wills), could readily estimate the extent of his father's "boundless capacity for taking pains" and the strenuous manner in which his editorial duties were discharged. In the introductory remarks prefacing the above mentioned series of letters, the younger Dickens says: "An amount of time and labour was devoted to the polishing and finishing other people's work in proof which would surprise many occupants of editorial chairs, and which, there

[1] "Charles Dickens as an Editor," in the *English Illustrated Magazine*, August 1899. With prefatory notes by Charles Dickens the younger.

is no doubt, very considerably astonished some of the contributors whose work required the greatest quantity of excision and 'writing-up.'" An instance of this "polishing" process is recalled by a letter to Forster written in 1856, in which Dickens refers to a story which took four hours to "hack and hew" into a presentable form—"and I am perfectly addled by its horrible want of continuity after all, and the dreadful spectacle I have made of the proofs which look like an inky fishing net." "During my own experience as subeditor of *All the Year Round*, during the last two years of my father's life," observes the son, "I hardly remember a week in which, after making up the number in London, he did not devote the two or three succeeding hours to going with the utmost care over the proof of each article selected; and even when, in his absences from town on reading tours, he had to be content to leave some of the proofs to me, his instructions as to the manner in which they were to be dealt with were so precise and definite that any work which was done upon them might still almost be said to be his own. . . . To enlist promising recruits; to help forward rising merit; to further the development of latent ability; and above all, to give every possible assistance to young writers who showed steadfast perseverance, and any of his own capacity for taking pains in small things as well as great; these objects were always foremost in my father's editorial mind. . . If any mistake was ever made, it was sure to be on the side of kindness, and it is certain that subsequent disappointment was not infrequently the outcome of an encouragement which was sometimes even too generous, of an appreciation which was sometimes expressed with even an excess of liberality.' The writer of those lines is undoubtedly correct in his surmise that many authors of repute, who went through the "fishing net" mill in their early days, would be willing to admit that the system favoured by "Boz" worked exceedingly well.

Mr. Justin McCarthy, who says of Dickens that he was "quick to encourage, slow to disparage," and that he had a kindly word for every struggling author of merit, is enabled to certify to the Novelist's exceptional powers as an orator, and assures us that "Boz" was "the best after dinner speaker he ever heard. His voice was rich, full, and deep, and his wonderful eyes seemed to flash upon every individual member of the audience. Dickens thoroughly understood the difficult art of public speaking—an art in which few (if any) excelled him, and he who stood paramount as the greatest orator of his time (Mr. Gladstone) referred to the Novelist's speech at the Royal Academy dinner in 1870 (his last public utterance) as "one of the most finished performances in its kind" that he ever knew.[1] The *doyen* of newspaper reporters, Mr. Thomas A. Reed, recollects that Dickens was a most effective speaker at a moderate rate of speed, and his sentences were carefully constructed. On several occasions his orations were reported by Mr. Reed, chiefly after dinner speeches, in which he specially excelled; but he never reported him with so much pleasure as on the occasion of the festival of the Children's Hospital

---

[1] Gladstone recognised Dickens as "a great fact in the literature of the century," and felt much angered when he read somewhere that Dante was as familiar a name in Florence as that of Dickens in London.

in 1858, when his address was magnificent, thoroughly characteristic, and extremely telling, and its subsequent publication has since brought many handsome contributions to the Hospital exchequer. Dickens's speeches usually bore marks of careful preparation, but he never referred to notes except in the case of quotations.[1] In explaining to Wilkie Collins his *modus operandi* in preparing important speeches, he said that his habit was to take a long walk in the morning, during which he would decide on the various heads to be dealt with, and these being arranged in their proper order, he would, in his "mind's eye," liken the whole subject to the tire of a cartwheel—he being the hub; from the hub to the tire he would run as many spokes as there were subjects to be treated, and during the progress of the speech he would deal with each spoke separately, elaborating them as he went round the wheel; when all the spokes dropped out one by one and nothing but the tire and space remained, he would know that he had accomplished his task—the speech was at an end.[2]

We have Forster's assurance that Charles Dickens's speeches "derived singular charm from the buoyancy of his perfect self-possession, and to this he added the advantages of a person and manner which had become as familiar and popular as his books." The Reverend Edward Bradley ("Cuthbert Bede") doubted if the Novelist could be excelled in the arts of elocution. "Possessed of a singular dramatic power gifted with a voice of much clearness and compass—with great facial expression—apt in the actor's artificial art, and yet with a nature thoroughly natural. . . .

[1] "Charles Dickens by Pen and Pencil," 1889-90.
[2] "Charles Dickens as I knew Him," by George Dolby, 1885.

Rare, indeed, is it to meet with one in whom these many qualifications are centred; and . . . I think that I am fully justified in saying that the Prince of Novelists may fairly be reckoned one of the most effective orators of our time."[1] Dr. A. W. Ward, the Master of Peterhouse and Vice-Chancellor of Cambridge University, points out that Dickens possessed (in addition to personal qualifications) "that strong and elastic imaginative power which enables a man to place himself at once in sympathy with his audience, and that gift of speech, pointed, playful, and, where necessary, impetuous, which pleads well in any assembly for any cause."[2] One who was present at Drury Lane Theatre, on the occasion of the delivery by Dickens of his speech on Administrative Reform, took mental notes of his peculiarities of voice and style, for, being seated immediately under the speaker, he could conveniently study the play of his features. "Dickens," he says, "had acquired the habit, peculiar to all good speakers, of opening wide his mouth to give full effect to the charm of oral delivery. This gave him rather the appearance of gnashing his teeth, but no doubt he knew full well what he was about, and how to display his powers, histrionic though they mainly were, to the best advantage."[3] As a matter of fact, the Novelist carried into effect the valuable advice which he afterwards tendered his son, Henry Fielding, when beginning his novitiate as a debater at the Union Club, Cambridge: "Take any amount of pains about it," he

---

[1] "Charles Dickens by Pen and Pencil," 1889-90.
[2] "Dickens" (English Men of Letters Series), by A. W. Wards, 1882.
[3] "Charles Dickens by Pen and Pencil," 1889-90.

said; "open your mouth well and roundly, speak to the last person visible, and give yourself time."[1]

When commenting upon this subject Edmund Yates records, in his "Recollections and Experiences," a remarkable instance of what he terms Dickens's "wonderful readiness." He says: "I was so much in the habit of going with him to public dinners, and the managers of those entertainments so frequently begged me to propose his health as chairman, that it became a joke between us as to whether I could possibly find anything new to say. On one occasion—it was at one of the Newsvendors' dinners—I said nothing at all! I duly rose, but, after a few words, my thoughts entirely deserted me, I entirely lost the thread of what I had intended saying, I felt as though a black veil were dropped over my head; all I could do was to mutter 'health,' 'Chairman,' and to sit down. I was tolerably well known to the guests at those dinners, and they were evidently much astonished. They cheered the toast, as in duty bound, and Dickens was on his feet in a moment. 'Often,' he said—'often as I have had the pleasure of having my health proposed by my friend, who has just sat down, I have never yet seen him so overcome by his affection and generous emotion as on the present occasion.' These words turned what would have been a fiasco into a triumph. 'I saved you that time, I think, sir!' he said to me as I walked away with him. 'Serves you well right for being overconfident!'"

[1] "The Letters of Charles Dickens."

CHAPTER 16

# THE PORTRAITURE AND PERSONALITY OF DICKENS

Since the publication of Forster's "Life" there have been placed on record a number of word-portraits of Charles Dickens, portraying him from his youth upwards, and these enable us to realise his outward semblance with tolerable distinctness and accuracy. In order, however, to complete the composite picture thus conveyed to the mental retina, it is essential that we should acquire some knowledge of his personal traits and idiosyncrasies, and this is rendered possible by the various reminiscences of "Boz," lovingly registered by his friends and contemporaries.

We have Dickens's own assurance that, as a child, he was "a very queer small boy," and in a letter to Washington Irving in 1841 he describes himself as "a very small and not-over-particularly-taken-care-of boy." Forster says that he was a very sickly lad, being subject to attacks of violent spasm, which prevented him from taking part in any games requiring much exertion, such as cricket or prisoner's base—indeed, it seems that he never excelled in any outdoor games, but enjoyed watching others at play. Of reading, however, he was especially fond, his weak health strongly inclining him thereto, and he never tired of devouring the contents of certain romances to which a more detailed reference is made in the first chapter.

His personal appearance as a schoolboy is truthfully suggested by "Phiz" in his etching representing little David Copperfield giving his "magnificent order" at the public house, where he is seen wearing a kind of Eton jacket, corduroy trousers, and a white beaver hat. He was a handsome boy, with long and light curly hair—eager, observant, amiable, intelligent, thoughtful, and sensitive to a degree, while at children's birthday parties and similar juvenile gatherings he proved a great acquisition, being excellent company, and having precocious abilities in the way of singing and recitation. *Apropos* of his schooldays at Wellington House Academy (1824-26) it is remembered that he usually held his head more erect than lads ordinarily do; there was a general smartness about him, and, owing to his high animal spirits, he was probably connected with every mischievous prank in the school.

The next pen-portrait of Dickens belongs to a rather later period, when he acted as clerk in an attorney's office, 1827-28. A fellow clerk, Mr. George Lear, thus describes his "prepossessing" appearance at that time: "He was rather a short but stout built boy, and carried himself very upright—his head well up— and the idea he gave me was that he must have been drilled by a military instructor. His dress, in some measure, perhaps, contributed to that impression. He wore a frockcoat (or surtout, as it was then generally called) buttoned up, of dark blue cloth, trousers to match, and (as was the fashion at the time) buttoned with leather straps over the boots; black neckerchief, but no shirt collar showing. His complexion was of a healthy pink—almost glowing—rather a round face, fine forehead, beautiful expressive eyes full of animation, a firmly set mouth, a good-sized rather straight nose, but not at all too large. His hair was a beautiful brown, and worn long, as was then the fashion. His cap was like the undress cap of an officer in the, army, of some shining material with a narrow shining leather strap running round the point of the chin. His appearance was altogether decidedly military. I always thought he must have adopted this from his having lived at Chatham. He looked very clean and well-fed and cared for."[1]

The first meeting between Dickens and his future biographer took place when the former was nineteen years of age, in his early reporting days, and Forster was much struck by his "keen animation of look," which would have arrested attention anywhere. There exists, however, a more tangible presentment of the future Novelist as he then appeared, in the form of a miniature on ivory by his aunt, Mrs. Edward Barrow, which shows the face, hairless yet, surmounted by rich clustering hair of a chestnut hue, while the high satin stock and the broad lappets of the coat mark the costume of the period. In 1833, the well-known *litterateur*, John Payne Collier, dined with Dickens and some of his relations, and formed a highly favourable opinion of the young stenographer's abilities; he records that, on meeting him soon afterwards, he remarked a great difference in his appearance and dress, for he wore a new hat and a very handsome blue cloak, with black velvet facings, the corner of which he threw over his shoulder *à l' Espagnol*. The fact is, his position meanwhile had improved, and there is reason to believe that his "Dora" (not the lady whom he married) had then come into his life. In 1835, that is, during his

[1] "Charles Dickens by Pen and Pencil," 1889-90.

engagement to Miss Catherine Hogarth (who became his wife a year later) he gave sittings to another painter on ivory, Rose Emma Drummond, the supposed prototype of Miss La Creevy in "Nicholas Nickleby"; in this miniature the face is seen with slight whiskers, the eyes are dark brown, and the hair chestnut coloured, the dark blue coat with high velvet collar, and the blue satin stock, constituting the accessories of a natural and pleasing portrait, to which, by the way, a peculiar interest attaches, for Dickens presented it to his *fiancée* as an "engagement" gift.

Of Dickens's face Mrs. Carlyle once said that "it was as if made of steel," and Leigh Hunt declared that it had "the life and soul in it of fifty human beings." The beautiful crayon portraits by Samuel Laurence, executed at this time, entirely endorse such statements respecting the fire and beauty of Dickens's physiognomy, and the full-length presentment by Maclise (now in the National Gallery) conveys an excellent impression not only of that physiognomy, but also of the everyday dress of the subject of the painting. "Look at the portrait of Mr. Dickens," wrote Thackeray, concerning the Maclise canvas. ". . . Here we have the real identical man Dickens: the artist must have understood the inward 'Boz' as well as the outward before he made this admirable representation of him. What cheerful intellectuality is about the man's eyes, and a large forehead! The mouth is too large and full, too eager and active, perhaps; the smile is very sweet and generous . . . the nose firm and well placed, the nostrils wide and full, as are the nostrils of all men of genius (this is Monsieur Balzac's maxim) . . . Long mayest thou, Oh Boz! Reign over thy comic kingdom. . . . Mighty prince, at thy imperial feet, Titmarsh, humblest of thy servants, offers his vows of loyalty and his humble tribute of praise."[1] Sala assures us that for grace, and refinement, and intellectual force we must go to Maclise's canvas, for this is the Charles Dickens "who was, in the early days of Queen Victoria's reign, one of the best-looking and best-dressed young fellows about town; or who, a few years later, in a blue frock, white vest, and white trousers, looked even nattier and comelier." In the Maclise portrait we behold the Novelist seated in an armchair and depicted as something of a dandy as regards his costume; but it must not be forgotten that those were "dressy" days, when gentlemen (of the younger generation at least) wore swallowtail coats with high velvet collars, voluminous satin stocks with double breastpins, brilliantly coloured waistcoats of silk or velvet, "Cossack" trousers, for which tightly fitting black pantaloons were substituted for evening wear. The aristocratic Count D'Orsay ("the Phoebus Apollo of Dandyism," as Carlyle designated him), who is said to have possessed the physique of a young Hercules and the comeliness of an Adonis, was undoubtedly the most magnificently attired man of the nineteenth century, and following his example in this respect were a few young men of rising reputation, who, with the Count, paid court to the "gorgeous" Lady Blessington at Gore House. Chief among these grandly-apparelled personages were Disraeli, Bulwer Lytton, Harrison Ainsworth, and Charles Dickens; as each seemed to vie with the other in the splendour of his clothing, their simultaneous presence at her ladyship's *levées* must have afforded a most effective spectacle. The kind of dress worn by these

[1] *Fraser's Magazine*, 1840.

butterflies of fashion was truly oriental in its wealth of colour; an emerald green coat with velvet collar, a cream-coloured waistcoat, mustard-coloured trousers, black satin stock, with a double diamond pin and the connecting light gold chain—thus did the "smart" young men of the early Victorian era exhibit themselves at society functions, such as the receptions at Gore House and in the rival *salon* of Holland House. Dickens's taste in sartorial matters was generally somewhat "loud," and he always prided himself upon his daring to wear vests of a pattern and colour so resplendent (as, for example, the black waistcoat embroidered with flowers which he wore at Judge Walker's party at Cincinnati in 1842) that his friends wondered at the courage he thus displayed at a period when a more sober form of attire became general. In an amusing document which the Novelist penned in 1844, giving an account of a meeting of the Mechanics' Institution at Liverpool, when he officiated as chairman, he wrote: "And this deponent further saith, that his white-and-black or magpie waistcoat did create a strong sensation, and that during the hours of promenading this deponent heard from persons surrounding him such exclamations as 'What is it! *Is* it a waistcoat? No, it's a shirt'—and the like— all of which this deponent believes to have been complimentary and gratifying."[1] A still more amusing illustration of this pronounced *penchant* is discoverable in the following letter to Macready, dated a year or so later, asking for the loan of a particularly striking garment for a special occasion:—

"You once—only once—gave the world assurance of a waistcoat. You wore it, sir, I think, in

[1] "The Letters of Charles Dickens."

'Money.' It was a remarkable and precious waistcoat, wherein certain broad stripes of blue or purple disported themselves as by a combination of extraordinary circumstances, too happy to occur again. I have seen it on your manly chest in private life. I saw it, sir, I think, the other day in the cold light of morning—with feelings easier to be imagined than described. Mr. Macready, sir, are you a father? If so, lend me that waistcoat for five minutes. I am bidden to a wedding (where fathers are made), and my artist cannot, I find (how should he?), imagine such a waistcoat. Let me show it to him as a sample of my tastes and wishes; and—ha, ha, ha, ha!—eclipse the bridegroom!

"I will send a trusty messenger at half-past nine precisely, in the morning. He is sworn to secrecy. He durst not for his life betray us, or swells in ambuscade would have the waistcoat at the cost of his heart's blood.

"Thine,

"The Unwaistcoated One."

During his visit to Italy in 1853, he called upon an acquaintance who (he averred) failed at first to recognise him because, forsooth, he was not wearing the customary coloured vest. "Why haven't you got a bright waistcoat on?" inquired the astonished friend, to whom Dickens forthwith apologised for his appearance with a black one. Mr. W. P. Frith, the veteran Royal Academician, relates that when (in 1859) the Novelist sat to him for his portrait, he arrived at the studio wearing a large sky-blue overcoat with bright red cuffs. "I protested that I could not manage the overcoat," says Mr. Frith, "and Dickens, with great

---

[1] "The Letters of Charles Dickens."

docility, agreed to abandon this favourite article of apparel, remarking, in explanation of its gaudy appearance, that he was very fond of colour." There is no doubt that the Novelist found it difficult to conform to the comparatively sombre dress as donned by the male sex at that time, and he practically admitted his want of appreciation of modern garb when, in a speech delivered at a public meeting held for the purpose of establishing the Royal Dramatic College, he alluded to "the silks, and velvets, and elegant costumes" of those who trod the theatrical boards, that must every night be exchanged for "the hideous coats and waistcoats of the present day."

Serjeant Ballantine has recorded in his diary for 1838, when he saw Charles Dickens for the first time, that he looked "quite a boy," although he had already won his spurs under the *sobriquet* of "Boz." "There was a brightness and geniality about him," continues the learned Serjeant-at-law, "that greatly fascinated his companions. His laugh was so cheery, and he seemed so thoroughly to enter into the feelings of those around. He told a story well and never prosily; he was a capital listener, and in conversation was not in the slightest degree dictatorial. . . ." Carlyle, when writing to his brother John in 1840, gave a terse and vivid pen-portrait of Dickens, whom he had just met at the home of the Stanleys: "He is a fine little fellow—Boz, I think. Clear blue, intelligent eyes, eyebrows that he arches amazingly, large protrusive rather loose mouth, a face of most extreme *mobility*, which he shuttles about—eyebrows, eyes, mouth and all—in a very singular manner while speaking. Surmount this with a loose coil of common-coloured hair, and set it on a small compact figure, very small, and dressed *à la* D'Orsay rather than well—this is Pickwick. For the rest, a quiet, shrewd looking little fellow, who seems to guess pretty well what he is and what others are."[1]

George Henry Lewes, soon after the completion of "Pickwick," called upon Dickens at Doughty Street, in response to an invitation, and gives the following pen-portrait of him: "Those who remember him at that period will understand the somewhat disturbing effect produced in my enthusiasm for the new author by the sight of his bookshelves, on which were ranged nothing but three volume novels and books of travel, all obviously the presentation copies from authors and publishers, with none of the treasures of the bookstall. . . . I did not expect to find a bookworm, nor even a student, in the marvellous 'Boz'; but, nevertheless, this collection of books was a shock. He shortly came in, and his sunny presence quickly dispelled all misgivings. He was then, as to the last, a delightful companion, full of sagacity as well as of animal spirits; but I came away more impressed with the fullness of life and energy than with any sense of distinction. I believe I only saw him once more before I went to Germany, and two years had elapsed when we next met. While waiting in his library (in Devonshire Terrace), I of course glanced at his books. The well-known paperboards of the three-volume novel no longer vulgarised the place; a goodly array of standard works, well-bound, showed a more respectable and conventional ambition; but there

---

[1] Dickens was not a "very small" man, being about the average middle height. Lady Martin (Helen Faucit), who knew Dickens at this time, failed to recognise Carlyle's description of his hair as "a loose coil of common-coloured hair," but would herself have called it a rich brown, very abundant, with a slight undulation in it.—*See* "Charles Dickens by Pen and Pencil," 1889-90.

was no physiognomy in the collection. A greater change was visible in Dickens himself. In these two years he had remarkably developed. His conversation turned on graver subjects than theatres and actors, periodicals, and London life. His interest in public affairs, especially in social questions, was keener. He still remained completely outside philosophy, science, and the higher literature, and was too unaffected a man to pretend to feel any interest in them. But the vivacity and sagacity which gave a charm to intercourse with him had become weighted with a seriousness which from that time forward became more and more prominent in his conversations and his writings. He had already learned to look upon the world as a scene where it was the duty of each man in his own way to make the lot of the miserable many a little less miserable; and, having learned that his genius gave him great power, he was bent on using that power effectively."[1]

A young American, Charles Edward Lester (subsequently U.S. Consul in Genoa), who visited Dickens about this time, regarded him as "incomparably the finest looking man he ever saw," and declared that no picture could do justice to the expression of his face while he was engaged in an interesting conversation; there was something about his eyes at all times which could not be reproduced in a portrait. After eulogising the Novelists handsome features and graceful figure, Mr. Lester proceeds to observe, phrenologically, that his forehead "indicates a clear beautiful intellect, in which the organs of perception, mirthfulness, ideality, and comparison predominate. . . But the charm of his person is in his full, soft,

---

[1] *The Fortnightly Review*, February 1872.

beaming eyes, which catch an expression from every passing object; and you can always see wit, half sleeping in ambush around them, when it is not shooting its wonted fires. . . ." Another American, James T. Fields (who became one of Dickens's closest friends), has recorded his impression of "Boz" as, in 1842, he bounded into the Tremont House, Boston, fresh from the steamer that had brought him to Transatlantic shores: "From top to toe every fibre of his body was unrestrained and alert. What vigour, what keenness, what freshness of spirit, possessed him! He laughed all over, and did not care who heard him! He seemed like the Emperor of Cheerfulness on a cruise of pleasure. . . ."

Richard Hengist Horne, author of "Orion" (the "farthing epic"), knew Dickens intimately, and recalled his genial conversation, his hatred of argument, his impulsiveness, his admirable method of telling a story (generally with humorous exaggerations), his broad sympathies, his singular personal activity, and his partiality for games of skill. "In private, the general impression of him is that of a first-rate practical intellect, with 'no nonsense' about him." Until 1844, the Novelist's face was almost destitute of a hirsute growth; in Italy, during that year, he encouraged the development of a moustache, which was removed on his return to England. He considered at the time that this appendage (especially when trimmed at the ends, "to improve the shape") enhanced his personal appearance, and that, without such an adornment, "life would be a blank." As regards Dickens, however, this certainly not the case. In the earliest photographic portrait of him (a daguerreotype by Mayall, *circa* 1849), the face, although clean shaven with the exception of slight whiskers, begins to look older and more masculine but there still remains the alert expression which always distinguished it. The portrait (representing the Novelist, as his friend Charles Kent said, "at his very best and brightest") is doubtless the one referred to by George Eliot in a letter dated 1871: "We have just got a photograph of Dickens, taken when he was writing, or had just written, 'David Copperfield'—satisfactory refutation of that keepsakey, impossible face which Maclise gave him, and which has been engraved for the 'Life' in all its odious beatification. This photograph is the young Dickens, corresponding to the older Dickens whom I knew—the same face, without the unusually severe wear and tear of years which his latest looks exhibited." Thus we perceive that the author of "Adam Bede" criticised Maclise's painting in no admiring spirit, and, curiously enough, she failed to discover anything worthy of special comment in the personality of Dickens himself, when she saw him at a public meeting in 1852. "His appearance is certainly disappointing," she declared,—"no benevolence in the face, and, I think, little in the head,—the anterior lobe not by any means remarkable. In fact, he is not distinguished looking in any way—neither handsome nor ugly, neither fat nor thin, neither tall nor short." We pass from this jarring note to the more sympathetic presentment by a young American lady (Miss Clarke, afterwards Mrs. L. K. Lippincott) who visited him at Tavistock House in the same year: "Mr. Dickens—how clearly he stands before me now, with his frank, encouraging smile, and the light of welcome in his eyes!—Was then slight in person, and rather pale than otherwise. The symmetrical form of his head, and the fine spirited bearing of the whole figure, struck me at once—then the hearty *bonhomie*, the wholesome sweetness of his smile; but more than anything else, the great beauty of his eyes."

In 1854, Edmund Yates obtained his first interview with the Novelist, whom he had long worshipped from afar, and by whom he was, from that time, numbered amongst his most intimate acquaintances. The editor of the *World*, having mentally conceived Dickens's personal appearance from Maclise's portrait, found that his physiognomy had changed considerably during the sixteen years which had elapsed since the picture was painted. Instead of the soft, delicate, hairless face as depicted by Maclise, he saw that the features were of a more masculine type, and that the hair, though worn still rather long, was beginning to be sparse; the cheeks were shaved, but a moustache and a "doorknocker" beard encircled the mouth and chin. His eyes, however, retained their wonderful brightness and the keen, eager outlook, while his bearing was hearty and somewhat aggressive. In the following year, the Novelist gave sittings in Paris to Ary Scheffer, the French historical painter, and the portrait (now in the National Portrait Gallery) represents "Boz" as described by Mr. Yates.[1]

Here is a little picture of Dickens, by Hain Friswell, as he appeared in the 'fifties: "On one occasion we were walking down Wellington Street, and just passing the office of *Household Words*, when a hansom cab stopped, and out stepped a gaily

---

[1] Dickens referred to this as "the nightmare portrait," as the sittings were given when he was busily occupied with "Little Dorrit," and could not easily spare the time. He did not regard it as a successful portrait; nor did Scheffer himself feel satisfied with it, and, during one of the sittings, said apologetically, and with a vexed air: "At this moment, *mon cher* Dickens, you look more like an energetic Dutch admiral than anything else." Technically, however, it is a highly artistic and refined work.

dressed gentleman; his bright green waistcoat and vivid scarlet tie anyone would have noticed, but the size of the nosegay in his buttonhole riveted my attention. My father introduced me, and I, who had only seen engravings of the Maclise portrait and photographs, was astonished to find myself face to face with Charles Dickens."[1]

The Novelist's friends now beheld the last of the youthful, clean-shaven countenance which marks the earlier portraits, for the "door-knocker" beard (or "goatee") and moustache had come to stay, and this, with the lines that were visible upon the face, tended to mark the progress of time. His friends protested against his evident intention to refrain from the use of the razor, rightly judging that the result would be to conceal the remarkable charm of mouth and chin; the beard added years to his age, and his friends "lost for good seeing the joke coming before it was spoken, which had such a specially humorous effect," in addition to which, there was imparted to his countenance a comparatively commonplace appearance, as testified by Baugniet's drawing of him in 1858. A year or two earlier Mr. W. P. Frith, R.A., received a commission from Forster to paint a portrait of the Novelist, and both the artist and his patron were horrified at the hirsute appendage, for it certainly had the effect of injuring a very handsome and characteristic mouth. Forster, who thought it was merely a whim of Dickens and that the fancy would pass, suggested waiting until the disfigurement was removed; but they waited in vain, the Novelist declaring (with a touch of jocularity) that "the beard saved him the trouble of shaving, and much as he admired his own

[1] "James Hain Friswell: A Memoir," 1898.

appearance before he allowed the beard to grow, he admired it much more now, and never neglected, when an opportunity offered, to gaze his fill at himself . . . ." He insinuated, too, that Mr. Frith would surely prefer to save himself the trouble of painting features that were so difficult as a mouth, and chin. "We waited," says the artist, "till the beard was allowed to grow upon the chin as well as upon the upper lip, so, fearing that if we delayed longer there would be little of the face to be painted, if whiskers were to be added to the rest, the order was given and the portrait begun." The painting, which occupies the most important place between the earlier presentments and the later photographic representations of Dickens, was bequeathed by Forster to the Nation, and is now included in the collection at the Victoria and Albert Museum, South Kensington.

Curiously diverse opinions have obtained regarding the colour of Dickens's eyes, which seemed to have chameleon-like qualities. In Miss Drummond's miniature they are represented as *blue*, and Carlyle described them as "clear *blue* intelligent eyes." T. Adolphus Trollope declares that they were "a distinct and brilliant *hazel*; Ary Scheffer depicted them as *brown*, and Mr. Frith as a *blue-grey*; an American writer, in 1842, called them *black*, and Mrs. James T. Fields subsequently alluded to them as "glowing *grey* eyes." It has been reasonably suggested that their hue actually altered according to the condition of his health, and in reply to my query as to the veritable tint of her father's eyes, the late Miss Mamie Dickens wrote: "When I began to think of the actual colour, I really was at a loss to define I never saw eyes so constantly changing in expression and in colour as his did. But I have it on true artistic authority, from one who knew him *intimately*, that his eyes were undoubtedly 'dark *slatey* blue, looking black at night—not in the least brown—only as the little orange line round the pupil was very strongly marked it gave a warm look to the eye. The pupils were also large and sometimes much dilated—that also made the eyes look darker than they really were— a *dark slatey blue.*' I have never seen any other eyes at all like them, as to expression, or variableness of expression, nor have I ever seen any other eyes altogether so beautiful."[1] The Novelist's daughter could recall his appearance before the cultivation of moustache and beard, "when both the sensitive, powerful, and beautiful mouth and the firm chin were visible; when he grew older and the beard and moustache were grizzled, and his hair became very thin, and the face was lined and worn, it still remained the most beautiful and lovable face of all faces in the world. It was always delightful to watch him, and the wonderful and quickly changing expression of his face as he talked, sometimes so grave, so earnest, with a searching look in his deep eyes as if he could look into your very heart, and as if it would be impossible to meet those eyes with a bad or mean thought in your own heart, sometimes with a smile and laughing eyes, which seemed to throw sunshine and merriment all about him, but always with a fascination no one could resist, and with the most delightful and most sympathetic voice that was ever heard."[2]

Sir Joseph Crowe remembered Dickens as being full of fun, and that he enjoyed his company vastly. His abundant hair of sable hue enframed a grand

---

[1] "Charles Dickens by Pen and Pencil," 1889-90.
[2] "Charles Dickens," by his Eldest Daughter, 1885.

face, somewhat drawn and thrown into capricious ridges. His dress was florid: a satin cravat of the deepest blue, relieved by embroideries, a green waistcoat with gold flowers, a dress coat with a velvet collar and satin facings, opulence of white cuff, rings in excess, made up rather a striking whole."[1]

Of Charles Dickens's mode of life at Gad's Hill much that is interesting might be written. His innate love of order was so strong that it became his invariable rule to make a daily morning round of inspection before settling down at his desk. To ensure punctual and methodical habits on the part of his domestic servants, he prepared with his own hand, for their guidance, written instructions regarding their respective duties, and nothing was permitted to go amiss by being left to chance. The pedestrian exercise in which he indulged naturally familiarised his appearance to everyone residing within a radius of ten or a dozen miles from Gad's Hill. His figure could be immediately recognised even at a distance by the rapid swing of his walk as he strode along, accompanied by his dogs, and, may be, by Miss Hogarth or a guest friend; erect of head, bright of eyes, brown of face, and with a beard which began to show signs of grey hairs in the 'fifties, he marched along the country roads or through Cobham, Park and Woods, carrying a blackthorn stick-the picture of health and strength. Such perambulations were by no means purposeless; his powers of observation were never idle, and the mental retina retained a vivid impression of all that the eye observed, while he stored up in his ever-active brain a wealth of material, to be drawn upon

---

[1] "Reminiscences of Thirty-Five Years of My Life," by Sir Joseph Crowe, K.C.M.G., C.B., 1895.

when writing "Great Expectations" and the delightful "Uncommercial Traveller" papers.

A severe illness in 1864 put a broad mark between his past life and what remained to him of the future. The torture occasioned by a frostbitten foot, resulting in a lameness which never left him, and the frightful shock to his nervous system caused by the Staplehurst railway accident, tended to age him prematurely. The excessive and prolonged strain of the public readings undoubtedly affected his health most alarmingly, so that in his fifty-fourth year he looked considerably older, and seemed to justify the name of "Wenerables," which (as we have seen) his grandchildren bestowed upon him. George Dolby describes the Novelist's figure at this time as being tall and sinewy—"his face, adorned with a wiry moustache and grizzly beard, struck one at once; deep lined and bronzed, it was a philosopher's; the eyes, whose depths no man could fathom, were large and eloquent, and side by side lurked the iron will of a demon and the tender pity of an angel. His face had all the romance of an ancient Norseman, while his whole mien reminded one of nothing so much as a Viking." The Novelist's American friends, when he visited them in 1867, detected the vast alteration effected in his appearance since they first beheld him twenty-five years before, and, instead of the smooth-faced, full-eyed, long-haired, boyish looking person as they remembered him to have been in 1842, they saw in him a man much sobered by time and arduous labour, a man whose hair was thinned and whitened, and on whose visage the thickly gathered wrinkles gave a deeper setting to the eyes; for although the complexion was florid, the whole face had become furrowed and shrunken. The picturesqueness (so to say) which then characterised the Novelist's head and face is happily perpetuated in a series of photographs taken by Mr. Ben Gurney of New York; when the negatives were secured, Dickens declared he would never be photographed again—and he never was! He, however, pronounced these particular portraits (for which he gave sittings after much persuasion) to be the best that had ever been produced.

Motley, the historian, once met Dickens at dinner, and thus wrote to a friend: "He looks about the age of Longfellow . . . His hair is not much grizzled, and is thick, although the crown of his head is getting bald. His features are good, the nose rather high, the eyes largish, greyish, and very expressive. He wears a moustache and beard, and dresses at dinner in exactly the same uniform which every man in London, or the civilised world, is bound to wear, as much as the inmates of a penitentiary are restricted to theirs. I mention this because I had heard that he was odd and extravagant in his costume. I liked him exceedingly. We sat next each other at table, and I found him genial, sympathetic, agreeable, unaffected, with plenty of light, easy talk, and touch-and-go fun, without any effort or humbug of any kind."[1]

Mr. Percy Fitzgerald spent many hours in Charles Dickens's company during the last few years of the Novelist's life, and clearly recalls the tall, wiry, energetic figure, the bronzed face, the keen, bright, searching eyes, and mouth hidden by a wiry moustache and grizzled beard. "He had much of the quiet resolute manner of command of a captain of a ship." remarks Mr. Fitzgerald. "He strode along briskly as he walked; as he listened his searching eye

---

[1] "Letters of J. L. Motley," 1889.

rested on you, and the sensitive nerves in his face quivered as those in the delicately formed nostrils of a dog do. There was a curl or two in his hair, on each side, which was characteristic; and the jaunty way he wore his little morning hat, rather on one side, added to the effect. But when there was anything droll suggested, a delightful sparkle of lurking humour began to kindle and spread to his mouth, so that you felt that something irresistibly droll was at hand." Sala affirmed that, even during his later years, Dickens's walking attire "was decidedly odd, and almost eccentric, being marked by strongly pronounced colours, and a fashioning of the garments which had somewhat of a sporting and somewhat of a theatrical guise." Mr. Fitzgerald's assertion that he never met a man so unlike a professional writer is strengthened by Sala's affirmation that those who did not know Charles Dickens might have mistaken him for "a prosperous sea captain home from a long voyage, some Western senator on a tour in Europe, some country gentleman of Devon or of Yorkshire, who now and then bred a colt or two, and won a cup, but never betted." When Blanchard Jerrold met the Novelist at Charing Cross about a month before that fateful day in June 1870, he noticed how much he had aged in appearance, as, with bent back and limping in pain at a snail's pace, oaken staff in hand, he wended his way to the office of *All the Year Round*. The thought lines in his face had so deepened and the hair had so whitened that Mr. Jerrold could hardly believe it was Dickens whom he then beheld. "It was he, however; but with a certain solemnity of expression in the face, and a deeper earnestness in the dark eyes. Those who had not seen him for some time were now almost struck with the sudden whiteness of his hair.

His sunburnt face seemed set in snow, beard and hair were blanched so perfectly."[1]

Concerning Charles Dickens's habit of life, Dr. A. W. Ward, Master of Peterhouse, has recorded some, interesting details: "He was an early riser, if for no other reason, because every man in whose work imagination plays its part must sometimes be alone; and Dickens told us that there was to him something incomparably solemn in the still solitude of the morning. But it was only exceptionally, and when hard pressed by the necessities of his literary labours, that he wrote before breakfast; in general he was contented with the ordinary working hours of the morning, not often writing after luncheon, and, except in early life, never in the evening. Ordinarily when engaged on a work of fiction, he considered three of his not very large MS. pages a good, and four an excellent, day's work; and, while very careful in making corrections clear and unmistakable, he never rewrote what a morning's labour had ultimately produced. On the other hand, he was frequently slow in beginning a story, being, as he himself says, affected by something like despondency at such times, or, as he elsewhere humorously puts it, 'going round and round the idea, as you see a bird in his cage go about and about the sugar before he touches it.' Walking exercise was at once his *forte* and his fanaticism; he is said to have constructed for himself a theory that, to every portion of the day given to intellectual labour should correspond an equal number of hours spent in walking. . . . The walks he loved best were long stretches on the cliffs, or across the downs by the sea, where, following

---

[1] The Novelist's hair never became perfectly white, but remained grizzled.

the track of his 'breathers,' one half expects to meet him coming along against the wind at four and a half miles an hour, the very embodiment of energy and brimful of life."[1] The Novelist's powers of endurance as a pedestrian were, indeed, extraordinary, and very few of his friends could successfully compete with him; readers of his books will remember that he endowed some of his characters with equally remarkable attainments, causing them to accomplish what, under the circumstances, may be regarded as impossible performances in walking.

Dickens, when writing, required absolute quietude, the slightest sound causing a fatal interruption of his thoughts. He was usually alone while busy at his desk, but his eldest daughter recalled the time, when, during convalescence following a protracted illness from which she suffered in her childhood, she was permitted to remain in his study, and there reposing upon the sofa, was enabled to watch her father at work. Thus, one morning she was startled by his suddenly jumping from his chair and, rushing to a mirror, making some extraordinary facial contortions—then returning rapidly to his desk, he wrote furiously for a few minutes, and again went to the mirror to repeat the strange performance, after which he began talking rapidly in a low voice (being totally unconscious of his daughter's presence), and proceeded with his task. It was a most curious experience for me," says Miss Dickens, "and one of which I did not, until later years, fully appreciate the purport. Then I knew that with his natural intensity he had thrown himself completely into the character he was creating, and that for the time being he had not only lost sight of his surroundings, but had actually

---

[1] "Dickens," by A. W. Ward, 1882.

become in action, as in imagination, the creature of his pen."[1] We learn from the same source that his manuscripts were usually written upon white "slips," though sometimes upon blue paper, and there were many mornings when it would be impossible for him to fill one of these, his brain refusing to work; he would, however, remain at his desk the usual number of hours, even if, in the end, nothing resulted except a few desultory scratchings or sketchings on his paper. He invariably wrote with a quill pen and blue ink, and never (it is believed) with a lead pencil, to the use of which he objected.[2] His handwriting was considered extremely difficult to read by many people, but those who were familiar with it experienced no such trouble. In his manuscripts (nearly all of which are at the Victoria and Albert Museum, South Kensington) there are so many erasures and interlineations (thus indicating the care and fastidiousness of the writer) that a special staff of compositors was used for putting his matter into type. For his personal correspondence he favoured a bluish notepaper, and sometimes signed his name in the left-hand corner at the bottom of the envelope.

Charles Dickens was, perhaps, one of the most tidy persons that ever lived. He hated disorder (says Dr. Ward) "as Sir Artegall hated injustice; and if there was anything against which he took up his parable with burning indignation, it was slovenliness, and half done work, and 'shoddiness' of all kinds. His love of order always made him the most regular of men."

---

[1] "My Father as I Recall Him," by Mamie Dickens.
[2] The particular blue ink which Dickens used had the advantages of drying quickly and of not clogging the pen.

"Everything with him," we are assured, "went as by clockwork; his movements, his absences from home, and the times of his return, were all fixed beforehand, and it was seldom that he failed to adhere to what he fixed." He prided himself on his punctuality, and as for his strong sense of order, he could not live in a house or occupy a room until everything was in its right place. The testimony of Sir Arthur Helps similarly certifies that he was one of the most precise and accurate men in the world, his love of order and neatness being almost painful, while unpunctuality made him unhappy. Charles Dickens the younger remarked of his father,[1] that "whatever he did he put his whole heart into, and did as well as ever he could. Whether it was for work or for play, he was always in earnest. . . . Speaking through the mouth of David Copperfield, my father described his own way of life with perfect accuracy when he said: 'I never could have done what I have done without the habits of punctuality, order, and diligence, without the determination to concentrate myself on one object at a time, no matter how quickly its successor should come upon its heels . . . Heaven knows I write this in no spirit of self laudation. . . . My meaning simply is, that whatever I have tried to do in life, I have tried with all my heart to do well; that whatever I have devoted myself to, I have devoted myself to completely; that, in great aims and in small, I have always been thoroughly in earnest. . . . Never to put one hand to anything on which I could throw my whole self; and never to affect depreciation of my work, whatever it was; I find now, to have been my golden rules.'"[2] The

---

[1] *North American Review*, May and June, 1895.
[2] "David Copperfield," chap. 42.

following quaint note to Wilkie Collins speaks for itself, as illustrating this methodical habit:—[1]

TAVISTOCK HOUSE, *Sixth June*, 1954.

MY DEAR COLLINS—

| | | |
|---|---|---|
| Day, | | Thursday. |
| Hour, | | Quarter-past 11 a.m. |
| Place, | | Dover Terminus, |
| London Bridge. | | |
| Destination, | | Tunbridge Wells. |
| Description of Railway Qualification, | | Return Ticket. |
| | (Signed) | CHARLES DICKENS. |
| Entd. | | |

Form of trip appointment, in compliance with Act of Parliament, Victoria, cap. 7, section 304.

In conversation, Dickens used the monosyllable "we" much more frequently than that of "I," and made use of his superiority to charm and quicken the society around him, but never to crush or overpower it with a sense of their inferiority; the most diffident girl was encouraged to express to him her modest opinion.[2] "In general society," observes James Payn, (especially if it has been of an artificial kind, I have known his manner to betray some sense of effort, but in a company with whom he would feel at home, I have never met a man more natural or more charming. He never wasted time in commonplaces—though a lively talker, he never uttered a platitude—and what he had to say he said as if he meant it. On an occasion . . . he once spoke of himself as 'very human'; he did so, of course, in a depreciatory sense; he was the last person in the world to affect to possess any other nature than that of his fellows."[3] Frederick Locker-Lampson, whose

---

[1] *Harper's Magazine*, August 1891.
[2] "Mary Boyle: Her Book," 1902.
[3] "Some Literary Recollections," by James Payn, 1885.

acquaintance with the Novelist gives weight to the assertion, speaks of his conversation as being "so affluent—so delightfully alive," "and declares that, when in congenial society, "he talked like a demon of delightfulness." To strangers he was somewhat reserved, but a warm reception ever met those who made the slightest advance. One especial characteristic was noted by Miss Boyle, which, in her opinion, added greatly to the charm of his society, viz., the remarkable gift he had of setting others at ease when in his company.

Carlyle, shortly after the death of the Novelist, thus wrote to Forster: "It is almost thirty years since my acquaintance with him began; and on my side, I may say, every new meeting ripened it into more and more clear discernment of his rare and great worth as a brother man; a most cordial, sincere, clear-sighted, quietly decisive, just, and loving man: till at length he had grown to such a recognition with me as I have rarely had for any man of my time. . . ." Again, on the completion of Forster's "Life," he wrote: ". . . So long as Dickens is interesting to his fellowmen, here will be seen face to face, what Dickens's manner of existing was. His bright and joyful sympathy with everything around him; his steady practicality, withal; the singularly solid business talent he continually had; and, deeper than all, if one has the eye to see deep enough, dark, fateful, silent elements, tranquil to look upon, and hiding, amid dazzling radiances as of the sun, the elements of death itself. . .."

Dickens has been described by some who knew him as aggressive, imperious, and intolerant; but this applies only in particular instances where there was justification for such an attitude; as, for example, in the case of bores and similar troublesome persons. To the question, "Was Dickens the man as lovable as Dickens the author?" Edmund Yates briefly replied: "Yes, wholly," and affirmed that all the leading qualities of his books were component parts of his nature. Those in trouble who sought his advice found in him a sympathetic listener and a wise and trustworthy counsellor; for he was gifted with an extraordinarily clear and well-balanced judgment, and his opinions were delivered with commendable promptitude, no matter how preoccupied his thoughts at the moment. "Whatever the doubts brought to him might be in their character," says Charles Kent, "they were surveyed in all their bearings, they were weighed in the minutest scruple, they were reduced to their intrinsic value, or, supposing them not to have any, they were utterly dissipated. Acting in this way, his common sense was like a powerful solvent."[1] The Novelist's brother-in-law, Henry Burnett, ever regarded with feelings of admiration and affection the personal idiosyncrasies of "Boz," and in describing them he said: "His nature was transparent; you found him today as you would find him tomorrow. If he felt the lead within, it was sounding his own depth, and the surface was calm. You never saw in him the pride of success; he never affected to be even what he must have known he was. In conversations about other favoured men there often appeared a gleam of pleasure, but none could detect the faintest scowl of jealousy or envy, nor do I believe it was ever felt within."[2] "He was, perhaps, the largest-hearted man I ever knew," is the pronouncement of Thomas Adolphus Trollope (brother of Anthony Trollope).

[1] "Charles Dickens, by Pen and Pencil," 1889-90.
[2] Ibid.

"I think he made a nearer approach to obeying the divine precept, 'Love thy neighbour as thyself,' than one man in a hundred thousand. His benevolence, his active, energising desire for good to all God's creatures, and restless anxiety to be in some way active for the achieving of it, were necessary and busy in his heart ever and always. . . . Dickens hated a mean action or a mean sentiment as one hated something that is physically loathsome to the sight and touch. And he could be angry, as those with whom he had been angry did not very readily forget."[1]

Dickens's two favourite expressions were "Please God" and "Surely, Surely." He admitted that he had "an indescribable dread of leave-takings," and would never say "goodbye" if he could help it, substituting therefore, as regards members of his own family, a kiss or a nod. On the day before his death, his daughter Kate said to her sister, as they were about to leave home for London, "I *must* say goodbye to papa," and went over to the Chalet where he was busy writing. As a rule, when thus engaged, he would just put up his cheek to be kissed; but this day (as though he had an intuition of what was impending) he took his daughter in his arms, saying, "God bless you, Katie." And there, "among the branches of the trees, among the birds and butterflies, and scent of flowers," she left him, never to look into his eyes again.[2]

. . . . . . . . .

For Politics, *per se,* Dickens entertained no special admiration, nor was he much of a politician in

---

[1] "What I Remember," by T. Adolphus Trollope.
[2] "My Father as I Recall Him," by Mamie Dickens.

the conventional sense; at the same time it is incorrect to assume that he regarded the whole business of parliamentary life with contempt. As a radical of the old school ("fire-eyed radicalism," he once termed it) he not unfrequently gave forcible expression to his opinions on practical politics and severely criticised the action (or inaction) of the Conservative Government. As readers of his books are aware, Dickens often made his novels the medium for ventilating social grievances and exposing gross abuses—to wit, the administration of the Poor Laws, the method of conducting Chancery business, Government "Circumlocution," and other matters of grave public concern, the majority of which, however, have since undergone a process of reform. In the early 'forties Dickens found an occasional vent for his radical proclivities by writing unsigned articles for the *Morning Chronicle*, which excited public comment,[1] and during the Tory interregnum in 1841 he contributed anonymously to the *Examiner* (then edited by Forster, and long since defunct) three political squibs in verse, which were intended to strengthen the cause of the Liberals. The first of these satirical productions was entitled "The Fine Old English Gentleman (to be said or sung at all Conservative dinners)"; the second was called "The Quack Doctor's Proclamation," and has a "Tol de rol" chorus, to be sung to the tune of "A Cobbler there was"; while the third he designated "Subjects for Painters (after Peter Pindar)." Forster doubts if Dickens "ever enjoyed anything more than the power of thus taking part occasionally, unknown to outsiders, in the sharp conflict the press was waging at the time."

---

[1] A leader written by him for that paper on March 9, 1844, has reference to Agricultural interests.

The *Daily News*, too, afforded him an opportunity of occasionally indulging his *penchant* for party politics, as witness his verses (signed "Catnach") on "The British Lion—A New Song, but an Old Story," which were to be sung to the tune of "The Great Sea-Snake."[1] Both in the *Daily News* and *The Times* may be found letters bearing his signature, dealing with important social questions, such as the Corn Laws, Crime and Education,[2] and Capital Punishment,[3] and his epistles did not fail to call serious attention to the points which they raised. His own journals, *Household Words* and *All the Year Round*, contain many articles bearing upon political and other public matters.

It is recorded that once, and once only, Dickens made a political speech, on the occasion of his presiding over the first public demonstration in favour of Administrative Reform, at Drury Lane Theatre in 1855, and in April of that year, writing to (Sir) A. H. Layard on that subject, he said: "There is nothing in the present time at once so galling and so alarming to me as the alienation of the people from their own public affairs," and affirmed his belief that public discontent was in danger of being turned into "such a devil of a conflagration as never has been beheld since" the first French Revolution. We are told by the authors of "The *Daily News* Jubilee" (1896) "that he grew impatient, often and naturally, at the slowness of the process by which parliamentary action worked itself out; the all but intolerable delay which was just in the way of even the most needed measure of reform;

---

[1] *Daily News*, January 24, 1846.
[2] Ibid., March 9, 13, 16,1846.
[3] *Times*, November 14, 19, 1849.

the perpetual rolling of the stone up the hill only to see it roll down again." It is stated by the same authorities that "he more than once expressed a willingness, and even a desire, to enter the House of Commons if a suitable opportunity were to offer itself." In 1841, the Novelist actually received an invitation from the town of Reading, to contest the seat at the ensuing election of a member to represent that constituency in Parliament, and twenty years later he was paid a like compliment by the electors of the Finsbury Division of London, but in each case he politely refused to entertain the proposal. In making a "short confession" of his political faith ("or perhaps I should better say want of faith"), he informed a Birmingham audience (a few months before his death) that he had very little confidence in the people who govern us—"please to observe 'people' there will be with a small 'p'"—but that he had great confidence in the People whom they govern—"please to observe 'people' there with a large 'P.'" The following reply to an invitation from Mr. (afterwards Sir) Robert Rawlinson, C.B., to witness the opening of Parliament, possesses a peculiar interest at the present time—the year of the Coronation of King Edward VII:—

TAVISTOCK HOUSE,
*January 25*, 1854.

"My dear Sir,—I assure you that we are all extremely sensible of your kind remembrance, and much indebted to you for your invitation; but, though reasonably loyal, we do not much care for such sights, and consequently feel that you ought to bestow the places you so obligingly offer us on some more deserving objects. The last ceremony of that kind I ever saw was the Queen's coronation, and I thought it looked poor in comparison with my usual country walk. As to Parliament, it does so little and talks so much that the most interesting ceremony I know of in connection with it was performed (with very little state indeed) by one man, who just cleared it out, locked up the place, and put the keys in his pocket."

That Dickens was a religious man in the truest sense no one who has read his works can fail to perceive. *Apropos* of this, I may call attention to an article entitled "Charles Dickens's Use of the Bible,"[1] the author of which denotes the frequency with which the Novelist quoted from, and referred to, the Book; and we at once recall certain quasi-religious characters (such as Brother Stiggins and the Rev. Mr. Chadband) whom he held up to ridicule mainly to expose such impostors, thus indicating how strongly he felt on the subject of sincerity in religion. Writing (in 1843) to a correspondent who had taken offence at the present-ment of Stiggins as "the Shepherd," Dickens pointed out that "the design of 'the Shepherd' and of this and every other allusion to him, is to show how sacred things are degraded, vulgarised, and rendered absurd when persons who are utterly incompetent to teach the commonest things take upon themselves to expound such mysteries, and how, in making mere cant phrases of divine words, these persons miss the spirit in which they had their origin."[2] Bred in the Church of England, he was not bigoted or intolerant, for he numbered among his dearest friends people of various religious

---

[1] *Temple Bar*, September 1869.
[2] "The Letters of Charles Dickens."

persuasions. He had a strong aversion, however, for what seemed to him dogmatism, and described himself as "morally wide asunder from Rome," while of Puritanism in its modern form he was an uncompromising opponent.

In common with all intelligent persons, he thoroughly abhorred so-called religious quarrels. Writing to M. de Cerjat in 1864, he said: "The spectacle presented by the indecent squabbles of priests of most denominations, and the exemplary unfairness and rancour with which they conduct their differences, utterly repels me. And the idea of the Protestant establishment, in the face of its own history, seeking to trample out discussion and private judgment, is an enormity so cool that I wonder the Right Reverends, Very Reverends, and all other Reverends, who commit it, can look in one another's faces without laughing, as the old soothsayers did. . . . The Church that is to have its part in the coming time must be a more Christian one, with less arbitrary pretensions and a stronger hold upon the mantle of our Saviour, as He walked and talked upon this earth."[1] Of Mission work, as generally transacted, it is interesting to learn that it did not find much favour with him, as evidenced by the following citation from a letter written in 1865: "So Exeter Hall holds us in mortal submission to missionaries, who (Livingstone always excepted) are perfect nuisances, and leave every place worse than they found it."[2]

Dickens was not an orthodox churchgoer, believing in the practical side of Religion rather than in its outward observance. During 1843, while living

[1] "The Letters of Charles Dickens."
[2] Ibid.

Copy of a page of the original manuscript of "David Copperfield"

| Kate Dickens | Mamie Dickens | Charles Dickens |
| H. F. Chorley | Charles A Collins | Georgina Hogarth |

A portrait group — In the porch at Gad's Hill Place

*From a photograph by Mason & Co. 1865 in the
possession of the Author*

at Devonshire Terrace, he took sittings for a time in the Little Portland Street Unitarian Chapel, whose officiating minister, the Rev. Edward Tagart, he regarded with an affection which continued long after he had ceased to be a member of his congregation. "On essential points," says Forster, "he had never any sympathy so strong as with the leading doctrine and discipline of the Church of England; to these, as time went on, he found himself able to accommodate all minor differences." His faith in Christianity itself, apart from all sects and schisms, was unswerving. "I have always striven in my writings to express veneration for the life and lessons of our Saviour; because I feel it, and because I rewrote that history for my children—everyone of whom knew it from having it repeated to them, long before they could read, and almost as soon as they could speak. But I have never made proclamation of this from the housetops."[1] Thus reads an epistle, written on the day of the fatal seizure, in reply to a letter addressed to him in reference to a passage in the tenth chapter of "Edwin Drood," in which his correspondent took exception to a particular figure of speech, drawn from Holy Writ, and which he thought had been employed irreverently. The manuscript of the "History of the New Testament" to which Dickens alludes is still in the possession of his family, who have received many earnest entreaties that it might be printed and published for the benefit of other children; but it was his particular wish that it should never be published (it having been composed solely for his own children), and that wish is held sacred and irrevocable. He had also written prayers for

---

[1] "The Letters of Charles Dickens."

his children as soon as they were old enough to say them, and when his boys were of an age to understand the inner meaning of religion, and especially when they left home and the beneficial influence of home surroundings, they were forcibly reminded of the desirability of leading a true Christian life. In October 1868 Henry Fielding Dickens entered Trinity Hall, Cambridge, as an undergraduate, and his father (who felt the parting sadly) gave him much wholesome advice upon many things, including religion: "As your brothers have gone away one by one," he said, "I have written to each of them what I am now going to write to you. You know that you have never been hampered with religious forms of restraint, and that with mere unmeaning forms I have no sympathy. But I most strongly and affectionately impress upon you the priceless value of the New Testament, and the study of that book as the one unfailing guide in life. Deeply respecting it, and bowing down before the character of our Saviour, as separated from the vain constructions and inventions of men, you cannot go very wrong, and will always preserve at heart a true spirit of veneration and humility. Similarly I impress upon you the habit of saying a Christian prayer every night and morning. These things have stood by me all through my life, and remember that I tried to render the New Testament intelligible to you and lovable by you when you were a mere baby."[1] On the day of the departure of his youngest son (Edward Bulwer Lytton Dickens) for Australia, he placed in the boy's hand a letter, stimulating him to do what was right in his new life, and saying that he had included a New Testament

---

[1] "The Letters of Charles Dickens."

among his books, "because it is the best book that ever was or ever will be known in the world, and because it teaches you the best lessons by which any human creature who tries to be truthful and faithful to duty can possibly be guided. . . ."[1] In his Will, too, the Novelist exhorted his "dear children humbly to try to guide themselves by the teaching of the New Testament in its broad spirit, and to put no faith in any man's narrow construction of its letter here or there."

Again adverting to the Novelist's Will, we find how pronounced was his objection to the paraphernalia of undertakers. Here he emphatically directed that those who attended his funeral obsequies should "wear no scarf, cloak, black bow, long hatband, or other such revolting absurdity;" he had noted his views on this subject in the thirty-first chapter of "David Copperfield," where David says that he did not attend Barkis's funeral "in character," thereby meaning that he was "not dressed up in a black coat and a streamer, to frighten the birds." In these days of Funeral Reform and Cremation, such ostensible manifestations of grief are no longer considered à la mode, although outward observances of this kind are still fondly cherished by the poorer classes.

Dickens's acquaintance with literature was restricted to a few English authors; of foreign classics his knowledge was superficial. An attentive reader of his books cannot fail to discover the fact that the Novelist seldom quotes from other writers. We may find occasional references to Swift, Scott, and Byron, and more frequently we meet with allusions to the stories in "The Arabian Nights' Entertainments," to "Robinson Crusoe," and the writings of Fielding and

[1] "The Letters of Charles Dickens."

Smollett, whose fascinating romances ever retained a charm for him. He found pleasure, however, in reading particular works of certain of his contemporaries, and once notified to Forster that he had derived much enjoyment from Douglas Jerrold's "Story of a Feather," concerning which he said, "Gauntwolf's sickness and the career of that snuffbox, masterly," and added that he had "been deep in Voyages and Travels, and in De Foe. Tennyson I have also been reading again and again. What a great creature he is!" He never faltered in his allegiance to the late Poet Laureate, and the present Lord Tennyson informs me that Dickens had the warmest admiration for "The Idylls of the King;" indeed, the Novelist confessed as much to Forster, when he said. "How fine the Idylls are! Lord! What a blessed thing it is to read a man who really can write. I thought nothing could be finer than the first poem, till I came to the third; but when I had read the last, it seemed to me to be absolutely unapproachable." For certain books of Carlyle, too (notably "The French Revolution") Dickens had an especial liking, and he used to say that he "would go at all times farther to see Carlyle than any man alive." In 1844 the Novelist intimated that he was "all eagerness to write a story about the length of that most delightful of all stories. 'The Vicar of Wakefield.'" He keenly appreciated Goldsmith's comedies, "She Stoops to Conquer" and "The Good-natured Man"— "both are so admirable and so delightfully written that they read wonderfully," he said in a letter to M. de Cerjat, whom ("as a brother reader of high distinction") he recommended to peruse them, adding that one night he read aloud to Forster (then on a sickbed) the first named comedy, "and we enjoyed it with that wonderful intensity that I believe he began to get better in the first scene, and was all right again in the fifth act." Scientific treatises did not appeal to him, but occasionally a new book on an abstruse subject would attract his attention, as shown by the following passage from a letter to the Hon. Mrs. Watson: "I think you will be interested with a controversy between Whewell and Brewster, on the question of the shining orbs being inhabited or no. Whewell's book is called, 'On the Plurality of Worlds'; Brewster's, 'More Worlds than One.' . . . They bring together a vast number of points of great interest in natural philosophy, and some very curious reasoning on both sides, and leave the matter pretty much where it was."[1] With reference to his literary proclivities, Mr. James T. Fields observes: "There were certain books of which Dickens liked to talk during his walks. Among his special favourites were the writings of Cobbett, De Quincey, the 'Lectures on Moral Philosophy' by Sydney Smith, and Carlyle's 'French Revolution.' . . . Mr. Barlow, in 'Sandford and Merton,' he said, was the favourite enemy of his boyhood and his first experience of a bore. He had an almost supernatural hatred for Barlow, 'because he was so very *instructive*, and always hinting doubts with regard to the veracity of 'Sindbad the Sailor,' and no belief whatever in 'The Wonderful Lamp,' or 'The Enchanted Horse.'"[2]

Concerning matters of Art, Dickens never claimed to possess a knowledge—certainly he knew nothing of the *technique*, but could appreciate a good

---

[1] "The Letters of Charles Dickens."

[2] "Yesterdays with Authors," by James T. Fields, 1872. And see Dickens's paper, entitled "Mr. Barlow," in the "New Uncommercial Samples" (*All the Year Round*, January 16, 1869), where he is referred to as "the instructive monomaniac."

picture when he saw it. Although including among his most cherished friends several of the most prominent painters of the day, it is remarkable that in his extensive portrait gallery we do not find the presentment of an artist, if we except that of the kind-hearted miniature-painter, Miss La Creevy—for that *dilettanti*, Henry Gowan (in "Little Dorrit") cannot be reckoned as a member of the profession. So far as I am aware, Dickens never essayed the use of brush or pencil; but, as an artist *in words*, he is perhaps unrivalled, many of his descriptive passages (in "Pictures from Italy," for example) suggesting subjects in which Rembrandt or Teniers would have revelled. Sometimes he posed as an art critic, and during his sojourn in Italy he became (as he expressed it) "brimful of cant about pictures," offering to enlighten Forster on the subject of the different schools at any length he pleased, and imparting to him, in a half-serious, half-humorous vein, his impressions of the famous paintings by the Old Masters such as he had seen in the Vatican and the various public and private galleries. He described Titian's great picture, at Venice, of the Assumption of the Virgin as "perfection," and Tintoretto's painting of the Assembly of the Blest as "grand and noble in the extreme—the most wonderful and charming picture ever painted." Judging from a letter addressed to Harrison Ainsworth in 1849, there is a picture which excited his admiration even more: "I have no Parisian wrinkle for you," he said, "unless it be an earnest entreaty to you to go to the School of Painting at the Palais des Beaux Arts across the river—seize the concierge by the throat, and demand to see a fresco ['The Hemicycle'] by Paul de la Roche, which I believe to be the greatest work of art in the world." Certain productions at Verona and Mantua he considered as "really too absurd and ridiculous even to laugh at. Hampton Court is a fool to 'em," he said—"and oh there are some rum 'uns there, my friend. Some werry rum 'uns." He believed that the rules of art were much too slavishly followed; "making it a pain to you, when you go into galleries day after day, to be so very precisely sure where this figure will be turning round, and that figure will be lying down, and that other will have a great lot of drapery twined about him, and so forth. This becomes a perfect nightmare." He found it difficult to commend too highly the portraits and heads by Titian, Rubens, Rembrandt, Vandyke, Guido, &c., and the subject-pictures by Raphael, Correggio, Murillo, and Paul Veronese. "Such tenderness and grace, such noble elevation, purity, and beauty, so shine upon me from some well remembered spots in the walls of these galleries, as to relieve my tortured memory from legions of whining friars and waxy holy families. I forgive, from the bottom of my soul, whole orchestras of earthly angels, and whole groves of St. Sebastians stuck as full of arrows according to pattern as a lying-in pincushion is stuck with pins. . . ." It will be perceived that Dickens did not hesitate to express his opinion of those world-famous canvases; he felt convinced that "one of the great uses of travelling is to encourage a man to think for himself, to be bold enough always to declare without offence that he *does* think for himself, and to overcome the villainous meanness of professing what other people have professed when he knows (if he has capacity to originate an opinion) that his profession is untrue." From a visit to the Paris Art Exposition in the winter of 1855 he arrived at the conclusion that English art, as compared with French, was insignificant and "niggling," while the general absence of ideas was horribly apparent; referring to the English school there represented (Leslie, Stanfield, Frith, Ward, Egg, &c.), he remarked that "what we know to be wanting in the men is wanting in their works—character, fire, purpose, and the power of using the vehicle and the model as mere means to an end. There is a horrible respectability about most of the best of them—a little, finite, systematic routine in them, strangely expressive to me of the state of England itself. . . . There are no end of bad pictures among the French, but, Lord! The goodness also! The fearlessness of them; the bold drawing; the dashing conception; the passion and action in them!" Respecting Dickens as an art critic, mention must be made of two friendly essays written by him and published in the *Examiner* in 1848. The first is a notice of the series of plates by George Cruikshank, entitled "The Drunkard's Children," and the second is a heartily eulogistic criticism of John Leech's designs depicting "The Rising Generation." Certain of the Cruikshank etchings he regarded as "masterpieces worthy of the greatest painter," and the power of the artist's conceptions led to a dissertation upon similarly remarkable qualities in the works of Hogarth. For Leech's "Rising Generation" he had nothing but praise, infinitely preferring that refined artist's productions to the grosser conceptions of Gillray and Rowlandson, which, he thought, are rendered "wearisome and unpleasant by a vast amount of personal ugliness." Dickens realised the fact that Leech possessed, in an extraordinary degree, the gift of being able to represent female beauty with a few slight but sure touches of his pencil, and that in all his designs, whatever that skilful draughtsman attempted, the result was satisfactory. "His drawing seems to us charming; . . . his wit is good-natured, and always the wit of a gentleman. He has a becoming sense of responsibility and self-restraint; he delights in agreeable things; he imparts some pleasant air of his own to things not pleasant in themselves; he is suggestive and full of matter. . . . Popular art in England has not had so rich an acquisition." He endorsed the comments of a *Quarterly Review*-er who voted it absurd to exclude from the ranks of Royal Academicians such men as these clever illustrators, and asks, in concluding this essay: "Will no Associates be found upon its books one of these days, the labours of whose oil and brushes will have sunk into the profoundest obscurity, when many pencil marks of Mr. Cruikshank and Mr. Leech will be still fresh in half the houses in the land?" Dickens's protest was penned in 1848, and the Royal Academy (still obdurate) declines to admit the claims of a mere draughtsman in black-and-white, however skilful, to be enrolled as a member of that august fraternity.

It has been surmised that Charles Dickens was partial to what Dick Swiveller terms "the flowing bowl"—a misapprehension, founded, maybe, on the numerous references to strong drink in "Pickwick" and on certain convivial allusions in his letters. Mr. George Dolby (who was in a position to know) assures us that Dickens was no epicure, and that, although he frequently both wrote and talked about eating and drinking, he seldom met any one more temperate, both in the matter of drink and diet, than he was. It is unnecessary, in this connection, to do more in the way of emphatic contradiction than quote the assertion of one who had seen him in every position where it might be supposed a weakness or failing of that kind would assert itself: "Never once can I call to mind a single instance of his having dulled his brain or made his tongue speak foolishly by such a vice. When sustaining the position of Chairman with its enticing duties he very frequently had by his right hand his own decanter of toast and water; with this he toasted." Many of the Novelist's friends have testified to his exceptional skill in brewing gin-punch—an art of which he was very proud, and to see him perform the operation you would think he had never done anything else all his life, his undivided attention being concentrated upon the effort; this particular beverage he usually concocted after dinner, being sometimes aided in its preparation by Mark Lemon, whose duty it was to squeeze the *lemons!* In the summertime his guests, on arriving at Gad's Hill Place about noontime, after a hot journey from town, would receive at his hands welcome refreshment in the form of "cider cup," which he had ordered to be in readiness—a delicious, cooling drink composed of cider, soda water, sherry, brandy, lemon peel, sugar, and ice, flavoured with borage, all judiciously mixed. "He liked to dilate in imagination over the brewing of a bowl of punch," wrote Mr. James T. Fields, "but I always noticed that when the punch was ready he drank less of it than anyone who might be present. It was the sentiment of the thing, and not the thing itself, that engaged his attention." "No man," says Forster, "advocated temperance, even as far as possible its legislative enforcement, with greater earnestness." He was no fanatic, however, in this deserving cause and never confounded it with that of Teetotalism; for he recognised the difference between the use and the abuse of drink, as proved by his attack upon Cruikshank's Fairy Library, which the Novelist described as being rewritten according to Total Abstinence, Peace Society, and Bloomer principles, and expressly for their propagation.[1] "For him, drunkenness had a teeming and reproachful history anterior to the drunken stage; and he thought it the first duty of the moralist bent upon annihilating the gin shop to 'strike deep and spare not,'" to suppress such remediable evils as unsanitary habitations and workshops, and to improve the demoralising environment amidst which the poorer classes are compelled to spend their existence. As a smoker, Dickens also practised moderation, a cigar after dinner, or an occasional cigarette, representing the extent of his nicotian habits. *La Pureza*, "manufactured from the finest blended tobacco," is advertised as his favourite cigar.

As a host, Dickens was incomparable. No guest under his roof beams ever felt otherwise than at home, and in the event of an invitation to the "Kentish freehold," ten thousand chances to one but the visitor would be punctually met at the Higham station by the Novelist himself, and driven over to Gad's Hill in the favourite jaunting car, with musical bells on the harness. At Christmas and New Year tides the house was always filled with guests, a cottage in the village being reserved for the use of the bachelor members of the holiday party. Dickens, who always deserted work for the week on such occasions, was the life and fun of

---

[1] "Frauds on the Fairies," in *Household Wards*, October 1, 1853.

those gatherings, concerning which his eldest daughter (Mamie) has recorded that "games passed the evenings merrily, 'Proverbs,' and 'Dumb Crambo' being very popular, her father's great imitative ability showing finely in the latter." All who stayed at Gad's Hill at this season ever remembered the genial host, as he stood in the hall on the New Year Eves, watch in hand, listening for the midnight chimes. As soon as they struck the ear there were a few minutes of breathless silence; then, as he stood by the open door (no matter what the weather might be), with all eyes fixed upon him, his voice would be heard saying, "A Happy New Year. God bless us all!" which was followed by such kissing and handshaking, such drinking of healths in hot mulled wine, such dancing very often, such kindness and goodwill!—The servants not forgotten, but getting a hearty good wish from "the master."[1] There are some who, as privileged guests at Gad's Hill, still remember these annual observances, and the earnestness with which he performed his part.[2]

The foregoing allusion to Yuletide amusements recalls Dickens's delight in outdoor games of the simpler kind. Battledore-and-shuttlecock was played constantly in the garden at Devonshire Terrace; the American game of bowls pleased him, and he was an expert at rounders; croquet he disliked, but he enjoyed cricket immensely as a spectator, always keeping one of the scores during the matches at Gad's Hill. He was not what might be termed a good dancer, and although very fond of dancing, never indulged therein

---

[1] "Charles Dickens." by his Eldest Daughter, 1885.

[2] Gad's Hill Place is now owned and tenanted by the Hon. Francis Lathom. In 1889, the house narrowly escaped destruction by fire; the old story—an escape of gas and a naked light. Happily the fire was subdued, but not before much damage had been effected.

"except at family gatherings in his own or his most intimate friends' homes." Graceful in motion, his dancing, such as it was, seemed natural to him, and at its best in the "Sir Roger de Coverley" (his favourite dance), and in what are known as country dances. "Dance music was delightful to his cheery, genial spirit," observes Miss Dickens; "the time and steps of a dance suited his tidy nature, if I may so speak. The action and. the exercise seemed to be a part of his abundant vitality." Once (as mentioned on a previous page) he induced his little daughters to teach him and John Leech the polka, in order to be perfect at the ensuing children's party; so anxious was he about his steps that he frequently jumped up and practised them by himself, whistling the time meanwhile, and one night he jumped out of bed in an agony of fear lest he had forgotten the step, and had a practice in the cold![1] Mr. G. D. Leslie, R.A., recollects that, at a birthday party at Tavistock House, Dickens performed with Mark Lemon an old English country dance in his shirt sleeves, and tripped away until the perspiration streamed down his face. Even quadrilles became *dances* when he footed them.

His eldest son's birthday celebrations on Twelfth Night always afforded the keenest delight, especially to the younger members of the household and their juvenile friends. Sometimes there was a magic lantern entertainment, and on a certain memorable occasion Dickens and Forster purchased between them the entire stock-in-trade of a conjuror, wherewith to amuse the assembled guests, for the Novelist numbered among his accomplishments the art of the prestidigitator. Writing to an American friend he

---

[1] "Charles Dickens," by his Eldest Daughter, 1885.

said: "If you could see me conjuring the company's watches into impossible tea-caddies, and causing pieces of money to fly, and burning pocket-handkerchiefs without burning 'em, and practising in my own room without anybody to admire, you would never forget it as long as you live." One of these conjuring tricks (always eagerly awaited) comprised the disappearance and reappearance of a tiny doll, which would announce most unexpected pieces of news and messages to the different children in the audience.

During his schooldays Dickens received instruction in music, an attempt being made to teach him the pianoforte; but the music master felt compelled to declare to the principal of the school that his efforts were fruitless—he could make nothing of him, and that it would be robbing the boy's parents to continue to give him lessons; so they were abruptly ended. It must not, however, be supposed that he had no aptitude for music—indeed, in after life he was intensely fond of it, and had a most excellent ear and good voice. As a young man he now and then condescended to sing seriocomic songs, interspersed with clever sketches of character, for the entertainment of his friends, and these performances were highly successful, conferring great pleasure even upon the most sedate amongst his audience. His eldest daughter, in referring to a later period, avers that her father would listen to playing or singing by the hour together, and was very critical as to the proper pronunciation and the distinct articulation of words. The playing of the violin by Joachim, who visited Gad's Hill, perfectly enchanted him. "I never remember seeing him so wrapt and absorbed as he was then, on hearing him play; and the wonderful simplicity and *un*-self-consciousness of the genius went straight to my father's heart, and made a fast bond of sympathy between those two great men."[1] George Linley's song of "Little Nell" was an especial favourite of his; Mendelssohn's "Lieder" charmed him, as did also Chopin's and Mozart's compositions, while he found delight in good dance music and the rendering of national airs.

Dickens's relations with children were ideal in character, and Miss Dickens recalled that he was a most kind, indulgent, and considerate father, always gentle to them about their small troubles and infantine terrors. She remembered how he would sing to them of an evening before bedtime, to their great delight, as, with one seated on his knee and the others grouped around, he would at their request go through no end of songs, mostly of a humorous kind, and laugh over them quite as much as his small listeners, enjoying them quite as much, too. "He contended that an intelligent child's observation was accurate and intense to a degree; that such a child should never be needlessly frightened, or sent into the dark against its will, but should be kindly and gently reasoned with, until all such childish fears and terrors should gradually melt away, from the very consideration and sympathy shown to the little creature."[2] Possessing such an insight into, and understanding of, juvenile character, it is not surprising that children "took" to him at once, for even the shyest of babies would hold out its arms to him with perfect faith and confidence. And then, again, in times of sickness and suffering," says Miss

[1] Miss Dickens, in "Charles Dickens by Pen and Pencil," 1889-90.
[2] "Charles Dickens," by his Eldest Daughter, 1885.

Dickens, "what a magic there was in his voice, in his touch, what sympathy expressed for the invalids, how they listened for his footstep, and how eagerly the little faces would turn to the door to welcome that bright and helping presence. And how useful he was in a sickroom! He always knew the right thing to be done, and did it so quietly and so cheerfully, was so ready and so handy, that he inspired everyone with unbounded confidence and hope in him." If additional testimony were wanting of Charles Dickens's love for children we may turn to the different child characters in his books (little Paul Dombey and the rest), which prove the wonderful fellow feeling he had for them in all their joys and griefs.

Of dumb creatures, too, he was ever the friend and partisan, and domestic pets invariably formed part of the household. To begin with the Devonshire Terrace days, there were the two ravens (of whom the immortal "Grip" was compounded), and an eagle, who lived in a grotto in the garden, chained by one leg, and whose life was made something of a burden by the tantalising tricks of Grip the second. On his return from America in 1842, the Novelist brought home to Devonshire Terrace a white Havannah spaniel called "Timber," which soon became very amicable with the children. The young folks kept rabbits and guinea pigs, but their father could not appreciate these. He much liked birds as pets, and on their account cats were not allowed in the house. But his strongest love among animals was doubtless for dogs. Coming to the Gad's Hill times there were "Turk," a beautiful mastiff, and "Linda," a good-tempered St. Bernard, both constant companions of the "master" during his walks, while next to be named is "Mrs. Bouncer," a dainty

Pomeranian—a special gift to Miss Dickens in the Tavistock House period—who speedily won her way into the affections of every member of the household, the Novelist becoming her special slave. A few years later came "Don," a Newfoundland, and then "Bumble," his son, named after the beadle in "Oliver Twist" because of a peculiarly pompous and overbearing manner he had of appearing to mount guard over the yard when he was an absolute infant.[1] Lastly, there was "Sultan," an Irish bloodhound (the gift of Mr. Percy Fitzgerald) who had a bitter experience with his life at Gad's Hill, as he was reluctantly sentenced to be shot for having fallen upon and severely bitten a little girl who was passing the house. Dickens was very fond of horses, and used to remark upon the strangeness of the fact that an animal "so noble in its qualities should be the cause of so much villainy." For the use of his children he obtained horses and ponies from time to time, but they were not of a very choice breed; these included "dear old 'Toby'"—a pretty pony—and "sober Newman Noggs," who drew the basket carriage at Gad's Hill.

During a summer holiday at Broadstairs, a bathing woman gave Dickens's daughters a young canary which developed into "a very king of birds," and became a most important member of the household. Although at one time its life was endangered by "two particularly tigerish and fearful cats" belonging to a neighbour, and against which a fierce war was waged, no harm came to "wonderful little Dick," of whom Miss Dickens says: "He was the nicest, cleverest, and tamest little bird you ever saw . . . was devoted to his mistress, and

[1] "My Father as I Recall Him," by Mamie Dickens.

would come flying to her from any part of the room if she only just held out a finger; he hopped about the table all breakfast time, and on to our heads and shoulders; sometimes he took a naughty fit, and hopped on his master's shoulder and pecked his cheek, then he used to have to retire to his cage in disgrace. . . . He used to go almost mad with joy when his mistress returned after any absence, and Charles Dickens would constantly go, into the room behind his daughter, to witness the meeting and the little bird's delight." "Dick" died of old age, having attained fifteen years, and was buried under a rose tree in the garden behind the house, the exact spot being marked by a tablet inscribed with an epitaph composed by his master: "This is the grave of Dick, the best of birds, born at Broadstairs, midsummer, 1851, died at Gad's Hill Place, 4th October 1866." While Dick lived, cats were of course tabooed, and were never allowed about the house; but after his death a white kitten (called Williamina) was given to one of the family. She was particularly attached to the master, and took her little progeny into his study to live, where, after several ineffectual rebuffs, they were allowed to remain. Before very long they became very rompish, swarming up the curtains, playing on the writing table, and making such a disturbance as was never heard in that sanctum before. They were never complained of, however, and were never turned out until it became necessary to find homes for the little creatures; one of them, being deaf, and in other respects "a very exceptional cat," was retained, it being known to the servants as "the master's cat," in consequence of its affection for him. He was always with his master, and used to follow him about the garden, and sit with him while he was writing. "One evening they were left alone together, the ladies of the house having gone to a ball in the neighbourhood. Charles Dickens was reading at a small table on which a lighted candle was placed, when suddenly the candle went out. He was much interested in his book, relit the candle, gave a pat to the cat, who he noticed was looking up at him with a most pathetic expression, and went on with his reading. A few minutes afterwards, the light getting dim, he looked up and was in time to see Puss deliberately put out the candle with his paw, and then gaze again appealingly at his master. This second appeal was understood, and had the desired effect. The book was shut, and Puss was made a fuss with and amused until bedtime. His master was full of this anecdote when we all met in the morning."[1]

Dickens owned that he had the primeval savage's love for bright, positive colours. His garden, therefore, gave plenty of scope for indulgence in brilliant blooms, entire beds being filled with scarlet geraniums—his favourite flower—which made a splendid blaze of colour all through the summer months. He really loved *all* flowers, but the gayest and the brightest coloured the best; his daughter never remembered him pick out a purely white flower as being especially pleasing to him. He had a passion for mirrors, so looking glasses were placed in every possible corner of the house, and five in the Chalet, where (as he told his friend, Mr. Fields) "they reflect and refract, in all kinds of ways, the leaves that are quivering at the windows, and the green fields of waving corn, and the sail-dotted river." Referring to these peculiar tastes, one of his daughters said

[1] "Charles Dickens," by his Eldest Daughter, 1885.

laughingly to her father, "I believe, papa, that when you become an angel your wings will be made of looking glass and your crown of scarlet geraniums." The Novelist's *penchant* for bright flowers was remembered when he lay in the chamber of death, and loving hands adorned the room with fresh coloured blooms, which were then so abundant. Every year on the 9th of June and on Christmas Day such flowers are strewn upon his grave in Poets' Corner by his children and his grandchildren, and by unknown hands; and every year beautifully tinted leaves are sent from across the Atlantic, to he similarly deposited upon the simply inscribed stone which marks the last resting place of Charles Dickens.

# INDEX

(note); reporting for, 28, 29 (and see note); Sketches in, 31, 32; political articles in, 144, 462 (and note)

Morris, Mowbray, 176

Motley, J. L., 397; recollections, 452

*Mr. Minns and his Cousin*, 30

*Mr. Nightingale's Diary*, acting of, 240, 412

*Mrs. Lirriper's Legacy* (Christmas Number), 323

*Mrs. Lirriper's Lodgings* (Christmas Number), 315-6

*Mudfog Papers, The*, 58

*Mugby Junction* (Christmas Number), 336; origin of, 337; characters in, 337; sale of, 337

*Mystery of Edwin Drood, The*, plot of, 385 (and see note); at work on, 387, 389, 397; plan for first number of, 387; payment for, 388; clause in agreement for, 388; dinner celebration, 389-90; Longfellow's opinion of, 402; illustrations for, 403; publishers' announcement concerning, 403; unfounded rumour respecting, 404; a passage from Holy Writ in, 467

Napier, Macvey, 117

Naples, 178, 225

New Testament, Children's, 151 (and see note); manuscript of, 467

*New Uncommercial Samples*, 377

New York, 97, 101, 178, 287, 360, 371; Harbour, 103; Boston Theatre, 112; public dinner at, 113; readings at, 354; banquet at Delmonico's, 367-8; Steinway Hall, 368

*New York Ledger, Hunted Down* written for, 288, 289

*New York Tribune*, "violated" letter in, 271

Niagara Falls, 65, 98, 105; wonderful effect of, 363

*Nicholas Nickleby*, 58-72, 73, 379, 406; announcement of, 58; agreement concerning, 59; characters in, 61, 64-6, 407,437; Dotheboys Hall in, 61-3; illustrations for, 63;

first cheap edition of, 65; at work on, 66; dinner celebration of, 67; payment for, 67; dramatisation of, 68 (and see note); plagiarisms and piracies of, 68-70

Norfolk Street (now Cleveland Street), 4

Normanby, Lord, presides at a farewell dinner, 127

Norton, C. E., at the Delmonico banquet, 367; at Gad's Hill, 374; Mrs., 374

*No Thoroughfare* (Christmas Number), 349-50; collaboration in, 350; dramatisation of, 350, 374

*Not so Bad as We Seem*, acting of 197 (and see note), 412

O'Connell, Daniel, and Little Nell, 79

*Old Curiosity Shop, The*, 18, 82; characters in, 18, 79; proposed titles for, 78; Little Nell in, 79, 161, 162; at work on, 80; sale of, 81; blank verse in, 156

Oliphant, Mrs., and *Hard Times*, 230 (note)

*Oliver Twist*, 19, 54-8, 60, 73; characters in, 42, 57; illustrations for, 54, 56; temporary suspension of, 54; payment for, 56; Cruikshank's claim concerning, 56-7; dramatisation of, 68 (and see note); first cheap edition of, 134; readings from, 376, 378-390, 419, 420

Osgood, J. R., and the walking-match, 359, 360

Osnaburgh Terrace, 127, 130

*O'Thello, The*, 406

*Our French Watering-Place*, 217

*Our Mutual Friend*, 3; first thoughts of, 314; proposed titles for, 314; characters in, 314-5, 320, 327; illustrations for, 319-20; at work on, 320-1, 322, 323, 326; manuscript of, 325, 326, 327

*Our School*, 20 (and see note)

*Our Watering-Place*, 185

*Our Young Folks, Holiday Romance* written for, 345

Ouvry, F., 348

# LIFE OF LORD JEFFREY

With a selection from his correspondence

Vol 1: ISBN 1-904995-00-4
Vol 2: ISBN 1-904995-01-2

Cockburn's biography of Lord Francis Jeffrey is the only publication available on the life of this well-regarded lawyer, literary critic and Whig supporter.

These publications offer the reader a fascinating insight into Scottish law, politics and literature. Lord Jeffrey was a founder of *The Edinburgh Review* and it's editor from 1803 – 1829 during which time he turned the world of criticism upside-down with his controversial reviews of literature, politics and law. He openly used *The Review* to support the Whigs in Scotland and to influence the politics of his time. His career in law eventually led to his appointment as Lord Advocate of Scotland.

Lord Jeffrey was a prolific letter writer and over 200 of his letters are included in volume two, including letters to politicians, authors, lawyers and close friends. His correspondence is clever, witty and honest.

He was a good friend of Charles Dickens and was the Godfather to Francis Jeffrey Dickens. Some of his personal and touching letters to Dickens are included.

Please visit www.lexden-publishing.co.uk for further information.

Printed in the United Kingdom
by Lightning Source UK Ltd.
120580UK00001B/36